I0883841

Sol Butler

SPORT AND SOCIETY

Series Editors
Aram Goudsouzian
Jaime Schultz
Founding Editors
Benjamin G. Rader
Randy Roberts

For a list of books in the series, please see our website at www.press.uillinois.edu.

Sol Butler

An Olympian's Odyssey through Jim Crow America

BRIAN HALLSTOOS

UNIVERSITY OF ILLINOIS PRESS
Urbana, Chicago, and Springfield

Manufactured in the United States of America
1 2 3 4 5 C P 5 4 3 2 1
♾ This book is printed on acid-free paper.

Cataloging data available from the Library of Congress

LCCN 2025025223
ISBN 978-0-252-04697-1 (cloth : alk.)
ISBN 978-0-252-08912-1 (paper : alk.)
ISBN 978-0-252-04862-3 (ebook)

The manufacturer's authorized representative in the EU for product safety is Mare Nostrum Group B.V., Mauritskade 21D, 1091 GC Amsterdam, The Netherlands. Email: gpsr@mare-nostrum.co.uk

In loving memory of *Shirley Harper Cox*

Gary Everett Stoos

Jean Helen Hall

For *Joplin*
Elise
Tatum
Sharon

Contents

Acknowledgments

I began researching the life of Sol Butler in 2013 after the late David Richard Rollins gave me his photographs of the inimitable Paul Robeson, who befriended and played college football with David's father. This generous gift sparked my poster presentation on Robeson and Butler, who graduated from the University of Dubuque (UD), at that year's American Historical Association conference in Washington, DC. Responding to my presentation, historian Brian Ingrassia encouraged me to write a biography on Butler and later offered valuable feedback on early chapter drafts. Librarian Jonathan Helmke and I created the exhibition *Racing Past the Color Line: Sol Butler and Paul Robeson in Collegiate Athletics*, and historian David Wiggins supported my initial book idea; years later, he gave important feedback on my entire manuscript. Robeson, Rollins, Ingrassia, Helmke, and Wiggins prompted my early efforts on this book.

The exceptionally generous support of Hal George has greatly improved this book by making possible developmental editing, additional research, and the book's enhanced visual appeal (which includes the commissioned cover art). Like his father before him, George continues to conscientiously manage Maple Grove Cemetery in Wichita, Kansas, where Butler and most of his family are buried. George reminds me that Sol Butler was part and product of a heroic family of overachievers. Despite my devoting considerable attention to Sol and his parents, I give much less space to Sol's sister Josephine, a heroic tuberculosis nurse. Despite its limitations, I hope that Hal finds the following story a fitting tribute to the Butler family.

The late Sherman Howard and Pixie Armstrong Freymann shared moving personal accounts regarding Butler. In a lengthy interview at his home near Chicago, Howard revealed how the sports legend trained him and other Black South Side youth. Freymann described witnessing the emotional impact

Butler's death had on his friend, her father, Johnny Armstrong. I am deeply grateful to them both for sharing these memories.

Steve and Rosemary Miller generously hosted my trip to Wichita and Hutchinson, Kansas. After giving informative tours of both cities, Steve drove us to Kingfisher, Oklahoma, for further research. David Sebben provided a similarly memorable tour of Rock Island, Illinois. Replete with visual and primary sources, David's book *"Nothing Great Is Easily Won": The Solomon Butler Story* offers valuable insight on the heroic athlete. These friends' unwavering support has improved my book in numerous ways.

During two visits in 2019 to Decatur, Alabama, I gained vital information and guidance from historian Wylheme Ragland and archivist John Allison. Ragland also shared his copy of Ben Sr.'s extensive Civil War pension file and introduced me to David Burleson, who gave me an unforgettable tour of his family's estate, where Ben Sr. was enslaved until his escape during the Civil War, and shared scholarship on the Burlesons' influential family. These men's research, generosity, and ongoing support have greatly enhanced the first chapter.

This book builds on prior research and commemorative efforts. UD students in the Black Presidium promoted Sol Butler's legacy, eventually naming a cultural house after him in the mid-1970s. Letters from alumnae Jane Pitts to the star athlete's former classmates produced lively written responses that shed light on how he impacted his college campus. Historian and activist Ocania Chalk drew attention to Butler through his book *Black College Sport* and his contribution to Arthur Ashe's important work *A Hard Road to Glory*. Former UD athletic director, the late James Odenkirk, wrote an essay on Butler, which developed into a chapter in the book *Before Jackie Robinson*. Paul Waggoner wrote several newspaper articles and a journal essay on Butler and shared his findings with the UD Archives and me.

My UD colleagues have supported my efforts from the start. Jon Barz shared his annotated list of articles on Butler from the *Chicago Defender* and his insightful essay on the Butler brothers' book, which underpins chapter 3. He offered sage feedback on a manuscript draft. Nolan Hauta skillfully turned my musical epigraph idea into a stunning reality. Paul Misner connected me with Hal George and long-term loaned his thick file of source material on Butler. Becky Canovan's generous assistance has ranged widely from research to securing copyright permissions. Meghann Toohey shared previously buried treasures in the UD Archives, while Sue Reiter and more recently Stephanie Austin-Reed handled my incessant book and document requests. Mark Ward provided ongoing support through UD's Office of Academic Affairs. Ann Kendell and Clarissa Ferguson handled financial concerns, and Sandy Hockenberry and Scott Rima generated interest among alumni. Dale Easley hosted a spirit-boosting public reading of my book's introduction. Joseph and Linda Chlapaty have supported Butler's legacy through their summer fellowship, which has resulted in published essays by Garrison Grubb and Gordon Musel. Kim Wulfekuhle-Isaac provided and interpreted historic transcripts and registration records. Lori Welsh offered invaluable guidance in formatting the manuscript. Thanks to a semester-long UD sabbatical, I made considerable progress on several chapters.

Additional thanks go to Chris Doll, the late Joel Samuels, Chad Gunnelson, Annalee Ward, Jeannine Pitas, Mary Bryant, Andrew Jones, Amy Ressler, Jason Crane, Nathan Ripperger, Thomas Robbins, Melissa Hemesath, Allison Jacobsen, Elesha Coffman, Jeffrey Bullock, Stacey Ortman, Morgan Pannell, Emily Highnam, Charles Barland, Gerald Zuercher, Adam Smith, Christine Darr, Josh Thomas, Kevin Cattani, Jim Romagna, Brian Kane, Joseph Letriz, Mallary Sturtz, Kristen Eby, Adam Kleinschmit, Gail Hayes, Adam Hoffman, Vance Thomas, and Travis Frampton.

My research on Butler has taken me to dozens of archives and research centers in eleven states and the District of Columbia. For making my visits productive, I owe thanks to Cheryl Beredo (Schomburg Center for Research in Black Culture) and John Calhoun (Billy Rose Theatre Division, New York Public Library); Kathy Shoemaker (Stuart A. Rose Manuscript, Archives, and Rare Book Library, Emory University); Mary Jones (Heinz History Center); Marilyn Holt (Carnegie Library of Pittsburgh); John Allison (Morgan County Archives, Alabama); staff of the Stark Pubic Library, Canton, Ohio; Cynthia Fife-Townsel (Vivian G. Harsh Research Collection, Woodson Branch) and Johanna Russ (Harold Washington Library Center's Special Collections, Chicago Public Library); Christine Colburn (Hanna Holburn Gray Special Collections Research Center, University of Chicago); Darmon Lewis (Center for Research Libraries in Chicago); Linda Stahnke Stepp (University of Illinois Archives); staff at the Milwaukee Public Library; Michael Gibson (Center for Dubuque History, Loras College); Noelle Sinclair (University of Iowa Law Library); Dan Gall (University of Iowa Library); Hang Nguyen (State Historical Society of Iowa); Ryan Bean (Kautz Family YMCA Archives) and staff at the Wilson Library and Elmer L. Anderson Library, University of Minnesota; staff at Minnesota History Center's Gale Family Library; Michael Church and Lauren Gray (Kansas Historical Society); Jeannie Boevers (Kingfisher County Courthouse, Oklahoma); Charlene Childs (Hutchinson Public Library); David Reed (Reno County Museum); Rose Mitchell (A C Bilbrew Library); Patricia Banuilos and Frank Harris (LA County Library); Louise Hilton (Margaret Herrick Library); Suzanne Noruschat and Susan Hikida (Doheny Memorial Library, USC Libraries Special Collections); Julianna Jenkins (UCLA Library Special Collections); and John Cahoon (Seaver Center for Western History Research).

Among the numerous archivists, librarians, directors, civil servants, and volunteers who made research possible via phone and email, I wish to thank

Carine Genevey Renaud (Olympic Foundation for Culture and Heritage); Angus Hamilton (State Library of Victoria); Rebecca Murray (Library and Archives Canada); Jessy Wheeler (Boston Public Library); Laura Russo (Howard Gotlieb Archival Research Center, Boston University); Jennifer Fauxsmith (Schlesinger Library on the History of Women in America); Robin Carlaw (Harvard University Archives); Genevieve Coyle (Yale University's Beinecke Rare Book and Manuscript Library); Raymond Butti (Brown University's John Hay Library); Patrice Kane (Fordham University); Hilary Dorscho Wong (Division of Rare Books and Special Collections, Cornell University); Katherine Collett (Hamilton College Archives); Timothy Horning (University of Pennsylvania's University Archives); Gloria Walker (Kappa Alpha Psi Inc.); Charlene Peacock (Presbyterian Historical Society); Eir Danielson (Bertrand Library, Bucknell University); Zach Brodt (University of Pittsburgh); Pam Williams (Frostburg State University); Thomas Haughton (National Archives); Paul Allen Sommerfeld (Music Division, Library of Congress); Gene Hyde (Ramsey Library, University of North Carolina–Asheville); Heather South (Western Regional Archives); Nate Pederson and Laura Garcia-Culler (Georgia Historical Society); Rebekah Scarborough-McGraw (Middle Georgia Regional Library); Dave Johnson (Penn Relays); Maureen Lerch (University of Akron–Wayne College Library); Jayne Ptolemy (Clements Library, University of Michigan); Joe Smith (University of Notre Dame's University Archives); Michelle McCoy (Chicago Public Library); Raquel Flores-Clemons (Chicago State University Archives); Dino Robinson (Shorefront Legacy Center); Anne Zald, Charla Wilson, and Janet Olson (Northwestern University Libraries); Kathy Clark (Aurora University); Harris Phillis (Thomas Tredway Library, Augustana College); Mary Mendelin (Rock Island–Milan School District); Phillip Cunningham (Tulane's Amistad Research Center); Jon Martens (Kenosha History Center); Peggy Bolhuis (Kenosha County Land Information); Katie Blank (Raynor Memorial Libraries, Marquette University); Melissa Olson (University of Wisconsin–Parkside Archives & Area Research Center); Ricki King (Roots to Branches Genealogy); Hope Grebner Bibens (Cowles Library, Drake University); Harlene Hanson (Stewart Library, Coe College); Molly Lambropoulos (Dubuque Community YMCA); Le Denniston (National WWI Museum and Memorial); Howard Trace (American Legion's Library and Museum); Jason Coleman and Kathy Coleman (Kansas State University); Anne Crane (Friends University); Bronwyn Page, Riah Morgan, David Reed, Ashley Maready, and Henry Platts (Reno County Museum); Carole Branda (Kansas African American Museum), Jami Frazier Tracy (Wichita-Sedgwick County Historical Museum); James Goodwin (*Oklahoma Eagle*); Robin Brilz (Fairmount Heritage Foundation, Denver); David Hays (University of Colorado Boulder Libraries); Dean Smith (The Bancroft Library, UD Berkeley); Lloyd Cayton and Herb Cobbs (Mayme A. Clayton Library and Museum); Salvador Güereña (California Ethnic and Multicultural Archives, University of California, Santa Barbara); Jim Tessalone (USC Sports Information); and Aimee Perez (UCLA Library Special Collections).

During our phone conversation, Black Fives historian Claude Johnson likened Sol Butler to a bee "going around pollinating flowers." To the degree this book is a late-blooming flower, I give huge credit to those who came through at key stages. The amazing discoveries of Carolyn Krumanocker at the Oklahoma Historical Society shed light on the Butler family's experience in Kingfisher County. Nancy Ingersoll shared copies of her late spouse Robert Ryland's memorable autobiography. Neal Rozendaal provided contact information for Sherman Howard (and a welcome biography on Duke Slater). Frank Potter delivered the pivotal lecture on Paul Robeson where I first met David Rollins. For timely advice, my thanks to David Brodnax, Ulrich Adelt, Nishani Frazier, Richard Breaux, Elliott Powell, and Erica Hannickel. Daniel Atkinson provided keen insight on blackface minstrelsy. Kristen Anderson-Bricker at Loras College shared her insightful research on the WWI flu pandemic. My friend and favorite college professor, Joel Eisinger, offered helpful feedback on early chapter drafts.

I would also like to thank the late Kerry Burt, Amie Allen, Zephrey Allen, Lanita Morris, R. G. Lucas, Thomas Wells, Rita Liberti, Maureen Smith, Ketra Armstrong, Mark Dyreson, Lou Antolihao, Leslie Schwalm, Corey Creekmur, Joann Ross; descendants of Charley Paddock, John Adelmann, Eric Lott, David Roediger, Shawn Leigh Alexander, Rob Ruck, Louis Moore, Andrew D. Linden, Gerald Gems, David Trowbridge, Jaden Janek, Joseph Cooper, James Carton, Boukary Sawadogo, John Kisch, Bob Wells, Davarian Baldwin, Christopher Husted, William Estrada, Randall Burkett, Dan Burleson, Chasidy Williams, Galyn Vessey, Barbara Dinneen, Gregory Bond, Michelle Updegrove, Bonnie Basemann, Gabrielle Martin, Noelle Martin, Silke Weineck, Craig Klein, Larry Lester, Michael Webber, Gary Ashwill, Heidi Pettitt, Hence Parson, Valerie Darnell, Jennifer Mack, Ben Weiss, Darlene Powell Garlington, Betsy Schlabach, Antoinette Toppin, artist Chris Rice, and rising entrepreneur Rafael Edy.

Special thanks go to Beth Marino, an exceptionally talented developmental editor, who strengthened my arguments in the process of helping shed about fifty thousand words from my manuscript. Furthermore, her wise and caring advice kept me moving forward. Wayne Anderson reconnected me with Beth, our mutual friend from American Studies at the University of Iowa.

Thank you to everyone at the University of Illinois Press who has helped turn my manuscript into this book. Danny Nasset, Gary Smith, and Tad Ringo shepherded me through the publication process, and I remain grateful that Danny, along with Sport and Society series editors Jaime Schultz and Aram Goudsouzian, took an interest in this project. Thanks go to the two anonymous readers of my manuscript for their insightful suggestions, as well as to Charrice Jones, Kevin Cunningham, Jennie Fisher, and Angela Burton for addressing my questions and concerns. Copyeditor Jill R. Hughes improved the manuscript in innumerable ways, and thanks to Jason Gabbert for the superb cover design.

Regarding the art that graces the cover, I owe a big thank-you to my friend Sharon Matt Atkins for putting me in touch with artist and project manager Jennifer Hoffman-Williamson (Goblin Party, New York), who introduced me to artist Khari Johnson-Ricks. The finished work exceeds my expectations and vividly evokes the intensity and kinetic brilliance of Sol Butler.

Two friends, Susan Renée and Donald Register, deserve special recognition. Susan's support through this project has been an unanticipated gift. Her willingness to share her exquisite writing on her own compelling, brave, and compassion-filled life has inspired my efforts and raised my spirits. Retired Presbyterian pastor Donald Register has been present for numerous family milestones, officiating at the blessing of marriage ceremony for my spouse, Sharon, and me as pastor of the church that descended from the one that gave rise to the Roamer Girls (see chapters 7 and 8). He exemplifies a life lived with dignity, love, and purpose.

I am forever grateful for the late (Aunt) Willie Mae Jackson and her life partner, (Uncle) Earl Taylor, making me always feel welcome and—over numerous story-filled meals in their kitchen—vividly evoking their experiences in Depression-era Orange Mound, Memphis, and Bronzeville Chicago. The love and support of my siblings, Michael Stoos and Jennifer Stoos, and siblings-in-law, Cheryl Stoos, Dan Tysver, Sherrie Hall, Lasandra Hall, and Chanell Hall, and my many beloved nieces and nephews buoy my efforts.

I offer this book in loving memory to my parents, who cherished the arts, and the mother-in-law I never got to meet. My mother, Shirley Harper Cox, and father, Gary Everett Stoos (former United Church of Christ pastors), taught me to admire and follow those who resist oppression and fight for justice. I am endlessly grateful for their love and support. Jean Helen Hall migrated from Covington, Tennessee, to Chicago's South Side, eventually becoming a registered nurse and purchasing a home for her family. She died suddenly at forty-two, not long before I started dating her second-born child of five, who is now my beloved spouse. Jean's legacy of perseverance, ingenuity, and strength lives on through the sacrifices and family-sustaining efforts of her descendants.

I dedicate this book to my wife, Sharon, whose love and encouragement made this book possible, and to our children, Tatum, Elise, and Joplin, whose lives make my scholarly efforts feel necessary and important. When reading this book, may you dearest ones sense why its creation—the product of several thousand hours of labor—is my hopeful investment in a fully desegregated world of equal opportunity. A parental commitment, this story symbolizes my steadfast love for you.

Following pages: Butler poised before broad (long) jumping on July 4, 1919, at the Inter-Allied Games in Paris, France. (Film still, University of Dubuque Archives)

Warm-Up

From "I'm Going to Land on a That Shore," spiritual arranged by Phil V. S. Lindsley (*National Jubilee Melodies*, 12th ed. [Nashville: National Baptist Publishing Board], p. 125)

In 1919, only days after being shackled by younger classmates in a college prank that evoked the specter of American slavery, Sol Butler began a journey that would bring him international fame. The twenty-four-year-old star Black athlete could still feel the pressure where the metal restraints had been sawed off his ankles when Amateur Athletic Union officials summoned him to compete on the American track and field team at the Inter-Allied Games in Paris. At a time when segregation both prompted and restricted Black movement, Butler journeyed in relative freedom and style from the Iowa campus of the University of Dubuque to Paris, France, by car, train, and passenger ship. At the international sporting competition, attended by the signers of the Versailles Treaty, he leaped to a commanding first-place finish in the broad jump. Already a Midwest celebrity, Butler quickly became known around the world.

Once in motion, Solomon Wellings "Sol" Butler stayed in motion. Born in Oklahoma in 1895, he and his family migrated to increasingly integrated Midwestern communities, where Butler achieved unprecedented success in high school track and field and football before dominating college sports at the University of Dubuque. His first-place finish at the 1919 Inter-Allied Games brought him long-lasting, Olympic-size fame even though war, injury, and charges of professionalism thwarted his dreams of claiming an Olympic medal. As a professional athlete during the 1920s and 1930s, Butler traveled from coast to coast and across the Midwest demonstrating the innovative play of "Black Fives" (i.e., all-Black) basketball and dazzling audiences of barely integrated National Football League (NFL) games and all-Black football teams alike. Athletic ambitions led him to Hollywood, into boxing, and back to Chicago, where he helped guide the next generation of top Black athletes to compete within and against segregated society.

Due to an infamous US Supreme Court ruling, Butler lived all but his earliest and final months of life in a nation that legally practiced and violently enforced racial separation. When and how segregation slowed him down depended on an unpredictable interplay of local custom, ideology, and business calculation. His inclusion on the NFL's Canton Bulldogs, for instance, did not prevent his exclusion from a game against the Giants in New York. Such instances echoed and reinforced the entrenched racial divide nationwide and the systemic racism that still dramatically increases poverty and incarceration rates of African Americans while reducing their levels of wealth, home ownership, health, and educational achievement. Butler's arduous and dangerous, if sometimes self-serving and unsuccessful, movement across the color line represented an imperfect yet compelling challenge to stubborn racial barriers for himself and those who followed.

Despite daily confrontations with injustice, Butler unrelentingly adapted to the shifting realities of white supremacy to create spaces of opportunity—level playing fields—for Black athletes. He negotiated contracts with white team owners, traveled across lands populated with sundown towns and histories of racial violence, and battled on gridirons where Black bodies were targets of racially motivated abuse, all of which served to subvert the system of segregation. By occupying sport spaces that dominant society groomed for whiteness, Butler and a few other early twentieth-century elite Black athletes, including many of his friends, helped mobilize the long civil rights movement.

Multidimensional Mobility and African American Opportunity

Sol Butler's life of constant travel—of speed and agility and of the dynamic social negotiations required of a Black man navigating racism in the first half of the twentieth century—is a study in mobility. Whether sprinting down a race track, traveling across the country to compete, or traversing racial and class lines in social interaction, he relied on an orchestrated blend of transport, ranging from trains, automobiles, and ocean liners to his fleet legs and gilded tongue.[1] His body in motion on fields of play attracted fans; fueled their imaginations and speculations; and, through newspaper accounts, photographs, and memory, left the most discernible record of his time on earth. Until the 1920s, perhaps no one else consistently leaped well over twenty feet, dashed one hundred yards in ten seconds or less, and escaped and shut down opponents on the gridiron and in the basketball "cage" with such dazzling dexterity. Butler practiced strategically, long and hard, excelled in a wide range of sports, and played at an elite level beyond the age when his peers retired from competition. Whether hustling over cleat-worn fields or sweat-soaked courts, he always pushed his body's limits.

As sport success created opportunity, Butler increasingly depended on transportation to reach distant destinations. From coal-fired to jet-fueled engines, travel evolved dramatically during his lifetime, enabling a realm of speedy, individualized transit. Yet it also served as a powerful tool for maintaining racial inequality. Shortly after Butler's birth in Oklahoma Territory, the US Supreme Court ruled against biracial citizen Homer Plessy in his challenge to Louisiana law requiring separate cars for Black people on trains. The court upheld segregated seating, thus affirming the state's claim of separate but equal accommodations, which in practice promoted segregation at the expense of equality. This ruling ushered in the nearly six decades of federally sanctioned segregation known as Jim Crow (a term coined from the song and dance "Jumping Jim Crow," popularized by an early blackface minstrel).

Mechanized travel also symbolized the means for subjugating and destroying Black bodies.[2] White mobs commandeered trains to bring victims to lynching sites or dragged mangled corpses behind cars. Large-spectacle lynchings, a form of recreation fueled by access to personal vehicles and mass transit,[3] also made palpable the links between transport and deadly power: mobility in the service of racial terrorism. Butler enjoyed a freedom of movement not possible for African Americans during slavery, but he still experienced racially coded impediments to travel. Hotels and restaurants excluded Black would-be customers across the Midwest. Railroads below the Mason-Dixon Line, which Butler occasionally crossed to attend sporting events, excluded Black passengers from cars serving whites. During his lifetime, thousands of white-on-Black murders went unpunished because the American legal system buttressed white supremacy. When he traveled, opportunity and risk coexisted.

Sol Butler's parents helped to mitigate such risk by migrating to places where their children could maintain cultural ties while accessing well-funded public education and safely enjoying additional opportunities typically denied to African Americans. Their move out of Wichita, Kansas, when schools became segregated, for instance, brought the family to Hutchinson, the only large community in that state where education remained integrated. Under their tutelage, Sol interacted daily with people from diverse backgrounds and in a variety of settings. He and his three siblings had to navigate schools filled with white students, teachers, and administrators. These social interactions sparked friendships and respect across racial lines that helped protect him from racially motivated harm on the playing fields and beyond.

Middle-class manners, expressed through studied gestures and verbal eloquence, along with an acute awareness of his audience, played an essential role in Butler's success as an athlete. His heroic journey into racially contested spaces—which were potentially anywhere he encountered white people—relied not only on what he accomplished with his legs but also on his comportment. From high school through his professional sports career, commentators noted how Butler's smile put people at ease and won them over. Those who knew him on a personal level wrote of his countenance as revealing his friendliness, openness, honesty, confidence, and all-around high character. The journalists who did not know him often said that his wide winning smile evidenced simplicity, docility, naïveté, and even subservience and dim-wittedness. At an international competition in France, Butler shook hands with a former king, just as he did a few days later with the commander of the American forces during World War I. In both instances, film shows that the champion athlete greeted these older white men with a seemingly relaxed grin and confident, direct gaze; the media misrepresented these staged performances of mutual respect as subservience and condescension. Like other Black cultural leaders, most famously the then-rising jazz revolutionary Louis "Satchmo" (i.e., satchel mouth) Armstrong, Butler's smile disarmed audiences, encouraging receptivity to his extraordinary skills.

White audiences often viewed Butler through the distorting lens of racism, but he navigated across the country and the Atlantic with precision, poise, and purpose. He adopted what literary scholar Koritha Mitchell identifies as a *critical demeanor of shamelessness* that "becomes possible when looking at oneself without the lens of dominant representations" and recognizing "the power of dominant assumptions but also how little they have to do with you and the communities to which you belong."[4] Coming of age when brazen world champion Black boxer Jack Johnson served as a lightning rod for white male anxiety and rage, Sol crafted a public persona of a modest, hardworking, and loyal athlete, but his decades of actions in the sports world consistently challenged Jim Crow forces that limited the movement of Black athletes and African Americans in general. He knew how to use the spotlight to his advantage.

A master of movement, Butler embodied the possibility for African American education, recreation, pleasure, employment, achievement, recognition, leadership, group organizing, and activism. Always on the go, he achieved early twentieth-century fame, yet reared to value communal bonds, he strove for much more than just personal glory. As he said in a memoir he cowrote with his older brother, he aimed to be a leader of his race.

In Jim Crow America, few Black athletes benefited from quality recreational facilities, strong organizational support, and access to elite competitions; even fewer had the opportunity to turn their athletic talents and abilities into a source of income. During the 1920s and 1930s, when professional sports and hero culture blossomed, Butler made a Herculean effort to support himself through sports, both on and off the fields of play. For years after his contemporaries and friends—including Judge Duke Slater, businessman Fritz Pollard, record producer J. Mayo Williams, and performing artist Paul Robeson—left athletics to pursue other professions, Butler continued to work as a player, organizer, manager, coach, trainer, and journalist in an industry that increasingly brought wealth to white athletes and their supporting casts. Segregation created economic inequality in athletics, just as it did more broadly in African American life. He pushed back against this reality, directly challenging the oppressive social and economic system with his continued presence in sports spaces funded and controlled by white people.

Black Sports Entrepreneurship and Desegregation

On October 10, 1913, one day before high school sophomore Sol Butler scored five touchdowns in a shutout victory over a team from a neighboring Kansas town, twenty-seven-year-old Austrian economist Joseph Schumpeter arrived in New York City on the ocean liner *Lusitania*. Invited to Columbia University as a visiting professor, Schumpeter would meet "glowing acclaim" over fall and spring semesters as he lectured at universities across the country.[5] A fan of American economists, who in turn embraced him and his work, Schumpeter expounded on his influential theories and prompted references to him as the father of modern entrepreneurial thought. In his book *The Theory of Economic Development* (1911), Schumpeter presented a powerful idea on economic change and its consequences.[6] He believed that development "occurred only as the economy absorbs the effects of a change that forever alters its structure, destroys the old equilibrium, and creates the conditions of a new equilibrium," writes Schumpeter biographer Robert Allen. "Development is what happens between the old and the new equilibrium" and depends on entrepreneurship.[7] According to Schumpeter's theory, the entrepreneur's one and only job was to spark development through *innovation*. While the self-assured European scholar did not aim to shape public policy or foster *social* change, he nonetheless believed his theory of economic development could be applied to all aspects of society, including politics and social life. Responsive to the dynamics of societal change, it provides an instructive foundation for conceiving of Butler as an entrepreneur.

Sol Butler was an incredible athlete, but considering the totality of his sports career, "social entrepreneur" is a fuller and more apt description of his efforts. While his fame resulted from his athletic accomplishments, his career choices suggest that fame was primarily a means to foster change in the social, political, and business realms. What good was fame if he and his friends and family continued to be treated as second-class citizens? When Butler raced past and jumped beyond competitors in track and field, his victories were arguments against segregation writ large.[8] The same held true when he coached a winning team, mentored youth, made a sale in business, or, as a journalist, drew attention to the victories of other Black athletes. Under Jim Crow, embodying and supporting African American achievement in any field, including sports, signaled the uplift of the race. Butler's efforts against segregation and toward justice, therefore, may be viewed as part and parcel of his social or, more precisely, *Black sports* entrepreneurship.[9]

Economist Schumpeter argued that there were different types of innovation: introducing a new good or method of production, opening a new market, controlling the supply source of raw materials, and the "carrying out of the new organization of any industry."[10] Black athletes did not have the same organizational control or access to consumer markets as their white peers, so we can read Butler's athletic accomplishments and career moves as innovations. His entrepreneurial spirit as he carried out new organizations of the sports industry radiate from activities as varied as his single-handedly winning integrated high school track and field meets and competing in the fragilely integrated NFL and on all-Black football and basketball teams against all-white teams to promoting the integration of professional tennis and automobile racing and surveying white sports figures on the topic of race. Like Los Angeles Lakers superstar Kobe Bryant,[11] Butler's support of women's athletics is one of his greatest legacies; through organizing, coaching, and advocating for compensation, he helped create conditions that led to the establishment of women's professional basketball. While not alone in the innovative ways he challenged segregation and gender inequality—in fact, we may better see his innovation as a vital part of a collective whole—Butler may be unique in the combined length and breadth of his professional sporting activity, which meant he was uniquely situated to innovate in the athletic arena.[12]

Butler's entrepreneurism depended on the cooperation of like-minded individuals. Jim Crow realities meant he had to work collaboratively and remain dutifully responsive to the African American community that supported him. His strategies were rooted in the traditions of Black ancestors who, through inventiveness, grit, daring, and faith, "made a way out of no way" to claim rights and freedoms. The capital Butler drew upon was cultural more than financial and reflected the motile strength of his relationships and ability to influence people. His innovations did not create financial wealth as much as they helped make possible a durable position in amateur and professional sports for future Black Americans. Like his parents' heroic efforts to raise a family with high aspirations, Sol's dynamic movement on integrated playing fields, in the social sphere, and across the country embodied his claims to full citizenship, for himself and for all Black Americans.

His daring behavior aimed at social change—Butler's "entrepreneurial action"—contributed to a collection of actions by Black athletes that led to the eventual breaking down of the color line in sports.[13] Whether coincidental or causally linked, the parallels between Butler's efforts and certain noteworthy developments raise questions. Would African American long jumpers have become so dominant in this event during the 1920s and 1930s if not for Butler's door-opening success? By bravely facing segregation and exclusion as an athlete in New Orleans, did Butler prepare the Amateur Athletic Union to reject that city's subsequent bid to host a national track and field meet? In fostering support for interracial athletics as a player and coach in Los Angeles during the Great Depression, did he play a role in the reintegration of the NFL? Would many promising African American youth—under the auspices of Ye Olde Tymers Club and the park system in Chicago—have blossomed into elite amateur and professional athletes without Butler's coaching and mentorship?

As white Americans adjusted to Butler and other Black sports entrepreneurs' movement into "white" spaces, they became, over time, more open to and supportive of Black presence in athletics, a reality popularly symbolized by Jackie Robinson's desegregation of Major League Baseball. Athletics became increasingly segregated during Butler's early decades of adulthood, but he helped spark a lasting reversal of this dispiriting trend. According to Schumpeter, "An entrepreneur is not a profession and as a rule not a lasting condition."[14] Most of what Butler did posed no threat to the system of segregation. Some of his actions, like performing minstrelsy on stage during his high school and college years, probably buttressed this system. But at his most daring, athletic best, with bodily and social transport deftly harmonized, Butler impacted—even dazzled—white audiences and provided them with tangible reason to question the absence and exclusion of other Black athletes.

Outline of This Book

Sol Butler: An Olympian's Odyssey through Jim Crow America illustrates how a star athlete fostered integration by disrupting the equilibrium of segregation. His development and success as an innovator or social entrepreneur may be understood in three stages, which structure this book. Part I: "Origins" (chapters 1–3) focuses on Butler's first twenty years and the lessons he learned from his family and in their interracial Oklahoma, Kansas, and Illinois communities. Only one generation removed from slavery, he dutifully imbibed the lessons of the Black middle class and witnessed how cultural leaders, including athletes, could transcend barriers imposed by white supremacy that kept African Americans from securing good jobs and homes and the benefits of broad social inclusion. Part II: "Amateur" (chapters 4–6) covers Butler's college years in Dubuque, Iowa, when he tested the limits of social and physical transport through amateur athletics. Operating during the World War I era within unusually integrated sport and educational spheres, a testament to his exceptional ability to discern where he might be most free, he achieved global fame and sports recognition that buttressed his subsequent entrepreneurial efforts. Addressing the next fifteen years of his life, part III: "Professional" (chapters 7–9) considers Butler's thorny transition into professional and segregated sports and the dynamic, often successful ways he capitalized on his celebrity in primarily all-Black communities of Chicago, New York, and Los Angeles. His incessant cultural engagement, even as his body slowed with age, attested to his fearless commitment to integration through sports.

The first chapter illustrates that mobility was a defining feature in the lives of Sol's parents, who created educational opportunities for their children through migration. In Kingfisher, Oklahoma, and Wichita, Kansas, Sol first encountered segregation while developing a belief that interacting with—even befriending—well-connected white people and adopting middle-class values was a ticket to upward mobility. Chapter 2 illustrates why he cultivated a public persona of humility as his unprecedented success in Hutchinson, Kansas, high school sports increasingly placed him in the spotlight. Adopting the ideology of the era that amateur sports both revealed and developed good character, he distanced himself from the racially inflammatory example of immodest Black heavyweight champion Jack Johnson (just as Joe Louis did years later). Chapter 3 focuses on his cowritten memoir about his high school athletic trials and triumphs, including in Rock Island, Illinois. Along with providing invaluable insight on his life and worldview, this genre-bending booklet represents an innovative way to capitalize on his regional athletic popularity for purposes of securing access to higher education, a perceived key to upward Black mobility.

Chapter 4 considers Butler's first two years at Dubuque German College (now the University of Dubuque), where he and his brother enjoyed unusually free movement as the only Black students in a school that celebrated its diversity. When not sharpening his physical and social skills among a polyglot student body, he traveled east to establish a national reputation in track and field while forming bonds with other burgeoning Black cultural leaders. The fifth chapter makes the case that mounting anti-Black sentiment and broad-scale threats of racial violence during World War I limited Butler's freedom. Even on a comparatively progressive, interracial campus—and despite his stellar national success in track and field and college graduation—he had to endure white supremacy's indignities, dangers, and prohibitions on the playing fields and even on campus amid white women and younger classmates. Chapter 6 follows Butler through his crowning athletic achievement at the Inter-Allied Games in Paris. His world-beating long jump, a symbolic strike against racist ideologies, contrasted with the oppression Black troops experienced in postwar Europe and demeaning media portrayals of his hypervisible Black success. Momentarily leaping over the color line made this barrier more obvious.

Chapter 7 traces how Sol's entrepreneurial ambitions prompted him to leave the predominantly white communities where he established his fame to focus his appreciable sport energies on rapidly growing all-Black communities. Capitalizing on the first wave of the Great Migration after a frustrating Olympics, he moved to Chicago, where he participated in the marketplace activism of the New Negro era, most notably through basketball. Chapter 8 shows Butler, who passes his physical peak and stops competing in elite amateur events, increasingly challenge segregated systems as an athlete and journalist. This new activist emphasis coincided with his entrance into commercial sales and product endorsements in New York and Chicago and his professional football career across the Midwest. The synergy between his myriad sports activities—on the playing fields and in the realm of culture and business—made this period the peak of his social entrepreneurism. Chapter 9 follows Butler during a period when economic woes mount and he attempts to wed his innovations with the sporting life. By the time of the Great Depression, he participated strictly on all-Black teams that pushed for integration by competing against white teams. Entering the realms of boxing and Hollywood, the once impeccably humble cultural leader embraced a degree of showiness to maintain his freedom of movement.

Addressing his final two decades of life in Chicago before his untimely death in a barroom gun fight, the concluding "Cooldown" considers Butler's integratory efforts through the lens of Black creative destruction, sports innovations that undermined both segregation and a vibrant all-Black sports world. In collaboration with many other sports entrepreneurs, he established the conditions for sturdy symbolic victories of sports integration, like Jackie Robinson entering Major League Baseball, and a new social equilibrium balanced on the presumption that no one should be excluded from athletics because of their race.

The Significance of Music

Music played a vital role in Sol Butler's life. Through school and into adulthood he publicly sang and danced, and late in life he even composed a song with two sisters from one of the great Black vaudeville troupes. Music developed in unprecedented ways over the course of Butler's life. He witnessed the proliferation of popular sheet music, the rise of phonograph records and radio, and the introduction of "talkies" (films that incorporated synchronized sound, which his friend Fritz Pollard helped popularize). He also experienced new forms of Black music that forever transformed American culture and global music. As a youth he would have heard ragtime piano, with its infectious syncopated rhythms, played by young performers like the musician who married his oldest sibling. Around the time he graduated from college and moved to Chicago and New York, jazz mobilized movement in surrounding venues, like the halls where he and his basketball teammates danced to hot bands. His professional football teammate and friend, Mayo Williams, who as "the most prominent and prolific Black record producer (and the most consequential producer of Black music) during the first half of the twentieth century" stimulated an early craze for blues music.[15] By the time Butler returned from Los Angeles to Chicago in the 1930s, local gospel composers, directors, and choirs were transforming Black sacred music practices around the country. All of these new, vital forms of music coalesced in response to the same conjuncture of modern societal forces—migration, industrialization, and segregation—that shaped the sporting culture in which Butler made his greatest impact.

The eleven musical epigraphs within provide a creative counterpoint to the evidence-based narrative of Butler's life. Some of the quoted songs connect directly with events in this biography, but in most cases the selections represent my attempt to evoke something meaningful. In some instances a particular lyric conjures an animating mood, theme, or idea in the chapter; in others, the creative brilliance of the notes themselves evokes the cultural landscape that Butler occupied in ways that words cannot. Nearly every piece testifies to the strength, depth, and richness of African American culture.

Together, these musical epigraphs remind us that as remarkable as the story of Sol Butler may be, we cannot fully appreciate his life—or any life—solely through what remains in the archival record. Undoubtedly, much of his dynamic existence has been lost to history. By invoking the changing soundscape that flourished throughout Sol Butler's life, the epigraphs invite us to conceive of the star athlete in symbiotic relationship with other forms of Black cultural production, which experienced their own mobile journeys through early twentieth-century America.

• • •

Less than six months after moving to Hutchinson, Kansas, Butler's seventy-year-old father, Ben Butler Sr., dictated a letter to the US Pension Bureau. "I believe a great injustice was done me in rejecting my claim for Increase of Pension Act of Feb_6_1907," the illiterate veteran began. If the secretary of the interior refused to reconsider Butler's petition to increase his monthly payments to fifteen dollars, which the new pension commissioner, James Davenport, had just rejected, Butler requested that his "claim be put in hands of a Special pension Examiner to determine its merits."

Two people witnessed the signing of Ben Butler's letter before a notary public. One, Mary Doran, was the wife of Samuel Doran, a land surveyor, former probate judge, and a member of the Union Signal Corps; Ben would have known him as a fellow member of an interracial post of Civil War veterans. The other witness, railroad clerk Theodore Talmage, would have crossed paths with Ben at his refreshment and shoeshine stand downtown. These reasonably wealthy, educated, white homeowners represented just two of the numerous people—including lawyers, doctors, and politicians—whom the Butlers summoned into duty over multiple decades and across many different hometowns to help ensure they received the hard-fought federal funds to which Ben's debilitating service to his country entitled them.

While his parents took deft steps, both physical and social, to secure the family's tenuous financial future as Ben Sr.'s declining health rendered him increasingly immobile, seventh-grade Sol had just finished his first season of football at his new school, giving onlookers a glimpse of his burgeoning kinetic brilliance. The youngest Butler first raced and eventually jumped with all of his physical, mental, and spiritual strength to pass a color line, which might be left in the proverbial dust only if he stayed on the move.

Sol Butler in the school yearbook, photo ca. 1917. (The *Key* [1919], p. 109, University of Dubuque Archives)

PART I

Origins

Spring 1895–Summer 1915

1

Endured Many Hardships

March 3, 1895–Summer 1909

From "Lift Every Voice and Sing" (1900) by James Weldon Johnson and J. Rosamond Johnson

"I was born in Oklahoma, seven miles from the present site of Kingfisher, March 3, 1895." So begins *Three Years of High School Athletics*, the memoir Solomon Wellings "Sol" Butler wrote with his older brother, Ben, in 1915. "My father was a slave, but my mother a free born woman. Our family, which is composed of two boys and two girls, endured many hardships that naturally follow the opening of a new country. By a piece of misfortune my father lost his farm and we moved to Kingfisher to live." The move to Kingfisher was not the first of Ben Butler Sr.'s migrations, and it wouldn't be his last. Bent on determining his own fate, he mounted several escapes from racial oppression and undertook many journeys toward economic opportunity, as did Sol's mother, Mary Elizabeth Butler (née Wellings). Together, the couple navigated across class and racial lines through the South to the Midwest. Mobility defined their adult lives. Free movement, though often hard won and fraught with danger, would come to define their son's life as well.[1]

Born on March 4, 1839, on a plantation in Morgan County, Alabama, in the Tennessee Valley, Sol Butler's father entered life as the property of another man, Arthur Stephenson. By the time of the 1830 census, Arthur owned twenty-one people; a quarter century later, he owned forty-one—Ben, his mother, and his siblings among them. The Stephensons owned a 2,347-acre farm on land the Cherokee and Chickasaw Indians lost through treaties with the US government in the early nineteenth century. Around the time Ben turned seventeen, Arthur died, and his estate, including human property, was divided up among his widow and children. Probate records identify Butler as "Boy Ben" under the inventory of "Negroes," with a value of nine hundred dollars, several hundred dollars less than adult males like "Man George," who topped the list at fourteen hundred dollars. At the time of his death, Arthur owned thirteen men, eight women, ten boys, six girls, and four young children. Ben, along with his mother and siblings, went to the oldest Stephenson child, Minerva, and her husband, William Byrd Burleson.[2]

The Burlesons lived approximately seven miles southeast of Decatur, Alabama, on a four-hundred-acre plantation given to William in the 1840s by his father, Jonathan Burleson. The elder Burleson owned three thousand contiguous acres that, on the west end, contained a stretch of Flint Creek, which flowed north to the Tennessee River; the eastern border of the Burleson land roughly bisected what became known as the Burleson Mountain, which rose to over eight hundred feet above sea level. William, Minerva, and their ten children lived in a house on the un-farmable eastern portion of their estate near a freshwater spring. The slave quarters were situated nearby on land that sloped up from the flat, cotton-growing farmland on the western half of the plantation. According to the 1860 census, Ben and his family were among fifteen enslaved Black people on William Burleson's plantation.[3]

Considered, in his own words, a trustworthy "honor slave," Ben probably traveled into Decatur and perhaps even Huntsville (about twenty-five miles away) to run errands for the Burlesons.[4] In Huntsville he might have seen the active slave market. In both towns he had opportunity to encounter free Black people, most of whom were biracial. Such encounters offered a glimpse of what freedom looked like, even if severely circumscribed in a society that failed to recognize anyone with African ancestry as a full citizen. The US Supreme Court made this explicit in Ben's late teens when Chief Justice Roger Taney wrote in the majority decision of the infamous Dred Scott case that Black people "had no rights which the white man was bound to respect." Reflecting and reinforcing this culture of white supremacy, the vast majority of African Americans in Alabama were enslaved, accounting for nearly 43 percent (51,800 enslaved people) of the total 1860 population of the Tennessee Valley. One-third of Morgan County's residents were enslaved.[5]

Ben spent the first two years of the Civil War on the Burleson plantation, which offered familiarity and a degree of stability during a period marked by intense chaos and unpredictability. Speaking many decades after the fact with a reporter in Kansas, he recalled:

> When the war began old master was too old to enlist but all the boys and his brothers went to the war. I run the plantation for old master and got out three crops after the war opened. It was in 1863 when the Yankee soldiers was

> only six miles away that Master told me I'd have to go off and take the stock to the Confederate army. He told me to take all the mules and other stock.[6]

Conjuring up a tortured mix of emotions, he declared the reason for his next bold move: "I didn't want to leave the plantation, and didn't want to get into any army, but I made up my mind that if I had to fight, I'd fight in the Yankee army 'cause I knowed they were coming to help my people out."[7]

Ben escaped in the fall of 1863. When he fled to the Yankee army, they sent him to Pulaski, Tennessee, where in mid-November he enlisted as a cook in Company B of the Second Iowa Volunteer Infantry Regiment. African American enlistment increased during the second occupation of North Alabama, and by war's end approximately five thousand Black people from the state had joined the Union Army. Like Ben Butler, many of these Southern Black enlistees were relegated to service jobs and denied a gun and the chance to fight, a reality that began to change as Black troops and all-Black regiments demonstrated their bravery and skill on the battlefield.[8]

His regiment left Pulaski in April 1864 to join the Sixteenth Corps of the District of Tennessee on its campaign to capture Atlanta. Ben served under Captain Oliver C. Lewis of Davenport, Iowa, and Colonel Noel B. Howard and was wounded during the Battle of Atlanta.[9] The unidentified injury may have caused the partial paralysis in his left leg that caused him to limp in later years. Union forces captured the city by early September. "I served in the rest of the war," Butler recalled, "and went with old Uncle Billie [*sic*] Sherman to the sea."[10] "Uncle Billie Sherman" was General William Tecumseh Sherman, who led over sixty thousand troops from Atlanta to Savannah, Georgia. It was in Savannah that Sherman issued Special Field Orders, No. 15, which allotted forty-acre plots of land seized from Confederates to thousands of newly freed people. Later that year, President Andrew Johnson revoked the orders, and Butler, like most of his fellow Black enlistees, would never benefit from a single acre.

From Savannah, Ben's regiment traveled toward Washington, DC. While they were en route, the war ended, and in the nation's capital the regiment participated in a large military pageant and remained in a camp until early June 1865. They then moved on to Camp McClellan in Davenport, Iowa, where Ben disbanded with his regiment on July 20, eight days after his honorable discharge in Louisville, Kentucky. Four decades later, in an effort to secure his military pension, he once again journeyed hundreds of miles to Davenport, where he was greeted by his white comrades of the Second Iowa Regiment. His experiences along the Mississippi River—burnished by the aura of a war that brought freedom to enslaved Black Americans and dignity to Black enlistees—gave Ben Butler reason to feel partial toward Iowa, the state where his two sons would attend college a half century after the war ended.[11]

As a Union soldier, Ben had served as "Ben Bullison," the name his enlisting officer wrote down phonetically since Ben could neither read nor write. But after the war ended, "he refused to be called by that name any longer."[12] He chose the surname Butler in honor of Benjamin Franklin Butler, the Civil War general and Republican congressman from Massachusetts. During the war, General Butler initiated the Union policy of designating captured slaves in Virginia as "contraband of war," which drove Northern support for the abolition of slavery. After the war, Congressman Butler helped shepherd the Civil Rights Act of 1875 through Congress and into law.[13] "In 1867 in Memphis Ten. I voluntary [*sic*] changed my name to Ben Butler," the Black veteran dictated to a notary in Kingfisher, Oklahoma, years later. "I did not want to ware my masters [*sic*] name any longer."[14] Ben Butler could not have foreseen the consequences of shedding the name of his former enslaver: a lifelong struggle to receive compensation for the military service he performed as Ben Bullison.

Within a few years of the war's end, and around the time he moved to Memphis (where he would live until the 1890s), Ben returned to the Burleson plantation one last time.[15] He arrived to find his former master's family in a state of grief and decline. William Burleson and his fifteen-year-old son had died on the same December day shortly after the war ended; a ten-year-old daughter had preceded them in death less than two months before. Finding herself alone with a toddler on a decimated farm, Minerva moved to Decatur.[16] Her young brother-in-law leased the Burleson farm to his business partner, George Lemon, a private in the Union Army, who was "lured by the prospect of realizing a quick profit by raising cotton."[17] Lemon and other former Union soldiers in the area "had high hopes that they could revolutionize cotton agriculture by transforming the former slave labor force into wage labor, thus aiding the freed people and proving once and for all the superiority of the North's ideas."

Butler could have stayed to earn wages farming the same land he had worked as an enslaved man, but he returned to North Alabama with only one goal in mind: to learn his birth date. He sought out his "old mistress," states one of the many affidavits he obtained in his long quest to receive his military pension. "She informed me that I was born a slave in Morgan County Alabama on her farm March 4th 1839, as she had the Records of my birth in the old family Bible."[18] He would later dictate that "my birth was only recorded in a stock book."[19] These written statements, sometimes procured from doctors, white acquaintances, and friends, and typically signed before a notary public or other witnesses, provided information necessary to secure a pension and attested to the veracity of Butler's claims.

In only a few years as a free man, Ben Butler had traveled from North Alabama, where he was enslaved for the first twenty-four years of his life, to Tennessee, Atlanta, Savannah, Washington, DC, and then halfway across the country to Iowa via Kentucky, with unknown and untold stops along the way. He continued to assert his independence through travel, choosing a new name in Memphis and claiming his birth date, a stolen piece of identity, upon returning to the Burleson plantation. Mobility expanded as it symbolized his freedom.

Sol Butler's mother, Mary Elizabeth Wellings, entered the world a free woman nearly three decades after Ben Butler's birth into bondage. Born in Macon, Georgia, on December 7, 1867, Mary grew up during Reconstruction, a period that held great promise for Black Americans, even if only a modicum of this promise was realized during her lifetime. Her father worked as a carpenter, a profession that swelled with the demand for caskets after a smallpox outbreak killed nearly five thousand of Macon's Black residents in the year following the war; her mother worked as a maid. Unlike Ben, Mary learned to read and write. She had a younger sister, Ida, and an older brother, Joe Bennett. In 1878 the Wellings family lived at the intersection of Oglethorpe and First streets on the south side of the city; two years later they lived in the Vineville District, along the west bank of the Ocmulgee River.[20]

Mary's education prepared her to enter the Black middle class. As historian Heather Andrea Williams notes, "African American parents often saw education as a commodity, making direct links between schooling and upward mobility."[21] Life before emancipation had made this link apparent, especially given the fiercely enforced prohibitions across the South against teaching the enslaved to read and write. As the only community in central Georgia that offered a school for Black children that went beyond sixth grade, Macon provided rare opportunities for some Black students, yet total enrollment figures mirrored inequality levels across the state. Only 40 percent of the city's 1,800 and the state's 197,125 African American children of school age in 1880 and 1878, respectively, attended school, compared to 62 percent of white children in Georgia. Thirteen-year-old Mary went to school, but her illiterate sixteen-year-old brother, Joe, worked as a servant.[22]

By the time Mary moved to Memphis in the 1880s, the city had witnessed considerable post–Civil War change and trauma. The Black population had grown from a few hundred to many thousands and, as in Macon, approached 50 percent of the overall population. The Reconstruction era brought Black men not only freedom and opportunities but also the vote. In the 1870s, Memphis elected its first Black officials, including city council members and magistrates. During the following decade, after Reconstruction ended, Memphians elected four Black state representatives who actively pushed for civil rights legislation. Boding well for Black mobility, in 1880 a Tennessee federal circuit court ruled in favor of Jane Brown, an African American woman who sued the Memphis and Charleston Railroad for removing her from the first-class ladies' car even though she had purchased a first-class ticket. (A few years later, prominent activist Ida B. Wells won a similar case involving racial exclusion on a passenger train.)[23]

These achievements reflected the vigorous political activity within the city's African American community, but Black progress in Memphis did not proceed unchecked. The precedent the Brown and Wells cases set would be reversed in subsequent state and federal court rulings. Decades earlier, in May 1866, a white mob descended on Black neighborhoods in South Memphis. After a four-day rampage with no police intervention, the mob left forty-six African Americans and two white people dead, at least five women raped, and numerous Black churches and schools destroyed. This occurred before Mary's birth and the family's move to Tennessee. Ben's whereabouts in the years immediately after the war remain unclear, and he too may have missed this horror, but he would have experienced the city's devastating yellow fever outbreaks, most notably in 1873 and 1878, which killed thousands of residents. The potency of these outbreaks reflected the extremely unsanitary conditions in the city; its unpaved streets filled with garbage and sewage provided ideal breeding grounds for killer germs.[24]

The details of how the barely twenty-one-year-old Mary Wellings from central Georgia and the forty-nine-year-old Ben Butler from northern Alabama came to be married in Memphis in 1888 are lost to history. Rev. Lee Mitchell officiated the wedding in Avery Chapel, an African Methodist Episcopal (AME) church with a thriving congregation. In Avery Chapel, which survived 156 years until late 2019, the Butlers could have met Ida B. Wells and grocery store owner Tommie Moss, who both taught Sunday school classes and would become central figures in the racial violence that soon transformed the city.[25]

Mary and Ben Butler remained together until Ben's death more than three decades later. Mary gave birth to at least seven children, four of whom survived past childhood. Ben helped support the family in Memphis through a range of work available to Black people in an increasingly segregated urban society. Late in life he reported that in his younger years he had worked as a farmhand. In his late thirties and early forties, he worked at different times as a porter, waiter, and laborer. Later, he worked as a huckster on Beale Street. Mary worked as a laundress.[26] Memphis was home for the growing Butler family—Mary, Ben, daughter Anna, and son Ben Jr., but on March 9, 1892, that would change forever.

A Promised Land for Blacks

In early 1892, Tommie Moss and ten other African Americans opened the Peoples Grocery across the street from a white-owned grocery store, which until then had had a monopoly in the neighborhood. What began as a fight between a Black boy and a white boy over a game of dice quickly spiraled into an excuse for a white mob to target the competition. Six white men, two of them armed, surrounded the Peoples Grocery, and the owners emerged to protect their store. Shots were exchanged, and two of the white men were shot in the melee. Moss and two of his fellow grocers were soon arrested. Shortly after, a mob descended on the prison, captured the three Black men, and murdered them. Moss's last words were reported to be: "Tell my people to go west; there is no justice for them here." After the triple lynching, gangs of armed white men ransacked the Peoples Grocery, which its surviving Black owners later sold for a small fraction of its initial value to William Barrett, the white owner of the neighboring grocery store, notorious for gambling and illegal liquor sales. Barrett played a key role in fueling the white hatred that led to the lynching and the literal elimination of his Black competitors.[27]

Stories about the lynchings and mob violence appeared in newspapers across the country, both in African American papers and in the mainstream (white) press. Many portrayed Memphis as a chilling example of the South's descent into bloody inequality. No journalist made this case more effectively than Ida B. Wells, the courageous and brilliant young African American co-owner and editor of the *Memphis Free Speech*. Wells, a good friend of Tommie Moss, wrote a series of editorials about the lynchings: "There is therefore only one thing left that we can do," she concluded, "save our money and leave a town which will neither protect our lives and property, nor give us a fair trial in the courts, but takes us out and murders us in cold blood when accused by white persons." Wells's work made an impact in more ways than one: white terrorists destroyed her newspaper, marked her as a target for racial violence, and drove her out of Memphis. She also helped inspire the exodus of about six thousand Black Memphians in the months that followed the lynchings; historian Paula Giddings credits Wells for leading the first antilynching movement.[28]

The lynchings were only one symptom of the virulent racism that was increasingly eliminating the modest political, social, and economic gains made by Black Americans through their hard-fought efforts during and following Reconstruction. Memphis, along with the rest of the South, was entering a long period of legal segregation. In response to Jane Brown's legal victory, white Tennessee legislators passed the nation's first law requiring separate but equal first-class passenger cars. Even more troubling, an 1883 Supreme Court ruling declared the Civil Rights Act of 1875 unconstitutional. Throughout the decade, "scientific" racism and white fears about imagined Black licentiousness prompted the passing of antimiscegenation laws. Increasingly, Black children in Memphis attended school, but in segregated facilities, and by 1886, Black families had no representation on the school board. When the Democratic Party assumed control of the state government in the late 1880s, new laws disenfranchised Black voters. For decades, Ben had lived in a Memphis with elected Black officials and a respected and highly engaged Black electorate; in

1892 he and his family heeded Wells's advice and fled a city with no hope of Black political representation and with diminishing Black access to the ballot. The triple lynching punctuated the city's decline into a period of "no justice" for African Americans.[29]

With a toddler and infant in tow, Ben and Mary gathered up whatever possessions their travel would allow and moved over five hundred miles west to Kingfisher, Oklahoma, joining hundreds of other Black Memphians who made the trek to begin life anew in the same region. If the Butlers followed the lead of most migrants, they traveled by train. Some families, however, traveled by carriage, which enabled them to transport more of their belongings, including the farming implements necessary to work the new land they hoped to occupy. Oklahoma Territory had been clawed back from Indian Territory, the land to which the Native Americans of the Southeast were forcibly resettled after Andrew Jackson's Indian Removal Act of 1830. After the Civil War, white settlers pushed the federal government to lay claim to millions of acres—referred to as "Unassigned Lands"—in the western portion of Indian Territory. This vast expanse of land was thrown open to settlement on April 22, 1889, and thousands of white people and some African Americans entered the former Indian lands to settle. The Butler family followed in the footsteps of Native Americans, but while the Cherokee and Chickasaw walked a Trail of Tears away from land and autonomy, the Butlers traveled toward freedom and opportunity.

Abutting the western border of Arkansas and therefore on the same latitude as former slave states, Oklahoma was a popular destination for many white Southerners. Yet for the thousands of African Americans who migrated to the territory in the early 1890s, it represented the possibility of escape from the oppressive realities of the South. Boosters, most notably politician and businessman Edwin P. McCabe, sparked increasing movement to the region. Black Kansan R. F. Foster motivated fifty black families from Birmingham, Alabama, to move to Kingfisher. Several months before the Peoples Grocery lynchings, four train carloads of Black migrants arrived in Oklahoma Territory from Memphis. About eighty people from this group stopped in Kingfisher. An article printed in newspapers across the Midwest and the East Coast reported that the Memphis migrants "claim to be well provided with money, horses and mules, farming implements, household goods and provisions . . . They are all well clothed and are evidently a superior looking class of colored people."[30]

Like many other Black migrants to the region, the Butlers "looked to Oklahoma and Indian Territory as the places to achieve their dreams of yeoman independence."[31] African Americans viewed land ownership as a crucial part of racial uplift, and perhaps no place at that time offered more promising prospects for would-be landowners. By the turn of the century, Oklahoma's Black farmers owned 1.5 million acres of land valued at about $11 million. Only a quarter of Oklahoma's Black farmers were sharecroppers and tenant farmers, while across the South, only a quarter of Black farmers owned their own land. The pervasive practice of sharecropping and tenant farming kept millions of African Americans poor, if not indebted to white landowners. Regarding land access, Oklahoma was "indeed a promised land for blacks."[32] From what the Butlers could discern about Oklahoma from a distance, they likely anticipated that a growing Black community, open farmland, and opportunity awaited them. Their thirteen years in Kingfisher testified to both the fulfillment and, as time went on, the increasing frustration of ever realizing these expectations.

Approximately four hundred thousand additional acres of Cheyenne and Arapaho lands were made available to settlement on April 19, 1892, three years after the initial land rush and less than six weeks after the triple lynching in Memphis. Tens of thousands of people gathered in preparation to lay claim to property. "Everything in the town is booming and simmering," wrote a visitor to Kingfisher from Missouri. "There are about a dozen saloons, innumerable gambling houses, all running day and night, and the streets are filled with free exhibitions of every kind," including wheels of fortune, fakirs, and confidence men.[33] Women and men, most of whom carried weapons, competed in horse races through town. Soldiers guarded (without complete success) the soon-to-open territory from those attempting to get an early jump. "Dances, songs and shouts were heard along the long line until long after midnight" on the eve of the great race for land. "A negro colony north of town sang plantation melodies nearly all night."[34]

Countering the optimism, hope, and excitement conveyed by early reports from the new territory in Oklahoma, less than a month later, newspapers were describing the destitution and starvation confronting hundreds of Black migrants from Memphis. The victims, which may have included the Butlers, had been lured by unscrupulous Black real estate agents who failed to deliver on promised land claims. Some settlers died, and a large group of survivors tracked down one of the duplicitous agents, James Holland; fastened a rope around his neck; dragged him around Kingfisher; and attempted to hang him from a telegraph pole until the police intervened.[35]

By a Piece of Misfortune

On July 19, 1892, Ben purchased 160 acres of farmland in Kingfisher County for $14.80 (roughly 80 percent of the average US monthly wage for farm laborers that year).[36] The Butlers' Cheyenne or Arapaho neighbor to the immediate east was called Killing Woman, but despite her menacing moniker, she had nothing to do with the "piece of misfortune" that eventually cost the family their farm. Less than a month after the Butlers moved onto their land, a Black man named Mathew Clowers purchased the same 160 acres. Surviving records do not indicate whether Clowers and Butler were the victims of willful deception or reckless negligence on the part of land agents, but either way, for nearly four years the two families farmed and presumably lived on the same land. The Butlers' second daughter, Josephine, was born on January 20, 1893. Their youngest child, Solomon, arrived on March 3, 1895 (although the earliest extant record placed his birth in 1894).[37] When Sol was an infant, Ben Butler sued Mathew Clowers for sole possession of the contested acreage. In 1896 the Kingfisher district court affirmed the decision of a lower court in *Benjamin Butler v. Mathew Clower* [*sic*] that ruled in favor of the defendant. The Butlers lost their farm, and the family moved into the town of Kingfisher.[38]

The Butlers' move from farm to town set the tone for Sol's life in three important ways: First, it placed him in an urban environment two decades before the start of the Great Migration, when millions of the rural Black majority became urbanites. He would live in many other towns and cities over his lifetime but never again in the countryside. Second, the move placed him in close proximity to white people. Race relations changed over time and between communities, but having to interact with white people remained constant, and his future success would depend on his ability to communicate across racial lines. Finally, his family's move to Kingfisher brought him face-to-face with segregated society. They entered town at the beginning of the Jim Crow era, which the federal Supreme Court sanctioned with *Plessy v. Ferguson* in 1896, and Sol Butler would spend the rest of his life attempting to navigate, if not hurdle, racial obstacles endemic to the nation's rampant white supremacy.

The largest town in the county, Kingfisher was founded the same year Oklahoma Territory was opened to settlement and had 1,134 residents months later by 1890. This same year, Kingfisher County, with a population of 8,332, had 1,304 Black residents. So even though white people made up the town's majority, African Americans played a significant role in the local economy and counted among Kingfisher's original residents. The largest business, Oklahoma Mill, depended on wheat grown locally and brought in by trains, which reached the town by October. Around the time the Butlers arrived in Oklahoma, the presidentially appointed governor, Abraham Jefferson Seay, built a three-story mansion west of town hoping that Kingfisher would become the territorial capital. Although the governor's hopes were never realized, the community more than doubled in size over the next decade.[39]

With this growth came the need for schools, which the town initially established in tents. Kingfisher College and a normal school for the education of teachers both opened in 1895. The town's first high school opened a few years later. Virtually from the start, schools were segregated. An act passed by the inaugural session of the territorial legislature gave counties the power to decide whether or not students of different races could attend school together.[40] Like most counties in the territory, Kingfisher voted against "mixed schools,"

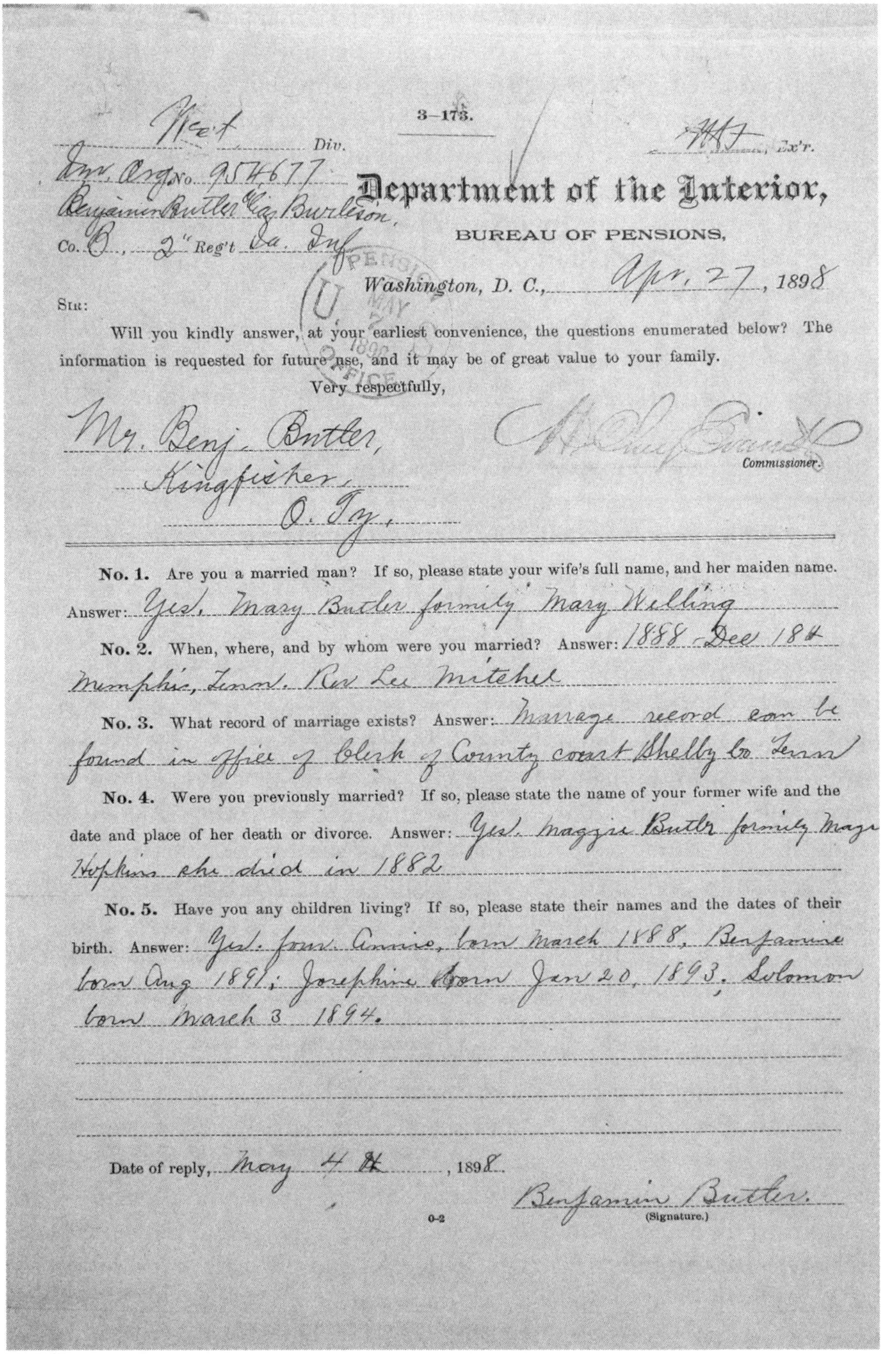

West Div. 3–173. Ex'r.

Inv. Org. No. 954677

Benjamin Butler Co. Burleson,

Co. B, 2nd Reg't Ia. Inf.

Department of the Interior,

BUREAU OF PENSIONS,

Washington, D. C., Apr. 27, 1898

Sir:

Will you kindly answer, at your earliest convenience, the questions enumerated below? The information is requested for future use, and it may be of great value to your family.

Very respectfully,

Mr. Benj. Butler,
Kingfisher,
O. Ty.

Commissioner.

No. 1. Are you a married man? If so, please state your wife's full name, and her maiden name.
Answer: Yes. Mary Butler formerly Mary Welling

No. 2. When, where, and by whom were you married? Answer: 1888 Dec 18th Memphis, Tenn. Rev Lee Mitchel

No. 3. What record of marriage exists? Answer: Marriage record can be found in office of Clerk of County court Shelby Co Tenn

No. 4. Were you previously married? If so, please state the name of your former wife and the date and place of her death or divorce. Answer: Yes. Maggie Butler formerly Maggie Hopkins she died in 1882

No. 5. Have you any children living? If so, please state their names and the dates of their birth. Answer: Yes. four. Annie, born March 1888, Benjamin born Aug 1891; Josephine born Jan 20, 1893, Solomon born March 3 1894.

Date of reply, May 4th, 1898.

Benjamin Butler.
(Signature.)

0-2

Benjamin Butler Sr. transcribed letter to the US Bureau of Pensions dated April 27, 1898, listing Sol's birthdate as March 3, 1894. (National Archives and Records Administration)

though the vote was not exactly aboveboard. The nonappearance of some election judges meant that the votes of "a large neighborhood of colored people" were not counted, though even without this apparent election tampering, Kingfisher may have landed on the side of segregation since "women were almost unanimous against mixed schools. The republican men were divided on the issue and the democrats were a unit in their opposition."[41] The first Black school in Kingfisher opened in 1896, the year the Butlers moved to town; thus Sol spent his first years of formal education in an all-Black primary school.

Segregation in schools followed the trend in politics. White supremacy festered and swelled in the territory, overshadowing initial signs of Black political progress. Many hopeful settlers arrived with the notion that Oklahoma might be Black-led and primarily peopled by African Americans. This possibility, popularized by newspapers, never came even close to reality, but it motivated African Americans to migrate and stirred white racial anxieties. White fears over Black empowerment and the growing strength of avowedly anti-Black Democrats and Populists fueled the Lily-White movement within the Republican Party, which historically had championed African American rights. The Lily-Whites sought to remove any Black presence from the party. Near the turn of the century, with "increasing resistance to the elevation of Negroes into even minor roles of power in the political structure," Black political power waned. African Americans began to question whether the Republican Party best served their concerns and deserved their vote. Some leaders encouraged African Americans to demand more from the party that seemed to be straying from its civil rights roots, even if this meant not voting for Republican candidates or creating a separate Republican convention or ticket.[42]

In September 1900, Kingfisher County's Black residents nominated an all-Black slate of candidates for the Abraham Lincoln Republican ticket, an alternative to the traditional, predominantly white Republican Party ticket. One of the most influential white Republicans in the county, newspaper editor Jacob V. Admire, attempting to discredit the men and motives behind the new ticket, portrayed its organizers as sore losers who wished to see white candidates defeated, blaming their own shortcomings (or failures of their race) on the Republican Party. In a Wichita newspaper that kept abreast of neighboring Kingfisher news, Admire wrote to dissuade Black voters from supporting the Abraham Lincoln Republican candidates by mentioning a man whom he assumed his readers would know and respect. The goal of the new ticket's organizers was, Admire explained, "to deceive and mislead," but their nefarious plans would "be laid so bare . . . that even Ben Butler will leave them in disgust."[43] Admire portrayed Ben Butler, who within a few years would move with his family to Wichita, as such a staunch supporter of the all-Black party in Kingfisher that only the most egregious misdeeds would prompt him to change his allegiance.

Ben Butler was increasingly hindered by poor health. The Dependent and Disability Pension Act of 1890 granted a monthly pension to soldiers who suffered from disabilities that prevented them from earning a living. A pension system for Union veterans had been in place since the war, but this new, less restrictive legislation led Butler to apply for the first time. While still in Memphis, he hired New Orleans attorneys, who helped him through his pension application process, and doctors' reports affirmed his maladies and inability to work full time, but the Medical Board of Surgeons in Memphis recommended that his application be rejected.[44] Butler later claimed that "their report was not favorable on account of their bias and prejudice." This rejection capped the opening round of the Butlers' arduous, decades-long battle to secure compensation for Ben's military service.[45]

Butler reapplied and was rejected at least nine more times over the course of a decade, a process that required numerous doctors' visits and testimonies in notarized affidavits that attested to his health problems and he included with his pension appeals.[46] These affidavits sworn by Ben's friends in Kingfisher affirm that he was a loyal and respected man and suggest additional qualities that made him a role model in the community. E. O. Tyler, who had known Ben since they attended the same church in Memphis and now lived within two blocks of each other in Kingfisher, asserted that Ben did not drink and engaged in "no vicious habits." Ben "is a *good christian gentleman* and is strictly temperate," wrote George F. Robinson, who had known him since the Butlers moved to Oklahoma. "He also has a good family and the reputation of good family government and morality."[47]

In addition to the struggle to prove his disability, Butler was also hindered in his pension quest by his post–Civil War name change from Burleson (or rather Burlison, Bullison, and Bulison, as it variously appeared in his service records). He eventually hired a Washington, DC, law firm, which would be compensated ten dollars once he began receiving his pension.[48] Butler's attorneys instructed him to get written support from a former military superior who could attest that Ben Butler and Ben Bullison were the same person, so when Sol was six, his father embarked on a trip from Kingfisher to Davenport, Iowa.

The trip to the Iowa town where he had disbanded from his regiment more than thirty-six years earlier took him nearly two months, suggesting he visited friends or relatives along the way. Ben reportedly was the "happiest man in Davenport" upon securing the needed signed affidavit from retired captain Joseph W. Davis.[49] "Evidently there is no mistake about the man's identity," noted the *Davenport Daily Republican*, "for his old comrades remember when he was cooking for them just as well as though it were yesterday."[50] These Iowa "comrades" also purchased a new set of clothes for Butler during his visit: "This trip exhausted my means," he soon after conveyed to the US Pension

Bureau. "I am old, crippled with rheumatism, suffering from poverty with a large family to support." In July 1902, after one more rejection and a decade of travel, doctors' visits, soliciting others for help, and reasoning with the pension bureau, Ben finally received his first monthly check of six dollars.[51]

They may have struggled, but the Butlers were not destitute, and they achieved a degree of upward mobility. By the turn of the century, they owned a house, surrounded by primarily home-owning Black neighbors, free of a mortgage.[52] They continued to submit claims to increase Ben's pension checks and, after additional rejections, managed to secure eight-dollar monthly payments by the end of 1903 and ten dollars each month by August 1905. Over the previous decade, various doctors had diagnosed Ben as suffering from rheumatism, lumbago, paralysis in his left leg, heart disease, liver and kidney problems, chronic diarrhea, partial blindness, and piles. A new diagnosis added "senile disability" and "disease of lung" as additional ailments.[53] Through all of this physical infirmity, Ben continued to work as a bootblack. In early 1905 he managed to purchase just over eighty acres of new farmland for seven dollars, located about two and a half times as far northwest from Kingfisher as the farm they had lost nine years earlier.[54] Given Ben's poor health and the absence of any reference to this second farm in Sol Butler's memoir, they apparently rented the land to neighboring farmers instead of working it themselves. They hung on to this rental property for seven years, long after they had left Oklahoma.

The youngest member of a poor, yet relatively stable family, Sol Butler left no record of how he filled his days in Kingfisher. He would have completed some, presumably segregated, schooling. Rather than having to plant, harvest, and tend to livestock, as his rural contemporaries did, he and his siblings instead would have assisted their mother and father around the house and in the various service and sales jobs they held over the years. Sol likely had ample time to play with friends, and though he would not play organized football until several years after leaving Oklahoma, he may have been exposed to the sport through the team at Kingfisher College, a small Congregational school. He certainly had opportunity to race his older brother, Ben, who, Sol recalled, used to outrun the future Olympian "any day of the week."[55]

After the segregating of Kingfisher schools, the territorial assembly passed additional legislation aimed at separating the races, including a marriage law that prohibited miscegenation and one that required separate schools in any district with eight or more Black children. Black transplants' high hopes for Oklahoma quickly evaporated. By 1904 the push for statehood was intensifying, and before Oklahoma could become a state with Jim Crow codified in its constitution, near the end of 1905, the Butlers hit the road again, this time headed for Wichita, Kansas.[56]

Roaming the Streets and Alleys

The Rock Island Railroad line connected the approximately 135 miles separating Kingfisher from Wichita. Kingfisher was home to the "colored folks' fair" at the end of September each year, which attracted plenty of Wichita residents, some of whom the Butlers might have encountered. And some of these visitors might have shared firsthand accounts of the city's Black prosperity and opportunity—because Wichita was booming. Incorporated as a city in 1870, from 1900 to 1910 the population of the city more than doubled to 52,450, including 2,457 African Americans. At the confluence of the Arkansas and Little Arkansas rivers and a busy railroad terminal, Wichita served as a transportation hub, first for cattle and then for wheat.[57]

The northerly move away from discrimination in the South was not entirely successful. In 1879 white residents cited the threat of illness as grounds for attempting to exclude early Black migrants to Wichita. At the same time, white Southerners used prison and racial violence to discourage outmigration, which to them represented a loss of cheap labor. These local and Southern efforts did not prevent thousands of African Americans from migrating to Kansas from Louisiana, Mississippi, Texas, and other Southern states in what historian Nell Irvin Painter calls "the most remarkable migration in the United States" in the decades shortly after the Civil War.[58] Known as "Exodusters," likening them to the biblical Israelites who fled Egypt, these migrants endured the cold, poverty, and relative lack of support in Kansas to avoid horrific conditions in the South after Reconstruction. Indian in name only and inhospitable to African Americans, Wichita nonetheless offered a degree of freedom from the brutal violence of the Jim Crow era.

African American cowboys, soldiers, construction workers, and homesteaders had been part of the city since its founding. An African Methodist Episcopal church (later known as St. Paul's AME), two Black Baptist churches, and the Prince Hall Masonic Lodge formed around 1880, all of them serving as centers for Black social and cultural activity. A Black business district formed along Main Street and North Water. W. N. Miller, the editor of the town's Black newspaper, the *Wichita Searchlight*, boasted, "Today the race can point with pride to a drug store, a grocery store, two pool halls, a meat market, two hotels, several rooming houuses [*sic*], two barber shops, one bath room, two restaurants."[59] The Black-run Court House Grocery opened up at 517 North Main Street around the time the Butlers arrived. Ben and Mary may have viewed it as something of a rebirth of Tommie Moss's Peoples Grocery Store, a beacon of Black prosperity.[60]

Though not as extreme as in the South, segregation still dictated human relations in Wichita. When the Butlers arrived, Black people tended to purchase or rent housing in only a few areas in the city (a reality undergirded by increasingly discriminatory social practice rather than by laws and regulations). Restaurants and stores denied them service; movie houses, theaters, and other venues consigned them to inferior seating or excluded them outright; and few occupied anything but the most menial municipal jobs. The court system excluded Black residents from juries, while the local white media portrayed them as criminally inclined and perpetuated other unsavory stereotypes. Popular culture, including Thomas Dixon's white supremacist play, *The Clansman*, which came to town in early 1907, further reinforced existing racism. When two years earlier Booker T. Washington spoke in Wichita, all area hotels refused him accommodation, so he left town on a 10:30 p.m. train. Even the Wichita dead confronted the color line in segregated cemeteries, except for the integrated Maple Grove Cemetery, where the body of each of the Butlers, save Ben Sr., would eventually be buried.[61]

Although Wichita, like the rest of the country, afforded Black citizens only second-class status at best, opportunity still existed across racial lines. On June 30, 1906, Garfield Post #25 mustered in Ben Butler as a member of the Grand Army of the Republic (GAR), an interracial organization for veterans of the Civil War. The nearly two hundred local members in good standing (a number that doubled by the time the Butlers left Wichita) bonded around their shared war experience to advocate for veterans' causes, which included pensions and, during Reconstruction, promoting the voting rights of Black veterans. By the time the family moved to Hutchinson three years later, Ben had secured the support of US representative Edmond H. Madison, who wrote to the commissioner of pensions, asking that he send a representative to Alabama to find Minerva Burleson's family Bible to support Ben's assertion that he had turned seventy and was therefore eligible for increased pension payments. (The commissioner declined Madison's request, disingenuously offering to consider 1860 census records, which would not have documented Ben's age while he was enslaved.)[62]

Public education in Wichita initially offered a promising refuge from segregation. When the Butlers arrived, primary and secondary schools were integrated. The four Butler kids, including ten-year-old Sol, encountered new social challenges when they entered integrated schools, where Black students constituted a small minority, for the first time in their lives.[63] But midway through the Butlers' first year in the city, the Wichita Board of Education, authorized by an 1879 state law regarding primary education in cities with more than fifteen thousand residents, voted to segregate elementary schools. The resolution came as a "bolt of lightning" to the Black community. "No greater surprise has ever been thrust upon any people than was this resolution," wrote W. N. Miller in the *Searchlight*.[64] At the Court House Grocery, Black leaders held a mass meeting to protest the school board's decision. Political efforts led to the electoral defeat of a school board member who voted for segregated schools, yet protesters failed in their primary objective, and integrated primary schools in Wichita soon vanished.[65]

Worse than being segregated, Black students in Wichita, except the thirty who would attend the segregated wing of Park Elementary School, entered the new school year without a school. "Today there are more than 600 bright faced, bright eyed, innocent Negro children who are either at their homes or roaming the streets and alleys of Wichita while more than 3000 bright faced and bright eyed white children are merrily answering the school bells and are wending their way back and forth from their respective schools, happy as happy can be," Miller wrote.[66]

The Black community raised money to challenge segregated schools in the courts. In September 1906, widow Sallie Rowles sued the school board in district court on behalf of her twelve-year-old daughter, Fannie, who was denied admission to Emerson Elementary School. (Fannie's older sister was a friend of Sol's sister Anna.) Shortly after the court ruled in favor of the school board, 45 percent of the city's Black elementary school students in attendance ignored this ruling and went to the school closest to their home. In the spirit of this peaceful yet firm resistance to separate schools, Black leaders raised additional funds to appeal the Rowles case. The next year, the Kansas Supreme Court overturned the lower court ruling and schools reintegrated until legislation in 1909 cleared the way again for a segregated school system.[67]

Make Us Feel Proud

In this increasingly hostile climate, racial pride and African American success served as powerful antidotes to the virulent racism that devalued Black lives. Ben Butler, who felt comfortable sharing stories of his enslaved past, embodied the rise from slavery and, as modest as his street-corner sales and service jobs may have been, the dignity in independent hard work. By 1906 he ran a "boot black stand . . . [with] the assistance of his two little boys," Ben Jr. and Sol.[68] Mary Butler laundered white people's clothes for modest pay, but she was literate, blessed with a beautiful voice, and actively participated in Black women's clubs; Mary helped situate the Butlers among the most respected Black families in Wichita.

The dozens of references to Mary Butler in the pages of the *Searchlight* document the busy schedule of a community leader. She was a singer, and within her first year in Wichita she had performed solos at several events. These successes led to her invitation to perform at a fraternal lodge's Labor Day event in Redman Hall, where she "was loudly encored and . . . called back a second time."[69] Newspaper coverage of the Butler family in Wichita gave no indication of Sol's early athletic promise, but it was in the *Searchlight* that Sol's name first appeared in print. Eleven years old, on Christmas break from fourth grade, and undoubtedly wearing his best Sunday clothes, "Master S. Butler" performed a recitation at a church event.[70] Shortly before he delivered his memorized lines to the audience crowding the St. Paul's sanctuary, his mother performed a vocal solo. St. Paul's AME Church often hosted cultural events, along with literary society meetings and tea parties, that prized dignity and refinement and were central to the Black middle-class social sphere that Sol's mother helped construct in Wichita.

Mary Butler belonged to three women's clubs; two of these clubs—the WTV and BTW—bore the names of prominent Black leaders, William Tecumseh Vernon and Booker Taliaferro Washington. Mary was appointed to a WTV committee; she was treasurer of the BTW, and she served as secretary of the city's home cooking club. The several homes the Butlers rented in succession served as meeting sites for dozens of clubwomen. These and other clubs in the city gave middle-class Black women an increased sense of authority and agency. "The negro women's clubs are doing a grand work for the people of their race," asserted Booker T. Washington's third wife, Margaret Murray Washington.[71] While ostensibly gathering for song, "fancy needlework," and conversation, the clubs provided women a forum for sharing information and ideas, developing organizational skills, promoting charity work, and raising political awareness.[72]

At the time Mary joined the WTV, its namesake, W. T. Vernon, was president of Western University in Quindaro, Kansas, which was often called the "Tuskegee of the West."[73] This AME Church school grew dramatically under Vernon's leadership "into one of the best institutions for Negroes west of the Mississippi," largely because he had secured state funding—which enabled the construction of several new buildings—in exchange for generating Black support for the Republican Party. His political skills led President Theodore Roosevelt to appoint him register of the United States Treasury Department.[74] The literary society of St. Paul's AME Church, which nearly all the WTV's members attended, held a debate that ended with the resolution that "W. T. Vernon was a greater race man than Booker T. Washington."[75]

Vernon and Washington worked toward similar ends but through somewhat different means. Both men gave highly anticipated speeches in Wichita, and the *Searchlight* kept readers regularly apprised of their whereabouts and doings. Their speeches, often on the subjects of education and race relations, appeared on the newspaper's front pages. Both men recognized the benefits of higher education and professional training for African Americans, while Washington more vigorously promoted industrial training, which provided the practical skills he thought necessary for the working-class Black masses. The Southern leader discouraged African Americans from protesting and pushing for social equality and racial integration and urged them to pursue self-improvement instead. Less conciliatory, Vernon primarily supported industrial training simply as a means of securing funding. He was among the Black reformers at segregated schools who pushed for "race pride, potential for higher education, and movement toward full integration," objectives that would guide Sol Butler's steps beyond Kansas and into adulthood.[76]

Improved conditions, Vernon and Washington both argued, would follow hard-earned success. "Youth must abstain from idleness which leads to crime," Vernon said in a speech at Garfield Hall in Wichita. "They must appreciate that industry, thrift and true worth that will lend competency and standing in the community and that color will be no bar to the real success of the worthy and deserving."[77] The underlying premise of what historians have dubbed "respectability politics" was that Black people would advance socially, economically, and politically by exhibiting virtues and values shared by white middle-class society. White people would come to recognize Black people's worthiness for fuller, more equitable participation, and Black people would move toward justice and equality.[78]

All available evidence indicates that Mary Butler subscribed to the widely held Black middle-class beliefs that Vernon and Washington championed, which promoted good manners, cultural achievement, and ethical behavior as a means of "elevating the race." Within months of her family's arrival in the city, seventeen-year-old Anna Butler joined sixteen young ladies and twelve young gentlemen at a "Jolly Three" party in honor of two out-of-town visitors. The "features of the evening were music and games. At a late hour a three-course luncheon was served. All reported a jolly time."[79] A few months later Mary Butler "tendered her daughter, Miss Anna, a pleasant surprise [birthday] party Friday evening . . . Quite a number of her friends were present. A delicate luncheon was served and a delightful time spent."[80] In June 1908, Ben Jr., Josephine, and Sol were among the twenty-eight boys and girls present to enjoy "social games" and honor a female friend's departure to Chicago. "At a reasonable hour," the newspaper reported, "refreshments were served after which the guest departed declaring the hostess[es] pleasing entertainers." The short accounts of these and other parties attended by the Butler children offer a glimpse into the tight-knit group that shaped the social skills and worldview of Wichita's middle-class Black youth.[81]

In 1907 the *Searchlight* ran an article on "Instances of Negro Success" featuring Black men and women who excelled in a wide array of fields, including educators, artists, performers, a surgeon, an architect, a lawyer, an inventor, and even a cotton raiser. But the article included no athletes.[82] Consistent with this telling omission, the *Searchlight* rarely ran any sports coverage, aside from an occasional mention of the "colored" baseball team in the area, such as the Wichita Blues; or the basketball and track teams led by the "young colored men of Wichita"; or the Black schoolgirls, placed on teams according to their Methodist or Baptist affiliation, who played basketball at Garfield

Two young women in Hutchinson, Kansas, approximately (perhaps *exactly*) the ages of Sol's sisters, Josephine Butler and Anna Gardner (neé Butler). (Photograph by Edith Bailey, ca. 1913, courtesy Reno County Museum and Strataca, used with permission.)

Hall.[83] One man became a striking exception to the *Searchlight*'s scant sports coverage: boxer Jack Johnson. Born in 1878 in Galveston, Texas, to formerly enslaved parents, Johnson gained international fame and notoriety in and beyond the boxing ring. After defeating Canadian Tommy Burns for the world heavyweight championship in Australia at the end of 1908, Johnson evoked fierce reactions worldwide, ranging from staunch Black pride to volatile white hatred and anxiety. Pitting one man against another in bloody competition, the popular sport of boxing viscerally highlighted entrenched notions of masculinity and race. Johnson's title magnified anxieties over the degenerating white male body, which fueled searches around the world for a "Great White Hope" to defeat him.[84]

As a Black man who triumphed in a sport that reformers roundly condemned and who flouted the most sacred of white supremacist taboos by romancing and marrying white women, Johnson drew a lot of criticism, and not just from white people. According to historian Geoffrey C. Ward, "The champion seemed the antithesis of everything [Booker T.] Washington had always said a black man should be: he was free-spending, not thrifty; brash instead of humble; defiant in the face of white laws and customs intended to hamper his movement and limit his choices."[85] His behavior defied the respectability politics that Mary Butler so firmly embraced.

African Americans' pride in Johnson's accomplishments frequently trumped any reservations. *Searchlight* editor W. N. Miller held popular race leaders like Washington and Vernon in the highest regard and had his own reservations about the champion and his sport; yet in an article about Johnson written nearly two years into the heavyweight champion's six-and-a-half-year reign, Miller defended the boxer:

> While we cannot say that we believe in pugilism between men nor that we encourage that class of sport—yet away down deep somewhere within there is some kind of feeling that makes us feel proud of that jet black Negro Jack Johnson who showed his physical manhood in the fighters ring Saturday night . . . There has, in times past been several Negroes who if they had been given the chance, would no doubt have royally and in flying colors have won this belt—be that as it will or may—it is the first Negro ever given the chance and he won the belt. That Jack Johnson is a Negro-full-blood—there is no question that he stands to day the Champion of the World in the ring all must agree. Being a Negro we, of course feel some personal pride in Jack Johnson's triumph . . . as we also feel that every Negro in this broad land feel[s]. We suggest three cheers for Jack Johnson.[86]

The boxer's full name is repeated four times in the space of a paragraph in a kind of alliterative incantation, as though Miller is catching a glimpse, through Johnson's unapologetic accomplishment, of what might be possible outside the rigid constraints of respectability politics. Miller celebrates the racial purity that Johnson's dark skin supposedly certified, which discouraged naysayers from contesting his Blackness, but even more than for simple racial chauvinism, Miller cheers Johnson because his title represents justice—the first Black boxer to have the opportunity to compete for the title—and Jack Johnson did not disappoint.

Miller wasn't the only Jack Johnson fan in Wichita. After watching a play followed by a Shakespeare comedy at Garfield Hall, an all-ages, likely all-Black audience stayed to watch a film of Johnson's twelve-round fight versus world middleweight champion Stanley Ketchell.[87] It isn't hard to imagine the cheers that erupted when Johnson delivered his knockout punch, demolishing the latest Great White Hope. In the years Sol Butler transitioned through puberty and into adulthood—figuring out what it meant to be a Black man in a world violently skewed toward maintaining white supremacy—Jack Johnson remained the most prominent African American presence in the media and popular imagination. In the words of historian Davarian Baldwin, "The 'sporting life' masculinity that Johnson represented . . . exalted personality, sexuality, and the physical exterior as the expression of a new race consciousness."[88]

With a muscular build, rounded features, and dark brown skin tone, Sol Butler somewhat resembled the champion Johnson, a point highlighted by both white and Black reporters throughout Butler's athletic career. Even if the teenage Butler failed to see a resemblance between himself and the famous boxer, the existence of a strong, successful, and increasingly wealthy Black man defying oppressive racial expectations would not have gone unnoticed by a Black boy trying to make his way in a white world.

Sol Butler attended the integrated Irving Elementary School with his older siblings Josephine and Ben Jr. (Anna previously left school after finishing tenth grade). While the school board worked to fully segregate Wichita's primary schools, more than fifty Black students were still attending Irving, although the school implemented a segregated graduation ceremony for the eighth-grade class the year Ben Jr. graduated.[89] The Butler children sat in classrooms amid a majority of white students who were, at best, indoctrinated to doubt Black ability and, at worst, raised to be violently racist. In his memoir, Sol has nothing to say about life in Wichita beyond the length of his stay. While he may have played baseball on a recreation team in Wichita, he did not play any sports at Irving, though a classmate recalled, many decades later, that Sol had been "a grade school marble champ."[90] Not long after the Butlers left Wichita, the town's schools instituted a policy of refusing to play teams that fielded Black players.

While the president of the school board during Sol's final semester at Irving Elementary tried to convince Black residents that schools would remain integrated, events across the community suggested otherwise. New state legislation paved the way for segregation, and two years later Wichita residents voted roughly three to one to fund the construction of separate Black schools, which children began attending in 1912. Segregated education returned to the city and would shape the experiences of families for decades to come. The *Searchlight* reported that Black businesses were being driven off Main Street and that "no colored man has yet been drawn as a juror in the District Court for several years past."[91]

When Ben Butler Sr. was fourteen years old, he had spent his entire life on the Morgan County plantation where he was enslaved. Denied an education and any meaningful freedom, he had scant reason to expect his future prospects could rise above a lifetime of forced labor in the service of white people. A half century later, against a Kansan backdrop of intensifying expressions of anti-Blackness, Ben and Mary Butler embodied the liberatory potential of movement and, after nearly four years in Wichita, packed up their family, including the fourteen-year-old Sol, and moved to the small, nearby city of Hutchinson, where Sol began seventh grade in a new, integrated school.

2

Good Behavior and Gentlemanly Conduct

Fall 1909–Summer 1914

From "Magnetic Rag" (1914) by Scott Joplin

Less than one year after the Butler family moved from Wichita to Hutchinson, Kansas, the *Hutchinson News* ran a feature about Ben Sr. titled "Longs for Old Days: This Ex-Slave's Heart Goes Back to Dixie and the Cotton." The white reporter recorded the alleged musings of Sol's father—"Sometimes, Ah think the old days is the best days, after all, and wish that Ah was back on the old plantation"—in a transcription that evoked the racializing use of eye dialect popularized by the short stories of Thomas Nelson Page.[1] Three days earlier, on July 4, 1910, Black boxer Jack Johnson had defeated another "great white hope," Jim Jeffries, in a fifteen-round bout in Reno, Nevada, to retain the heavyweight crown. During the fight, a reported one thousand Black Kansans gathered to pray and sing hymns for Johnson in a tent erected by a Hutchinson church. This large and racially charged public event drew considerable attention in a town of 16,364 residents, including only 840 African Americans. Upon receiving a telegraph with word of his victory, according to one condescending account in a Kansas City paper, the "negroes cheered for half an hour, hit each other and rolled on the ground, shouting, 'The Lord is with the black man.'"[2] When the *Hutchinson News* reporter asked Ben Butler about the new world champion, he contradicted his earlier statement to a rival paper by allegedly replying, "Go long. What good's Mistah Johnsing doin' this yere nigger?"[3]

Just emerging as a sports star in his own right, Ben Butler's fifteen-year-old son, Sol, witnessed the incendiary power of a Black athlete challenging the primacy of white manhood. Jeffries's defeat marked "the waste of a godlike heritage," lamented novelist Rex Beach in the *Chicago Tribune*.[4] Lawman and professional gambler Bat Masterson augured, "It [will] be a long time before the white race comes into its own again."[5] Racial violence erupted across the country in the aftermath of Johnson's victory.[6] The young Butler could not have failed to notice the African American community's conflicting responses to Johnson's win, from the jubilation of the throng in the tent to the public ambivalence exhibited by Black leaders like his father; nor could he have failed to notice how the boxer triggered alarm in white America. While Jack Johnson unapologetically basked in his global celebrity from a sport that rewarded larger-than-life personas and the flouting of convention, the young, still anonymous Sol Butler was trying to make his mark on the mostly white, small-town gridirons and track fields of middle America. Johnson "embodied American individualism in its purest form," wrote biographer Geoffrey Ward.[7] Nevertheless, the reaction to his world-beating and "self-invented" professional success closed the doors of championship opportunity to the next generation of Black boxers in the white-controlled sport. In stark contrast, determined to cultivate cross-racial community support, Sol helped open doors in amateur team sports that would bring African American athletes fame and influence.

From the time the Butler family moved to Hutchinson—affording their children the integrated education they were going to be denied in Wichita—until Sol entered college five years later, he would develop into one of the Midwest's most successful young athletes, enabled by the stunning social mobility he cultivated alongside his physical talents. As Butler accumulated victories, he developed a persona that was informed by the middle-class values of the era, both Black and white, especially regarding sports as a crucible that formed and revealed the character of young men. Heralded by his community for both his remarkable athletic talent and for his modest, hardworking ways, Butler was able to succeed in an overwhelmingly white world because he fashioned himself mostly in opposition to the public image of Johnson as impudent and brash, which made the veteran fighter's ostentatious displays of wealth and relationships with white women all the more intolerable to white America. Had Sol Butler claimed after winning a big race, "I outclassed [my opponent] in every department," as Johnson did after beating Jeffries,[8] he would have risked losing the community support necessary to enter increasingly prestigious and far-flung track and field meets.

Butler relied on others to state the obvious: He was in a class by himself. Coaches, organizers, and fans of the era expected humility from athletes, especially from young Black athletes. Butler's image—the humble, young Black sports hero—was a triumph of social mobility that allowed him to move and compete in white worlds, where he was not only accepted but celebrated as well.

Progression of the Young People

Sol Butler's parents quickly rooted the family in their new community. Ben Sr. became "a conspicuous figure in Hutchinson" at his shoeshine and drink stand across from the courthouse.[9] While he lacked the means to create the electrified and well-appointed "Shoe-blacking Emporium" that Booker T. Washington promoted when he encouraged African American bootblacks to follow the example of white workers by modernizing their establishments,[10] Ben Butler did make his mark with a memorable drink. White newspaper columnist John Bentley, who recalled the eldest Butler as short, "almost round," white-haired, and always grinning, recalled:

> In the alley next to my own dad's office, Ben Butler conducted a combination shoe shining and cold drink stand but the only refreshment he offered was a bright red concoction whose base was soda pop. This he dipped from a ten gallon crock. Ben called this sweet poison "Strawberry Finish." His sales talk was convincing. It's many a belly ache this jolly old Negro talked me into with his smooth argument about the tonic qualities of Strawberry Finish.[11]

One of Ben Butler's obituaries noted that he "numbered his friends by thousands," which included his clientele of primarily white businesspeople.[12] "His cheery disposition and homely philosophy was as effective as though couched in choisest [*sic*] English," the obituary read, "and many is the dignified judge and jurist who has stopped after a hard session of court to relax by conversing with Ben."[13]

As it had in Wichita, Ben Sr.'s status as a Civil War veteran brought him social connections and a degree of respect. Transferring his Grand Army of the Republic membership on November 26, 1909, from Wichita's Garfield Post to Hutchinson's Joe Hooker Post, he joined more than two hundred aging, almost entirely white Union soldiers in good standing.[14] Fellow GAR members immediately embraced Ben Butler as a likable leader. Within a few months of transferring posts, he was nominated for a three-year position as a trustee and elected as an alternate delegate to the annual state encampment, and when Ben Butler was faced with financial difficulties, the Joe Hooker Post formed a Ben Butler Committee that raised six dollars for the struggling veteran. Through Ben Butler's own tenacity and the powerful white support he commanded in Hutchinson and among his GAR comrades, at seventy-three he finally secured an increase in pension payments, from thirteen to twenty-four dollars a month.[15]

The Butlers moved out of their rented house at 1214 Fourth Avenue East and purchased a small home at 324 West Avenue B. Within less than five hundred square feet, bordered by a small porch, entryway, and kitchen, slept eight people: the five Butlers, along with Anna's husband, John Gardner, and their daughter, Velna Mae, who was born within six months before or after her parents' wedding on June 15, 1911.[16] From the refreshment stand to the GAR, Ben Butler's cross-racial social mobility made him "a leader amongst his people" and a model for a teenager whose athletic success would depend on successfully navigating a white world.[17]

As she had in Wichita, Mary Butler secured the family's position within Hutchinson's Black elite. Local church members welcomed her to Hutchinson at a mid-October reception featuring music, toasts, and a luncheon. The following week, the Imperial Art Club invited Mary to its meeting for a two-course lunch.[18] At the club's next meeting, she sang as part of "an entertainment" that included other vocal and piano soloists, before "Dr. G. [W.] Allison made a short talk on the progression of the young people. After which ice cream and cake was served."[19] Success at this event led to Mary presenting a recitation and song for the club at Lyons, Kansas, a few weeks later.[20]

Mary's efforts toward social respectability, along with other community-building activity reported by the Black press, served to counterbalance attention in white newspapers, which tended to focus on African Americans only when there was bad news to report. A few days before Anna and John Gardner wed, he was arrested in response to a complaint from "a negro girl." Earlier in the year, he had served several weeks in jail after an alleged armed assault. When reporting on the wedding, a local paper drew attention to the groom's criminal record.[21] The following spring, another white news outlet reported the arrest of Ben Jr., who was "charged with failure to support his wife." The reporter identified Ben Jr. as the "son of the old ex-slave who runs a refreshment and shoe shine on Main street."[22] Another story suggested that Ben Sr. misled Reno County officials by "drawing support from the county for many months" without disclosing all his sources of income, including his monthly pension and one-dollar-per-night job as a night watchman.[23] White supremacy and relative poverty were enormous, ever-present hurdles for Sol Butler and his family to overcome in their efforts to maintain the dignified, modest image that would allow their youngest son to move with relative freedom in the world of high school sports.

Mary and Ben Sr. frequently returned to Wichita not only to visit with old friends but also to take advantage of economic opportunities they lacked in Hutchinson, which was less than a third the size of Wichita.[24] Mary once again earned money by taking in laundry, while Ben's primary income came from his shoe-shine stand and military pension. In mid-October 1910, just over a year after the Butlers' move to Hutchinson, the first of what became weekly advertisements for a new restaurant called the Sunflower Stand, co-owned by Mary Butler and another Tennessee native, Ella Woodard, appeared on the front page of the *Wichita Searchlight*.[25] The Sunflower Stand was located at 509 North Main Street, a hundred-mile round-trip commute via the Missouri Pacific Railroad from Mary's home in Hutchinson, and within feet of the once Black-owned Court House Grocery, which since the Butlers' arrival in Kansas had been purchased by white grocer Joseph C. Ludes. Mary and Ella kept the Sunflower Stand going at least through March of the following year, when their advertisements stopped running.[26] Economics clearly did not dictate the Butlers' move to Hutchinson; all signs instead point to another salient factor—schools.

Sol Butler entered seventh grade at Maple Street School, a brick structure built in 1887 on a football field-size lot less than a mile east of the Arkansas River. Like all schools in Reno County, Kansas, Maple Street was integrated.[27] Perhaps integration was a practical necessity in Hutchinson, where Black residents accounted for only about 5 percent of the total population. Or perhaps the county's integrated schools reflected the area's relatively more progressive, less racist values than those of other Kansas communities, but signs point to a town that suffered under the same anti-Black racism that plagued most of the country during this era. For example, Hutchinson school superintendent Justus Otto Hall published a well-publicized history textbook that included a passage in which Hall argued that the spread and growth of Southern slavery occurred because most of the labor "was unskilled and so could be done nearly, if not quite, as well by the slaves as by the more intelligent whites."[28] It probably came as no surprise to Reno County's Black residents when in 1913 two African American leaders lost their bid to become members of the county's board of education.[29]

But Reno County schools remained integrated as others across Kansas were moving to segregate, and unlike rural areas in the state, where over half of teachers had attended little to no high school, Hutchinson schools attracted relatively well-educated teachers, wooed in part by competitive salaries that in the high school averaged $106 per month (a nearly 50 percent increase over just a few years). One-third of the county's tax revenue went toward the school system.[30] Superintendent Hall attested to the administration's academic ambition: "Within the schools themselves the ideal has been to a great extent preparation for college, development of ability to pass [college entrance] examinations, and training preparatory to entering professional life."[31] Notably, Kansas sent a higher percentage of students to college than any other state. The city's rapid growth prompted the building of a new high school, at a cost

Sol Butler (back row, middle) with teachers and other students at Maple Street School. (Photograph by Edith Bailey, ca. 1911, courtesy Reno County Museum and Strataca, used with permission.)

of $147,000, which became a source of local pride and a model of excellence statewide. Four hundred seventy students enrolled in the school's first year, and that number continued to climb during Sol's high school years.[32]

The fact that Sol and his siblings even attended high school was an impressive accomplishment, given the low rates of matriculation by students of all races, but especially among students of color. In 1910, 10 percent of all students nationwide attended high school and only 5 percent graduated. About three thousand African Americans took courses in college or professional programs in 1915, and most of these students were in the South.

The Butler children benefited from the era's widespread reform efforts. Progressive reformers pushed for abolishing child labor and making school attendance mandatory, goals more fully realized in coming decades. Freedpeople in the South and subsequent generations of Black leaders played an essential role in developing and expanding public education.[33] They helped fuel the Progressive movement, even though white Progressives often ignored or excluded African Americans, including in the realm of education. Black church leaders; clubwomen, like Mary; and other Black Progressives "worked to improve social conditions and institutions in their communities," including Hutchinson's integrated school system.[34] The Butler parents brought their four children to a state that was tied for first in the nation for school attendance, with 70.6 percent of school-age residents attending school; Kansas also boasted the lowest high school dropout rate in the country. Living in this city and state shaped the children's upward educational mobility as they achieved what had been impossible for their parents.[35]

Exceedingly Anxious to Succeed

When Sol Butler started high school, Hutchinson High had just begun offering "complete courses in physical training and gymnasium work for both boys and girls," required for all freshmen and sophomores and optional for juniors and seniors.[36] Around the same time, articles in the *Interstate Schoolman*, a monthly journal published in Hutchinson, began touting the virtues of industrial and manual training that deemphasized liberal arts education. Less than a year after asserting the importance of college preparation, Superintendent Hall changed course: "High school with a single aim, such as preparation for college, defeats its purpose as a high school," he wrote. The ideal institution now also "must develop industrial skill and business efficiency; it must serve the church, the state and society . . . In its broadest sense, the purpose of the modern high school is social service."[37] Butler arrived at Hutchinson High School during its transformation into a comprehensive institution, which mirrored the broader national trend of high schools moving away from strict college preparation and toward a wide array of offerings that included the nurturing of physical activity.[38]

This transformation reflected the era's changing attitudes toward recreation and sport; Sol Butler entered high school athletics at a time when educators increasingly viewed sports as a tool for shaping and revealing the character of youth. Historian Benjamin Rader writes that Progressive Era educators believed that interscholastic athletics "could create an *esprit de corps*, 'a mass spirit in which each individual surrenders himself' to a common goal. Such a communal spirit encouraged a positive attitude toward the high school and a peaceful acquiescence of the students to adult direction."[39] The *Interstate Schoolman* reprinted articles by Luther Halsey Gullick, an eminent "social engineer" in physical education and recreation. "There is no one thing in school life which inculcates loyalty more effectively than good school athletics," wrote Gullick, who helped found the Boys Scouts of America and the Campfire Girls. "By being true to his gang—a gang which is clean and moral—by being faithful to his class and his school, the boy develops loyalty to the larger social units, and acquires an actively social conscience."[40] The journal also promoted Alden Arthur Knipe's novel *Captain of the Eleven*, which features the heroics of prep school football captain Bunny Reeves, who models character traits like honesty, courage, and perseverance.[41]

The reality on the ground in Hutchinson quickly adapted to the era's ideals. The spring after Sol's dazzling debut season in high school football, the Reno County Teachers Association met in Hutchinson to discuss games and athletics; the inventor of basketball and head of the Physical Department at the University of Kansas, James Naismith, gave the principal address, titled "Influence of Athletics upon Character." A few months later, Hutchinson High School was accredited by the North Central Association of Colleges and Secondary Schools, which promoted athletics under the control of councils composed of faculty, alumni, and students.[42]

"I was in the seventh grade when I went to Hutchinson and I immediately became interested in playing . . . football," Sol wrote in his coauthored memoir, self-published in the spring of 1915 during his senior year in high school. "I gained a very good idea of the game and determined to do my best to master every feature of it." Describing his early football career, Butler carefully presented himself as the kind of humble, hardworking schoolboy sports hero who might have been friends with Bunny Reeves. He walked readers through his introduction to the varsity team:

> I was exceedingly anxious to succeed, because it is not every freshman who has the honor or chance to rub shoulders with the jolly juniors or the grave seniors. The first evening I donned a pair of football pants I felt that life could not hold any greater boon than the wearing of this respected armor. But the worst was yet to follow, in the form of scrimmages and learning to tackle. After about two hours of hard work I began to realize the truth of the saying, "that nothing great is lightly won." We kept this practice up every afternoon for about two weeks.[43]

Butler also addressed what was often elided in the era's conversations about the link between sports, character, and success: ideas about race. Emphasizing the seemingly transformative power of good character, he described how racism initially threatened his standing on the football team and how the team's shared "principles of good behavior and gentlemanly conduct" ultimately transcended race:

> On account of my being a colored boy a few of the boys objected to my playing on the team, but after they had learned to know me better, and found I at all times was guided by the same principles of good behavior and gentlemanly conduct as themselves, they welcomed me as one of them. I can truthfully say that there never was a "whiter" bunch of boys than those

> who represented the gold and blue during the time I took part in athletics as a representative of Hutchinson high school.[44]

Butler's use of the now archaic and offensive term "white" to mean fine and upstanding signals the extent to which white supremacy framed how he presented, and perhaps thought about, his experiences.

Throughout his memoir, Butler addressed encounters with racism without emotion and with a consistent deference to the transcendence of good character, as though racism were just another aspect of the playing field, where he could establish not only his superior athletic abilities but also his superior character. Butler recalled the first football game of his high school career, against Stafford High School:

> I was unable to take part in the game because the visitors objected to playing against colored boys . . . I did not feel the least bit discouraged, because I realized that there are certain conditions that every man and every race has to overcome, and I was determined to prove to all Kansas that there was not a player in the state who had received any better home training than myself, or any better ideas of what constituted true sportsmanship and fair play.[45]

Butler touted his "home training"—the education in manners and "principles of good behavior and gentlemanly conduct" that Mary Butler in particular would have overseen, no doubt influenced by Booker T. Washington, W. T. Vernon, and the respectability politics of their namesake women's clubs.[46] Grounded in a relatively conservative ideology of racial uplift championed by the Black middle class, Butler's rhetoric evoked a genteel, community-oriented, middle-class social mobility through athletics that stood in stark contrast to that of the emphatically self-made example of working-class cynosure Jack Johnson.

After being forced to the sidelines in the team's first game, Butler faced the same fate in the second game of the season, against Lyons High School. This time Hutchinson's coach, Don Yeoman, "pulled our team off the field and refused to play" until Lyons agreed to compete against Hutchinson with Butler and his African American teammate, Clarence Phillips, on the field. "From that time on we never had any more trouble that year," Butler claimed, "[because] Yeoman, who was one of the squarest men I have ever had the pleasure of working with, championed our cause when any argument of this nature arose."[47] The cause Yeoman championed, perhaps at the urging of local Black leaders like Butler's parents, spoke to interests that extended well beyond those of the team.

With the help of Butler and Phillips, the team put together the school's best football season in six years. In his book, *Huddle Up Hutch*, football coach and author Steve Miller describes Sol Butler as the "greatest and most accomplished athlete ever to play football at Hutchinson High School."[48] At left half (the equivalent of a running back), peers considered him "the fastest man in the state . . . No player could stop him in his long runs." After narrowly winning the first game at home without Butler against Stafford and then ending with a scoreless tie at the Lyons home field, the Hutchinson Salters (now the Salthawks) handily defeated Sterling and Kingman high schools. "Best high school team I ever saw," reported a referee at the latter game, in which Hutchinson deployed a hurry-up offense that demoralized the unprepared Kingman squad. The rematch against Lyons again ended in a scoreless tie, and the rematch against Stafford was notable for the blizzard the Hutchinson team had failed to anticipate and for the untrained substitute referees. The under-clad and freezing Salters played poorly, and with the team down by five points, Coach Yeoman forfeited the game. The Salters won their final two games, trouncing Sterling and, on Thanksgiving Day, Great Bend 35–0. "By having the best percentage of any football team in the state, and by going through the season undefeated," Butler argued, "we were the recognized state champions."[49] According to Miller, who counted the loss with the five victories and two ties, Hutchinson claimed the championships of central Kansas and western Kansas.

When the football season ended, Butler declined to try basketball and instead went out for track and field in the spring of 1912:

> I thought that I could be of greater service to the school as a track man. I had never taken part in any track events before this time, but a number of critics who had seen my work on the football field thought I could make good. With this encouragement I started out at the opening of the season to do my best to make the team and help "put Hutchinson on the map."[50]

In purported service to his school and town—and with an explanation that could have been ripped from the pages of Luther Halsey Gullick—Butler went on to win first place in nearly every event he entered. In the process, he set in motion two patterns that became as predictable as the seasons: The first, lasting through high school and his four years of college, saw him earn through running, jumping, and throwing (and without exception) more points for his team than all his other teammates combined; and the second, even longer pattern was his transition each winter and spring between football and track and field. By college and into his professional years, basketball and other sports, like tennis, would carve out space in his annual athletic schedule. While he would stop competing in track by the mid-1920s, once he could no longer win at the most elite levels, his competitive spirit and entrepreneurial bent kept him cycling through a wide range of sports as an athlete, coach, and trainer for at least three more decades.

After winning the opening meet at Stafford, the Salters traveled the next Saturday to a district meet in Sterling, where they again won with ease. Taking first place in the 100- and 220-yard dashes, the 220-yard hurdles, and the broad (now long) jump, Butler earned a gold medal, and the team received a cup. Butler recalled, "The winning of this meet caused great rejoicing in the camp of the Hutchinson high school and it made us feel as if we could accomplish anything when so loyally supported by the student body and faculty."[51] The relatively new Central Kansas Athletic Association sponsored the next meet, its second annual, with ten schools participating at the state fairgrounds in Hutchinson. James Naismith served as referee. Rainy weather slowed down the track but did not prevent Butler from earning first place in the 100-yard dash, 220-yard hurdles, and broad jump and a gold medal for top individual performance. He finished in second place in the 220-yard dash behind Ed Porter, an African American athlete from Great Bend.[52]

The penultimate track and field meet, at the University of Kansas in Lawrence, determined the top high school teams and athletes in the state. "The day was ideal and the sun shone warm and bright. The track was in fine condition," Butler recalled.[53] He took first place in the 50-yard dash, 100-yard dash, 220-yard dash, and 220-yard hurdles and won the meet's individual cup. "This meet, as no other could, shows Butler in his true light," wrote a *Hutchinson Gazette* reporter in a front-page article. "It is a remarkable thing for one boy to capture all the dashes and the hurdles."[54] Sensing a receptive audience, "Butler made quite a hit when he made a speech accepting the Individual cup."[55] After seeing Sol dominate in two successive meets, James Naismith named him to his all-Kansas interscholastic track team.[56]

The attention and respect Sol garnered in these meets did not shield him from what Hutchinson athletes identified as "a raw deal" at the season's final meet. After he seemingly won first in the 220-yard dash, the judge ruled the race a tie between him and a sprinter from the local Wichita high school. According to a Hutchinson newspaper, Butler "quit" as a result, and "Coach Yeoman left the field at this time to go to his home in Kingman."[57] Butler wrote, "Yeoman refused to continue in the meet and we withdrew."[58] The Salters ended up in third place after having been in the lead.

Nevertheless, Butler finished his season on a constructive note. Coach Yeoman assigned him and six of his teammates to coach track at area grade schools in preparation for an annual meet at the state fairgrounds; Butler worked at his alma mater, Maple Street School. Two years later, he was assigned to coach the Hutchinson freshmen track squad.[59] In both cases, he would have been coaching mostly white teams, serving as a rare, if not lone, example of Black leadership for white youth. Butler's assiduous efforts to maintain his image as a hardworking, humble team player did not go unnoticed: His coach was willing to withdraw the whole team from a meet on his behalf, and Butler was seen not just as an athletic superstar but also as a leader with the good character needed to help mold the next generation of young athletes.

We Predict Great Things for Young Butler

If Butler stood out in his first year of high school football, he dominated in his second. An article after a mid-season game against Pratt High School summed it up: "As usual, Butler . . . was the whole game and carried the ball three-fourths of the time."[60] With Butler at left halfback, Hutchinson lost only one out of ten games in the fall of 1912 and more than quadrupled their opponents' total points. Butler scored thirty-one touchdowns, earning well over half of the team's total points for the season. The Salters' offense was not only successful but also exciting to watch as the team transitioned from old-fashioned up-the-middle line plunges to end runs and passes. This increasingly open style, prompted by Butler's explosive speed, power, and dexterity, allowed him to rack up many long and memorable gains. He scored seven touchdowns in the opening 78–0 victory over Sterling High School. Among his documented long gains over the season were two runs for 80 yards, one for 70 yards, and a 60-yard touchdown reception. Butler alone came within 14 yards of reaching the total yards gained by arguably their toughest opponent of the season.[61]

In the season's penultimate game, an uncharacteristically low-scoring, 13–7 victory over the previously undefeated Pratt team, before a crowd of around two thousand, the Salters gained 343 total yards. Pratt had agreed to put their undefeated season on the line only after Coach Yeoman offered them first $100 and then $150.[62] Recalling a thrilling long run that led to the game's first touchdown in the fourth quarter, Butler wrote, "The great cheer that went up from the grand-stand and the congratulations of my team mates made me feel that I could sacrifice anything in return for such loyal support."[63] A *Pratt Union* article about Pratt's first loss of the season reported on the Hutchinson team: "The negro must be credited with 248 yards, leaving 95 yards for 'the help.' When we add that these gains were made with rather ragged interference [blocking], much of the yardage indeed being made after being tackled by one, two or three Pratt men, and you have a fair idea of Sol's importance."[64] The reporter's several references to Butler's teammates as "the help" signaled a gridiron power inversion of the usual racial order. Not relishing this new arrangement, the writer concluded, "May his tribe not increase, and may he, in time, absorb enough knowledge to graduate, and so pass from the arena of high school athletics."

In Hutchinson's final game, their second against Kingman, Coach Yeoman showed mercy on the opponents by having Butler sit out in the scoreless first quarter. With Butler on the field in the second quarter, the team scored five touchdowns, including three scored by Butler. With the win safely secured by halftime, he sat out for the remainder of the game, and the scoring stopped. As one of his schoolmates put it in the pages of the school newspaper, the *High School Buzz*, "The fellows seemed lost on the offensive without the whirlwind half[back] during the rest of the game."[65]

Almost singularly responsible for Hutchinson High School's athletic success, Butler earned the attention and respect of white people in the region. He continued to present himself in ways that the media increasingly valorized as manly, clean (in terms of avoiding unnecessarily rough and unethical play), diligent, respectable, and, most importantly, humble. The editor of a Black newspaper from Topeka wrote, "We predict great things for young Butler in the future and the white students as well as the citizens of Hutchinson speak in the highest [terms] of him and say he is always polite and kind and they show him that they appreciate anythng [*sic*] good that a colored man can do and will give him credit when merited just as readily as the white man who earns these things."[66] But the positive attention was mingled with derision and paternalism from many white journalists. One from Stafford, who introduced Butler as "the speedy nig," wrote, "If the young buck does not swell up and bust over all this attention there will be some hope for him."[67] On the other hand, Butler's accomplishments prompted some white writers to acknowledge the pervasiveness of anti-Black racism. "Throughout his career, Sol has had to fight his way for recognition because of his color," observed a contributor to the *Buzz*.[68]

His good character opened doors, making wide recognition possible, but there were limits to the social mobility it afforded him. During Butler's sophomore year of high school, Hutchinson's deputy sheriff fired a shotgun at a Black teenager whom he suspected had written a threatening letter to a white farmer. The unidentified child, "on his way home from a church festival," knew nothing about the letter and mistook the officer for a drunk man along the railroad tracks. The *Hutchinson News* presented the incident as a humorous gaffe. The victim was, "after all, only a sixteen year old colored school boy."[69] While it had been a decade since a Black man had been lynched in the state, white officers could regularly threaten, if not engage in, casual racial violence without running the risk of public censure.

Around the same time, a staged photograph of Butler in his football gear appeared on the front page of the *High School Buzz*.[70] He cradles a football in his left arm while his right hand hangs loose at his side. His right leg bends slightly to suggest forward movement toward the viewer's left; the heel of his raised football cleat, tied neatly to the top of his ankle, reveals the metal studs that enable his quick acceleration and direction changes on the grass fields. His body-hugging jersey emphasizes his lithe, well-muscled torso. Most arresting is his unsmiling gaze, directly into the camera with chin slightly raised. Butler's

Butler the sophomore in football uniform. (*High School Buzz*, November 1, 1912, p. 1)

dignity made no compromise with his vaunted humility. He would cultivate an image that would allow him relative freedom of movement in the mostly white world of high school sports in Kansas, but he would never venture into the realm of timidity or subservience. Sol Butler knew he couldn't be a Jack Johnson figure in Hutchinson, Kansas; he couldn't afford to be polarizing or confrontational because he depended on the support of his white coaches, teammates, and neighbors. But like Johnson, and perhaps with an eye toward eventual celebrity on par with the great boxer, Butler was always unapologetically himself.

Already a regional athletic star, Butler had yet to complete his sophomore year in high school. The spring 1913 track and field season opened with a telling sign of the sport's increasing prestige and popularity. Hutchinson High School did not field a team in baseball, the era's most popular sport, in part because "the students are more generally interested in track work."[71] This spoke to the highly publicized success of the school's track team and its star, Sol Butler. They continued their winning ways in the opening meet at Pratt, where they won eight of fourteen events in front of a crowd of twenty-five hundred that included eighty students and teachers who had traveled by train from Hutchinson. Butler finished first in the 50- and 100-yard dashes, the shot put, and the 220-yard hurdles. The team brought home five of the eight silver cups, which were valued at an estimated four hundred dollars combined.[72] Over his first season and one meet, Butler had won four individual cups and twenty-one medals: "The collection is now on display at the Book and Art store on North Main street." Butler's trophies were on public display again the following year at H. D. Winslow's bookstore.[73] He had succeeded not only on the field but also in the arena of public opinion. The young Black man was the pride of his mostly white community, a bona fide hometown hero.

Butler performed remarkably well throughout the rest of the season. At the University of Kansas interscholastic meet in Lawrence, he again placed first in the 100- and 220-yard dashes and the 220-yard hurdles. In the Arkansas Valley Interscholastic meet at Fairmont College, in front of two thousand spectators, he finished first in the broad jump, 100- and 220-yard dashes, and 120-yard hurdles, dramatically lowering the state record in this hurdles event.[74] Hutchinson newspapers devoted virtually no attention to the season's final meet in Manhattan, Kansas, after news emerged that the team's star would be excluded from the event in deference to the racist expectations of a team from Missouri. But Butler did participate in the end (perhaps in response to the public's demand to see the most exciting athlete) and won first in the 50- and 100-yard dashes, 220-yard hurdles, and 12-pound shot put and ran a leg on the first-place relay team. Hutchinson narrowly missed winning first place at the meet, while Butler easily secured the individual honors.[75] "Although the *Topeka Daily Capitol* [*sic*] advertised that they would give a cup to the individual point winner, I have yet the first time to see it," he recalled of his season-ending accomplishment.[76] A rival newspaper reported that racism accounted for their withholding the valuable award.[77] Writing about the incident in his memoir, Butler again demonstrated the limits of his humility and selflessness: "That paper owes me the cup and I hope that I will receive it at some future date, when the promise is remembered."[78]

The 1913 football season began with commanding victories at St. John High School and at home versus Stafford, whom they defeated 41–0, with Butler scoring five of the team's six touchdowns.[79] "Sol is undoubtedly the fastest back in the state and we are proud of the fact that he bucks the line, carrying the ball for Hutchinson," enthused the school newspaper.[80] However, two of their next three scheduled games yielded disappointment. The game against Marion represented the season's only loss, which reportedly resulted from injuries, the muddy field, overconfidence, and the absence of two starters because they "were behind in their studies and the teachers would not sign their cards [that gave them permission to play]."[81] Word had already spread that such a fate would not befall Butler, who was known as "a first rank student." Noting that this "clean player . . . practically carries the team," a reporter from the *Great Bend Tribune* wrote, "His color is all that will keep him from becoming one of the best known athletes in the state."[82] Shortly after this article appeared, Lawrence High School officials announced they would not play against Hutchinson with Butler and Phillips on the field; Lawrence did not yield when promised half of their opponent's home-field ticket earnings. Hutchinson would not exclude their Black players, and the game was canceled. Later in the season, Pratt, whose undefeated record had been toppled by the Salters after Pratt had agreed to play for $150, refused to play Hutchinson that season because two of Pratt's best players allegedly "could not stand to play a 'negro' boy." But both Lawrence and Pratt had played against teams with a Black player earlier in the season.[83] Butler recalled, "It seemed that a number of the schools had banded together and adopted resolutions refusing to play against colored boys."[84] The objections came from teams aiming for a championship, using discrimination as a tool to avoid failure.

In their blowout victories over soldiers from Fort Riley and the team from Emporia High School, the Hutchinson Salters vividly displayed their exciting, fully developed offensive style, characterized by shifts in formation, passing, and lateral and improvised open-field running. The soldiers relied primarily on running the ball through the line with a wall of blockers.[85] Butler intercepted one of the soldiers' only passes, running it back for a touchdown. High schools like Hutchinson adopted the open style of play from three sources: the college game, which implemented it to improve safety;[86] Chicago high schools like Oak Park, which introduced the forward pass to the East Coast in 1910;[87] and the terrifically successful Carlisle Indian Industrial School, a Native American boarding school team led by the inimitable Jim Thorpe that featured "an extraordinary new offense, an exercise in sophisticated fakery, exact timing, artfully disguised ball handling, and, above all, speed."[88] With these innovations, exceptional athletes like Butler and his future friend Fritz Pollard at Lane Tech High School in Chicago pushed the precollege game to dazzling new heights. In the game against Emporia, Butler and quarterback

Johnny Armstrong twice executed "a criss cross," which involved a fake handoff and resulted in Armstrong gaining long yardage, including one touchdown run: "On a fake forward pass, Butler ran through a broken field for a 40-yard gain and on the next play smashed through tackle for 25 yards and a touchdown."[89] He also ran back the opening kickoff of the second half and scored a third touchdown.

The 1913 Salters finished the season on a high note. They scored a combined eighty-one points, to their opponents' combined total of six, in their victories over Kingman and Nickerson high schools. In the final seconds of the season-ending game before a crowd of three thousand at Salina High, Butler ran a kick back 90 yards for a touchdown, one of four he scored in the second half.[90] The players wrapped up the season in the Hutchinson High School auditorium with a fund-raiser, which attracted greater media attention than any one of their games. Raising money to purchase letterman sweaters, the twenty-one members of the Hutchinson football team spent several weeks practicing for a performance that included jokes, music (including "good 'coon' songs") accompanied by violin and piano, and dancing.[91]

Such racially charged gestures of goodwill did not end with the fading strains of the high schoolers' "coon" songs. A few days later, Indiana Church of Christ evangelist Charles Reign Scoville came to town to lead the Christian Union evangelistic campaign, an extended revival that one local businessman considered "the biggest thing we have had in Hutchinson."[92] On a Monday night in First Methodist Church before an interracial audience, Scoville joined Black pastors J. C. Rogers of Second Baptist and Rev. H. Franklin Bray of the Butlers' church, Bethel AME, to deliver an address aimed primarily at the perils of corrupt male behavior. "You have your work to do, as well as we [white people] . . . You can work among your own people more effectively than can we," declared Scoville, before evoking a seemingly more integrationist version of Booker T. Washington's famous five-fingered metaphor from his Atlanta Exposition speech: "Let the colored Christians and the white Christians of Hutchinson join hands with the common purpose to take Hutchinson for Christ." Ben Butler Sr. was invited to the front of the sanctuary to lead the congregation in song. According to one local news report, "The old ex-slave, with tears streaming down his face shouted: 'Praise the Lord. Now come take me. Come and get me. I'm ready to go right now. The day I've been praying for these many years is here. I see the white people and the colored people worshipping together. Praise the Lord. This is heaven for me.'"[93] He then led in the foundational Black sacred music practice of call and response. "Swing low, sweet chariot," Ben sang, to which the congregation responded in unison: "Coming for to carry me home."

Concluding the service, Scoville invited all "colored people of the city" to another upcoming service in Convention Hall, where a "section of one of the balconies will be reserved for them."[94] Similar to those teams that refused to play the Salters, the pastor promulgated segregation in Kansas, tacitly giving expression to the famous words Washington uttered years earlier in the South: "In all things that are purely social we can be as separate as the fingers."

Son of Thunder

In early 1914 Sol Butler was invited to attend "the biggest indoor interscholastic track, field and swimming tournament,"[95] a two-day meet with over three hundred young male athletes from high schools and college preparatory schools in seven states, held at Northwestern University in Evanston, Illinois, and organized by Northwestern's athletic director, Lewis Omer, one of the era's most influential organizers of high school sports.[96] Sol traveled to Evanston with his brother, Ben, his "at all times . . . constant companion," and their trip was financed by contributions from high school classmates, teachers, and Hutchinson businessmen.[97] A college town just north of Chicago, Evanston maintained policies of segregation that necessitated the creation of Black businesses, organizations, and churches.[98] Excluded from boarding on campus and at local hotels, the Butler brothers stayed at the home of Abe L. Jones, "one of the wealthiest and most influential colored citizens of Evanston" and a sports enthusiast.[99]

Black Evanston residents had reason to take interest in the heralded athlete's performance at their town's prominent university, which then enrolled perhaps only two Black people, students in the Garrett Biblical Institute.[100] Butler did not disappoint. He "started the night's entertainment by sprinting down the sixty yard pathway in :06 2/5 [6.4 seconds], a world's record," noted the *Chicago Tribune*. Before the evening was over, the "redoubtable Butler smashed a record [by over ten inches] in the broad jump, the last event of the meet."[101] His one-man team earned fourth place in the meet, and he claimed the individual title, which came with a trophy and a fifty-dollar award.[102] After the meet, Lewis Omer wrote effusive recruiting letters to Butler and his coach, Herbert Roe: "Butler is the fastest athlete west of Chicago, either amateur or professional . . . one of the best runners I ever saw."[103] Omer promised to make Butler a "special shield . . . a more imposing looking trophy," for an upcoming meet,[104] and he urged Butler to enroll at Northwestern: "If you come to Northwestern I will see that you get on the Olympic team, if I have to raise the money by subscription to send you to Berlin."[105]

Word of his success at the Northwestern meet spread far and fast. "There is another Howard Drew out in the Middle West, at least in the making," wrote the *Boston Globe*, comparing Sol to the 1912 Black Olympian.[106] The *Hutchinson Gazette* reprinted a lengthy account of the meet from the *Chicago Record-Herald* and claimed that Butler "was featured in all of Chicago's Sunday papers."[107] Coach Roe told the *Hutchinson News*, "Sol did more than we expected of him." The *News* noted that Butler's father was "the happiest man in Hutchinson." After a humorous recounting of his son's accomplishments and hyperbolic parental bragging, Ben Sr. dutifully testified to Sol's unfailing modesty: "And the beauty about it all is, Sol ain't swelled up over what he does. He never says a word to nobody when he wins them races. He's just happy to be able to win points for high school. He never tells me about it."[108]

When Butler returned to Hutchinson, he was feted by local Black residents in "a parade of triumph," which started at the Butlers' home, proceeded down Main Street, and ended at the high school.[109] African American city collector Walter Evans led the procession, followed by "Sol's colored friends." Butler rode "perched precariously on the long hood of a big touring car driven by [white classmate] Norvel Sifers, the honest contenance [*sic*] of the ebony hued athletic star beamed with pleasure." Silver and gold medals hung around his neck, and a shelf arranged at the front of the hood displayed a dozen silver cups. Butler's father, whose "jolly old brown face was the picture of extreme happiness on this earth," rode in the back of the car with Reverend Bray of Bethel AME. Handbills announced a public reception that night in the high school auditorium, where Bray introduced Butler as "that ebony-hued son of thunder" to an interracial audience of around two hundred.[110] A banquet followed at Bethel AME, where Butler received "a huge bouquet of American beauty roses presented by white friends."[111] The *High School Buzz* wrote, "We give all honors to Sol Butler. The school has every reason to be proud of him, not only for his athletic ability, but for his character and gentlemanly conduct . . . Throughout his career, Sol has had to fight his way for recognition because of his color, and that is all the more in his favor."[112]

Butler lived up to Olympic-size expectations in the outdoor track and field season. On a beautiful late April day in Pratt at the conference meet against eight other teams, he finished first in six events. Before nearly two thousand spectators, he set a world interscholastic record in the 50-yard dash at 5⅖ seconds, tied the high school record in the 100-yard dash at 9⅘ seconds, and broke five state records.[113] Fans of other teams increasingly applauded him: "Since he made good at Chicago, Sol has been given representative territory in all of Kansas and is gradually winning national fame."[114] The next Saturday at Lawrence he duplicated his six first-place finishes in the same events at the state level, and the five-person Hutchinson team narrowly defeated the large Lawrence team, which had won the previous eleven state meets.[115] Another leading article on the front page of the *Hutchinson Gazette* summed up his performance as "unparalleled" and "another step forward toward earning the reputation of being the greatest all-around high school athlete in the United States."[116] A few days later, Butler set another world record at the Arkansas River Valley interscholastic meet. According to four of six judges at the finish, he lowered the 120-yard low hurdles amateur record set in 1909 by two-fifths of a second. He also took first in the 100-yard and 220-yard dashes, the broad jump, and shot put.[117]

His success at the Lawrence meet made a lasting impression on one of the day's officials, John C. Grover, whom the *Kansas City Star* identified as the "outstanding official of college football and track in this section for the last twenty-five years and holder of more continuous service refereeing records than any other man in intercollegiate sports."[118] Years later, Grover still remembered Butler's speech at a banquet thrown that night by the University of Kansas for a thousand guests, only a few of whom were Black. "It was a delicate situation," he wrote, wondering if Butler would "be boastful or modest? Would he boast a bit over his remarkable string of victories or would he minimize his efforts?" Quoting Butler "word for word," Grover wrote: "'My coach has taught me three things,' he said, 'first, my God; second, my country; third, my school. Today I did the best I could for my school.' He sat down, a thunderous applause ringing in his ears. He had met the situation gloriously, topping his wonderful work of the day by as fine and unaffected a speech as any athlete ever made."[119]

Attesting to his increasingly prodigious reputation, Sol became the focal point of the first film by Marion William Bailey, a professional photographer from Hutchinson who had recently purchased moving picture equipment. A few years earlier, his daughter Edith Bailey had taken what may be the earliest extant photograph of Butler, standing amid his eighth-grade class.[120] Shortly after Butler's success in Evanston, Marion captured finishes at the interclass competition held at the high school and traveled to Pratt to record the district meet. Capitalizing on Butler's recent dominance and the team's success in Lawrence, Bailey screened his (subsequently lost) film—the first made in that part of the state—at the De Luxe Theater along Main Street on a Wednesday night.[121] Under the cover of dark, the audience could marvel unabashedly at his gravity-defying leaps and lightning quickness, which sparked hopes for a journey to the 1916 Berlin Olympics.

On June 8, Butler headed east by train with Coach Roe and four teammates to compete at the University of Chicago. Named after the influential athletic director who organized it, Amos Alonzo Stagg, the Stagg meet—recognized as the largest and most prestigious high school track tournament in the country—included more than five hundred athletes from 116 schools and nearly every state. For the Hutchinson businessmen and boosters who helped fund the team's trip, Butler's participation represented a chance to put their town on the map.[122] They realized "that reports of the meet will go in every large newspaper in the country and that Hutchinson will be recognized as a live, wide-awake town if the boys make a credible showing."[123]

Butler recalled that when "the long anticipated day arrived" for the interscholastic track and field meet on Stagg Field, "it began to rain and we knew that we would have to fight on another heavy track."[124] Only about a thousand spectators witnessed Butler earn honors for most individual points by placing first in the 100-yard dash and broad jump (his jump measured nearly two feet longer than that of the next best competitor) and second in the 220-yard

"They're Still Talking," cartoon based on Butler's performance at Lawrence, Kansas, in 1914 as described by John Grover in 1931. (*Des Moines Register*, August 8, 1937, p. 71)

dash.[125] Writing for the *Chicago Tribune*, football great and sportswriter Walter Eckersoll highlighted Butler's extraordinary performance in the often-derisive fashion of white journalists, calling him "the demon colored athlete" and "Sambo Butler."[126]

An article next to Eckersoll's covered a separate track and field meet held that same day at the Negro League's American Giants ballpark, featuring youth who, if not for the reality of segregation, might have joined Butler, perhaps the only Black competitor at the Stagg meet, and the white athletes at Stagg Field.[127] Sol Butler was among the nation's few African Americans fortunate enough to navigate the pervasive and systemic ways that racism excluded students and athletes of color. The conjuncture of multiple factors—including exceptional family support, the relatively progressive racial attitudes of his home community, favorable connections between his coach and athletic organizers, and his own careful efforts to present himself as the hardworking, humble student-athlete who could earn favor with white fans, coaches, and teammates—created the unlikely opportunity for his talent and hard work to pay off. When he wrote about the Chicago meet—"It seemed that all my years of training were not in vain"[128]—some readers could appreciate how the remarkableness of this feat went well beyond his physical capabilities. It spoke to a hurdling, if only briefly, of a seemingly unbreachable social barrier.

Square Deal

Buoyed by their success, Sol Butler and Coach Roe decided to stay in Evanston for the summer. Roe would take courses in physical training at the university; Butler was "anxious to get in touch with athletics in Chicago," and for the first time in his life, he competed against an athlete of national renown.[129] On July 25 at the Chicago Athletic Club meet in Grant Park, along the shore of Lake Michigan, Butler raced Joe Loomis of the Chicago Athletic Association and winner of the 100-yard dash at the national Amateur Athletic Union meet in Baltimore. The two men finished in a virtual tie with a world record–matching time. In a split decision, and with many spectators and officials declaring Butler the victor, the judges awarded Loomis first place.[130] While praising Loomis as "fair and square, and a magnificent runner," Butler claimed that the race was unwinnable because he had to "run [against] the whole family. Pa Loomis was one of the judges." A photograph of the finish later proved that Butler won the race by about two feet.[131] The use of photographs during this period reflected a newly established reliance on the "objective authority of the image in sport," which accompanied the proliferation of sports associations and federations, rules and regulations.[132]

"When I began to see the exceptional chances for an athlete in Illinois I decided that I would attend school somewhere in the state the following year," Sol wrote in his memoir.[133] Herbert Roe had accepted a job as school athletic director in Rock Island, Illinois, along the Mississippi River.[134] "I soon afterward asked my coach if he would care if I wrote to the superintendent there to see if there was a good chance for me to help pay my way, and if my brother Ben would have a chance," Butler wrote.[135] Both white administrators "were agreeable to the plan." With the assurance of financial assistance, the brothers headed north to complete their secondary education.

Sol explained the move as "simply a case of deep gratitude and friendship I feel for Mr. Roe and the desire to stay with him, together with my plan for running in the bigger meets in the middle west," but there were forces pushing him out of Kansas. As Butler's athletic success grew, so, too, did the number of teams that refused to play Hutchinson. "This did not make me feel badly on my own account, because I have been subjected to numerous difficulties of this nature since birth," wrote Butler, "but I felt that Hutchinson was not getting a square deal in the matter."[136] Looking beyond his final year of high school, Butler knew he would be excluded from the University of Kansas because William Oliver Hamilton, the manager of athletics and track coach at this flagship institution, made it known that he would not recruit any Black athletes.[137] "Taking these things into consideration made up my mind that, as much as I hated to leave, I would do better to enter athletics in a different state, where I would have a better chance of continuing my work without such an abundance of objections and hard feelings."[138]

The Butlers' move to Hutchinson afforded Sol not only an integrated education but also integrated playing fields, where he was given the opportunity to shine on much bigger stages than those he might have encountered playing in an increasingly segregated Wichita. He capitalized on that opportunity by moving again, this time on his own initiative, to find even bigger stages with even fewer barriers. Sol Butler made good use of the advantages afforded him by his parents' and his own physical mobility by leveraging his remarkable, canny social mobility, especially in white-controlled spaces where he might otherwise have been excluded. The violent backlash to Jack Johnson's bold success in the ring and as a self-made Black man made the danger clear, so Butler carefully cultivated his image as an impeccably humble team player to avoid charges of impudence that could have derailed his sport dreams.

And yet, in order to keep moving in the direction of his goals, Butler needed to achieve individual recognition at a level almost approaching Johnson's celebrity without sacrificing all his vaunted modesty. This dilemma would lead Sol Butler to continue pursuing athletic greatness by honing his bodily mobility through dogged practice and by traveling farther from home to compete in elite regional and national competitions. His search for new spaces and sport opportunities prompted bold innovation beyond the fields and in literary form.

3

Exceptional Chances for an Athlete

Fall 1914–Summer 1915

From "Freight Train" (ca. 1910) by Elizabeth Cotten. (Copyright © 1957 Figs D Music and Sanga Music Inc. Copyright Renewed. This arrangement © 2024 Figs D Music and Sanga Music Inc. All Rights Reserved. Reprinted by Permission of Hal Leonard LLC.)

Sol and Ben arrived by train in Rock Island in early September 1914, several weeks before the leaves began changing color along the town's Mississippi River banks. During the Civil War, Rock Island was home to one of six Northern prisons for Confederate soldiers. Nearly a thousand formerly enslaved and free-born Black troops served in the 108th United States Colored Troops, a Rock Island regiment that helped guard the prisoners. On the heels of his military journeys to Savannah, Georgia, and Washington, DC, Ben Sr. just missed seeing the 108th when he disbanded from his own regiment across the river in Davenport, Iowa. In 1910, not long after Ben Sr. returned to the area for purposes of securing his military pension, the Black population in Rock Island was 397, less than 2 percent of the city's residents. Davenport and neighboring Moline, Illinois, which with Rock Island made up the area's Tri-Cities (now Quad Cities), had similarly small Black populations, but over the next decade the number of African Americans in the area would nearly double. Schools in the Tri-Cities were integrated, but the rest of the community remained segregated for several more decades.[1]

Both Rock Island and Moline supported semiprofessional football teams for over ten years, and the Rock Island Independents became one of the founding members of the National Football League. Sol Butler, Rock Island High School's new quarterback, arrived just in time for football season in a football-crazed town.[2] The *Rock Island Argus* and other papers, along with word-of-mouth excitement, generated quite a preseason buzz, and attendance at Rock Island High School football games that fall surpassed attendance at Hutchinson games and rivaled the crowds at the semiprofessional games in Rock Island, Moline, and Davenport. Butler did not disappoint Rock Island fans. He led the team to six wins—including some spectacular shutouts—two losses, and a tie against a college squad. In one game he scored eight touchdowns, including on a play that Butler biographer David Sebben notes "had never been seen before in local sports" and resembled what came to be known as the "Immaculate Reception" by Franco Harris in the 1972 playoffs.[3] One official from Chicago wrote that he considered Butler "the greatest high school player he had ever seen."[4]

The stakes were high for the final two games of the season against Davenport, Iowa, and Moline. "The rivalry among the several schools is intense and all are ever struggling for supremacy," wrote Butler.[5] After a disappointing defeat by Davenport (a game in which he scored his team's only touchdown on a 95-yard run from scrimmage), the Independents (also known as the "Islanders") learned from their mistakes, shifted players around, and "easily won the most coveted game of the football year" against Moline in front of four thousand fans.[6] Playing end instead of quarterback, Butler plowed "like a veritable truck horse in advancing the ball, a tower of strength in running interference," wrote the *Rock Island Argus*, "and pulled off some of the prettiest tackles ever witnessed on the Browning field."[7] The game's referee later wrote, "Butler took his life in his hands to win that game . . . Headfirst he dove over both lines of forwards and landed three feet beyond the goal line for a touchdown . . . I never expect to see so sensational a play again if I referee for fifty years."[8] Rock Island celebrated the win with a parade down Second Avenue that featured the football team, pep band, and "a great crowd of followers," who then gathered on the levee of the Mississippi River for a raucous, music-filled celebration around a bonfire.[9]

Near the end of Butler's senior year in Rock Island, a glee chorus claiming to be from the Tuskegee Institute in Alabama visited the Tri-Cities for several days of performances. The musical program included "plantation melodies, negro folk songs, and dialect readings,"[10] followed by a "short talk" by Walter L. Hutcherson, purporting to be the institution's regional field secretary, who "urged financial cooperation of those who were interested in helping the black man."[11] The talk ended with Hutcherson making the link between their performance, audience donations, and achieving higher goals: "In telling the story of my life, and struggles for what education I have been able to obtain, I am telling you the story of every boy and girl of my race who must earn his or her education."

Like members of the Tuskegee glee club, Sol Butler understood that his performances—on the athletic field and in the social realm—were essential to securing the white patronage he needed, particularly from business leaders, to advance his educational and athletic goals. The funds that allowed Butler and his brother to complete their high school education in Rock Island were contingent on Sol, like the Tuskegee singers, entertaining audiences without violating codes of racial decorum. Graduation appeared imminent, yet finding the means to enter and succeed in college—another four-year endeavor hampered by limited resources, an unpredictable racial climate, and unknown bodily limits up against ever-increasing athletic expectations—must have appeared especially daunting. On the verge of an exciting, yet nerve-wracking life transition, the Butler brothers turned to the literary arts to burnish their image and garner public support.[12]

Take Our Stand

A few months after the football season ended, Sol Butler published a book titled *Three Years of High School Athletics*, a "narrative of athletic experiences on the gridiron and track," which covered his first three years at Hutchinson High School and one season of football at Rock Island.[13] A thousand copies of the fifty-three-page book, which Sol Butler cowrote with his brother, Ben, were released on March 29 to satisfy a "great many" preorders.[14] Fifty black-and-white photographs, ranging in format from small portraits of Sol's educators, coaches, and teammates to full-page team shots and action collages, accompany more than fifteen thousand words of text. "I'm going to turn loose 2,000 of the books right in Hutchinson," Ben Butler Sr. told a reporter, indicating his anticipation of additional printings of the book. Referring to the joint production as "Sol's book," Ben Sr. proudly said, "I know it is good," before he saw it. "Just think of the source."[15] The Butler patriarch assumed that many of his white patrons and acquaintances would be interested in reading about the athletic triumphs of his youngest child and former Hutchinson star, and he did succeed in selling over a hundred copies in April. An unknown number of the books were sold at bookstores in Hutchinson, the Rock Island YMCA, and the high schools in both communities.[16] But as literary scholar Jonathan Barz suggests, "Perhaps the most remarkable aspect of Sol and Ben Butler's book is that it exists at all."[17]

The existence of *Three Years of High School Athletics* signaled the Butler brothers' remarkable foray into Black sports entrepreneurism, their most explicit acknowledgment that they could shape Sol's sports success beyond his performances on the fields of play. The gridiron and track and field star single-handedly won team events, consistently broke records, and set expectations to impossible heights, but therein lay a problem: His success made him increasingly visible yet known in surface and superficial ways. Audiences knew him through box scores, word of mouth, or a trip to see a game or meet and did not appreciate the person behind the dazzling performances. Newspapers sometimes addressed his good character, yet journalists unfailingly identified him as a notable "negro" or "colored" athlete, with all the stereotypes that white audiences read into these racial qualifiers substituting for what friends and family knew to be true about him. His media attention was a boon to the schools and communities he represented but did not always benefit Sol and other African Americans. As entrepreneurs attuned to the racial dynamics of athletics and drawing on the cultural capital of physical and social mobility, he and Ben Jr. asserted control over public perception, fashioning a fleshed-out image of a superb athlete to supplant flat, misleading, and even demeaning media representation. Rather than fame and fortune, their Black sport autobiography fueled their ascent into higher education and as cultural leaders.

While the fact of writing and publishing a book represented an entrepreneurial attempt to realize Black middle-class aspirations, evidence suggests that the funds to produce *Three Years* materialized thanks to Butler's success on the football field in his new hometown and the white patronage it inspired. The first three images in the book, all portraits, depict white men, including A. J. Hill, identified as supervisor of the manual art department and business manager of the athletic association. Due to the unprecedented leadership of the school's star quarterback, during the 1914 football season the athletic association turned its largest profit in school history, around one thousand dollars.[18] It's likely that the group agreed to cover the printing costs for *Three Years* as a token of their appreciation. The Butlers' story cast the school's athletics program in glowing terms, publicity that would generate interest in future events and help secure ongoing community support. Hill would have overseen the layout and typesetting of the book, as he did for the Rock Island High School newspaper and yearbook, the *Watch Tower*, and he used the services of the Driffill Printing Company for both publications.[19]

Told in the first person, the story blends both brothers' voices into one. The March 1915 issue of the *Watch Tower* reported that Ben Butler "has accomplished something which probably none of the rest of us have," suggesting that he alone authored the book.[20] The *Chicago Defender* soon after reported that Ben "wrote a book on his brother's athletic feats."[21] Other sources, including the book itself, clarify that the two brothers collaborated.[22] The relatively unknown brother, Ben, who presented himself as the agent and promoter of the widely celebrated brother, Sol, had incentive to boost his academic credentials and claim sole authorship.

The Butler brothers identified their goal on the title page: "We hope some day to take our stand as leaders of our race. To do this we must have a liberal education. We have written this book as a means to this end."[23] The publication represented their ticket to college in two ways: First, it raised money; as Sol put it in a letter to the *Hutchinson News*, "The price of the books will be fifty cents each, and the money [is] to be used to give us a college education without the necessity of myself becoming a professional athlete."[24] Second, it functioned like an especially lengthy and ambitious college admission essay, signaling how difficult and unlikely it was for two Black men to transition to the next academic level.[25]

By asserting their need for a liberal education to become leaders, Sol and Ben entered the contested ideological arena of racial uplift. They implicitly rejected the industrial education championed by gradualist Booker T. Washington and placed themselves in line with the ideas of towering Black intellectual W.E.B. Du Bois, who emphasized the need for a classical education. The brothers' college aspirations fit with the notion championed by Du Bois of the "talented tenth," which held that a college-educated Black elite should pull "all that are worth the saving up to their vantage ground."[26] Elevating the masses was a top-down process. Given the social circles in which the Butler family ran, they certainly knew of Du Bois and his work, and Sol would soon appear in the pages of *The Crisis*, the magazine that Du Bois founded and edited for the National Association for the Advancement of Colored People (NAACP).[27]

A large and dynamic group of Black Kansan educators who taught at all-Black schools and "equipped their students with the pride and strategies needed to sustain the twentieth-century fight for legal and social equality" also influenced the Butlers.[28] These educators included Western University president W. T. Vernon, whom Mary Butler and other clubwomen held in such high regard; Greene B. Buster, who taught African American history at Sumner High School in Kansas City; and teachers at the Kansas Industrial and Educational Institute in Topeka. In profession and training, they embodied Du Bois's talented tenth, deemphasizing industrial training and focusing instead on preparing students for college and leadership. True to the spirit of these educators from their former home state, the brothers innovated by wedding, in the minds of readers, this educational pursuit with Sol's exceptional physical mobility.

In a broad sense, the Butlers published *Three Years* as a means to move more freely beyond the playing fields. To this end, the narrative linked Sol's breathtaking athletic accomplishments with lessons in character that discouraged racialized thinking. At every turn, the book reminded readers that Sol's success should be attributed to hard work, discipline, sacrifice, service, careful observation, preparation, perseverance, reliability, humility, and compassion, rather than natural talent or racial attributes. It exuded optimism and faith in meritocracy and embraced the respectability politics of Washington and Vernon, implying that racism could be overcome through good character. *Three Years* connected character to notions of cleanliness, which symbolized a rejection of vice and corruption. When explaining the Rock Island football team's loss against Rockford, for instance, Butler concluded that "clean living produces strength, valor and manhood, while clean minds and morals are the parents of high ideals, unselfishness, modesty and fair-mindedness."[29] His success-filled, "clean" journey provided a template that other young people, especially young Black men, could emulate.

The literary genre of the Black personal narrative had been well established through the formative influence of slave narratives and subsequent works by Black leaders like Booker T. Washington. Echoing the conventions of slave narratives, *Three Years* begins with the brothers' assertion of authorship on the title page, followed by a white authority, coach Herbert Roe, attesting to the virtues of the book and the good character of Sol and Ben Butler, whom he identifies as the authors (Roe only indirectly vouches for the book's veracity). On a subsequent page, Sol credits Roe as "the man who has done most in my development," which regarded the younger man's maturation and athletic development but also may have included his ambition and strength as a writer.[30] The narrative's opening sentence begins "I was born," another convention in many works by the formerly enslaved.[31] Mimicking slave narratives in these ways suggested that the Butlers meant for readers to accept their account as accurate. "Telling the truth did not necessarily mean telling the whole truth, or every truth; it meant telling a truth that made sense to a white audience, with particular racialist preconceptions and literary expectations," writes author Benjamin Soskis about the nineteenth-century genre.[32] Like their predecessors, the brothers balanced desires to express their subjective truth and impact their audience.

They also had other literary influences. *Three Years* is an early example of sports biography that, according to Barz, "would become a significant force in American publishing in the next 100 years."[33] At the time, this relatively new genre almost exclusively focused on the lives of baseball players. One notable exception was *Reminiscences of an Athlete: Twenty Years on Track and Field* (1911) by white author Ellery Harding Clark, who won the gold medal in the broad jump and high jump at the 1896 Olympics.[34] Like the Butlers, Clark includes statistical results, describes key competitions, and places service to one's school before personal gain. The authors similarly evoke the exaltation of wearing team regalia for the first time—the team letter for Clark and football pants for Butler—and Clark, of a piece with the Butlers' emphasis on good character, identifies skill, brains, and mathematics as more important to athletic success than strength, muscle, and inspiration. *Reminiscences of an Athlete* appeared to serve as a model for Butler's book, unlike Jack Johnson's

In the fifty it is necessary to give every ounce of strength from the very start, hurling yourself at the tape when nearing the finish.

50 Yard Dash, Time 5 2-5

THE 100 YARD DASH.

The century is the greatest race known to the track, and supremacy in this is coveted by a great many sprinters. The start should be as quick as possible, every muscle in the lower

100 Yard Dash, Time 9 4-5

part of the body in action on the instant. The chest muscles should be relaxed until within fifteen yards from the finish.

A page from *Three Years of High School Athletics* (1915) by Sol and Ben Butler. (University of Dubuque Archives) first autobiography, *My Life and Battles* (published in French a year earlier),[35] and *Our Home Colony*, a 1908 treatise promoting African American emigration to Africa, by Moses Fleetwood Walker, the first openly Black Major League Baseball player in the 1880s and the last one before Jackie Robinson reintegrated the majors.[36]

Three Years was also indebted to the popular genre of sport fiction, represented by dime-novel author Gilbert Patten's (pen name Burt L. Standish) hundreds of serialized stories starring Frank Merriwell, a paragon of Progressive Era convictions about the power of athletics to shape and reveal character. "In athletics strength and skill win, regardless of money or family," went one of these tales about the protagonist's first year at Yale; "so it happened that the poorest man in the university stood a show of becoming the lion and idol of the whole body of young men."[37] Conjuring the type of brilliant sport success that Sol Butler, against all odds, enjoyed in high school, the Merriwell stories spoke to the democratizing power of athletics that Butler hoped to harness in his own sporting life and evoke in his book.

The final eight pages of *Three Years* are as instructional as they are biographical. In a section titled "HOW I RUN THE DASHES," illustrated with photographs of Butler winning races, the book advises readers on how to approach different stages of races. The book's final three pages, titled "METHOD OF TRAINING," offer advice on diet, sleep, and the importance of not competing in too many events in one meet. "I eat reasonable amounts of wholesome food with very little fatty or sweet stuff," Butler noted, before including meal suggestions and addressing the topic of sleep, which he considered more important than diet: "I usually go to bed about 10 o'clock and never later than 10:30 and always get up at seven."[38]

This shift toward health and training evoked many widely available sports books and journal articles published in the United States in the early twentieth century.[39] The Butlers' book shared several features with the recently published *Athletic Training* (1914), by the influential coach Mike Murphy, who wrote his book "primarily for the benefit of those who have not had the advantage of professional coaches," a tool to help realize the supposedly democratizing power of athletics.[40] Like *Athletic Training*, *Three Years* featured a line drawing of the ancient Greek sculpture Discobolus on its cover. Both books provide nontechnical advice on how to approach various track and field events. Sol and Ben also may have consulted the first book "written by a Black man which dealt specifically with Black athletics,"[41] the *Spalding Official Handbook of the Inter-Scholastic Athletic Association of Middle Atlantic States*, published from 1910 to 1913. Created and co-edited by visionary athletic organizer Edwin Bancroft Henderson, each edition included how-to articles on health, training, ethics, and other topics aimed to spur the growth of African American teams and leagues.[42]

The Butlers' varied and diverse literary influences point to the key feature at the entrepreneurial heart of *Three Years*: innovation. They introduced a new product, a unique combination of sports autobiography, sports fiction, and athletic training manual informed by the conventions of slave narratives. This innovation added a crucial dimension to sportswriting since white writers tended to exclude a Black presence and subjectivity. Sol's presence in integrated education and sports represented a challenge to a society structured by white supremacy, thereby disrupting readers' racially oppressive equilibrium. *Three Years* represented the type of intervention that, according to the theory of economist Joseph Schumpeter, sparked development; sports-infused African American literature might lead to a more inclusive equilibrium, where white readers accepted Black citizens pushing past segregation to reach their educational goals and freely express themselves. This particular innovation was more notable in its attempt than for the results achieved, judging by the lack of critical reception following its release. However, the Butlers succeeded in entering college, where a local newspaper amply referenced the book, and their literary efforts did presage the subsequent autobiographical works of other Black athletes.

The Climax

A month before the book came out, Butler, who was playing and starring in his first season of high school basketball,[43] traveled to Chicago to compete at the First Regiment Armory scratch meet. A newspaper photograph showed him finishing a preliminary heat at night on the brilliantly lit drill floor of the massive, turreted structure designed by Daniel Burnham and John Root. The next day, Butler won first place in three events, the 40-yard dash, 300-yard dash, and, in a highly touted race in which Joe Loomis finished second, the 40-yard high hurdles. These victories earned him individual honors and his one-man team a fourth-place finish just behind the University of Chicago.[44]

Butler returned to the Chicago area a month later with three teammates and coaches to compete at Northwestern in their sixth annual indoor interscholastic meet. Competing against the best athletes from thirty-seven schools, Butler claimed first place in the 60-yard dash, 60-yard high hurdles, broad jump, and, a new event for Butler, the twelve-pound shot put. He tied the world record in the 60-yard dash and set an interscholastic record in the broad jump before the two thousand spectators gathered in Patton Gym. His twenty total points single-handedly gave his team the victory, edging out Chicago's second-place Lewis Institute.[45] In emphasizing the dominance of his performance, the *Chicago Tribune* playfully suggested, "Rock Island may be tempted to honor him by changing the name of the town."[46] Evanston's African American community tendered him a "demonstration second to the one given Jack Johnson when he put Jeffries away."[47] Sol predicted that a fine performance like this would be "the climax of his high school career."[48]

If not the climax, his performance certainly elevated interest in a high school athlete who many considered the best in the country. The business-savvy Butler brothers released *Three Years of High School Athletics* just two days after the meet, thus making explicit that Sol's mobility drove their entrepreneurism. On the same day as the book release, athletic director Lewis Omer announced that Sol would enroll at Northwestern in the fall. Within the week there was talk of Sol trying out for the Olympics in track and field.[49] He also "received liberal offers from the Chicago and Illinois athletic clubs to represent them at the world's fair meet in San Francisco this spring."[50]

Unparalleled success opened the door to new opportunities, but it also raised expectations beyond reach. A crowd of Tri-City residents traveled to Galesburg, Illinois, many on a special train car, to see the next conference meet at Knox College. Despite winning first place in the 50- and 100-yard dashes, 220-yard hurdles, and broad jump and second in the shot put, "Butler proved something of a disappointment to many who expected the dusky gentleman from Kansas to break records in every event in which he entered."[51] Explaining why Butler did not place in the 220-yard dash, a Davenport reporter wrote, "Considerable credit . . . must be given to Butler for racing as he had come directly from the 100 yard dash and broad jump, both of which he won."[52]

At one of the last athletic competitions of his high school career, an interscholastic meet in Iowa City, Butler nearly replicated his earlier feat of single-handedly winning a meet for his team. The team ended up tied for second place, just behind Davenport. After qualifying in the morning for five events, Sol placed first that afternoon in the 100- and 220-yard dashes, 220-yard hurdles, and broad jump, setting a meet record by over a foot in this final event. As the *Hutchinson News* reported, "The interest of the crowd throughout was centered on Butler, who in each of his events gave an exhibition of racing never seen before by the track fans at the meet."[53] According to the *Rock Island Argus*, his anchor leg in the half-mile "was an exhibition of the most wonderful running ever witnessed on the university field."[54] By the time the third runner passed the baton to Sol, the Independents were in seventh place and trailing by more than one hundred feet with only a little over 200 yards to run:

> Sol then took up the race and set the crowd wild by passing up the five men in front of him in short order. He then gave all that was in him in an endeavor to pass the Cedar Rapids man who was leading, and he cut down yard after yard of his opponent's lead. But the advantage was just a little too great and the race a little too short . . . and the Cedar Rapids man breasted the tape about a foot in the advance of the colored streak. Experienced track officials said after the meet that they never had seen and never expected to see again such an exhibition of running as Sol exhibited.[55]

Scrapbook photograph of winners of the 100-yard dash at the University of Chicago 1915 interscholastic track and field meet. (Amos Alonzo Stagg Papers, University of Chicago)

Days before Sol's and Ben's graduation, the Ladies' Progressive Art Club entertained the five Black members of Rock Island High School's 1915 graduating class at the Masonic Hall. Ben Jr. gave an address, and Ulysses Clark, Sol's lone Black track teammate, performed a cornet solo, which complemented the additional music "furnished by the colored band," all in celebration of the first Black students to graduate from Rock Island High School.[56] Their accomplishment warranted such fanfare, as at the time, the median number of years American children spent in school was just over eight, a number that was considerably lower for African Americans. While early twentieth-century educational statistics, especially regarding race, are incomplete, they suggest that a lower percentage of Black students graduated from high school in 1915 than earned a PhD a century later.[57] The brothers' parents would have been elated by this accomplishment, an essential step toward their adult children assuming the mantel of "race men"—in short, becoming African American leaders. The family's multiple migrations in pursuit of integrated schooling and numerous other untold sacrifices had yielded desired results.

The first Thursday after his high school commencement, Sol departed for Chicago by train to compete in his second Stagg meet, his final high school track and field competition.[58] Numerous sources predicted that he would once again win the individual title. After a poor start and second-place finish in the 100-yard dash, Sol finished first in the 220-yard dash and second in the broad jump. His thirteen total points tied him for first place with Evan Pearson, a nineteen-year-old high school sophomore from Washington State. Photographs of Butler taken at the end of the meet show him stern-faced next to the other athletes who placed, perhaps disappointed with his performance, perhaps anticipating the inevitable disappointments to come.[59]

No Help Whatever

In mid-July at the Central Amateur Athletic Union meet in Chicago, where he smashed the union's record in the broad jump by leaping over twenty-four feet, Butler qualified to compete in the track and field meet to be held that summer at the Panama-Pacific International Exposition in San Francisco.[60] Touted as a premier track and field event, the meet attracted top athletes from around the country to compete in the new world's fair facility. The question of how Butler would pay for the trip dogged him in the months leading up to the exposition. His new Illinois community did not support him to the degree anticipated, which in part reflected the view that he already had enough financial backing. Reports that all qualifying athletes would receive one hundred dollars from event organizers may have discouraged would-be sponsors' contributions, even though a reporter made clear that this amount would "barely cover the necessary expenses" for the trip.[61] Whether Chicago-area athletic clubs rescinded their "liberal offers" or Sol rejected these offers in order to represent Rock Island, media attention to this potential opportunity helped paint the image of Sol as someone with ample resources.[62] Fund-raising for the world's fair trip became increasingly desperate.

Rock Island High School alumni, led by cigar store employee Morris Cook, pushed for community support in the pages of the *Argus*:[63] "Other entrants, almost without exception, have the backing of strong athletic clubs or other organizations. Butler, so far, has had no help whatever."[64] Just three days before he was scheduled to depart by train for the coast, only thirty dollars had been raised out of the one-hundred-dollar goal. The newspaper tried to correct misinformation and false impressions while implying that potential donors did not want to support a Black man and highlighting the harm that a lack of support might pose to the city's image. "Many have taken the wrong view of the matter. The money is not being raised for the sprinter's personal use alone," a supporter clarified:

> Should Butler go to the coast without any backing outside of the $100 allowed by the A.A.U. the situation will naturally reflect on this city for failing to overlook some valuable advertising and showing the proper boosting spirit. In Chicago and other cities[,] athletes, regardless of their color or social standing, are given backing of clubs and private subscriptions without exception. Butler has an excellent chance to win the broad jump and should he be successful the name of Rock Island will be flashed all over the world.[65]

On the verge of a trip that held the promise of propelling him to new heights, Sol ran into the roadblock of flagging community support. His exceptional physical and social mobilities, symbolized by the production of a book, did not yet guarantee his ability to travel when and where necessary. Entrepreneurism that depended on the goodwill and patronage of white folks had its limits. True to the resilient nature of his family, he maintained faith and pressed on.

Butler managed to scrape together enough for the trip, though he did not raise enough funds to bring his brother, who had been living with him in Coach Roe's house; he therefore departed from Rock Island alone at 3:05 a.m. on Thursday, July 29, on a westbound train, joining other qualifying athletes who had departed from Chicago.[66] Whatever money the brothers had raised from sales of *Three Years* was meant to support their journey into college, not this trip to the West Coast. After stopping in Denver, Colorado, to raise money at the Shorter AME Church,[67] Sol presumably continued westward, avoiding Southern states, where he would have been forced to endure "the unspeakable torture of the Jim Crow car."[68] On Monday, Butler contacted his family to let them know that he had arrived in San Francisco.[69]

The Panama-Pacific Exposition celebrated the completion of the Panama Canal, a symbolic victory for American imperialism and a changing world order fostered by military and commercial might. According to the exposition president, Charles Moore, the goal of holding the event during a period of an escalating world war was "to help keep the torch of civilization burning and the feeling of international amity alive."[70] For many African Americans, the fair also offered a chance to celebrate Black achievement, which *Oakland Tribune* columnist and historian Delilah Beasley documented in her book, *The Negro Trail-Blazers of California*. Virginia Stephens, "a colored school girl" from Oakland, came up with the name "Jewel City" for the event; exposition officials chose the name out of thirteen thousand submissions for the 288-day event, which drew nearly nineteen million visitors. Beasley also documented exhibits that featured Black invention, erudition, and achievement in education, medicine, animal breeding, and art. A local woman won first prize for her Persian cat, and artist Henry Ossawa Tanner earned a gold medal for his painting *Christ at the Home of Lazarus*. Beasley noted that the five Black track athletes at the exposition, including Olympic sprinter Howard Drew, received "much publicity."[71]

Sol made it to San Francisco on time and prepared to make history, but in the end, nineteen-year-old African American runner Robert Morse made the biggest mark at the meet by winning first place in both the senior 220-yard dash and junior 100-yard dash and third place in the senior 100-yard dash. A Black sportswriter for the *New York Age* crowned him the "new speed king."[72] Butler placed first in the junior broad jump, which was open to athletes under twenty-one. He competed but did not place in any events the second day during the senior meet.[73] While "running at full speed[, he] pulled a tendon in his leg and was taken to the hospital for the remainder of the day," reported the *Hutchinson Gazette*.[74] This would not be the last time an injury sabotaged Butler's expectations.

During their eleven months in Rock Island, the Butler brothers had taken their first entrepreneurial strides, setting the stage for going to a college where Sol might succeed in sports at a higher level. The Illinois city had served its purpose, and the two men moved from the area for good, but not before they linked Sol's success and their educational ambition in attempting to shape public perception through their innovative autobiography, *Three Years of High School Athletics*. Despite the brevity of their stay, Tri-City residents remembered Sol. Three years after his departure at a commencement event, a chorus from Moline High School sang an original song titled "Solomon Butler."[75] On the lips of students from a rival sister-city school, the fame of the former Rock Island star rippled across the Upper Mississippi River.

Yet racial realities threatened to sour any tune. Moline High's yearbook featured a two-page illustrated account of its "most successful" blackface minstrel performance "in the annals of the high school" followed by a student drawing of a hooded rider mounted on a caparisoned steed emblazoned with the letters "KKK."[76] In a similar vein, by the time Butler competed for Hutchinson High School, its official yell, "The Allagaroo," contained the word "Nigger," which students chanted for decades to come; the popular chant with the anti-Black term somehow migrated with the Butlers to Rock Island.[77] Whatever degree of pride and respect white students in Illinois and Kansas exhibited toward Butler emerged from a school culture normalized like others in white supremacy.

• • •

The brothers kept their eyes on the Tri-Cities and would eventually return for football. Attempting to capitalize on his brother's increasing track and field fame in the run up to the 1920 Olympics, Ben Jr. visited Davenport in attempting to secure the most lucrative contract for Sol from a semiprofessional football team.[78] A few years later, Sol returned to join the Rock Island professional team in the budding NFL and played a vital role in the Independents' victory over the powerful Chicago Bears. From early on, the Butlers spotted the entrepreneurial synergy that Sol's multisport mobility made possible in the area, where he might excel on tracks, fields, gridirons, and in the sphere of public opinion.

Before tapping into the professional sport potential of this or any other community, however, Sol had to see how far he might go in the vaunted arena of amateur athletics. In the summer of 1915, the logical step in that direction was to complete his "liberal education." This required finding a college that welcomed nonwhite students and had an athletic program that would support Sol's expanding mobility. Northwestern University, where he had first achieved regional fame a year earlier at the spring indoor meet, seemed a likely destination. Yet it was here that a white administrator disinvited him from staying on campus with the hundreds of other athletes. Athletic powerhouses in the Midwest—including Northwestern; University of Chicago; and state institutions in Iowa, Minnesota, Wisconsin, and Illinois—allowed a few Black students to join sports teams while they segregated housing and excluded them from other extracurricular activities. Even if they permitted Butler to attend classes and play sports, on the whole these schools were less than welcoming.

Black collegians and would-be students who faced such exclusion occasionally found sympathetic white support. After learning that athletic director Louis Omer had placed Butler with an off-campus African American host in Evanston, allegedly because Omer believed that the young white men would mistreat him, the dean of Northwestern Law School, John Henry Wigmore, wrote a scathing editorial about what this incident revealed.[79t] He likened the school's intolerant white students to children "stunted" and "maimed" by the prejudices of their elders. The university compounded problems by "stipulat[ing] in advance that no colored student visitor [participating in the meet] should be placed in the university quarters with our white students." Butler did not address being segregated at Northwestern in his autobiography, although he may not have known until after the book's release that his treatment was codified into a policy. "It is my purpose to call attention to the facts," wrote Wigmore to a privileged and, to his mind, mistaught white audience:

> Here are groups of young men living in a land which bled its best blood for equal treatment of white and black,—studying the ideals of all the past ages—aiming to be self-respecting gentlemen—cultivating the bravest and the highest principles of humanity—acknowledging the religious faith which proclaims all mankind as brethren. And yet they start out in life with practicing the most pitible [*sic*] kind of snobbery—the snobbery of color.[80]

Sol and Ben Jr. came from a family that avoided the snobbery of color, uprooting to settle in communities free from the kind of behavior that Wigmore denounced. As *Three Years of High School Athletics* implied, they aimed to be self-respecting gentlemen who bravely cultivated the highest of human principles. Finding a college or university that would honor these principles by affording them the same opportunities as all other students was a tall order, even in the North. Due to systemic inequality, historically Black colleges and universities (HBCUs)—at least those within easy reach of their Kansas home, like Western University in Quindaro—could not provide them with opportunities to compete at the highest levels in track and field. Learning of a Christian college in the region with a burgeoning sports program and that proclaimed "all mankind as brothers," the Butlers soon headed to a new community farther up the Mississippi River.

PART II

Amateur

Fall 1915–Spring 1920

4

Welded into One Blood

Fall 1915–Summer 1917

From "Alma Mater" (1914–1917) by Vicente J. Bernal (lyrics) and Mark James (music)

The media gave conflicting reports on where Sol Butler would attend college. In early April, the *Chicago Defender* shared his intentions to enter Harvard University. Two months later, Hutchinson newspapers claimed that he and Ben were heading to Lake Forest College in Illinois.[1] A Davenport newspaper relayed that Sol received "good offers from several universities" but had yet to decide.[2] The NAACP's *Crisis* magazine reported that Butler would be headed to Northwestern. These plans fell through, perhaps due to reservations over his anticipated campus reception (apropos of the anti-Black sentiment that Dean Wigmore excoriated in his editorial) or a curricular gap in the star athlete's high school transcripts.[3] "Butler stated that he will enter some preparatory school this coming year," reported the Rock Island *Argus*, "and will eventually take a course at Harvard."[4] Three days after this announcement, he and his brother quietly entered Dubuque German College, a small Presbyterian school in northeastern Iowa, where the Butler brothers would be the first and only Black students.

When the Butler brothers arrived in Dubuque in early September 1915, they had the chance to show their parents the young and growing campus clad in red brick on the western edge of the Mississippi River town. The tour might have included Severance Hall, the three-year-old four-story dormitory, along with the classrooms, library, dining hall, and offices of the main building, the massive multipurpose structure built in 1906 when the college moved away from the river and up the hill. On the opposite end of campus, the newly installed Kane Heights Field offered a panoramic view south over the farm fields and rolling hills of the ancient Driftless Area, a contiguous region in Iowa, Illinois, Wisconsin, and Minnesota untouched by glaciers. Lining a pedestrian mall behind the main building sat the chapel, the heating plant, and the months-old McCormick Gymnasium, which school officials dubbed "the finest building of its kind in the Middle West."[5]

Less than a year had passed since the Hawkeye Conference welcomed Dubuque German College into its ranks, and the gym provided a space for virtually all athletics, including basketball, baseball, track, boxing, wrestling, swimming, and gymnastics.[6] This prized facility was made possible by a gift from Nettie McCormick, widow of a Chicago businessman who made a fortune after patenting a reaper invented by his father and Jo Anderson, the brilliant Black man his father enslaved.[7] "With the erection and completion of the gymnasium," wrote longtime university librarian and archivist Joseph Mihelic, "athletics began to receive more and more attention in the educational program of the school."[8] Not long after the Butlers arrived, the administration reportedly spent thirty thousand dollars to create what may have been the fastest outdoor track in the state.[9] "What a splendid athletic field and running track we now have!" wrote an editor of the *Dubuque Evangelist*. "It gives the young men splendid opportunities for developing the physical man."[10]

At the same time, Dubuque German College—including the academy (equivalent to a high school), college, and seminary, with a total of 248 students (78 in the college)—strove to stay true to its origins and sacred mission.[11] The school was founded in the mid-nineteenth century to offer theological training for German-speaking pastors. Amid the dramatic influx of immigrants starting in the late nineteenth century, in 1901 the General Assembly of the Presbyterian Church requested that the school train other non–English speaking ministers and committed to provide "opportunity to all students with high potential regardless of race."[12] The diversity of the school attested to its commitment to serve all students.

During their college years, Sol and Ben may have spent more time dining, attending classes and chapel, and engaging in all other aspects of student life with people born abroad or raised in German- or Spanish-speaking communities in the United States than with native-born students and faculty whose first language was English. Immigrant students primarily came from Eastern Europe, Latin America, and East Asia. A few Pima Indians and at least one unnamed African American student enrolled in the academy. Most of the school's many Latino students—from the American Southwest, Mexico, Puerto Rico, Colombia, Cuba, Brazil, and Peru—participated in a literary organization named after Miguel de Cervantes, in which about half of the meetings were conducted in Spanish. There were enough students from Hungary, Slovenia, and Bohemia to establish individual and combined clubs that celebrated those countries' history and literature. A large contingent of students and most of the staff spoke German. The monthly student publication had recently switched its name from *Der Seminarian* to the *Dubuque Student*, and nearly half of its articles still appeared in German. Female students began enrolling in the college by 1912.[13]

"The genius of the school is the intermingling of thirty-four types of foreigners who are being educated in the American life and spirit," Dubuque German College president Cornelius Steffens wrote in a 1917 editorial, "The Genius of Dubuque."[14] Among the thirty-four "nationalities" he identified were Bohemian, Cuban, Filipino, Hungarian, Korean, Mexican, Persian, Puerto Rican, Russian Jew, Syrian, and "Negro." The president of Dubuque's board of directors, William Hiram Foulkes, called the school "a great fountain source of patriotic, Christian citizenship where the many bloods of the races of earth are being welded into one blood."[15] A publicity catalog boasted of "a large number of men, of varied nationality, of divers [*sic*] racial temperament and peculiarities, coming from various environments and differing from each other to a greater degree than the average student body of an American college, yet as unified and harmonious a student body as may be found anywhere."[16] President Steffens proudly highlighted that his school was seventh in the nation for the number of foreign-born students after the much larger Columbia, Pennsylvania, Harvard, Illinois, Cornell, and Michigan universities (and Dubuque allegedly rose to second place within a few years).[17]

In the spring semester of the Butlers' first year at Dubuque, Walter Rauschenbusch, the famed theologian, Baptist pastor, and a leader of the Social Gospel movement, delivered his speech "The Social Principles of Jesus" during compulsory Saturday morning chapel. He argued for "the existence of a spiritual solidarity of the human race" and proclaimed, "We are all united together."[18] In a history of the freshman class written for the yearbook, Ben Butler echoed this language. The freshman class, he wrote, "can boast of an unusual composition, in respect to races and nationalities. There exists among them a feeling of brotherly love and respect for each other that cannot be elsewhere found."[19]

When Sol and Ben Butler arrived on campus in the fall of 1915, for the first time in their lives they were surrounded by many non-Black students who had *not* grown up steeped in American white supremacy, but the school's outward embrace of its diversity did not mean that the campus was immune to the racism that pervaded American life. In a 1917 report by the Freedman Committee of the Presbytery of Dubuque, which was organized to oversee the denomination's efforts to support African Americans, the group referred to Black people as a "backward and fallen race," plagued by the "shallow soil" of their minds.[20] Since the Freedman Committee maintained close ties with the school, which benefited from the committee's financial support, and included many administrators and faculty, similar views likely found expression on campus.[21] On Saturday, September 20, less than three weeks after Dubuque's two Black students first arrived on campus, Walter Hutcherson, who had appeared a few months earlier in Rock Island with the alleged Tuskegee Choir, "gave a brief but intensely interesting discussion on the struggles of the colored man to obtain an education" in chapel at morning devotional hour. The *Dubuque Student* reported that Hutcherson, "who has obtained an education thru his pluck and perseverance, is now making it his business to represent to the people of this section of the country, the better side of the colored man."[22]

In the spring of 1916, at the end of the Butlers' first year, the college's valedictorian address, delivered by Texan Francis Hegar, was titled "Spirit of the South." Hegar's speech echoed the widespread sympathy toward white Southerners found in most contemporary histories of the postbellum era. Reconstruction, Hegar argued, was "a dark blot" with days "even darker than those of the Civil War," a "curse" that the government "forced upon the southern man, who was sufficiently humiliated."[23] He tapped into popular racist sentiment most forcefully stoked by the increasingly popular film *The Birth of a Nation* (1915). At times Hegar's speech, which the *Dubuque Student* printed in full, read like a title card from D. W. Griffith's infamously racist silent film: "The Negro, who before the war was no problem at all, was there to be civilized and to be made accustomed to his changed surroundings."[24]

While the singularly influential film celebrated lynching, Hegar did not condone violence and even expressed at least nominal concern for the well-being of Black Southerners, acknowledging that "sometimes the Negro does receive unfair treatment." The most conciliatory passage came toward the end of his speech: "The colored race has made tremendous progress, both socially and industrially. From the low status at the close of the Civil War, the Negro has risen to such a degree of culture, that he ranks not far below his white fellow-citizen . . . [The Negro] knows that unless he strives for better things and tries to develop himself in industrial, social and intellectual life, he will always have the prejudice of his white neighbor against him." Hegar returned the next year to teach at the college.

Dubuque had the distinction of being home to Iowa's first African American community, yet it had nearly as old a record for anti-Black violence.[25] In 1840 a mob lynched an African American man, Nathaniel Morgan, who with his spouse, Charlotte, were among the earliest settlers and community pillars in the burgeoning town.[26] Hostile attitudes toward Black people remained through and after the Civil War as European Americans rallied around whiteness, a unifying concept that allayed ethnic and religious tensions between Catholics and Protestants. In the words of historian David Peavler (now Trowbridge), white Dubuquers mounted "Jim Crow's final stand in Iowa" by successfully opposing integrated schools until Black residents' monthlong school boycott and an Iowa Supreme Court ruling ended segregated schools in 1877, but the African American community in Dubuque never grew beyond modest numbers.[27] By the time the Butlers entered college, only around seventy other Black people lived in the city.[28]

On June 1, 1916, Dubuque German College held its first annual banquet for varsity athletes, including the Butler brothers, downtown at the historic and newly rebuilt Hotel Julien. The event was meant to impress—organizers decorated tables in blue and white and provided more than forty guests with menu cards bearing a "huge letter 'D'."[29] In the evening's congratulatory and impromptu speeches, no one mentioned the most historically notable aspect of the banquet: the hotel's desegregated dining. A decade earlier, another Dubuque hotel had refused to allow an African American high school student from Savanna, Illinois, to join his football teammates for dinner.[30] In 1907 the Dixie Jubilee Singers, a seven-member, all-Black choral group, were refused lodging before and after a concert at Dubuque's St. Joseph's College. They waited in the station until 3:00 a.m. for a departing train to Chicago. "This is the first time we have ever been unable to secure hotel accommodations in a northern town," said the group's manager. "We have experienced difficulty in the south, but never in the north . . . It was no surprise to us . . . for we had learned from other colored people who have visited Dubuque that there is no race equality here."[31]

Sol did not find racial equality in Dubuque, but he did enjoy a level of social mobility previously unavailable to him and other African Americans in the area. Welcomed into sports-hungry campus life with a diverse, multilingual student body, he continued to move in white worlds but now also claimed certain privileges of whiteness that made this movement freer and not predicated on public displays of modesty. While at times engaging in activities steeped in racial denigration, notably blackface minstrelsy, he asserted his right to belong in white spaces by choosing a school that created unity out of difference and then fully engaging in campus life.[32] In this way, he and his brother expanded on the strategic migration modeled by their parents. On the heels of his trip to San Francisco, Sol increasingly visited distant cities to compete in elite track and field events and connect with Black leaders and culture. A burgeoning cosmopolite, he witnessed new examples of how to be a race man as early waves of determinedly mobile African Americans, pioneers of the Great Migration, culturally transformed these urban environments. Dubuque German College served as a relatively safe, supportive community from which to venture out and test the limits of a sublimely talented Black man's physical, social, and mechanical transport. On the move in Chicago, Pittsburgh, and New York, Sol could study racial leadership that transcended the respectability politics of his Midwest upbringing.

The Most Striking Figure

The Butler brothers left no direct testimony about why they chose Dubuque German College. According to one former classmate's account, Ben Lindeman, a recent seminary graduate who wanted to boost his alma mater's athletic program, "found Sol in a shine parlor, shining shoes and talked to him about coming to Dubuque."[33] Another former classmate expressed his belief that the school's football coach "went to Hutchinson and arranged for Sol to accept a scholarship at Dubuque," which he did once the coach agreed to include his brother, Ben, in the scholarship.[34] Located at the intersection of Wisconsin, Illinois, and Iowa and between Des Moines and Chicago, where the biggest regional track meets were held, the city certainly had geographic advantages for a rising athletic star who wanted to remain close to family in Kansas.

In a coauthored book written after he left the school—under a cloud of suspicion and accusations that he had sacrificed the academic and financial integrity of the institution for athletics—President Steffens offered a provocative and suspect recollection about how Sol and Ben Butler wound up in Dubuque.[35] After expressing support for college football because of "its manifest benefits in the way of health, entertainment and college spirit," Steffens described his first encounter with Sol Butler in the third person:

> [Coach John S. Chalmers] entered the President's office to present a colored boy who had been recommended to the coach by an alumnus as promising football material. The Negro was one of the nation's best broad jumpers, who several years later was to win Olympic honors at Paris for America. But to the President's consternation the boy demanded that an agreement for a stipulated sum of money be signed, in recognition of his athletic ability, before he should enter the college classes.
>
> "Never have I signed such a contract!" the President exclaimed. "I will sign none for you."
>
> Yet the colored boy was not at once dismissed from the room. "You misunderstand the purpose of Dubuque," its President explained. "Its aim is to help students get an education, whether or not they have money to pay for it. Now, if you really want to go to college, if you have the character necessary for making an education worth while, but have no money, we can help you. I will assure you of an education, just as I have done with other boys, but not on account of athletics. You must come to us *because you want to go to college*, or not at all."

> "Well," the boy replied, not at all abashed, "I have an offer of one thousand dollars from a big university, and I certainly ought to have enough money to pay my expenses, if I'm going to stay here."
>
> "If that is the way you feel about it, I cannot talk with you any more. But," the President added impressively, "if you do come to Dubuque, and if on even the first day of football practice you happen to break your leg or are otherwise incapacitated by physical injury, you need have no fear. We will see that your injury does not make you leave college; we will continue to care for you, and pay your expenses as if you were still able to do the manual labor to which you are assigned. That's all."
>
> Coach and athlete left the office, but in a few minutes returned. "Well," the colored boy rather patronizingly announced, "I'll trust you!"
>
> He became quarterback on the football team, and a faithful student and worker.[36]

Steffens may be the only person on record to have recalled the famously modest athlete with an abundant sense of entitlement—a foil to the former president's picture of his own upstanding character and incorruptible morals. While Sol may have shown a side of himself that he typically kept hidden, it is also possible that Ben, rather than Sol, addressed Steffens on Sol's behalf; as Sol's promoter, Ben's assertions to the press often bordered on braggadocio, and as Sol's manager, he had reason to fight for the best arrangements. Perhaps Steffens conflated the two brothers in his book, whether due to a poor memory or wittingly for rhetorical effect, or perhaps he just embellished his actual encounter with Butler in order to refute claims that he had compromised the school's academic integrity for the sake of athletics.

Regardless of why he actually wound up at Dubuque German College, Sol Butler became the instant leader of the football team in his role as quarterback. "Perhaps the most striking figure of all [on the incoming football team] is that of Sol Butler," wrote sports editor Henry Reemtsma in the *Dubuque Student*, "who proudly carries upon his uniform some ninety-seven medals."[37] The Butlers headed to Dubuque with Sol's entire collection of medals, eighteen cups, and four shields.[38] In providing visible proof of a singular reputation, the ostentatious display announced his—and, by association, Ben's—right to be among the small minority who were overwhelmingly white, fortunate, and worthy enough to be in college.

The team photo for the year shows Ben Butler sitting cross-legged in the center of the front row, directly below the team captain, wearing a suit and tie, surrounded by players in uniform. The caption lists him as "Trainer."[39] Team practices began on September 9, just a few days after classes began. Each day Sol and the hopefuls for the varsity and reserve teams reported to Coach Chalmers for the 4:00–6:00 p.m. "steady grind."[40] The season opener

The Butler brothers with Sol's trophies, cups, plaques, and ribbons (ca. 1916). (University of Dubuque Archives)

against Iowa State Teachers College (now the University of Northern Iowa) was the team's first victory in what became a perfect season, which concluded with the Thanksgiving Day Hawkeye Conference championship game against Dubuque German College's hometown rivals—Dubuque College (formerly St. Joseph's and now Loras College).[41]

In the days leading up to the game, the *Telegraph Herald* printed two articles that introduced readers to Sol Butler. The first article ran alongside his photograph and summarized his biography and accomplishments as described in *Three Years of High School Athletics*. It ended with former coach Herbert Roe's testimony from the book: "He is the most reliable and conscientious of all the athletes I have worked with . . . and in addition to being a wonderful performer, has exceptional qualities that stand for character and manhood."[42] The second article simply reprinted the section from *Three Years* titled "METHOD OF TRAINING," in which Butler described the "set rules" to proper athletic training: "right living, a proper mental attitude, proper food and sufficient rest, all combined with hard work."[43] Readers also learned about Butler's love of ice cream and his regular nine-hour window of sleep. These articles generated anticipation and excitement for the game, but they also humanized the lone Black player on both teams for readers who might have been inclined to let racial tensions, or even violence, mar a day that was set to drive plenty of revenue for not only the schools but also downtown businesses.[44] The previous year, another Black Iowa player, future football great Duke Slater, had narrowly avoided disaster in Illinois when an angry crowd targeted him after a game.[45] Concern for Butler's safety prompted efforts at Dubuque German College and the newspaper to preempt a similar encounter in a city known for its racial intolerance.

On Thanksgiving Day, the audience of over six thousand, most of whom paid the one-dollar admission fee, included many out-of-town visitors—among them, hundreds of alumni and a group from Rock Island. According to one report, many in attendance had never before witnessed a football game. The sport had been played in the Midwest for decades but for less than a decade locally at the collegiate level. Students from the two colleges sat on opposite sides of the city field on bleachers, some of which, along with a fence surrounding the field, had been built just before the game. A packed grandstand occupied one end of the field. With a capacity crowd, many stood along the sidelines just outside the new fence. Pep bands led students in chants and cheers.[46]

The game remained close to the end. The Germans had an early opportunity to score after Butler intercepted a pass; he ran the ball from Dubuque College's 40- to their 12-yard line, but his team could not put the ball in the end zone. A Rock Island reporter noted that in the first quarter Butler showed "great generalship in mixing his plays and assisting in advancing the ball."[47] Early in the fourth quarter Butler led his team down the field, and a teammate ran the remaining 15 yards for a touchdown and the final points of the game, which ended 13–7 in favor of Dubuque German College. As quarterback, Butler kept his team to a ground game. Defensively, the team did well in limiting the opponent's running game but even better in disrupting the pass. The rival quarterback, Sol's former high school teammate, completed only one pass, while throwing two interceptions, including one to Sol, who intercepted a third pass from a would-be punter.[48] This was ironic given the reputation of Dubuque College's coaches, who transformed this aspect of the college game as football stars at Notre Dame. The head coach, Charlie "Gus" Dorais, who had led his Notre Dame team as quarterback, invited his favorite receiving target and future football coaching legend, Knute Rockne, to serve as assistant coach leading up to and during the championship game in Dubuque. Rockne's trip to Dubuque represented a broader pattern by star athletes, especially those from Notre Dame, who traveled by train around the Midwest to earn money as itinerant consulting coaches. Two years earlier, Dorais and Rockne had attracted national attention when they used the forward pass to defeat a favored Army team at West Point.[49]

Sol flanked by one and possibly two future University of Dubuque presidents on October 24, 1915, the morning after a football victory. (*The Key* [1917], p. 96, University of Dubuque Archives)

The media depicted the game between Dubuque German College and Dubuque College as hard fought and cleanly played. Using the crowd's behavior as evidence of the town's reigning civility and intelligence, a reporter wrote, "Each of the teams had loyal and strong lunged supporters who, with few exceptions, rooted fairly and cleanly and after the game was over there were no undue exultations on the part of the boosters for the winners or complaints from the adherents of the losers."[50] The victorious fans apparently muted their jubilation by the river (while the losing team's rooters departed early[51]) but erupted in glee when they returned up the hill to campus. A local business donated fireworks, and students and others "danced around the roaring blaze" of a bonfire, sang songs like "A Hot Time in the Old Town Tonight," and yelled college cheers.[52] "The football stars were lionized" and "roundly cheered," and "vaudeville stunts were pulled off that helped make the occasion a memorable one." Boosters and students organized additional celebrations to honor the team, whose members were "royally entertained" with a four-course dinner sponsored by local businessmen and their wives.[53] Again there were college songs and yells, and a hostess read the poem she wrote in honor of her guests. Back on campus, the team captain and Henry Reemtsma "gave a spread and smoker to the members of the squad."[54]

Winning the Hawkeye Conference championship served to extinguish any lingering doubts skeptics may have had about the school's lone Black player leading the team as quarterback. Along with profits from gambling, the game sparked monies for the competing schools.[55] Sol Butler "was chosen by all critics as quarter on the All-Conference Team and rated by all news-paper critics as the best quarterback in the State."[56]

The Genius of Dubuque

Surviving photographs suggest that Butler was also embraced by his teammates. One especially compelling image shows the team dressed in suits and hats, lined up on a pier next to a passenger boat. The accompanying handwritten caption simply reads "Homeward Bound," indicating that the team is in a neighboring river town, about to climb aboard the boat that will take them home to Dubuque.[57] The bluffs of North McGregor (now Marquette), Iowa, appear across the Mississippi River in the background. The season's only away game along the Mississippi River was against Campion College in Prairie du Chien, Wisconsin. The players' relaxed postures attest to the team's easy victory there. No player wears a more confident smile than Butler, who played a key role in the win. One teammate, future Dubuque German College president Karl Wettstone, stands behind Butler's right shoulder with his hand on Butler's left shoulder; another teammate (perhaps future president Paul Buchholz) holds Butler's left arm. In another yearbook photo, team captain Cornelius Hook and Butler are lying on the grass in hat, sweater, and slacks. Hook looks back at Butler, smiling. The handwritten caption reads "lazy boobs."[58] At a time when depictions of African Americans tended to range narrowly between buffoonery, vice, and violence, and virtually never as the embodiment of a nonhierarchical interracial amity, these images testify to a special team chemistry and represent singular illustrations of collegiate camaraderie between Black and white men.

Dubuque German College "fell on and ahead of the curve of African American inclusion and equality in campus life," contends historian Richard Breaux.[59] The Butlers were integrated into the social fabric of the school more so than most other Black men at predominantly white institutions. They lived in Severance Hall with a majority of the Dubuque students. Joseph Duke, who entered the following year, recalled spending time with Sol socializing in each other's rooms.[60] Such casual interracial interaction in living spaces was unknown to students in coming years at the University of Iowa, which maintained segregated housing no later than 1924 until after World War II. Like other African Americans at the state school, Duke Slater lived off campus in private homes. At Dubuque, the Butlers enjoyed the privileges granted to the small minority fortunate enough to attend college and live in a dorm.

Freeing students up for more work or play, a washerwoman took care of their laundry.[61] By the Butlers' second semester, on-campus housing swelled to capacity, leading administrators to rent an entire floor of the downtown YMCA building in order to offer "suitable rooms" to new students, but the school's two Black students remained comfortably on campus.[62] More than two decades before Viola Gibson led the desegregation of a public pool in neighboring Cedar Rapids, the Butlers swam with their white classmates in the pool at the McCormick Gym.[63]

Extracurricular activities provided another avenue for the Butlers to be integrated into campus life. Organized in 1872, the Philophronia Society was the oldest student group at the school. Twenty-seven members appeared in the 1915–1916 group photo; Ben, who served as secretary, appeared between two of the organization's seven women.[64] In October the Philophronia organized a "wienie and marshmallow roast" for all active and prospective members. True to the spirit of the literary organization, a football teammate romantically recounted the event:

> At 6:30 o'clock, when the sun had glided behind the blue hills in the west, we stole down the rocky cliffs to a place west of Dubuque, called "Sunny Brook." Between two young mountains on nature's carpet we pitched our camp. Not a few volunteers busied themselves kindling a fire. The evening was spent in the playing of games, singing, story-telling and feasting. A parting song—and at a late hour the sparkling dew-drops were shaken from the grass by weary feet as they were homeward bound.[65]

In early February the group "made merry" and enjoyed "light refreshments" in the Severance Hall parlor in honor of the Thanksgiving Day football victory.[66] After giving a "short, humorous program," students played games until 11:00 p.m. These activities attested to members' belief in "recreation, which strengthens the chords of friendship."[67] Eating, singing, storytelling, playing games, and, in general, making merry with a bunch of white students represented an extremely rare experience for two Black men. Yet a playful spirit animated their lives in various contexts, judging by the range of surviving formal and impromptu photographs. Playfulness on campus and beyond served as a tool to confound classmates' racism and forge bonds of friendship across differences.[68] The Butlers continued to claim privileges of whiteness, enjoying interracial social mobility that their choice in school, sport success, and conduct made possible.

Although the degree to which Sol Butler was integrated into life on Dubuque's largely white campus was unique, his role on the football squad was not. Black athletes across the country were both the only Black and the best players on their football teams, including Butler's future friends Frederich Douglass "Fritz" Pollard at Brown, Paul Robeson at Rutgers, and "Duke"

Slater at the University of Iowa. Robeson, admitted to Rutgers on the strength of his academics, had to earn a spot on a football team that fiercely resisted his presence. His teammates assaulted him in practice, breaking his nose, dislocating his shoulder, and stomping on his hand with cleats, thus ripping off his fingernails. Infuriated by the ongoing abuse, Robeson grabbed one of the perpetrators and hoisted him over his head until the coach intervened, announcing that Robeson had made the team. Attesting to the sometimes fickle nature of racism, his teammates soon embraced him as their own, cheering him on with the affectionate nickname "Robey."[69]

Butler experienced no documented physical abuse from his own teammates, but given the violent nature of the game, coupled with the era's cavalier and even approving attitude toward expressions of white supremacy, it is all but certain that Butler was at least the occasional target of racially motivated abuse from opponents. Even though the extant record remains silent about such incidents, he likely suffered more than his fair share of late hits, clotheslines, choke holds, elbows and fists to the face, cleats to his feet and hands, or similar violence. Frequent references to Butler and his team's play as "clean" and free of fighting suggest that he never retaliated.

Any abuse on the gridiron echoed incessant racial violence nationwide, including in the Butlers' hometown. Just before Sol's first college football game, an unarmed Black man was shot and killed on the grounds of the Kansas State Fair in Hutchinson. While newspaper coverage presented the twenty-year-old Black man as a foul-mouthed aggressor and the shooting as self-defense, evidence existed to the contrary. Responding to pressure from the local African American community, the state indicted the shooter for first-degree murder.[70] Shortly after this incident, the media began announcing the plans of many Black Hutchinson families, including those of prominent community leaders, to relocate to new, all-Black settlements in the western part of the state.[71]

Rather than leaving Hutchinson for a fresh start, the Butler family took steps to strengthen the existing African American community. When Sol and Ben visited for their first winter break, the whole family participated in a three-day oratorical and musical event sponsored by the Interstate Literary Association, for which Mary performed a vocal solo, Ben Jr. delivered an oration titled "The Negro in America," and Sol recited a poem by Frank Desprez, "Lasca."[72]

Ever-Changing Spectacle

Butler joined the varsity basketball team at Dubuque German College after the football season ended,[73] but his track career always came first. In February Sol traveled to Chicago for the Amateur Athletic Union Handicap and Scratch meet at the First Regiment Armory, where he performed well for the first time in a major competition since entering college. He finished second in the 40-yard dash in 4.75 seconds, second in the 40-yard low hurdles, and first in the 40-yard high hurdles. His excellent results earned him an individual honor trophy and fifth place for his school.[74] Butler's next indoor meet, the National Amateur Union Championship, brought Butler to New York City for the first time. En route he stopped in Chicago, where he lunched as a guest of the *Chicago Defender* and purchased new running shoes before continuing on by train to midtown Manhattan's Pennsylvania Station.[75]

In New York, Sol encountered a city more vertically oriented (the recently completed Woolworth Building was the tallest building in the world) and even more densely populated than Chicago; Manhattan alone had roughly the same population as the Midwestern metropolis but living on a strip of land less than an eighth of the size of Chicago. Whether he traveled to the Twenty-Second Regiment Armory in upper Manhattan by streetcar, bus, taxicab, horse and wagon, or the growing subway system, Sol would have seen signs of the city's rapidly increasing African American presence, especially in Harlem. There, Marcus Garvey, who had just arrived from Jamaica, was establishing his Black nationalist organization, the Universal Negro Improvement Association, in the United States. Several more years would pass before Harlem became widely identified as the epicenter of the "New Negro Movement," which dismissed the respectability politics of Booker T. Washington in favor of a social and political consciousness that rejected racial inferiority, asserted Black pride, and argued for equal rights, which sprang from the unprecedented artistic and cultural flourishing known as the Harlem Renaissance. As for the meet, Butler's ankles were "bothering him consederably [*sic*]," so he had to withdraw from the 70-yard hurdles after finishing second in the 60-yard dash and failing to place in the 300-yard run.[76]

Traveling across the country to New York was costly and time-consuming, but it served a bigger purpose than just giving Butler the chance to compete in this one meet; it connected him with other aspiring and seasoned Black leaders, who reminded Sol that athletics served as a tool for racial uplift. Victories in the sports realm vividly refuted notions of Black inferiority that buttressed segregation and racial violence. His interactions with Chicagoans and New Yorkers, perhaps including W.E.B. Du Bois at NAACP headquarters, helped him understand the links between his multifaceted mobility and civil rights.

Butler's sports schedule only became busier as the spring semester wore on. By April he was practicing daily with the varsity baseball team, but his track schedule was too busy for him to play enough games to letter.[77] Over one baseball weekend at the end of April, the Butlers and four other track teammates traveled to Pennsylvania to compete in the Penn Relay Carnival. (Ben served as his brother's trainer, but in Iowa he had started competing in conference meets.) Held at Franklin Field on the University of Pennsylvania campus, this twenty-one-year-old annual event was the largest in US track and field and brought together approximately twenty-five hundred high school and college competitors from across the country. There, Sol took fourth in both the broad jump and 100-yard dash,[78] but the Penn Relays also offered Butler the opportunity to meet with other African American athletes. At least two dozen African American collegians, including those from historically black colleges like Hampton Normal and Agricultural Institute, and many more high schoolers attended the event. Among these competitors was Paul Robeson of Rutgers College and Sol's friend Binga Dismond of the University of Chicago,[79] who also would compete again in this integrated meet that decades later was dubbed "the black Woodstock of West Philly."[80]

In addition to national meets in Chicago, New York, and Philadelphia, Sol's efforts on behalf of the Dubuque track team immediately transformed the fledgling program into the powerhouse of the conference. On May 13 Dubuque German College beat the team from Iowa State Teachers College in Cedar Falls; Butler earned five first-place and one second-place finish.[81] Two weeks later the team won the conference, and Butler was, as the *Rock Island Argus* described it, "the individual star."[82] He earned twenty-six points by placing first in the broad jump (setting a conference record), 100-yard dash, low hurdles, and high hurdles and finishing second in the high jump and shot put. The *Telegraph Herald* noted with admiration that "he went from one event to another, but appeared to be as fresh at the finish of his hard afternoon's work as he was at the start."[83]

As soon as Butler brought home the conference track and field title, he began preparing for the ninth annual Tri-State Track and Field meet at Forbes Field in Pittsburgh. Sponsored by the *Pittsburg Press*, the event received over a week of daily, increasingly hyperbolic coverage that billed it as the most significant athletic event of its kind after the Olympics. Sol Butler was one of the only competing athletes, whom the *Press* likened to Roman gladiators, mentioned by name in the days leading up to the meet. He and the meet's only other Black college athletes competed for the Scholastic Athletic Association, a team organized and coached by Hunter Johnson, the African American athletic director of the Delaney Rifles, an independent Black military organization, and trainer for the University of Pittsburgh track and field team. Johnson's team included sprinters Dismond, Fritz Pollard, Howard Drew, Irvin T. Howe, brothers Graham and Jim Burwell, Roy Morse, distance runner R. Earl Johnson, and other standouts. It was a well-educated team that included former and two future Olympians; its members would go on to succeed in business, law, medicine, the arts, and as community leaders.[84] This represented the first time that Sol was on an all-Black team. He could not have asked for a more astute group of men with whom to strive for sports glory while sharpening his activism and community-minded race consciousness.

In future years, he would compete with and against several of these athletes in track and field and in football.

In an effort to fill the bleachers and grandstand, *Pittsburg Press* reporters touted the meet's various appeals, ranging from its democratic spirit (no entry fee and no preferential seating) to the allure of the athletes' scantily clad, muscle-bound bodies.[85] One article referred to "motion picture men" creating a film of the crowd and finish lines to show "on the screens of the leading theaters of the country."[86] The newspaper's promotional efforts were successful, and on the day of the meet, the field presented an "ever-changing spectacle that will never be forgotten by those so fortunate as to be present," according to one of the more florid accounts:

> The immense grandstand was packed to its capacity with happy men, women and children. A sea of surging, cheering, shouting humanity greeted the eye wherever it fell and fairly bewildered with the grand composite effect of its mighty and multitudinous demonstrations. Not a moment passed but the air was rent with sudden catapulting shouts of elation and rejoicing.[87]

The Scholastic Athletic Association (AA) and approximately three hundred other athletes paraded past the massive crowd to the "swinging strains" of the Danny Nirella Band and Orchestra's "pulse quickening march," but Sol had little time to revel in the charged atmosphere.[88] He entered the day's first track event, a trial for the 100-yard dash, with a 2-yard advantage over the few top runners who had no handicap and therefore were listed as "scratch." Shortening distances for most runners or tacking on additional length or height to most throws or jumps represented one way that officials kept some meets competitive and exciting. Sol won his trial heat and the semifinal and then won first "by about the handicap distance" in the final heat.[89] The final race for the 120-yard low hurdles became the most celebrated of the day because the winner, Butler's teammate Harry Martin from Howard University, broke a world record. Butler took third place, and there was "not . . . a yard separating the first and third men."[90] When the record was announced, "The spectators jumped to their feet and cheered and hurled their hats and programs in the air in sheer excitement." Within a span of three hours, Butler competed in a total of seven events, more than any other athlete, and earned at least nine of his team's thirty-five points, more points than any other individual. Thanks to his efforts, the Scholastic AA tied the Tioga AA club for first-place honors in the meet, and Butler earned himself solid gold, silver, and bronze medals.[91]

Decades later, Hunter Johnson recalled his team's victory as one of the highlights of his distinguished athletic career. In his telling, Butler had asked him at the last minute if he could compete in a throwing event: "Well Sol slung the discuss [*sic*] and won a point and for the first time in college history, a group of colored track stars had beaten a major college array of athletes in an open meet." This series of events allegedly got Johnson in trouble with his employer, the University of Pittsburgh, but it accomplished his goal: "He proved to Pitt and the world that colored athletes have the stuff which champions are made of . . . and all they need is an opportunity to prove it."[92]

Butler might have been headed straight to Berlin from Pittsburgh,[93] but the escalating war in Europe meant the 1916 Summer Olympics in Berlin were canceled, and in September 1916 Butler was back in Dubuque for the start of the football season. Coach Chalmers and assistant coach Elmore Niebruegge adjusted to a more open-field style of offense for their star to use his running skills, and the second-year quarterback was more comfortable in calling plays that suited his strengths. After a late-season blowout victory, the *Chicago Defender* reported that Sol "put his men through a series of spread formation plays. These plays bewildered the opponents and before they had time to recover the locals planted the pig skin back of the goal line twice."[94] Butler saved his most memorable run for the season's final game, a 39–0 victory over the previously undefeated Buena Vista (Iowa) College on November 18. In the second half, a Buena Vista player "punted almost to Dubuque's goalline [*sic*]. Sol picked up the ball and tucking it under his arm, circled around to the goalline and then with the aid of splendid interference started down the field . . . 100 yards for a touchdown."[95] With only one loss,[96] Dubuque German College tied neighboring Dubuque College for the Hawkeye Conference championship. Sports editor Reemtsma put together an All-Conference team and picked Butler as the obvious choice for quarterback and captain, in part due to his "speed, ability at dodging and stellar tackling" but also because "his running of the team in all the games showed his remarkable head-work."[97]

The basketball season started as soon as football ended. Butler's exceptional jumping ability at center became as important as his phenomenal speed, and Dubuque had its "most successful basketball season" ever with a record of nine wins and six losses.[98] The school's track season began one day after the basketball season ended with an indoor interclass track meet in McCormick Gym, which the sophomores won to earn a silver cup. Butler led the team to a decisive conference championship, but an alleged registration error prevented him from participating in the state meet.[99] The new season brought a tongue-in-cheek warning in the March issue of the *Dubuque Student*: "Special Notice To All Track Men! Don't let your studies interfere with your Education."[100] When registering for the fall semester at the recently accredited institution, Butler declared his history major and took courses on American politics and the Constitution.[101]

Sol achieved his greatest individual track glory of the season in two outdoor meets. At the Penn Relays in Philadelphia, where he first met J. Mayo ("Ink") Williams,[102] he won his preliminary heat in the 100-yard dash and ended up third in the final race behind Brooke Brewer of Maryland State and Eddie

Teschner of Harvard.[103] The next day, the *Evening Star* in Washington, DC, wrote that Sol had been "shut out from a victory in the final by getting a late start."[104] He had reason to sense that victory over elite Eastern opponents was within his reach, and his performance in the broad jump would have only buoyed his optimism. He took first place by leaping 23' 5¾", living up to the advance praise the local newspaper gave him for his "customary brilliant style."[105] In early June he traveled to the Western Collegiate College (Big Nine) Conference meet at the University of Chicago, where he competed against athletes from eighteen different institutions, although the wartime enlistment of young men reduced the number of participants to 172, less than half the total from the previous year. Butler earned second place in the 100-yard dash, only to later learn, by virtue of a photograph, that he had actually finished first. Although he had not made good on his publicized plans to become the "world's champion sprint man" by the end of the track season, he did do well enough to suggest that the goal might be possible. More notably, he demonstrated that he could beat anyone in the broad jump.[106]

Leading Fun-Makers

In the midst of Butler's hectic schedule during his sophomore winter, he paid a visit to the Dubuque Masons, who "gave a smoker at their hall to discuss methods of maintaining social unity." According to the *Chicago Defender*, Butler addressed the audience of white men and told them that "a clean life open[s] up greater avenues for the black man."[107] At the end of the semester, varsity athletes gathered for their second annual lettermen banquet. During the celebration, Butler, along with the other team captains, gave a speech.[108] In addition to participating in the kinds of activities that would have been expected of a young Black man steeped in respectability politics—athletics, glee club, the Philophronia Society, and orations extolling the virtues of clean living for Black men—Sol Butler also joined a campus minstrel troupe.

Two photographs of the group appear in the 1916–1917 yearbook amid a photo-collage section that documents the social experience of Dubuque students.[109] In one picture, six minstrels in hats and dark sport coats are seated shoulder-to-shoulder on a stage, with Sol third from the right. Across the bottom of the image, someone handwrote the word "Darkies." Mainstream white American cinema, theater, cartoons, sheet music, records, and, in the coming decades, radio depicted Black people within a limited range of debasing stereotypes, which found expression on Dubuque's campus during Halloween of 1916 when Sol and four white peers performed on stage as blackface minstrels. Although not unknown, integrated minstrel troupes were rare.[110]

It wasn't the first time Butler had performed in a minstrel show. In high school in Hutchinson, Sol and Black teammate Clarence Phillips, capital-

Yearbook photocollage image of Butler with white teammates in blackface in October 1916. (*The Key* [1918], n.p., University of Dubuque Archives)

izing on their local celebrity, raised money in their off-season by performing in minstrel shows with other young Black men. Tickets sold for 25, 35, and 50 cents.[111] Butler's earliest publicized show benefited a musical group, the "Colored band," and featured dance and music by a concert band, glee club, and Toole's Orchestra; Phillips and two other performers "won the house" by closing the show with "Mammy's Shuffling Dance."[112] Flouting social decorum, this performance certainly contrasted with the waltz competition held at the town's armory a few weeks later, which Butler won while partnered with the spouse of a local Black physician and band leader.[113]

Whether or not the Black cast applied any blackening agent to their hands and faces, they drew upon the conventions of blackface minstrelsy, which had dominated American stages for generations. An interlocutor served as master of ceremonies and was flanked by end men, including Butler and Phillips, who performed in a series of vaudeville-style routines for audiences of both Black and white Kansans, likely arranged in segregated seats,[114] as many public spaces operated with de facto segregation policies. The group also appeared at the Home Theatre, "the most ornate and modern theatre between Kansas City and Denver," where theatergoers entered "through the arched doorway into a commodious lobby" and "theatre fans who sat in the cheaper plank seats in the top of the auditorium entered by a side door, never contacting the better paying customers."[115] The *Topeka Plaindealer*, a Black paper, reported, "As usual Clarence Phillips and Sol Butler were the leading fun-makers."[116] The *Hutchinson News* said, "From the opening . . . to the final curtain, the big crowd was convulsed in laughter or soothed by the harmony of the colored minstrel men."[117] The first half of the show was filled with musical numbers; Butler's solo appears to have been the recently published and rhythmically fresh "Waiting for the Robert E. Lee," about a cotton-carrying riverboat in the antebellum South. The second half of the show started with a monologue and dance before finishing with a comedy sketch involving an African prince in a club. Phillips played the role of a cook who was mistaken for the prince, while Butler portrayed a waiter named Brownskin. "[Bert] Williams and [George] Walker in their palmiest days never gave more satisfaction to an audience," wrote one journalist, referring to the era's most successful African American minstrels.[118]

While adhering to the racist tropes of blackface minstrelsy, Black performers also often worked to subvert those conventions, especially for Black audiences. Theater historian David Krasner maintains that "black performers entered into the blackface caricature and refashioned it."[119] The "big crowd of both white and colored people," who gave the Hutchinson minstrels "many ovations," undoubtedly made varied and even conflicting meanings of the shows.[120] Nostalgic references to "Mammy," the Confederacy, and picking cotton in Alabama might affirm the benignity of slavery for white audiences; for African American audiences, such references might playfully camouflage a critique of white people in, for example, their social pretensions and inability or unwillingness to see Black suffering or to roast the out-of-step behavior of an older generation of Black Americans. The *Topeka Plaindealer* noted that the local minstrels "played as 'old timers' at the game."[121] A likely target was septuagenarian Ben Sr., who reportedly attended and attracted attention at all of his son's high school football games and track meets. White blackface minstrelsy "was a fundamentally racist undertaking, neutering a race's identity by limiting it to demeaning stereotypes," write Yuval Taylor and Jake Austen in *Darkest America: Blackface Minstrelsy from Slavery to Hip-Hop*. But top Black minstrels "knew exactly what they were doing: they often had alternatives, and had good reasons for choosing to draw from the minstrel tradition."[122]

For Sol, minstrelsy could serve multiple functions. As a vehicle for social mobility, it could further ingratiate Butler to white audiences, who might have seen his performances as a signal that he was willing to comply with their racist expectations, that he was willing to stay in his "place." And yet minstrelsy also offered Butler a safe, socially accepted avenue to flout, through lowbrow humor, the respectability politics championed by his mother or to play at the kind of flamboyant celebrity that boxer Jack Johnson embodied. If on the fields of sport, where Butler's talents far outstripped those of nearly all of his white teammates and competitors, he needed always to put a modest face forward; the stage offered him the opportunity to be an unabashed star.

Among many other interpretations of blackface minstrelsy, scholars have identified how the cultural practice served immigrant and ethnic communities, like the Irish in the nineteenth century and Jews in the twentieth century, as a means of assimilating, asserting whiteness, and claiming the power, privilege, and access to upward mobility that whiteness conferred, at the expense of those who could not claim whiteness.[123] By foregrounding a hyper-distorted blackness on stage, minstrels pointed to a difference that was unassimilable within the logic of a pervasively white supremacist America. Through the ritual of "blacking up" and performing in ways that reified racial stereotypes, immigrant performers distanced and distinguished themselves from this difference. Given Dubuque's significant immigrant population and the college's explicit goal to educate foreign students in "the American life and spirit," it is reasonable to view the school's minstrels as participants in a nationwide process of creating white Americans and Sol Butler as availing himself of the opportunity to make a claim, however tenuous, to a piece of the privilege that whiteness conveyed.[124]

Enacting his tenuous privilege, Sol traveled with four classmates over the summer of 1917 to the Central YMCA College camp in Lake Geneva, Wisconsin, where they joined hundreds of American and dozens of foreign students and leaders from across the denominational spectrum. Their Dubuque contingent included one of Sol's biggest boosters, Henry Reemtsma, and football teammate and future college president Paul Buchholz.[125] Divided into small groups by tents with graduate leaders, they received training and opportunity for Bible study. The seventy-five-acre campus contained a small gymnasium and accommodated a wide range of outdoor activities. The nine-acre athletic field included an eight-lane running track, baseball diamond, eleven tennis courts, a six-hole golf course, and "all necessary appliances for field games and events."[126] Situated on a lake, the camp also boasted a fleet of row boats, several sailing yachts, a swimming pier with diving boards, and "safety appliances." Butler, who was raised a Methodist, would return again the next summer, this time accompanied by Dale Welch, another future president of Dubuque German College. Over a year into US participation in the world war, 40 percent of the campers focused on what organizers identified as "war work." A yearbook photo shows Welch and Butler crouched behind a school banner amid hundreds of campers.[127]

The YMCA camp provided international and nonwhite students, including a few Black students, inclusive opportunities that the larger Christian-sponsored organization and most predominantly white institutions of higher education did not.[128] Sol's inclusion did not portend a rise in Black participation in integrated camps or, over the next few decades, on his own college campus. The "genius of Dubuque" identified by President Steffens purportedly spoke to the institution's ability to thrive off of cultural diversity, but it might as well have referred to its most visible student, who navigated an always potential anti-Black environment to claim a space for people who shared his complexion. His challenge only increased in coming years as the nation's war effort intensified and his family experienced loss.

5

Unusual Amount of Stamina

Fall 1917–Spring 1919

From "On Patrol in No Man's Land" (1919) by James Reese Europe

On August 23, 1917, in Houston, just a few months after the United States entered the Great War, a white police officer shot a Black serviceman who intervened in the violent arrest of a Black woman. With frustrations already elevated over chronic Jim Crow abuse, this event led to more than 100 soldiers of the Third Battalion of the all-Black Twenty-Fourth Infantry Regiment to march in violent mutiny toward the city's police station. Four mutineers and 15 white people, including policemen and civilians, were killed in the melee; the presence of an Illinois National Guard unit prevented retaliation by white mobs. The army immediately removed the Third Battalion from Houston and a military tribunal convicted 110 soldiers for participating in the mutiny; 19 Black soldiers were hanged and 63 were sent to prison. The men, represented by a single officer, had no chance to appeal. The mainstream media roundly condemned the soldiers; a few of the battalion's outspoken Black supporters, who wrote editorials portraying them as manly and heroic justice fighters, were arrested on charges of violating the Espionage Act.[1]

Over the course of the war, nearly four hundred thousand African Americans served in the US military, comprising about 10 percent of all US forces, and two hundred thousand Black soldiers served in the American Expeditionary Forces overseas. According to historian Adriane Lentz-Smith, these soldiers "would join themselves to the American national project in all its light and shadows in return for earning full citizenship rights," but they would come up against the intractable reality of American white supremacy, which would allow Black people to claim certain rights only if they tolerated harsh and demeaning treatment under segregation.[2] Enemies on the European war front became increasingly indistinguishable from enemies on the US home front as African Americans' efforts to claim the privileges of whiteness met forceful resistance. An eroded faith in the country living up to its egalitarian ideals led some to mutiny, but Butler continued moving assertively in white Midwestern spaces and anticipating the rewards of recognition and respect for his athletic success. While deserved recognition and respect did not always come to him, he remained steadfast in his course, trusting that freedom sprang from the full exercise of his mobility. Along the way, he demonstrated considerable stamina by tolerating the racial slights and indignities aimed to immobilize him.

News from Houston dominated the Dubuque papers for several days, but by the time the Butler brothers and their peers arrived for college classes a couple of weeks later, local attention had shifted back to the war front overseas. During the first twelve months of the Great War, more than fifty Dubuque students volunteered or were drafted for service, a sizable number for a school with a total student body, including the academy and seminary, of around three hundred. Due to rampant anti-German sentiment, school officials dropped "German" from the institution's name more than a year before Iowa governor William Harding forbade the use of foreign languages in schools, churches, and other public places.[3] In a letter to the editor of the *Chicago Tribune*, Dubuque's President Steffens complained about the paper using the school's old name, insisting that "we are injured now every time the word 'German' is written or spoken as part of our name."[4]

The war also posed a financial burden on the school; the cost for provisions increased by 60 percent, and three substantial donors from New York withdrew their support "particularly because of prejudice against the foreigner."[5] Dubuque imposed a 33 percent tuition hike and sought creative cost-saving solutions. The administration turned eight acres of the athletic field—which contained one of the newest, finest tracks in the state—into a potato garden, for instance, while faculty wives darned sweaters, socks, and leggings for the school's athletes.[6] An editor of the *Dubuque Evangelist* wrote, "So dear to the American heart is this brotherhood of the race that we are cheerfully sacrificing blood and treasure to maintain it."[7] Professor Herman Styles Ficke later recalled that "by a policy of good will, of mutual respect, of reserve on the issue of racial superiority, life in the class room and on the campus produced no clashes even during the trying days of World War I."[8]

Fans Will Remember It

A few weeks into the fall semester, the glee club, with Sol singing second tenor, performed in Peters Commons for President Steffens and his wife. With the orchestra providing accompaniment from the balcony, the singers "made the beamed ceiling ring to the echo," an occasion that was one of the college's few large social events during the war.[9] Some student groups had donated their entire "social budget" to a YMCA fund in order to "alleviate suffering overseas."[10] This scaling back of social activities included a more modest athletic schedule than in previous years, but the enthusiasm for sports on campus was as strong as ever. The fall 1917 football season witnessed some of the most decisive victories in school history. The team held its first three opponents scoreless, easily defeating Platteville (Wisconsin) Normal by forty points, La Crosse (Wisconsin) Normal by forty-one points, and Ellsworth (Iowa) College by forty points. Butler assumed multiple roles on the team as quarterback, punt returner, and kicker and continued to dominate the field on both offense and defense; in La Crosse he kicked several extra points after quickly scoring touchdowns on a running play, a punt return, and a pass to teammate Johnny Armstrong, who had followed him to Dubuque from Hutchinson.[11]

Dubuque's fourth game, which ended in a 13–13 tie, proved to be the highlight of the season. A reporter for *The Key* wrote, "Ever since the beginning of the season everything pointed to November 3rd" when Cornell College from Mount Vernon, Iowa, arrived in Dubuque at full strength and with a reputation for being one of the strongest teams in the state.[12] The locals were missing four regular players due to injuries and unspecified conference rules. The field, a "solid mass of mud, prevented the stars of either team from showing at their best."[13] Despite these conditions, Butler got to a drier side of the field, where he could "use his legs," and "tore through the spread-out players, avoiding those who managed to get near him" for a 60-yard punt return. He kicked a goal for a 13–0 lead. Later in the game, his teammate Paul Krebs fielded a kickoff and handed the ball to Butler, who gained 55 yards. Overall, Dubuque reportedly amassed 200 yards to Cornell's 50 yards, but in the final six minutes, the Cornell quarterback made "two beautiful and brilliant passes in quick succession" for touchdowns. Several fumbles and a quickly darkening, unlit field prevented any further scoring.[14]

The tie against Cornell spurred greater celebration than any of the season's victories. One student organized a belated Halloween party in McCormick Gym, where Coach Chalmers and biology professor John Horsfall gave speeches, Butler's choir mates Dan Jansen and Paul Buchholz sang duets, and

Sol and Ben "did the Carolina cake walk," presumably to a ragtime piano piece. The performance of this already antiquated dance, which originated before emancipation and became a mass sensation in the decades that followed, was likely reminiscent of Sol's minstrel performances. The night concluded with games and "light refreshments."[15]

The next game, against Buena Vista, proved to be the most lopsided victory in school history. Buena Vista had lost all but two players from the previous year's squad due to graduation and the war, which led to its one "dismal season . . . in an otherwise golden era" of football.[16] Rather than a competition, the game was more of a "track meet," in which Dubuque scored 125 points and held their opponent scoreless. "Butler made a touchdown everytime he got his hands on the ball," *The Key* reported, "and incidentally gave the best exhibition of running that has ever been seen in and around Dubuque."[17] The yearbook reprinted a self-deprecating account of the game from a Buena Vista student periodical that noted when Dubuque "wanted a touchdown they gave it to the streak of blackening." In another account of the game, a Buena Vista player referred to Butler as a "nigger."[18] Perhaps Dubuque, with an unrelenting and unaccustomed lack of mercy, ran up the score because of the opposing team's blatant racism before or during the game, or perhaps the Dubuque coaches just wanted to deliver a big win for the final home game of the season.

Since an anticipated Thanksgiving Day game against Parsons (Iowa) College never materialized, the final game in late November against Upper Iowa University ended the season. Dozens of local rooters traveled to the college in Fayette "by Fords, Cadillacs and coal cars" to witness the conference championship game.[19] Butler scored five touchdowns in Dubuque's 43–13 victory, and his team finished the season with a total of 302 points versus 26 total points for their opponents and the conference title. "The question with those who have seen Butler in action is not how he ranks in the State," reflected an unidentified member of the college press club, "but among football players of all time. Able critics who have seen the best in the East and in the West have pronounced Sol one of the greatest players they have ever seen in football shoes."[20]

On the Tuesday after Thanksgiving, Butler received a call from Des Moines announcing that he had been selected to compete on the all-state team. Composed of the best football players in Iowa colleges as chosen by sportswriters, the all-state team was scheduled to compete on the coming Saturday against a team of army soldiers from Camp Dodge in the stadium at Drake University. Butler reportedly left immediately for Des Moines and was the first of the players to arrive. The team quartered on Drake's campus and attended social engagements arranged in their honor; on Friday the local chamber of commerce hosted a pep rally.[21]

The initial practice on the cold and snowy field began late Wednesday, and Sol "ran the team at quarter during the greater part of the afternoon."[22]

He "apparently more than made good" at the "pivot position," the *Telegraph-Herald* reported, and "will probably start the game as quarterback, and if he does it is safe to say that he will finish, unless knocked out."[23] Headlines for this article and one in the Davenport *Daily Times* stated with greater certainty that Butler would respectively "RUN" and "LEAD" the team.[24] The earliest *Des Moines Register* coverage of the game listed Butler as the only potential quarterback among the players "who no doubt will make up the all state squad."[25] In the end, though, Lester Watt from Grinnell College was selected to start the game at quarterback instead of Butler. "There was a divided opinion among the coaches and officials consulted," noted *Des Moines Register* sportswriter Sec Taylor, "and it was necessary to split hairs closely to decide which men were entitled to first choice."[26] Taylor drew special attention to the choice between Watt and Butler and, after identifying Watt's strengths, acknowledged that "Butler also is a great player and in the opinion of some of the coaches deserved first place ahead of Watt." The writer warned that "some of the men placed on the second team are likely to make a much better showing than those placed on the first team and if they do the fans will remember it." Intended as a fund-raiser for Camp Dodge athletics, the game ended up being a financial flop because only a few hundred fans braved subzero blizzard conditions to see the all-state team defeat the soldiers 7–0. According to Taylor's subsequent postgame account, Watt played well at quarterback. Butler saw only limited game time, subbing in at halfback.[27]

Dubuque German College football team photo, 1918. (*Clavis* [1920], p. 118, University of Dubuque Archives)

The following year's football season would be severely disrupted by war and the 1918 flu pandemic, and the Dubuque team would end up playing only three out of seven scheduled games.[28] Butler would serve as both quarterback and captain for his truncated senior season, which likely made him the first Black player to quarterback a white college team for four years.[29] He did so at a time when most colleges did not admit African American students, many teams refused to play against an opponent with a Black player, and popular culture and the mainstream media spewed a steady barrage of anti-Black messages that pointed to supposed mental and physical racial inferiority. His benching in Des Moines received media attention, but undocumented instances of racial exclusion were likely more common. Pete Peterson, who coached Butler's final two years of basketball at Dubuque, recalled that he "had to find alternative lodging and sometimes eating places for Sol when the team was on the road."[30] The football and track and field coaches presumably made similar arrangements for away games and conference competitions. Two decades would pass before another African American quarterback, Wilmeth Sidat-Singh, would gain widespread attention for leading a team at a predominantly white institution, Syracuse (New York) University, and not until the 1970s would there be a noteworthy number of Black college quarterbacks beyond the HBCUs.[31]

Sol's college success stood as a powerful refutation of the era's dominant racial narratives, but his benching in Des Moines, when accounts pointed to his being Iowa's best college quarterback, spoke to the limits of desegregation through mobility within a system of white supremacy. Incessantly testing the limits of harmonized bodily, mechanical, and social transport created opportunities and sometimes also occasioned his crashing against unbreachable racial barriers.

Not a Composite of All the Races

A few weeks into the spring semester, Dubuque's administration announced that the school would close early on May 1, 1918: "It is a step which seems fully justified by the great need of agricultural labor" during the war.[32] "In order not to lower the value of the semester's work," officials explained, "a program of speeding up has been adopted." Students attended classes six days each week and "all extra activities" were officially paused. Athletics and the glee club continued as usual, however, which led to an exceptionally busy schedule for Sol.[33] He had to miss the final game of the basketball season in Rock Island in order to attend the Big Ten indoor track meet in Urbana, Illinois, where he placed third in the 75-yard dash and first in the running broad jump, breaking the meet record by four inches.[34] The editor of the *Dubuque Evangelist* wrote that Butler "has brought honor to our school whenever he has gone to represent her."[35]

In early April, Sol joined the baseball team for its home opener against St. Ambrose College in Davenport, Iowa. The *Quad-City Times* considered Butler one of "the stars" on the Dubuque team, noting that he "is a dangerous man on the bases as he can steal second with one jump and make 100 yards in a fraction less than ten seconds if necessary."[36] Butler "was again an athletic hero, unloading two base hits and exhibiting plenty of speed on the paths," but a five-run bottom of the seventh inning gave St. Ambrose the 10–8 victory.[37] Butler devoted the rest of the month to practicing for the Drake Relays in Des Moines on April 20.[38] When the day arrived, a "driving snow from the north" covered the field and left inches-deep patches of water, yet nearly a thousand people attended the annual track event, eager to see 1912 Olympian and Drake University law student Howard Drew compete against some of the region's fastest sprinters, including Butler.[39] Despite efforts to clear the track with shovels and scrapers, snow continued to fall and obscured the lime lines marking the lanes. Butler finished the lane-less race in fourth. Drew stopped running after 75 yards.[40] After serving in the army, Drew graduated and went on to a successful career as an attorney and judge. His greatest athletic glory, however, lay in the past. Butler's two races may have suggested the same. In the half-mile relay, Butler entered the final 220-yard leg of the race with too much distance to close with front-running Grinnell College, and his team finished in second place.[41]

A few weeks after the Drake Relays, the Butler brothers went home for the summer.[42] Ben did not return to Dubuque College to complete his degree. Like Sol, Ben had been interwoven into campus life, and the yearbook gives the impression that his final year was characterized by fun and a degree of mischief. "Prof. Baker assisted by Benzine Ben get the students underway in physics lab," went one entry. In a photo above the caption "Anti-German Band," Ben and three other students stand in the snow and blow into musical instruments.[43] Decades later, a younger former classmate remembered Ben as "somewhat of a rascal."[44] It's not clear why Ben Butler finished his college education forty-one credit hours shy of a degree.[45] His father's failing health and rising tuition costs were possible factors, but it's also conceivable that he was forced out.[46]

One scenario that could have led to Ben's quiet expulsion might have been too loaded to acknowledge on record: interracial intimacy. More than twenty women were taking courses at Dubuque by 1918.[47] School publications and photographs document the Butler brothers in regular contact with white women through the Philophronia Society, the choir, and other social events, though Ben and Sol had reason to avoid dances or other events that would bring them into more intimate contact with white women. White mobs had lynched Black men around the country for far less sexually charged acts than a mutual embrace with a white woman on a dance floor. Their contemporary

Paul Robeson avoided racist backlash by staying off the dance floor at Rutgers University, choosing instead to serenade dancers from a balcony.[48] Speaking to the enduring anxieties of white men regarding Black men with white women (which in America dated back at least to the colonial era when anti-interracial marriage laws first appeared), Black jazz sideman William Oscar Smith took pains in the mid-1950s to convince an administrator at the University of Iowa that he did not have romantic ties with the white woman he brought to a departmental party; he rightly worried about being kicked out of his graduate program.[49] If there was even a hint that Ben had violated this stubborn taboo, the administration at Dubuque would likely have responded with a swift, resolute decision that he would not be invited back to campus.

Perhaps the closest that school officials came to publicly addressing the topic of interracial relationships was in a pro-eugenics editorial in the *Dubuque Evangelist*, which read in part, "The future American that we hope to develop out of the complexity of racial conditions is not a composite of all the races, but a composite of all the good qualities of all the races."[50] This focus on universal qualities rather than on physical bodies implied that certain racial groups would be excluded from the composite resulting from an imagined, institutionally sanctioned procreation. Nearly a century earlier, the Protestant Foreign Mission School in Cornwall, Connecticut—pejoratively dubbed the "Heathen School" because it drew many nonwhite students from non-Christian areas around the globe—came to an unceremonious end soon after two Cherokee students married local white women.[51] As more and more white women attended Dubuque College, leadership likely sought to prevent their intimacy with the school's Latino, Asian, or Native American students (once Sol graduated, nearly a decade passed before another African American enrolled) and to reassure donors and alumni—who might celebrate the heterogeneous and platonic mix of students united in Christian faith but recoil from the prospect of miscegenation—that no racial composites would be developing at Dubuque.

On July 5, 1918, the army required approximately forty thousand soldiers at Camp Dodge in Des Moines to witness the hanging of three Black soldiers accused of raping an unidentified white woman. The historical record leaves room for doubt about the men's guilt. Noting how the military's hasty, improvised handling of the situation, from arrest to sentencing to execution, recalled the actions of a lynch mob, one historian claimed that "for Alabama African Americans, southern 'justice' applied even when they were in the North."[52] Among the masses of forced witnesses to the hanging were three thousand African American troops from the Ninety-Second Division. Unlike their white counterparts, the Black soldiers were forbidden from carrying weapons to the event, adding to the horror, vulnerability, and subservient status the hanging was calculated to instill in them. Events like this one made clear that Black

Butler enjoying a laugh with choir members (ca. 1918). (*Clavis* [1920], p. 92, University of Dubuque Archives)

males, even star athletes, had to carefully measure their interactions with white women.

This reality might have increased Sol's motivation for traveling beyond Iowa to compete in regional and national meets, where he could socialize with women of color; the racially volatile sexual prohibitions imposed by white supremacy sometimes necessitated his moving within and to safer social realms. Nonetheless, photographs of Sol in the presence of smiling female classmates, along with certain playful accounts of coeducational club activity, suggest that interracial desires might be sparked on campus in pleasurable disregard of tacit administrative prohibitions. Sol's athletic skills and the glory he brought to Dubuque shielded him to a degree from racial intolerance.[53]

At home for the summer in Hutchinson, Sol probably stayed with his mother and father, who was almost eighty. He might have seen his sister Josephine, who earlier in the year became "the only colored girl from Kansas in the united army nursing corps."[54] Just before her brothers moved to Dubuque for the first time, Josephine went to Washington, DC, where she attended and graduated from the Freedmen's Hospital Training School. After returning to Kansas, she passed the examination in Sedalia to become a registered nurse, the only African American in her class of eighty-five. She would become a sought-after public health official, who over the coming decades specialized in tuberculosis care and challenged segregation while serving at a US veterans hospital in North Carolina during World War II.[55] Like her college-educated brothers, she blazed a prominent, upwardly mobile path that would have made her parents proud.

In Hutchinson, Sol and Ben Jr. began planning a "mass meeting which has for its purpose the stimulating of ideas which will be beneficial to the race."[56] The meeting would be attended by "all the progressive members" of Hutchinson's African American community—those who expected social progress to stem from African American participation in the war but could not ignore incidents like the hanging in Des Moines that portended ongoing racial violence and oppression.[57] Ben opened the meeting with a "short talk" that "emphasized the need of organization and competent intelligent leadership of the race." In the meeting hall that bore his name, Rev. H. Broadus warned young people about "the evils of thoughtlessness in regard to the future." Sol spoke about race leaders across the country and his hope for Hutchinson to produce "leaders who would be trusted by members of both races, and who could raise the standing of his people."[58] The free event ended with refreshments.

In addressing the subject of Black leadership, the Butler brothers would have evoked W. T. Vernon and others who effectively pushed for African American advancement by working within the traditional political sphere. Given their goal to become race leaders, as stated a few years earlier in Sol's autobiography, *Three Years of High School Athletics*, they also would have had themselves in mind. They both had successfully navigated several years of higher education. Consistently "trusted by members of both races," Sol kept demonstrating through multidimensional mobility how athletics might open doors to Black advancement.[59] Some doors remained closed, but he remained set on staying the course toward extending his and others' freedom of movement.

Shining Light

The big change on the Dubuque College campus in the fall of 1918 was the introduction of the Student Army Training Corps (SATC), a program that trained students for military leadership on hundreds of college campuses across the nation. Enlistees received government-issued uniforms and equipment but no pay.[60] "College trained men have shown their superiority in every branch of the service," said Col. H. A. Ripley of Camp Dodge, "and if there is anything the army needs right now, it is efficient officers."[61] The SATC operated "in full swing" by mid-October, housing over a hundred students in McCormick Gym.[62] Sol was among the students who moved out of the dorms and into the athletic-facility-turned-barracks. The YMCA furnished rooms for SATC students' entertainment with magazines, an Edison player with "a large variety of records," stationery for letter writing, a piano to accompany communal singing, and "games of various sort."[63] Physical training primarily consisted of long hikes up hills around Dubuque, an activity that the men accompanied with loud unison singing. The students complained and joked about their lack of uniforms (which apparently arrived after the November 11 armistice).

Over the summer, a number of professors and students, including Sol's basketball coach and several teammates, had entered the Student Officers' Training Camp at Fort Sheridan, Illinois; segregation prevented Butler from joining them. He may have considered applying for the Fort Des Moines Provisional Officer Training School, the country's only program for African American officers, but Butler did not go to Fort Des Moines. Perhaps he worried about how the demands of military training might undermine his athletic aspirations, or perhaps he opposed the idea of applying for a program that segregated soldiers by design, even in as prestigious a pursuit as officer training.[64]

The beginning of the fall semester coincided with the most harrowing period on campus during the deadliest influenza pandemic, which killed up to 100 million people worldwide.[65] City officials canceled religious services, day students had to be housed on campus, and all public places around town were closed. Approximately 15 percent of Dubuque's residents contracted influenza, leading to at least 134 deaths.[66] But the pandemic did not prevent students from holding a YMCA-sponsored Halloween party in McCormick Gym.[67] "When the orchestra began to play, punch and everything was forgotten in the wild scramble for partners."[68] Students from Benjamin Hall, the new dorm for women, drolly recalled a slightly different scene: "We surely felt very welcome, for the boys showed their delight in having us as their guests by glancing up occasionally from the letters they were writing, the books they were reading and the games they were playing. Oh! We never had such a time in all our lives!"[69]

After the war and influenza quarantine ended in November, the festivities continued. The YMCA put on a "Stunt" Party on Friday, December 13, and Butler once again joined classmates in blackface. He and a teammate named Dempsey, "as end men in the minstrel show, certainly brought down the house."[70] The following Thursday the SATC held an "informal dancing party" in McCormick Gym, where the men in just-arrived military uniforms "entertained their lady friends."[71] The odor of Fatima and Camel cigarettes "permeated the place," noted one account. "Music was furnished by one of the leading orchestras in the city, and during the intermission several of the S.A.T.C. boys themselves added to the program with songs and other musical numbers." By December 21, Butler and other members of the company received an honorable military discharge. The bugle stopped sounding in the morning and at night, marching and saluting ceased, and guards no longer

Butler in military uniform next to an unidentified female and Tommy Parker (ca. 1919). (Collection of the author)

paced in front of Severance Hall and the gym, which returned to its original function in the service of athletics.[72]

The spring semester began like the previous semester had ended, with considerable festive energy. The Philophronia Society threw a social in the Severance Hall parlor on the second Friday of the new year. Reflecting both the growing momentum of the women's suffrage movement and the increasing presence of women on campus, the event's central activity involved testing the homemaking skills of the male students, who would soon assume the "duty to be the home-makers" since "women were taking [their] place in the business world."[73] Male students demonstrated their skills in cooking, button sewing, and other domestic tasks. "Tommy Parker easily excelled Sol Butler in dishwashing," the yearbook reported.

About a week after the campus social, Butler was summoned back to Hutchinson "on account of the serious illness of his father,"[74] who would die two months later. The Monday night after Sol arrived in Hutchinson, the *Wichita Daily Eagle* announced an unusual "double entertainment" at Douglas

High School: a concert by the African American violinist and composer Clarence Cameron White—who had attended Oberlin (Ohio) College, performed for President McKinley, and studied with the influential Afro-British composer Samuel Coleridge-Taylor—and "a moving picture film showing Sol Butler, the famous negro athlete in action."[75] The origins and specific content of this film remain a mystery, but Sol may have been filmed by the author and film director Oscar Micheaux, who had family in southern Kansas. Micheaux was about to debut his first feature-length film, *The Homesteader*, at Chicago's Eighth Regiment Armory, where in a few years Butler would play on elite all-Black basketball teams. Decades later, a reporter identified Butler as among Micheaux's stable of actors.[76] As for Clarence Cameron White, he represented the type of race leader Sol championed at the Broadus Hall meeting at the end of the summer: He operated in an educated Black cultural sphere that aligned with white middle-class tastes and values; he navigated without provocation among white people; and he sought racial uplift through cultural achievement rather than by challenging societal norms. Whether White's playing preceded or followed the sports film or the one accompanied the other, the synergy between these two cultural products presaged Butler's entrepreneurism; in future years his celebrity and sport success fueled his efforts in theater, film, music, and journalism.

When Butler returned to Dubuque, he joined the basketball team several games into their season,[77] practiced for a busy spring concert series with the glee club, and participated in a new seventy-five-member mixed men and women's chorus.[78] His first track and field competition of the season was in Des Moines at the Drake Relays on April 19, less than three weeks after his father died in Hutchinson.[79] He appeared to channel his grief into athletic greatness. With his team trailing in the half-mile relay, Butler "passed his competitors with so much speed that they appeared not to be moving."[80] The following Friday he traveled by train hundreds of miles to compete at the Penn Relays, where he won the broad jump (establishing a pentathlon record), finished first in the 100-yard dash, and just missed first place in the 200-meter run. His two first-place victories, which conferred a status that was tantamount to national champion,[81] brought him special attention on the front page of sports sections across the country.[82] New York sportswriter A. C. Cavagnaro ascribed to Butler a trait typically denied to Black men in popular debates when he wrote that the heroic athlete possessed "an unusual amount of stamina . . . [He] proved himself the more iron man by winning the 100-yard dash against an especially fast field after capturing the running broad jump, an event that shatters the equilibrium of a sprinter."[83]

He continued to demonstrate extraordinary endurance over the Iowa Conference track season that followed in May. The Saturday after the Penn Relays, the Dubuque College track team headed to Cedar Rapids to take on Coe

College, which won the meet. Butler single-handedly kept things competitive, taking first place in the 100-yard dash, 120-yard hurdles, shot put, 220-yard hurdles, and broad jump, second in high jump and discus, and third place in javelin, and earning thirty-two of his team's fifty-two points.[84] He apparently exerted just enough effort to win his best events, because he "seemed entirely unfatigued at the end of the meet."[85] The following Friday the Dubuque team returned to Cedar Rapids for a conference meet, where Butler won first in his five individual events, tied a conference record set by former Olympian Clement Wilson in the 100-yard dash, and broke the broad jump record.[86] Butler earned more individual points than the bottom four teams combined, burnishing his reputation as "the shining light of all the trackmen in Iowa."[87]

We Would Not Injure Sol

Sol Butler concluded his college athletic career by attending the letter winners varsity sports banquet at the Hotel Julien. "It was simply one of those good 'get-together' dinners in which all formalities were discarded," wrote the *Telegraph-Herald.*[88] "Tobacco smoke and good fellowship flooded the banquet hall, interspersed by occasional streams of oratory" from president and "toastmaster" Steffens, coaches, team captains, and even Ben Butler, who returned to Dubuque for the occasion. Sol "delivered a heart-to-heart talk in which he thanked his college mates for the treatment they had accorded him during his four years in their midst and he assured them that he would devote his all to the support of Dubuque college." Echoing the brief and celebrated speech he gave at a banquet in Hutchinson five years earlier, "he closed his talk with the quotation, 'First, the Almighty; second, your country, and then the college you represent.'"[89] On a less serious note, Butler also offered to make a wager. For each of the previous three years, members of the freshman class had abducted leading members of the senior class on the night of the junior-senior banquet, attempting to keep them from the festivities, while the sophomore class swooped in to save them. Butler was willing to bet five dollars that the freshmen couldn't keep him from the banquet.[90]

The next morning, as Butler walked down the steps from his dorm room floor in Severance Hall, a group of freshmen jumped out; one "pinned Sol's arm to his side, while the four below shackled his feet and tied his arms," went an account published two years after the fact by one of Sol's abductors.[91] "We picked him up and proceeded to Epworth in eighteen minutes" in a Packard car. According to the *Telegraph-Herald*, the freshmen also "gagged" Sol before capturing the senior class president, George Sisler, and a few other seniors.[92] When the sophomores arrived, they threw several freshmen into a pond, and "Sol was taken to a machine shop to have the shackles sawed off." (The earlier newspaper account claimed that Butler freed himself with a file that Sisler

Butler shackled, sitting on a wagon with a classmate (1919). (*The Key* [1921], p. 139, University of Dubuque Archives)

smuggled in.[93]) Butler and the other seniors made it to that night's banquet, albeit a bit dirtied up.

Various accounts of the abduction, along with yearbook photographs, confirm that Butler was shackled, but no evidence exists to suggest that his white classmates suffered the same fate. The white freshmen who shackled the only Black member of the senior class likely understood that the chains evoked chattel slavery, a condition from which Sol was only one generation removed. The shackles also may have conjured up the thousands of contemporary Black men who were forced—often for the smallest infractions and on the flimsiest of evidence—as prisoners into a slave-like, often deadly, convict labor system. But in yearbook photographs, Butler appears relaxed and good-natured about his ordeal. The 1919 senior class abduction was recounted in both the 1920 and 1921 yearbooks, and both yearbook accounts indicate that the seniors went along with the ritual and received relatively good treatment: The "Freshmen had located to a meadow . . . and were spending the time taking pictures of their captives and playing cards with them."[94] The emphasis in the 1920 narrative, written by a member of the rescuing sophomore class, then shifts to the captors' humiliating defeat at the hands of the sophomores, who rendered them "wet and forlorn." Apparently deprived of their car, all of them boarded a freight train, except for one who was left in his underwear and had to walk miles back to campus.

In contrast, the 1921 yearbook account, included in a class reminiscence and written by one of the 1919 freshmen abductors, shifted the focus from the captors' defeat and humiliation to a disturbing fixation on Butler. The author took pains to clarify how the freshmen treated their famous captive well, noting that once they arrived in Epworth, "Sol was taken to the hotel for a breakfast of ham and eggs," and urging readers "to see how well Sol was enjoying himself, look upon some of the pictures taken of him during his captivity."[95] But the author concluded on an ominous note: "You see Sol was to sail for France to represent our school at the Army Meet, so we freshmen solemnly promised ourselves that we would not injure Sol in any way. Me thinks, had it not been for this promise Sol's physiognomy would not have been one to present at a Junior-Senior banquet."[96] The author clarifies with some relish that Butler emerged unscathed from his abduction only because the freshmen put their impulse for violence in check with a solemn vow. This impulse is especially chilling in light of the military executions of Black soldiers near Houston and in Des Moines and the fact that, as Sol was being shackled outside his dormitory, the United States was entering one of the bloodiest periods of racial violence in the nation's history.

Sol Butler left Dubuque having set school records for the 100-yard dash, 200-yard dash, shot put, discus throw, broad jump, 120-yard hurdles, and 220-yard hurdles. He was widely acknowledged as one of the greatest all-around athletes—the nation's top broad jumper and an elite sprinter. He led the football team as quarterback for four years of dazzling success. Butler accomplished all of this surrounded by white peers, many of whom took pride in his accomplishments and considered him a friend. But none of these white students could fathom his daily challenges as a dark-skinned Black man in a white world or grasp the high stakes hinging on his success. Undoubtedly some students viewed Butler as inferior, despite his superior accomplishments; the freshmen's impulse to make their disdain visible by reaching for a symbol of slavery or committing the kind of racial violence that characterized the brutal reign of Jim Crow could not have been new or unique during Butler's years at Dubuque.

We can imagine the litany of racist slurs and aggressions that Sol must have suffered—an underbelly of resentment and lurking violence—as he moved through these white worlds, attempting to claim his place as a student, athlete, and citizen. These slights served as reminders that no matter how many minstrel shows he performed, races and games he won, coeducational and extracurricular events he enlivened—or, more broadly, no matter how many Black soldiers fought and died for their country—the unfettered freedom of movement enjoyed by most white men in America remained out of reach. The expressions of hostility, mostly unrecorded, belied the image of interracial harmony depicted in yearbook photographs and championed by school faculty and administration. For all of Sol Butler's deft and exceptional mobility, both physical and social, and the relative freedom of movement that afforded him—to attend college and travel the country for track and field meets—white supremacy imposed unbreachable limits that tested his endurance.[97]

The morning after the junior-senior banquet, "Sol Butler had reason to forget that less than twenty-four hours ago he was a prisoner of the freshmen somewhere in the hinterlands."[98] Amateur Athletic Union officials in New York sent Sol a telegram announcing that he had been selected to represent the United States at the Inter-Allied Games "as a member of the greatest band of athletes which was ever assembled." This telegram was a formality; the final official word on an invitation he and others had assumed had been extended months before, but it still felt good.[99] An article from the Associated Press, which appeared in dozens of newspapers across the country, declared, "The team is the nearest approach to an American Olympic squad that has been sent abroad since the Olympic games in Stockholm" in 1912 and noted that "among the outstanding stars named are Sol Butler, the negro sprinter and broad jumper from Dubuque."[100] Sol went to the offices of the *Telegraph-Herald* to share the good news "with the telegram in his hand, grinning from ear to ear, his face radiant with the new honor that had been bestowed upon him."[101]

The Inter-Allied Games confirmation announcement came at an auspicious moment during Booster Week, when students of Dubuque College announced their plan to attract five hundred new students to join them in the fall.[102] As one journalist noted, Butler's inclusion in the Inter-Allied Games gave the school "immeasurable" publicity: "It is hard to conceive of any other way that the name of the institution could be more widely heralded."[103] On his way to the train station, "Sol was carried down the street in an automobile bearing the sign, 'Bound for Paris,'" reported the *Dubuque Times-Journal*.[104] "Immediately following there came a street car with the band and an eager crowd of supporters who were going to the depot to say good-bye. Butler boarded the train when it arrived at 12 o'clock and pandemonium reigned until it steamed out five minutes later." Sol or Ben Butler relayed news of the event to the *Chicago Defender*, which claimed that when he left, "a band, the college students and thousands of citizens were at the train to see him off and bade him farewell and good cheer."[105]

While this report probably exaggerated the size of the crowd, it conveyed the jubilation and even wonder of the moment—Butler riding high in the seat of honor and followed by an ebullient, diverse (mostly white) throng shouting his praises through a town with a long history of anti-Black sentiment. "It is hoped," continued the *Defender*, "that other boys will enter this college, which knows no color line, and 'make good' as has Mr. Butler."[106] Sol had endured the constraints on his free movement, including the benching at the all-state football game and racially circumscribed interactions with white women, and now enjoyed a triumphant send-off that his relentless attempts at social and physical mobility made possible.

While Sol was in New York, waiting to depart for the Inter-Allied Games in France, Dubuque College held its 1919 graduation ceremony without him, where he and nine others received recognition for earning bachelor's degrees. School officials had invited four students, including Butler, to present orations. Since Butler wasn't there to give his speech, an editor of the *Dubuque Evangelist* expressed an unfulfilled hope to publish it, but "The Negro, a Factor in the Life of America" is now lost to history.[107] Reflecting pride in their "cosmopolitan" makeup, the school newspaper listed the graduates' nationalities: "African, American, Bohemian, German, Holland, Hungarian, Mexican, Scandinavian, and Swiss."[108] Sol would soon see this embrace of cultural diversity expressed on a grand scale and under the eyes of the world. At the same time, he would witness American racism transported overseas, hampering the lives of Black military personnel and tainting the joy he would experience from his crowning athletic achievement.

6

The Democracy of Sport

Summer 1919–Spring 1920

From “Something Within” (1919) by Lucie Campbell

As hundreds of thousands of American servicemen in postwar Europe awaited safe passage home, a prominent Black family in Dubuque, Iowa, celebrated the birth of their newest member, Robert L. Martin. Born outside of town, where he and his mother might receive proper care, Martin embodied a spirit of free movement within a system of inequality. As a young adult, he attracted attention as allegedly the “only colored ski jumper in the world.”[1] During World War II he joined the segregated US Air Force and as a Tuskegee Airman flew sixty-three combat missions in a P-51 Mustang before being shot down over Yugoslavia. His quick thinking, a sturdy parachute, and friendly Europeans made possible his safe return to the United States, where among many awards he received the Distinguished Flying Cross. A post office and airport terminal now bear his name. Like Butler, who almost certainly knew the aviator’s podiatrist father, Henry A. Martin, Robert sped past typically unbreachable barriers to demonstrate Black excellence. They both achieved their greatest glory overseas, one man with his powerful legs and the other navigating a fighter plane, and refuted white supremacy through flight.[2]

While sparking resistance to racial oppression, the world wars also prompted ferocious white backlash. Toward the end of his life, Butler would see wartime activism and heroics, like Martin exhibited, transform into a civil rights movement. Yet the First World War, especially in its immediate wake, appeared to usher in unbridled intolerance and domestic terror. By the summer of 1919, approximately half a million Southern African Americans had moved to cities, mostly in the North, and filled jobs vacated by white servicemen. Racial resentment flared up over job competition, and white fears mounted in response to the imagined spread of communism and returning Black servicemen, who had enjoyed greater freedom in Europe than at home and had acquired military training. During the period of demobilization, when one and a half million US troops returned from France, Germany, and Italy, lynchings increased and white mobs massacred hundreds of Black Americans across the country. According to historian Jennifer Keene, "The war had a 'radicalizing' effect within the United States of America as the mobilization process politicized both civilians and soldiers. The violence . . . stemmed from a war culture that amplified class, ethnic, and racial divisions by associating challenges to the existing social order with questions of national security."[3]

It was the type of racial climate that in previous decades Butler's parents tried to escape through migration. Sol now traveled across the Atlantic Ocean with white teammates as an unlikely and hypervisible agent of international peace and goodwill at the Inter-Allied Games (also known as the "Military Olympics") and a conflicted symbol of American democracy. Sol evoked racial ambivalence from the media, a mixture of admiration and condescension that spoke to broader white attitudes toward Black veterans. The aspiring race leader—who would appear soaring over the broad jump pit in photo stills and one dazzling moving picture—represented the promise of unimpeded mobility, even as racial realities on the ground augured ongoing violent exclusion.

Landed on French Soil

The US team set sail on June 4, 1919, from Hoboken, New Jersey, for the Inter-Allied Games in France. The nearly fifty members—including three dozen in track and field—represented a handpicked group of athletes, many of whom secured their position the previous Friday at an intercollegiate competition in Harvard Stadium. Sol Butler did not compete in this meet and appeared to have been at the top of the list well before the Amateur Athletic Union (AAU) sent his official invitation.[4] Sprinter Charley Paddock recalled that the athletes "held a final workout at Travers Island, the summer home of the New York Athletic Club."[5] If Sol arrived in time to participate, his presence represented a change from a longtime club policy of excluding Black athletes.[6] The day before the trip, the athletes gathered at AAU headquarters in Manhattan to get their passports and final instructions. The next day, they met again at 290 Broadway Avenue and were driven from there to Hoboken in "sightseeing automobiles, preceded by a band."[7] Colonel Joseph H. Thompson, who commanded the team, "used every means to provide for the comfort and care of the athletes on board" the *SS Great Northern*. They "have been quartered in individual cabins and every possible endeavor has been made to eliminate the feeling of being cramped aboard ship."[8] Despite these efforts, "Sol suffered terribly from sea-sickness during the voyage between New York and Brest and was pretty well 'used up' when the Americans landed on French soil."[9]

The team arrived in Brest, France, on July 11.[10] Steaming into Brest harbor, they passed by the Trez Hir Leave Center, "a leave hotel . . . on the order of a country club," where white American soldiers, sailors, and YMCA workers found "rest and diversion." Established in order "to maintain morals and prevent mental and physical deterioration," according to an unpublished history, "one of the main features of the vacation was to be freedom."[11] Rose Glass, the YMCA social and entertainment secretary, in coordination with the Y's "canteen girls," brought groups to play baseball, swim, dance, sing, tell stories, watch shows, and "eat a picnic lunch out under the trees in the back garden." This idyllic setting for rest and entertainment excluded African Americans in the military, including the stevedores in Camp President Lincoln, which bordered Brest harbor. These Black dockworkers had no nearby relief stations open to them. Instead, musicians organized the singing of spirituals; the "relief" that was offered to Black servicemen tended toward a metaphorical rather than a literal escape from work and stress.[12]

Meanwhile, at Trez Hir, Glass and her assistants provided wigs and costumes "suitable for decking boys out as minstrels" for the "continuous round of minstrel shows."[13] Rather than an exception, these were the rule. "The army insisted on organizing minstrel shows," asserts Black studies scholar Cedric Robinson, thus illustrating "the extent of official involvement in promoting racism."[14] As official peace neared, the two hundred thousand African Americans who served overseas were still subject to the same segregation, restricted mobility, and casual racism they faced at home, and the progress many Black leaders had hoped for at the beginning of the war seemed even more out of reach.[15] As the only Black man on a team of elite athletes chosen to represent the United States at a turning point in the nation's role on the international stage, Sol Butler experienced relative freedom of movement at home and abroad. However, even with his exceptional physical mobility on global display at the Inter-Allied Games, his presence on the team constituted an act of protest that met with celebration but also predictable backlash.

When Butler returned to Dubuque from France more than two months after he left the cheering throng in the train station, he visited the offices of the *Telegraph Herald* to share an account of his heroic trip.[16] What Butler left unsaid, or the newspaper left unprinted, was whether he was housed with his white teammates or with Black servicemen in segregated barracks and canteens. Given the requirements and logistics of training, it's likely that Butler stayed with his teammates at Clignancourt Barracks, a former French hospital transformed into a barracks for US troops during the war. An official Inter-Allied Games publication noted that Clignancourt included a "special mess, separate from the mess of the troops at the barracks . . . for the athletes."[17] The separation maintained by this "special mess" also may have accommodated the military's desire to prevent Butler from mingling with the segregated white troops. Avoiding racial conflict was a primary objective for Elwood Brown, the YMCA administrator who proposed the Inter-Allied Games.[18] Rather than promoting segregation, however, Brown sought integration, at least in the realm of athletics. In the Philippines he had organized the Far Eastern Championship Games, which brought Filipinos, Japanese, Chinese, and other Asian athletes together in an Olympic-style competition.[19] He later explained his belief that "athletics was the first thing that would bring [the various countries in the Far East] together, those opposing races, the different religions, political and social ideas."[20]

Other African Americans overseas did not have access to the integrated opportunities that Butler likely enjoyed as a member of the US team, and Elwood Brown's desire to bring races together through sport did not appear to impact any other aspect of operations at the YMCA, which played a central role in serving US soldiers during and after the war and a major role in enforcing racial segregation abroad. "In accordance with its jim crow policy," writes historian Nina Mjagkij, "the YMCA maintained segregation in its work among American soldiers throughout the war and the period of demobilization. YMCA services for African-American troops 'were in almost every case inferior' and suffered from a shortage of personnel."[21] Accommodations around Pershing Stadium, the site of the Inter-Allied Games, were no different: The hundreds of troops from the four Black companies—and perhaps Butler, too—had access to only one segregated, understaffed YMCA hut; the Black troops could not attend the YMCA Inter-Allied Hut, named "the melting pot," where "the best of the A.E.F. [American Expeditionary Forces] shows were staged."[22] More than twenty YMCA secretaries, along with nearly a hundred "American girls," ran this tent, which had been moved from Brest and showed nightly movies "when other formal entertainments were not scheduled." The YMCA women served lemonade to the troops and athletes and served as dance partners to non-Black men from around the world.

Implementing broad-scale competitions across postwar Europe, crowned by the Inter-Allied Games, required the support of the US military. General Pershing and other army officials approved of Brown's proposal in large part because the games helped keep many of the nearly two million overseas troops engaged in constructive activity after the armistice.[23] These competitions served an additional purpose for the military: the projection of American might. According to scholar Robert Elias, the anticipated dominance of US athletes helped motivate the staging of the games as a display of "American superiority and to establish a United States presence for the Paris Peace conference."[24] While US soldiers competed in athletic contests, Woodrow Wilson, Lloyd George, Georges Clemenceau, Vittorio Emanuele Orlando, and delegates from other Allied nations met in Paris to hash out the terms of peace. These talks culminated in late June with the signing of the Treaty of Versailles, which officially ended the war. As Wilson played a leading role in shaping the terms of international peace, US athletes did, as expected, dominate in the Inter-Allied Games, winning first place in half of the events listed in the program and sweeping the first three places in 21 percent of events.[25] US athletic success provided symbolic support for the debatable claim that US military intervention was necessary for Allied victory and symbolic justification for the country's outsize influence at the Paris Peace Conference. Sol Butler's presence on the US team in the highly publicized games served to bolster both the spirit of inclusion that Elwood Brown endeavored to foster and the dominance that the American Expeditionary Forces aimed to project.

The Best Jump Ever Made in France

After landing in Brest, Sol Butler and his teammates devoted a week to "the hardest kind of training" at Colombes Field in the northwestern suburbs of Paris.[26] Final tryouts for the Inter-Allied Games occurred at the end of the week, when the elite squad from the States matched up against soldiers who had been stationed in Europe since the end of the war. Scouted from trials across American-occupied Europe—the military reportedly repurposed 150 airplane hangars for indoor events[27]—the competitors in the final Inter-Allied tryouts represented the best male athletes in the United States, which led javelin thrower George Bronder to speculate that the tryouts would "result in more spectacular competition than the Inter-Allied meet itself."[28] Butler's efforts in the 100-meter dash helped create the spectacle that Bronder anticipated. Butler and sprinter Charley Paddock, who was soon to be known as the fastest man alive, each ran the race in 10 4/5 seconds, coming within one-fifth of a second from tying the world record.[29]

Early in the afternoon on Sunday, June 22, Sol Butler joined nearly fifteen hundred athletes from eighteen nations and colonies for the opening ceremonies of the Inter-Allied Games in the massive Pershing Stadium. Built by American and French troops with the financial support of the YMCA, the stadium hosted a crowd that far surpassed its official capacity, with a reported ninety thousand spectators, who "filled every possible seating space in the huge concrete stands, overflowed on the grounds, or stormed in vain outside the circular walls in efforts to get a glimpse of the ceremonies inside."[30] The athletes paraded around the 500-meter track; the chief secretary of the AEF-YMCA,

Edward Carter, presented the deed of the stadium to General Pershing, who then gifted the stadium to France. An air show with US and French planes followed, which ended with an American pilot crashing a Fokker into a tree on a race track. The crowds "tore" the completely wrecked plane "to pieces for souvenirs."[31]

The next day, the opening spectacle was the trials for the 100-meter dash. "The track did not match the setting," wrote Charley Paddock several years later. "Almost any old kind of cinders had been used, and it was both soft and heavy."[32] Officials believed that "the cinder path was fairly fast but not exceptionally so," noting that the newness of the track discouraged world records.[33] Butler finished first in the third of five heats in the semifinals with a time of eleven seconds even. To maintain spectators' interest between events, organizers staged sword dancing, camel racing, and "a colorful representation of a desert fight with the combatants mounted on camels."[34] Later that day, Butler qualified for the finals after finishing third in the semifinals behind Eddie Teschner of the United States and John Lindsay of New Zealand, one of the Inter-Allied Games' handful of Black athletes. After the semifinals, Butler had the chance to be a spectator. Walking around the massive complex, he witnessed a baseball game "going on in one corner and boxing, wrestling, running, shot-putting and all kinds of games going on at the same time."[35] He noted that one of the French pilots flew an airplane so low over the field that the baseball shortstop touched it with his glove.[36]

The finals for the 100-meter dash took place on Wednesday, after being delayed a day by Elwood Brown because of rain.[37] Under the gaze of world leaders on the brink of finalizing peace—and generals Marshal Ferdinand Foch, Douglas Haig, John Pershing of France, Britain, and the United States, respectively, "and other notables who left the Hall of Mirrors at Versailles to witness the contest"—and amid "forty thousand soldier boys, wearing the uniforms of all the Allied nations," Butler faced two other Americans, Charley Paddock and Eddie Teschner, along with John Lindsay; John Armstrong "Army" Howard from Canada, another Black athlete; and René Caste from France.[38] Paddock remembered that the track "was like mush, though fortunately the cinders were too large to cling to spikes."

After a false start by Lindsay, the six men lined up again, feet braced in the holes they dug in their roped lanes (starting blocks were not yet in wide use). When the starter's gun sounded, they left their "holes as one man," recalled Paddock, but "Butler had started out slowly for him."[39] According to the massive almanac that documented the games, "The start in the final was almost perfect and brought the spectators to their feet in cheers. Flashing down the straightaway to the 75-meter mark, the sprinters were almost neck and neck."[40] Ten and four-fifth seconds after it began, Paddock breasted the yarn hung four feet above the finish line to take first place. Teschner came in second and Howard in third. Butler finished fourth. Failing to place, his hopes for glory on an international stage now rested on his final and strongest event, the running broad jump.[41]

Butler had to wait three days for the broad jump trials. As expected, he earned first place in the Saturday trials, with a jump of over 23 feet. American Harry Worthington, a twenty-nine-year-old Dartmouth graduate who had finished fourth in the 1912 Olympics, finished second. Shortly after the event on June 28, 1919, "an official announcement was made to the immense Saturday throng that Germany had just signed the Peace Treaty."[42] The war had officially come to an end, and amid the excitement a baritone from the Opéra Comique sang the French national anthem from the boxing ring.[43] At this moment, King Nicholas I of Montenegro summoned Butler, Canadian John Armstrong, and several other star athletes to be knighted.[44] The monarch had been deposed from his position seven months earlier at the Podgorica Nicholas Assembly and excluded from the day's momentous signing of the Treaty of Versailles. Nicholas I's efforts to reassert his rule led the seventy-six-year-old dignitary to daily exercise his right to a ceremonial entry to Pershing Stadium, which other royalty declined, announced by a bugle call for spectators to stand at attention until he arrived at his seat.[45] His decision to knight Butler and a few other athletes represented a deposed king's desperate attempt at soft power statecraft.

Nicholas failed to reestablish the monarchy in Montenegro, but he brought a king-size degree of attention to Butler. "An unusual combination, this, of a King and an American negro," read a New York newspaper caption.[46] US media coverage, influenced by the Inter-Allied Games press and publicity committee, composed of nearly forty military members, tended to present the encounter in stereotypes that evoked a paternalism reminiscent of the antebellum South. "The grin on the hulky negro's face was ear-wide as King Nicholas patted him," said one widely reprinted account.[47] Photographs show Butler smiling but not in a gesture of gleeful deference; he stands erect and dignified. The dethroned king is also smiling and appears equally happy with the encounter, which held far more significance for him than it did for the increasingly popular American athlete. The condescending coverage of the event reflected a widespread, blackface minstrelsy–inspired practice of media representation. For instance, the inaugural issue of the *American Legion Weekly* tempered Butler's athletic accomplishment by casting him as a patted buffoon; subsequent issues denigrated Black troops and suggested that Black people were only good for a laugh.[48] For example, a crude caricature of a Black man was accompanied by the account of a white officer who allegedly heard "one big buck" aboard a ship praying to the Lord to "call this ocean to attention."[49] The next issue showed a Black soldier grinning in a way that evoked the hyper-exaggerated smile of the famous Black minstrel comedian Billy Kersands.[50]

Butler being knighted by deposed king Nicholas I of Montenegro (1919). (Bibliothèque nationale de France, Gallica Digital Library, ID btv1b53017736h)

Since high school, when he dazzled fans in Kansas and Illinois, Butler had received media coverage ranging in sentiment from adulation to derision, but his encounter with Nicholas and subsequent athletic triumph brought a new level of attention that mixed admiration tempered by the enduring racial stereotype known as the "Tom." Named after the central character in Harriet Beecher Stowe's 1852 novel, *Uncle Tom's Cabin*, this caricature evoked a nonthreatening Black man who happily aimed to please white people.[51] According to most US media accounts, when shown king-size recognition, Butler smiled deferentially. After studiously avoiding a public persona that might conjure the image of a brash and dangerous Blackness, epitomized by former heavyweight champion Jack Johnson, Butler's image now fell victim to popular racist representation that denied his full humanity. At a time when, abroad and increasingly at home, the presence of proud and assertive Black troops amplified the reactionary force of increasingly violent white supremacy, mainstream media often presented Butler's undeniable success in a way that privileged whiteness. His unique, star-making mobility could be cast as predicated on subservience and in contrast with the dignified self-assurance he displayed under the spotlight and the mounting civil rights energy among Black service members.

The following day, Sunday, June 29, Butler achieved his life's most celebrated athletic accomplishment. Broad jump rules specified that all jumpers could take as long a run as they wished but had to leap before stepping beyond the joist placed flush with the ground in front of the pit. The four athletes who jumped farthest after three attempts qualified for "three more trials."[52] Butler and two other Americans, Leo Johnson and Harry Worthington, advanced to the final three trials. By this point it was clear that Butler would win first place; the only question was how far he would go. "As he went back for his last trial he threw away all of his marks, and kicked his sweater aside. He went back 15 yards further for his sprint, [and] tore over the jumpers' path" on his way to "the best jump ever made in France."[53] The official length of his leap was 7.557 meters, or 24' 9³⁄₁₆", just over a foot longer than the second-place finisher and nearly 3½ feet longer than the fourth-place finisher.[54] On an imperfect, saturated field in front of thirty thousand spectators, Butler came within 3 inches of setting a world record. Years later, Charley Paddock noted, and sportswriter Alan Gould confirmed, that Butler had "cleared 25 feet in practice," a length that no one in the world had leaped in any officially sanctioned contest.[55]

Film footage exists of one of Butler's last three running broad jumps in the finals. Photographers from the US Signal Corps were "kept constantly on the field at Pershing Stadium taking pictures of every event" to ensure a "complete pictorial history," and they captured Butler in mid-flight.[56] Apparently only one film crew, however, documented him in motion and recorded what is likely his earliest extant appearance on reel-to-reel film. In January the YMCA hired the Community Motion Picture Bureau to film the postwar operations of the Allied armies at home and abroad.[57] The film crew captured the final stages of construction on Pershing Stadium and many of the splendors of the opening day, including the parade of athletes and soldiers and the dedication ceremony. It also filmed many of the athletic events, including twenty-two seconds of the three American finalists in the running broad jump. After showing Leo Johnson sprint down the path, leap into the pit, and bounce out of the sand on his left leg, the camera—situated about chest level approximately 10 feet beyond the back-left corner of the pit—cuts to Butler, who wears a white sleeveless T-shirt with dark trim, imprinted with "US" in bold letters that span his ribcage, and khaki shorts pulled up above the navel. He stands at what appears to be the start of the runway, over 40 yards away. A group of servicemen standing around the race track beyond the broad jump runway wander and converse, seemingly oblivious to the action on the field. In contrast, a dozen US and French servicemen attentively line the side of the landing pit, squatting or standing as close as they can without impeding the work of the two men who measure the distance of each leap. Johnson and Worthington stand together to watch Butler. Three squatting photographers in

Butler leaps at the Inter-Allied Games in Paris, France (1919). (Bibliothèque nationale de France, Gallica Digital Library, ID btv1b53017813)

sport coats and hats appear on the bottom left corner of the frame, prepared to capture Butler in mid-leap. They nearly obscure the three small US flags, planted in the ground to mark top distances, which flap violently to reveal the stiff crosswind whipping through the stadium.[58]

Amid the stadium's commotion, Butler stands facing the runway with his feet together and arms slightly bent, palms against his thighs. For more than three seconds, he remains completely still, frozen in a symmetrical, statuesque poise, before beginning his sprint to the pit. Johnson had raced down the right side of the runway and Worthington the left side, but Butler takes off down the middle. As he builds speed, the servicemen lining half of the pit quickly wriggle back, including a French soldier in a kepi hat who rises from a squat to create space for Butler's run. About halfway through his approach, Butler's body has straightened from his early, more crouched steps, and he tips his head up slightly. In the final meters before flight, he pushes off somewhat laterally with his left leg, angling his body to the right; perhaps he spots a promising patch of cinder runway from which to take off or adjusts his steps in order to avoid scratching. In his penultimate step on his right leg, Butler readjusts to channel all of his momentum straight ahead and looks down to spot his point of departure. His left foot falls on a chalked line marking the end of the runway as his head snaps back. His right leg lifts as he leaves the ground, a bit of chalk flying in his wake. Both arms go up as he ascends, and his hands disappear from view while his head nearly scrapes the top of the frame—the cameraman failed to anticipate the height of his jump.

At the apex, Butler gazes up to his right, the grimace on his face contradicting the state of relaxed weightlessness conveyed by his body. Now descending, both legs lift to his chest, and his arms come down and fan out at different angles for balance. In the final stages of flight, Butler spots his landing. His left arm swings back while his legs straighten, bracing for impact. He lands with both feet squarely planted but with a little more momentum on his right side, which forces his bending torso to twist a bit to his left before he begins to pop up. Only his feet have touched the ground. Momentum leads him into two jogging steps forward as he looks back to see officials with a tape measure enter the pit. Butler walks off to his left as the surrounding servicemen appear transfixed by where he landed.

Call It a Race Riot

The Inter-Allied Games ended on July 6. Film from two different moving picture cameras capture General Pershing on a stage in front of the grandstand presenting to Butler and other victorious athletes their engraved medals cast in bronze.[59] In one of these clips, the silent film intertitle introduces "the dusky Sol Butler, United States, winner of the broad jump" before footage that shows Butler salute the general, receive an award, shake Pershing's hand, and walk off the stage. Butler appears to smile briefly as he looks the general in the eye. He also received an award from the French minister of war and, according to one account, another "decoration" from Nicholas I.[60] An official publication noted that Butler's smile "was contagious. The crowd [of thirty thousand spectators] cheered him."[61] Another account, which was printed in many US newspapers and took aim at Butler's masculinity, claimed that he, "the giant black boy who copped the broad jump, got as many cheers as Pershing when he went up to get his prizes. The colored lad was standing beside Brig. Gen. Wolf, our rifle crack, when the medals were passed out, which shows amongst other things, the democracy of sport, hey?"[62] Ostensibly laudatory articles like this one, which also infantilized Butler, evoked a widespread white ambivalence about his celebrity. He could be praised, they seemed to suggest, as long as he was perceived as an unthreatening, twenty-four-year-old child. Black manhood had to remain unvaunted.

The US team stayed in France for a few weeks after the Inter-Allied Games ended. The details of their itinerary are lost to history, but Butler recalled one event in particular as a high point of the trip—a 90-yard dash in the Tuileries Garden during the historic postwar Bastille Day celebrations. The dash was so memorable for Butler because he outran his teammate, champion sprinter Charley Paddock, a feat he later described as the proudest moment in his long athletic career.[63] The annual Bastille Day military parade, coming right on the heels of the peace treaty, was notable that year for its epic scale. Following French military leaders General Joseph Joffre and Supreme Allied Commander Ferdinand Foch, generals from the Allied nations led twenty thousand soldiers through a newly opened Arc de Triomphe and down the Avenue de Elysees to the Place de la Concorde before heading north on the Rue Royale. More than one million spectators witnessed the parade. A newspaper account noted that "giant stands were erected on the terrace of the Tuileries gardens and around the Place de la Concorde."[64] The holiday atmosphere and incomparably vast crowd, in addition to his remarkable victory over Paddock, likely contributed to the sense that this was the climax of the trip for Butler. (Other English-speaking newspapers do not record the race, indicating that it failed to capture the attention of journalists or he misremembered.) After Bastille Day, Butler traveled with "the entire party of American athletes on a trip over the western front and then down through southern France."[65] He also ran into his high school friend Clarence Phillips, who had served in the war.[66]

While Butler was traveling through France with his white teammates, on a trip sponsored by the Knights of Columbus, other Black Americans overseas were experiencing the same restrictions on their mobility that they faced at home. In a letter to Black YMCA secretary R. B. DeFrantz, musician Joshua Blanton described an incident when a white major commanded a white lieutenant to remove a Black doctor and four Black YMCA secretaries from a French train car. Blanton also relayed his absurd, circuitous journey home from France:

> To make a long story short [the YMCA] sent seven of us "Colored men" to St. Marlo the place where the white secretaries were sent for clearing for home. We got there, the white men objected to living in the same hotel with us and they were moved away. We were then sent back to Paris enroute to Marsailles [*sic*] where we had sailings for America on July 8th, when we got to Paris we were told that our sailings had been cancelled and we would have to remain in France until later. We were then held in Paris until the early August . . . simply because a few white fellows objected to being sent home with "Negro Secretaries" on the same ship. We would not have cared a rap by that time as we wanted to get home but to be in France working for a "So-Called" Y.M.C.A., and to be cuffed about as we were, then to finally have to get our tickets third class when we could have gotten second class easily and first class without any trouble was pretty bad. Mr. Bryan of South Carolina was the secretary in charge of the sailings at Bordeaux and he told the French officials that third class was just what he wanted for the "Niggers."[67]

Sol Butler traveled home from France with his teammates at the end of July, aboard the steamship *Imperator*. In addition to the athletes and thousands of soldiers, the 5,062 passengers included 50 prisoners, 78 soldiers' wives, 15 soldiers' children, and 384 welfare workers, presumably including many white YMCA secretaries.[68] The combination of Butler's star status and his being the only Black athlete on an otherwise all-white team buffeted him somewhat from the everyday, pervasive expressions of white supremacy. He did not need to look far, however, to witness second-class treatment of most African Americans, like Blanton and the seven other Black secretaries who had to wait.

The team arrived in Hoboken, New Jersey, on the morning of Sunday, August 10. After eating lunch at the Hotel Astor, the athletes purchased their train tickets home, enjoyed a sightseeing bus tour, and returned to the hotel for dinner.[69] By Thursday morning Butler had reached Dubuque. On Tuesday, August 19, he arrived in Hutchinson.[70] While Butler was still sailing home from France, a Missouri newspaper printed a one-liner: "When Sol Butler, negro sprinter, won the 100-yard dash in the A.E.F. track meet, did the spectators call it a race riot?"[71] Just three days earlier, a weeklong riot on Chicago's South Side had finally ended, leaving thirty-eight people dead, hundreds more injured, and at least a thousand African American homes destroyed in fires set by white rioters. Racial tensions had been building in the city, especially in South Side neighborhoods, where increasing numbers of Black migrants fleeing the Jim Crow South were met with rising resistance, racism, and violence from white Chicagoans, including, in the two years leading up to the riot, the bombings of Black homes and attacks on Black Chicagoans by white mobs.[72]

The riot began on July 27, set in motion by the drowning death of a Black teenager who had been stoned by a white man for crossing into "white" waters on a Lake Michigan beach. Historian Thomas Guglielmo explains: "The riot divided the entire city unmistakably between 'whites' and Negroes' . . . When it came to attacking African Americans, former enemies—Poles, Irish, Swedes, Jews, Italians, and others—quickly found common cause."[73] As native-born Americans brought racism to Europe, they also taught the masses of European immigrants at home to claim whiteness by rejecting and reviling Blackness and accessing privileges, like affordable home ownership, which were kept out of African Americans' reach. The tens of thousands of Black migrants who moved to Chicago during the war and hundreds of thousands more who arrived in subsequent waves of the Great Migration would feel the sting of this process of ghettoization.[74]

The Chicago riot was not an isolated incident. White-on-Black violence rose dramatically in the wake of the war when African American servicemen came home expecting and demanding rights and opportunities previously denied them. Racial terrorism swelled in response, with whites killing hundreds of African Americans across the country during what later became known as the "Red Summer." Race riots erupted and devastated Black communities in dozens of cities.[75] The worst bloodshed occurred near the Mississippi River in Phillips County, Arkansas, at the beginning of October, where Black sharecroppers had been meeting in the hopes of securing higher wages from white landowners. In what became known as the "Elaine Massacre," armed whites, perhaps including the national guard troops called in by the governor, killed with impunity up to several hundred African Americans and arrested hundreds more. Black migrants, war-tested soldiers, and poor, yet determined Southern farm laborers embraced a spirit of collective action, which weaponized white supremacy spared no energy to squelch.[76] Through this unwaveringly hostile terrain, the distance Butler traveled and racial trip wires he avoided in crisscrossing the color line to achieve global celebrity was dazzling, but it was also enough to make him and his loved ones shudder.

The Services of Sol

Butler returned to Dubuque in the fall of 1919 to attend seminary. While school officials did not, as far as the record shows, directly denounce the period's rampant white-on-Black racial violence, Dubuque president Cornelius Steffens wrote on the "Unity in Diversity" in the first month of classes, and soon after, the *Dubuque Evangelist* printed a piece by Rev. John Jowett that characterized rising intolerance as un-Christian: "We are gazing upon widening gulfs of hatred and suspicion. Races are drawing apart. We are thinking more of many bloods than of one blood."[77] The Presbyterian Church launched a multiyear denominational initiative—to establish "a true Christian brotherhood" and eliminate "interracial enmities"—called the New Era Movement.[78] The university's vice president, John H. Burma, in an article directed at young people, under the topic heading "The Christian Athlete and His Training," wrote: "Sol Butler who won international honors for our our [*sic*] school across the sea, did not win them because he was born different from other men, not at all; he won them largely because he sacrificed more and trained harder than other men. Few people can realize what these victories cost him in hard work and self denial."[79] Burma's assessment of Butler echoed an editorial from the *Chicago Herald and Examiner* predicting that the United States would be the "overwhelming winner" in the Inter-Allied Games "largely due to the scientific zeal with which American athletes practice . . . Where, except in America, could you find a jumper like Sol Butler (a negro, by the way), who could boast of having kept an exact record of over 2,000 practice jumps?"[80]

These acknowledgments of hard work and training were a departure from how the media usually covered Butler's success and pointed to a dual source of his mobility. He combined an exceptional work ethic (inculcated by his parents and informed by cultural leaders like W. T. Vernon and Booker T.

Washington) with record keeping and quantification, practices that characterized the ethos of the modern age of sports. This led to improved results on the fields of play and expanded his reach of influence by winning over cultural gatekeepers, such as relatively antiracist college administrators and journalists, who admired his approach.

A full-page article in the Dubuque yearbook related Butler's recent accomplishments and predicted success at the 1920 Belgian Olympics. An accompanying photograph roughly mirrored the large one printed in the September issue of the NAACP's *Crisis* magazine, in which Butler appears looking off into the distance in his sleeveless "US" shirt, shorts, and cleats at Pershing Stadium. The yearbook photograph shows him in the same outfit, standing on the wood plank sidewalk in front of McCormick Gymnasium with Peters Commons in the distance. With the sun dipping behind the camera in the southwestern sky, Butler casts a long shadow across the snow-swept grass on the campus quadrangle. He gazes sunward to his right, wearing a faint, relaxed smile. The low, raking sun's rays create a strong contrast between light and dark, highlighting his muscular physique. Most notably, he is positioned with the smokestack from the heating plant appearing on his immediate left, smoke pouring out at his eye level.[81]

The phallic imagery might evoke virile manhood, but for some the billowing smokestack may have instead conjured a nickname from the star athlete's high school years: "Smoke" Butler. Regardless of the photographer's intention, this possible reading of the image squares with the yearbook's notable increase in derogatory references to Black people: "Football practice after dark, Pop' asks the coach to hang a lantern on Sol," read one joke.[82] A poem titled "African Championship" relayed in six couplets the story of a violent dice game that ended with "a negro [getting] ten days in the jail."[83] While these items were meant to be funny, their casual racism served as a reminder that for all of its institutional celebration of diversity, Dubuque was hardly immune to the rising tide of white supremacy sweeping the rest of the country.

No longer eligible to play college sports, Butler served as an assistant football coach and lived a few blocks east of campus.[84] A week after the college football season ended, he teamed up with his friends and former teammates Johnny Armstrong and Vera Lowe to play a game for Dubuque's American Legion football team on Thanksgiving Day. The team's head coach was Ira Davenport, the earliest Olympian with Dubuque ties; in the 1912 Olympics, Davenport had earned a bronze medal in the 800-meter race. Now, in 1919, pregame newspaper attention across the state helped turn out a crowd of more than a thousand fans, who wagered more than three thousand dollars in advance of game day. With an inch of snow on the ground and the temperature hovering around ten degrees, the field conditions were brutal, as was the outcome for visiting rivals the Moline (Illinois) Indians, who had another star Black player,

Butler in Inter-Allied Games uniform on Dubuque German College campus (1919). (*The Key* [1921], p. 116, University of Dubuque Archives)

Hart Johnson, on the field, perhaps making this the first time an athletic event in Dubuque included more than one Black player.[85]

The *Telegraph Herald* included the fullest account of the 46–0 rout: "Sol Butler twinkled his talented feet repeatedly for long gains . . . A couple of times he darted through the entire opposition before being stopped, using a pivot whirl which sent tacklers reeling." In the first quarter, Butler ran 30 yards on a punt return, "wriggling in and out with the nimbleness of a jackrabbit." On a kickoff to start the second quarter, Butler brought down the Moline kick returner on the 15-yard line "with a spectacular tackle." During the third quarter, he gained 25 yards on a run from scrimmage, returned a kick 30 yards, and scored two touchdowns on short runs up the middle.[86]

Butler kept busy through the fall semester. He earned middling grades in his courses: Hebrew Grammar, Teachers' Use of Bible, Homiletics, Homilitical Exercisis [*sic*], and Encyclopedia.[87] He gave public talks in Dubuque and Hutchinson and joined an all-Black professional basketball team, the Forty Club,[88] which was sponsored by "Chicago's most exclusive social club" of the same name, "composed of aggressive business men [*sic*]" and "young men of social and business prominence."[89] His basketball skills had improved during his college years, and he could hold his own against the best in the region. Brother Ben was back on the scene acting as Sol's manager; he attended a conference with officials of the Davenport Athletic Club to offer "the services of Sol" to their football team the next year, after the Olympics.[90] "Benjamin made no bones over the fact that Sol would sign with the highest bidding club but that he preferred a tri-city team to any other and picked Davenport as the most likely." Sol Butler was capitalizing on his growing celebrity and moving increasingly into the professional arena, but his primary focus was a 1920 Olympic run.[91] He asked to be excused from classes at the beginning of spring semester, which the seminary faculty granted "on condition of his doing satisfactory work."[92]

Butler and 1912 Olympian Howard Drew were both invited to compete in a Fifteenth Infantry meet of Black athletes at the Second Regiment Armory in New York. A Kentucky newspaper billed the Iowa pair as the "premier colored runners of the country" and anticipated an audience of many thousands.[93] Financial or academic concerns prevented Butler from attending, but he and Drew both served as "starters" at an indoor meet in Kansas City. Held in Convention Hall, the meet featured track and field events for African American college, high school, and even grade school athletes from Kansas and Missouri. Large advertisements began to appear in newspapers more than a month in advance.[94] In the days leading up to the Kansas City meet, Butler visited his mother in Hutchinson, where "a number of the young colored people of the city gave him a surprise party."[95] The *Hutchinson News* identified him as a "hero of the colored youth" and announced that he was to be "guest of honor at a ball" in Wichita.[96] He and Drew did not compete against each other at the Kansas City event, the Interstate Athletic Association's inaugural meet, but ran in separate races as "a special attraction."[97] Drew defeated his Drake teammate Leo Patterson in the 50-yard and 220-yard dashes, while Butler got a bad start and "lost by inches" to a high school sprinter from Lawrence in the 50-yard dash.[98] Around sixty-five young Black athletes participated in front of about fifteen hundred spectators.

The two high-profile role models, Butler and Drew, understood that their route to sport success through predominantly white spaces (notably high school and college) was not available to most Black youth, especially during this period of rising intolerance and fear over European immigration and African American migration. Their new athletic association, which lasted at least three more years, provided the structured opportunity for competition that their white counterparts already enjoyed in these increasingly segregated states. Lending celebrity capital to efforts aimed to increase others' freedom of movement, their participation represented the type of cultural leadership that Butler would engage in over the coming decades. His athletic success enabled his transition into becoming a social entrepreneur.

Two months passed before Butler competed again, at the late-June tryouts for the Olympic team at the Central Amateur Athletic Union meet in Chicago, where he was among three African American Iowans, including Drew and University of Iowa football star Duke Slater, hoping to advance to final tryouts at Harvard Stadium the next month. As numerous pundits predicted, he easily earned his trip to Cambridge, leaping nearly 24 feet, more than 2 feet farther than the next competitor. In the 100-yard dash, Howard Drew finished second, but Butler did not advance, despite winning his trial heat. All of his hopes of achieving Olympic glory in Antwerp, Belgium, rested on the broad jump.[99]

The Dubuque Chamber of Commerce helped fund Butler's trip to the Olympic trials, but when Butler left Dubuque at the end of his first year in seminary and after four and a half years of residency, he would never again live in the town whose name he had spread around the world. Chicago, New York, and Los Angeles became his new homes. No longer incessantly navigating predominantly white spaces, he now made his way through urban areas that had been profoundly transformed by Black migration amid a swelling tide of white supremacy. Resisting segregation and mitigating its effects increasingly required working strategically within a separate racial sphere, on all-Black teams and for African American audiences. Even in coming decades, once his physical abilities faded, Butler remained devoted to sports. In this realm—as athlete, journalist, editor, organizer, coach, trainer, and mentor—his personal ambitions served collective ends. He soon realized that creating opportunities for himself and others in (at times) innovative ways required shedding his status as an amateur.

PART III

Professional

Summer 1920–1935

7

The Olympic Urge

Summer 1920–Winter 1922

From "Baltimore Buzz" by Noble Sissle and Eubie Blake, in *Shuffle Along* (1921)

Black dentist Willis Cummings, nearly seventy and determined to make known his youthful contribution in varsity cross-country, surprised authorities at his alma mater with his scrapbook. His brittling assemblage of clippings, telegrams, letters, and ephemera revealed how, decades earlier as a student at the University of Pennsylvania, he flourished academically and athletically. Thanks to his visit, future generations would know that in 1918 he served as the first Black captain of what became the Ivy League Conference, winning multiple prominent meets during his final two years on the varsity squad while finishing in the top 3 percent of his graduate class in dentistry. Cummings and Sol Butler participated in two of the same Penn Relays and a few years later competed together in a consequential New York meet.[1]

The University of Pennsylvania had actively tried to forget Cummings. During his year as captain, the athletic department did not photograph the team—as was done for cross-country in the years before and after and for every other varsity team that year—since this would have visually placed a Black man in the central position. The US Naval Academy's team refused to compete against Pennsylvania in a dual meet until the latter team agreed to bench him. After Cummings graduated, school authorities eliminated nearly all traces of his participation in athletics.[2]

At a football rally in 1922, the final speaker, a white university chaplain, "persisted in using the word 'nigger'" to entertain the mass throng. The indignant Black alumnus "showed rare grit and race pride" in censuring him:

> Standing in the midst of 2,000 white students, [Cummings] yelled at the top of his voice, "I object to such language. There are other words you can use instead of that." Some of the students standing near by were furious. It look[ed] for a time they would attack the courageous little dentist. Someone yelled, "who are you anyway?" Dr. Cummings . . . showed them his club pin. "That's who I am," he said, "while I was in school I ran my legs off for Penn and I don't intend to allow anyone out here to insult me or my race."[3]

Like the trophies and good press that protected Sol Butler from white antipathy, if not physical harm, Cummings's club pin placated the potential mob. "We hate to imagine," shuddered an African American journalist, "what would have happened if Dr. Cummings did not have the presence of mind to show his Varsity pin."

Butler and all would-be Black sport entrepreneurs sought their own version of a magical pin—tangible evidence of worth and belonging—to shield them from the ever-present danger of white supremacy. The problem for Sol, now removed from the relative safety of his alma mater in pursuit of new goals, was that the available avenues to proving his worth and right to operate in a socially integrated world kept narrowing.

In the weeks leading up to his departure for Belgium, Butler had reason to imagine millions of Americans soon celebrating news of his international victories, which would expose the lie of white supremacy as they brought glory to the nation. Would he supplant Jack Johnson in the racially charged public imagination? Would his athletic success open doors in sports, business, and beyond for other African Americans to enter? No point in his life appeared so primed for sports greatness and racial uplift nor as rife with potentially great disappointment.

If Pushed

Nearly thirty thousand spectators entered Harvard Stadium on July 17, 1920, to watch the US Olympic track and field trials. Three weeks earlier, facing no serious competition, Butler had easily earned a place at the trials after finishing first in the broad jump on the University of Chicago field.[4] The 1920 games in Belgium were the sixth of the modern Olympics and the first since 1912; Germany and other Central Powers nations were not invited to participate.

When Sol Butler—the celebrated twenty-five-year-old Black athlete who was poised to compete in his first Olympic games—arrived at Harvard Stadium early to warm up, he was stopped by an Irish American policeman. "I guess you do not know who I am?" Butler said. "No," the policeman said, "and I do not care who you are." "Well," Butler replied, "you may not know me now, but you will know me before I leave."[5]

The twenty-five-cent souvenir program listed fifteen broad jump competitors, including Robert LeGendre and Edward Orval "Ned" Gourdin.[6] LeGendre had won the pentathlon at the Inter-Allied Games and would later set a world record in the broad jump. Gourdin, one of the seven Black athletes at the Olympic trials, would later become the first person in a sanctioned event to jump more than 25 feet. But on that day at Harvard Stadium, Sol Butler was the broad jump man of the hour when he jumped 24' 8", an American record, securing his place on the Olympic team.[7] Butler and middle-distance runner R. Earl Johnson would be the only Black track and field athletes, and two of only five total Black athletes, on the 1920 US Olympic team.

The American Olympic Committee (AOC), working closely with the Amateur Athletic Union, oversaw US involvement in the games.[8] Formed in 1888 in New York, the AAU sought to organize and maintain standards over amateur sports that included track and field, basketball, and boxing. The volunteer organization "exploited the emerging infrastructure and the popularity of the Olympic Games to solidify its power and control of track," writes scholar Joseph Turrini, and the organization billed the Olympic track and field trials as its national championship.[9] Before the souvenir program for the trials listed the names of any athletes, it devoted more than a full page to naming the dozens of AAU officials and members who headed committees, judged, timed, inspected, and scored, including the current president and former president serving on the two planning committees.[10] For more than a decade, these rich and powerful white men had organized, financed, and controlled Olympic tryouts and American track athletes.

The small group of Black athletes who were able to break into the almost exclusively white world of elite amateur athletics and had been excluded from white-run athletic associations and clubs would have been only more vulnerable to the control exerted by AAU officials. According to the *Boston Globe*, after Butler had set the American record and easily qualified for the Olympic team at the Harvard Stadium trials, "the Olympic committeemen [demanded] that he make one try for the world's record."[11] He couldn't refuse, and the one extra jump proved to be fateful: Butler pulled a tendon, an injury that would cast a long shadow over his first and last Olympics.[12]

Two dangerous, racist tropes with antebellum origins existed: Black people were inherently lazy and needed prodding into action, and Black people felt less pain than white people. In the early decades of the twentieth century, the immense success of Black athletes began to transform these stereotypes into a new, seemingly positive notion of Black people, especially men, as possessing extraordinary, almost superhuman physical gifts. Scholar Joseph Cooper argues that "it is a long-standing and deadly stereotype in American society that views black males as subhuman and superhuman all at once."[13] Newspaper illustrator Robert Ripley, who went on to fame with his syndicated column, *Believe It or Not*, traveled to Antwerp with the US Olympic team and covered the athletes and games through a series of newspaper cartoons.[14] In his coverage of Butler, Ripley vividly illustrated the sub/superhuman beliefs about Black men that likely motivated AAU officials to strong-arm Butler into attempting his ill-fated extra jump at Harvard Stadium.[15]

In the roughly five-hundred-word article printed directly below the cartoon, Ripley described Butler as "a 'monkey' athlete—the type that makes good in a pinch," whose best jumps were made in response to "the stimulus of the moment" and enabled by the "suppleness and spring that lie in the muscles and sinews which ripple and writhe like live things under the ebony sheath that cloaks his stalwart frame." Ripley predicted that Butler's best leaps, including "that untouched 25-foot target," would come "under the lash of the Olympic urge." The cartoonist drew a picture of Butler bowing before the deposed King Nicholas, who reaches to place his hand on Butler's head, a gesture presumably meant to evoke the "patting" that many newspapers reported on during the Inter-Allied Games. Another vignette in the cartoon shows General Pershing looming over a minstrelized head of Butler, who gazes up with exaggerated lips in an open-mouthed smile, a far cry from the dignified encounter between the two men caught on film at the Inter-Allied Games. "We doubt if even the rosiest pickanniny dreams of Sol Butler ever conjured visions of appearing before royalty and having kings crown his kinky head with laurel wreaths," the accompanying text reads.[16]

Ripley's depictions of Butler illustrate what American studies scholar Davarian Baldwin calls the "paradox of playfulness," where Black failure in sport was connected to an "inherent biological or cultural inferiority," but the same racial "science" was used to explain Black athletic success as "due to an innate mental deficiency, the ancestral legacy of a 'primitive' African past, and/or measurable anatomical differences in black bodies."[17] In Ripley's telling, Butler's fame rested on a new, sports-related form of enslavement, where the Olympic "lash" was required to harness the potential of his rippling and writhing muscles and sinews.

After the trials at Harvard Stadium, Butler spent the weeks before the Olympics suffering the consequences of these racist assumptions about Black athletes. According to R. Earl Johnson, team trainer Jake Weber "spent the best part of twenty-one days, from the date of the injury until the games, trying to get Butler in shape."[18] Fearful that he would be cut from the team,

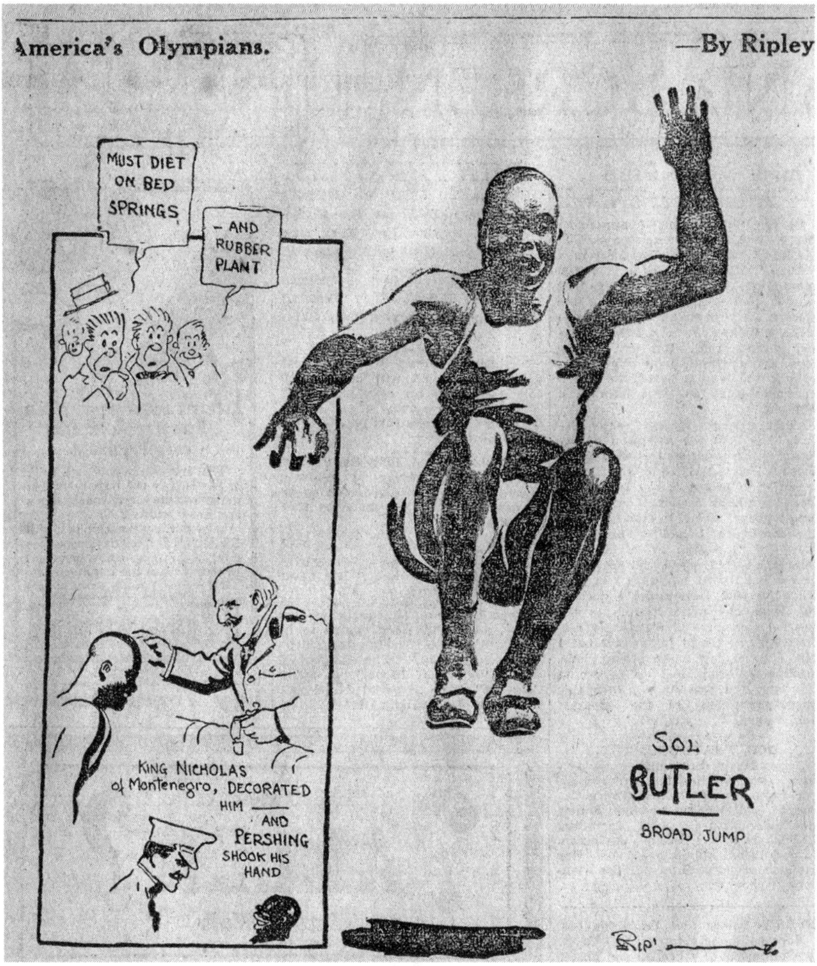

Robert Ripley, "America's Olympian," *Akron Evening Times*, August 13, 1920, p. 15. (Courtesy of Ohio History Connection)

Butler kept his injury a secret from everyone except Weber. The team's head coach, John Francis "Jack" Moakley, who spoke about Butler's victory in the broad jump as all but guaranteed, was clearly in the dark. Citing his triumph at Harvard Stadium, Moakley predicted that his star jumper would "bring a world's record home from Antwerp."[19]

Butler attended the celebratory "farewell meeting" held at the Manhattan Opera House in New York on July 26. Two military bands accompanied the athletes as they paraded from the shore on East Thirty-Sixth Street to the performance hall, where the athletes and audience of formally attired "friends, wives, clubmates, and well-wishers" listened to telegrams of encouragement from thirteen governors, a US senator, Assistant Secretary of State Franklin Delano Roosevelt, and New York mayor John Francis Hylan.[20] A photograph of the event shows the team on stage wearing suits and ties, with many athletes holding US flags.[21] From the opera house, the team paraded to the dock on West Thirty-Fourth Street surrounded by "thousands who cheered the athletes on their way, while hundreds of others looked down from office windows."[22] After a short ferry ride to Hoboken, the team boarded the *Princess Matoika*, which took them out to sea amid "a deafening chorus of river craft." Fifty-seven years after Ben Butler Sr. escaped enslavement in Alabama, and twenty-eight years after Ben and Mary Butler moved their growing family from Memphis to Oklahoma Territory, their youngest son embarked on his second voyage to Europe.

When Sol returned for good to the States, he entered a new phase of life: No longer a student garnering institutional support, he now had to earn a living in pursuit of his athletic goals. He had spent a decade under the spotlight as a sports star in small Midwest cities, where he deftly navigated white spaces—endearing himself with diverse audiences—by dazzling on the playing fields and in the social realm, with a charisma leavened by modesty, integrity, and playfulness. From this point on he would live in the largest US cities and within vibrant Black communities, buzzing from dramatic migrant growth, ripe with incalculable human potential, yet staggering under white supremacy, which kept living spaces cramped, rents high, and good jobs desperately scarce. Butler began figuring out how to navigate these new Black spaces to his benefit and in service to racial uplift. Drawing upon his celebrity capital and testing the limits of his multidimensional mobility, he became a sports entrepreneur. In the process, he lost patience with the unrealistic demands imposed by the white institutional guardians of track and field; his desire to control his own sports fate required sacrificing his unsated amateur ambitions. Whatever pain and frustration he felt in giving up on world record plans or winning Olympic gold in the broad jump—the event that had brought him his greatest glory—was compounded by the tragedy of what happened to him in Belgium.

Homeric Effort

On the *Princess Matoika*, an aging military vessel described as "a scarcely seaworthy tub,"[23] the majority of athletes roomed below deck, which Charley Paddock recalled as a "stifling hole, thick with the reeking past, powerful proof of the ship's recent cargo": corpses returning home from the war.[24] An AOC report described the trip as "hot and uncomfortable," in part because of the southerly route the ship took in order to avoid ice floes and because of regular rain that kept hatches and portholes closed.[25] Rats accompanied the athletes during mealtime, and one the size of a puppy reportedly bit hammer thrower Patrick "Paddy" Ryan on the hand.[26] In response to complaints, the AOC assigned thirty-four athletes, those who "made the best showing at the tryouts in the various events," to the sick bay, where they had more room and better accommodations.[27] It is unclear whether Butler, who arguably made the best showing of any athlete at the trials, got to enjoy these superior quarters or remained in the "stifling hole" for the duration of the trip.[28] In addition to the abysmal conditions on board, Butler also had to contend with seasickness. "Probably one of the sickest men for the first few days was Sol Butler. He did not care whether the boat went down or floated," wrote John Hallahan for the *Boston Globe* in an article subtitled "Water Had No Charm for Butler."[29]

Once the team arrived on dry land, conditions weren't much better. One athlete reported that the schoolhouse where the American athletes were housed in Antwerp "stunk to the skies."[30] Human waste overtaxed the plumbing; cots had no mattresses; showers consisted of a cold trickle; and breakfast was one roll, coffee, and a single sardine. But what prompted the only violent outburst at the schoolhouse, which sprinter Henry Farrell described in a widely circulated story as the "insurrection," had nothing to do with the "abominable" conditions at the schoolhouse. Farrell recalled:

> There was a terrible roar. Paddy Ryan, the hammer-thrower, grabbed his hammer and dragged it through the streets looking for Fred Rubien, secretary of the committee, when he found that he was bunked next to Sol Butler, the big Negro broad jumper. "I'll smack that dootch Rubien in the face with this hammer if I have to throw it into Holland," Ryan roared, as he tore through the strets [*sic*], driving even the gendarmes to cover in fright.[31]

The AOC responded by moving Ryan and two of his fellow throwers into superior accommodations at a hotel. In his record of the trip, which was published in the *Baltimore Afro-American*, R. Earl Johnson, who shared a room in the schoolhouse with Butler and eight white men, gave a rosy impression of Antwerp and made no mention of Ryan's racist outburst: "We are all treated well . . . [We'd] never know we are colored because the fellows take us along with them every place they go. Always we are comrades . . . The food is good . . . The [Belgians] try in every way possible to make things pleasant for us." Of Butler, Johnson claimed, "He is the most popular fellow on the trip. He is known by almost everybody. His smile and manner attracts all these people, some of whom have never seen a colored man."[32]

In Antwerp, Butler had a little over a week to prepare for the biggest athletic opportunity of his life. Only three weeks had passed since his injury at the Olympic trials, which was still a secret. Hurdler Walker Smith remembered the practice track as "very rough," and cold, rainy weather increased the risk of injury.[33] Butler's first warm-up jumps "drew a crowd of interested athletes" in the practice area, and he "showed the best performance of the day," according to a reporter for the *New York Herald*.[34] "On his third trial he cleared the splendid distance of 24 feet 1/4 inch," a jump that fell nearly 8 inches short of his record-setting leap at the trials but would have still won him the gold in Belgium had he repeated it in the finals.[35]

As it turned out, Butler would not make it to the finals. "The trials were held at 9 o'clock in the morning," R. Earl Johnson wrote.[36] "The mornings there [in Antwerp] are very cool. I don't think Butler had warmed up enough before he made his initial effort," Johnson speculated. Butler appeared to get a solid start: "His run was short and snappy. With little effort he hit the board and sailed thru the air." But his landing was a different story. "The beefy Dubuque College star sank deep in the sand as he landed and his left leg turned under him. He lay on the ground writhing in pain," the *New York Tribune* reported.[37] "His teammates rushed forward and carried him to the dressing room, where rubbers worked desperately over the injured leg . . . Butler begged pitifully to be given another chance." After being bandaged in the dressing room and returning to the trials, Butler "passed up all his jumps until the last one when he gamely tried to qualify," Johnson wrote.[38] "His best effort was a bunny hop of not more than 10 ft," after which, the *Herald* reported, "the American champion collapsed and retired crying."[39] Journalist Alvin Moses later described this futile, post-injury jump as "one of the most homeric efforts on record."[40]

A photographer from a Belgian agency captured some of the agony on film.[41] In one photograph, Butler writhes on his back, clutching his quadricep muscle just below the back of the knee. Another photograph taken from the track depicts a wind-still, sparsely populated stadium with the jumping pit in the background. Two white teammates in derbies, suits, and ties carry Butler off the track. The raking morning light emphasizes the tension on his face, the furrowing of his brow above his downcast eyes. "The whole team was pulling for Butler to win," wrote Johnson, "and when they learned he was injured you can bet there was gloom in the camp."[42] Johnson himself failed to qualify for the 10,000-meter finals. He dropped out of the third heat after about 6,000 meters, "having been seized with cramps in the stomach."[43] He would earn a silver and a bronze medal at the 1924 Olympics in Paris. Charley Paddock won gold in the 100-meter race and the 4 × 100-meter relay and silver in the 200-meter run, and Duke Kahanamoku won two gold medals, in the 100-meter freestyle and 4 × 200-meter freestyle relay.

America gave a warm welcome to returning Olympic athletes, but for the medal-less Butler, this homecoming was bittersweet. On October 2 he joined more than a hundred other athletes parading down Fifth Avenue, where he, Duke Kahanamoku, weight thrower Matt McGrath, and female swimmer Ethelda Bleibtrey (who won three gold medals) "were repeatedly cheered."[44]

Butler being carried from the Olympic broad jump pit after reinjuring his leg (1920). (Agence de presse Meurisse, Gallica Digital Library, ID btv1b9034300d)

That evening the Olympic team attended a banquet in their honor at the Waldorf-Astoria Hotel, where Mayor Hylan, like the media, presented the athletes as defenders of democracy who "have shown how a citizen should live, and love, revere and respect his native land."[45] The mayor shook Butler's hand twice after learning that he had attended seminary.

Butler and R. Earl Johnson soon left New York for Chicago, where Butler planned to rest for a few weeks before heading west to Dubuque as "a welcome visitor."[46] When he finally arrived home to see his family in Hutchinson, the *Iowa Bystander* had just announced his departure from seminary in Dubuque and his wish to "enter the Pennsylvania law school," which never came to fruition.[47] When asked about his injury and disappointing finish in Belgium, Butler said, "I don't like to talk about it . . . It nearly broke my heart when that leg got hurt. I wasn't able to walk for several days, and was laid up for two or three weeks."[48]

Butler still harbored hopes of breaking the broad jump world record and participating in the next Olympics, which meant maintaining his amateur status with the AAU, despite his frustrations with the organization. He therefore avoided the fledgling American Professional Football Association, which had just held its inaugural game between two Ohio teams, the Akron Pros and the Canton Bulldogs. But, out of school for the first time in his adult life, he would need to support himself while he pursued his athletic goals. Butler knew he could not thrive professionally in Hutchinson, Dubuque, or any other small, predominantly white community, where people of color had virtually no access to skilled and highly sought-after jobs. He soon left Kansas for Chicago, prepared to translate his fame and reputation into professional stability and continued amateur glory.[49]

Athletic Solidarity

Butler had spent plenty of time training and competing in Chicago and neighboring Evanston, but when he moved to the Midwestern metropolis in the fall of 1920, it was a momentous step in the young athlete's life. With his first solo move, his first time living in a major urban center, and his first time navigating the job market, Butler arrived in Chicago at an auspicious moment. The Great Migration and influx of African Americans into the city's segregated racial geography created a fertile market for leisure and entertainment. (In contrast, due to a dearth of new construction and discriminatory housing practices that limited most Black residents to a small area, this influx caused a "home famine" that would have increased his challenge in finding residence.)[50] Many of these mostly Southern Black migrants made their homes in and around a South Side district that stretched between Twenty-Second and Fifty-Fifth streets along State Street and east toward Lake Michigan and contained the YMCA branch, newspaper office, armory, church, and other institutions that had most shaped Butler's experience.

The media's creation of sport celebrities, combined with growing prosperity and a burgeoning consumer culture, created unprecedented opportunities for top athletes to make a living on playing fields and courts. "With the inception of pro basketball in Chicago in the 1920s," along with pay-for-play football and baseball, "sport provided year-round opportunities for profit," writes sports historian Gerald Gems.[51] But the explosion of opportunities in the athletic arena presented a potential minefield for athletes like Butler, who were dedicated to maintaining their amateur status, and the expansion of professional sports sparked anxiety among Black fans and boosters whose churches, media, and social clubs supported amateur teams.

While professional baseball "has been so closely allied to the saloon and underground dives," wrote *New York Amsterdam News* sportswriter Romeo Dougherty, amateur basketball "is fostered by religious and other institutions working for the uplift of our people."[52] But as professional sports expanded and amateur teams faced increased competition when it came to attracting and retaining the top talent, Black basketball organizers and promoters from the East to the Midwest saw professionalism creeping into the amateur ranks. In fact, some Black sports entrepreneurs saw the commercial elements of the game as inevitable. Basketball pioneer Will Madden wrote that when clubs started generating income from the game, "the power of the dollar" became too great to resist "because the very success of the thing creates the idea of commercialism, which in turn is bound to create professionalism."[53] During the 1920–1921 basketball season, large Black amateur clubs in New York began subsidizing player expenses. The storied St. Christopher Club spoke out against this perceived threat to amateurism, worked with two other Black teams on reforms to prevent professionalism, and removed most of their star players from the team roster, including Butler's friend Paul Robeson. The sporting editor at the *Chicago Defender* wrote, "All fair minded lovers of the game are anxious to see professionalism go now, once and forever more—amen."[54]

To help him navigate the increasingly complicated sporting world in his new city, Butler consulted with Robert Abbott, founder and publisher of the *Chicago Defender*, whose editorial leadership helped propel the Great Migration in general and to Chicago in particular. Abbott encouraged Butler to stick with the Forty Club, the talent-laden, all-Black amateur basketball team he had joined the previous season.[55] After a lifetime of competing on white teams, where he was one of two, or even the only, Black athlete, Butler would be spending all of his sporting hours surrounded by Black teammates. His interracial basketball experience in Dubuque was unusual. Beginning nearly two decades earlier, and buoyed by the same physical education movement that shaped Butler's dazzling high school athletic experience, the first Black Fives teams gained organizational structure and momentum from the pioneering efforts of Edwin Bancroft Henderson and the formation of the Interscholastic Athletic Association in Washington, DC, and Black athletic clubs in New York. Amateurism thrived in the 1910s under the banner of fair play and good sportsmanship but would be overshadowed during the 1920s by the entrepreneurially oriented and purposefully entertaining professional game.[56] Abbott and Butler spoke about more than just basketball. Butler soon began writing for the *Defender* and later served a short stint as the editor of the newspaper's new children's section, "Defender Junior."[57]

Led by their captain, former Lane Tech High School star Virgil Blueitt, and managed by Dr. Albert Johnson, the Forty Club practiced four nights a week at the armory that served the all-Black Eighth Infantry Regiment of the National Guard. (During World War I it became the 370th Infantry Regiment and fought valliantly with the French.) By the time Butler joined, the team had eight other players, including Bob Anderson, who had previously played for New York's St. Christopher Athletic Club, former all-state player George Duff, and the speedy Creed Hubbard of Ohio's Wilberforce University.[58] Over the coming decades, Butler and Anderson would join forces through athletics in building community and supporting Black youth.

In early December, Butler penned an article for the *Defender* advertising the Forty Club's first game. "The greatest society event of the season will be pulled off Monday evening at the Eighth Regiment Armory, when the well-known Forty Club sends its crack five against the Evanston quintet, supposed to be one of the fastest fives in the state," Butler wrote.[59] "The followers of the [Forty] club will wear purple and white streamers. A special elevated train will bring down the Evanston rooters." Seventeen female "society buds" would serve as ushers, and, true to the cultural practice that had developed alongside Black Fives basketball in Eastern cities, the game was to include a dance. The Charles Elgar Dreamland Jazz Orchestra would keep the players and their fans on their toes and entertained "till 2 a.m." After a narrow 25–23 victory over the Evanston Arrows, the only other Black amateur team in the Chicago area sanctioned by the AAU, the team played "75 per cent better" in the next game at home, defeating "the pride of New York, the famous St. Christopher five," by a score of 36–26 in the Eighth Regiment Armory before a reported crowd of two thousand.[60] Despite St. Christopher's rhetoric and initial strides toward reform, by the time the team headed to Chicago, the New York club had "retreated from its hard line against professionalism and reinstated most of its regulars."[61]

After one more home court victory over a YMCA team from Indianapolis, the Forty Club left Chicago to take on the best Black amateur teams in the East. During the three-week trip, they won ten out of twelve games; their only losses came against the Atlantic City Vandals and the Loendis of Pittsburgh, a team that many sport authorities considered the best in the country.[62]

Though Butler was not the team's best player, nobody approached his name recognition, and the media took note. "Olympic athlete and holder of the broad jump record and well known in this city," read an article in the *Chicago Defender* and the *New York Age*,[63] while another identified him as "a star of the Forty Club."[64] When the team went to Pittsburgh to play the formidable Loendi Big Five on March 3, the *Pittsburgh Press* noted that the Forty Club was "headed by that all-around and seemingly invincible athlete, Sol Butler."[65]

Pittsburgh boasted a vibrant amateur basketball scene, with men's and women's leagues for different age groups and weight classes. The *Pittsburgh Dispatch* devoted entire pages to covering amateur basketball.[66] For the Forty Club–Loendi game, local organizers expected an overflow crowd and added two hundred more seats to the arena. Attendees included officials from the Allegheny Mountain Association (AMA), the regional body of the AAU. The AMA was helmed by President William Samuel Haddock, who "labored earnestly . . . to keep amateur athletics free from the taint of commercialism";[67]

he also served for four years as the strike-breaking sheriff of Allegheny County, who ushered in "a complete suppression of civil liberties and a reign of terror."[68] During the 1919–1920 basketball season, the AMA/AAU had stripped Loendi of its amateur status after the club played a white team that employed professional players.

That season, Loendi was back in the running for the national amateur Black basketball championship, but the Forty Club landed on the AAU's radar when AMA officials, perhaps including Haddock himself, learned that Butler and Blueitt were being paid, at least for the Loendi game, which prompted an investigation and led to a sixty-day suspension of Butler's amateur status.[69] This kept him out of spring track and field events, the most painful result for someone aiming to enter the next Olympics. Apparently, Butler assumed that the aura of amateurism around basketball would shelter him from the scrutiny he would face if playing football or baseball, which post-college bore the stigma of professionalism. (Despite brother Ben's pecuniary inquiries in Davenport just before the Olympic Games, in the coming football season, the only team he would play for was an explicitly amateur all-Black squad coached by Fritz Pollard.)[70]

The suspension also ended Butler's basketball season as a player, but it did not stop him from extending his season as the organizer and coach of one of the most successful Black women's basketball teams of the decade, Chicago's Roamer Girls. The team developed out of the Sunday school at Grace Presbyterian Church, the congregation that supported the Forty Club.[71] The Roamers played the Cosmopolitans of the Olivet AME Sunday school on March 19 in "the first big game staged by the girls," which "equaled any played in the armory in the past." (The first game between all-Black women's basketball teams took place a decade earlier in New York.)[72] With the star play of Isadore "Izzy" Channels, the Presbyterians beat the Methodists 26–22. Historian Susan Cahn cites Butler's coaching of the Roamer Girls as an example of Black men and women forging "an athletic solidarity in the overall interest of advancing the race."[73] Leading the young church women in building character through competitive sports shifted focus away from the AAU's censure.

More significantly, the team challenged prevailing gender ideologies, which held that women playing competitive sports were unsightly, unfeminine, and threatened their reproductive capacity. "By the 1920s," notes sports historian Jaime Schultz, "'moderation' became the primary curricular focus as educators attempted to suppress competitive and intercollegiate contests" of all women.[74] Segregation and prejudice added another hurdle for Black women to overcome. Following in the footsteps of teams like the New York Girls, Jersey Girls, Washington Belles, and Pittsburgh's Della Robia Girls and Delaney Rifles, which Butler may have learned about from physical educator James A. Dorsey or his onetime coach Hunter Johnson, the Roamer Girls' leader helped usher in an era of dynamic women's basketball in Chicago.[75] The players would soon be on the front lines in using sports as a tool of desegregation.

Buy a Ticket

Butler maintained a relatively low profile until the opening of the 1921–1922 basketball season. In July he traveled to Boston with three friends: Fritz Pollard, the former Lane Tech and Brown University star athlete, who was then playing for the Akron Pros; Mayo Williams, former Brown athlete, then-current professional football player, and future prodigious music producer; and sportswriter Frank A. "Fay" Young. The four men played doubles tennis on July 23 and then headed to Harvard Stadium to see a track and field meet—Harvard–Yale versus Cambridge–Oxford. Of particular interest was a Harvard broad jumper, African American Edward Gourdin. In May, Gourdin had leaped 24' 6", just 2 inches shy of Butler's record jump.[76] Young recalled the four friends' conversation in Harvard Stadium: "Fritz said that Gourdin would break Sol's record that day, and Mayo joined in with him. Sol and I did not think so, and Fritz said, 'All right, you wait and see.'"[77] Gourdin jumped 25' 3", smashing the world record. "In the language of our forefather, 'We have sure seed,'" Young wrote. A poem by C. Leslie Frazier in the *Afro-American*, "I Wish I Could Have Been There," memorialized Gourdin's historic jump: "Oh, how I'd love to have been there and pictured other clean bronze lads, / who will follow in your footsteps and gladden the hearts of their dads, / because such fellows as Pollard, Sol Butler and clean cut Drew, / went through with colors flying in the same fair way as you."[78] Gourdin's record was situated as a link in a chain of Black male athletic achievement, made possible by the efforts of his predecessors and showing the way to future glory.

Butler was not ready to concede an antecedent place on this chain. Though he hadn't competed in any running broad jump events since leaving Europe a year earlier, he registered for the Central Athletic Association's outdoor track and field championship on August 13 at Stagg Field. His sixty-day AAU suspension had elapsed, and in the days leading up to the meet, he had "been jumping close to the record in his daily tests on Stagg field."[79] He intended to "shatter the world's record,"[80] but a heavy rain fell just before the meet, and he won the broad jump but fell far short of the record.[81]

When the basketball season opened, Butler was back on the court with the Forty Club, now known as the Defender Athletic Club (AC). The new athletic club held its first meeting at the Wabash Avenue YMCA, where it formed committees on rules and regulations. Six years earlier in this "Y" facility, the first one open to Black Chicagoans, Carter G. Woodson established the Association for the Study of Negro Life; five years later he would lead in establishing Negro History Week, a precursor to Black History Month.[82] Dr. Albert Johnson led a discussion that Sol Butler concluded, and the "ladies were represented and are heartily in accord with the organization" since it pledged "its support of the 'women in athletics.'"[83] As the first game against the Evanston Arrows approached, the *Chicago Defender* touted the team that now bore its name: "The general rank and file of our group in Chicago does not realize that within our gates is one of the best and fastest basketball fives in the country."[84]

The *Defender* advertised a game against a visiting team from Cincinnati as an opportunity to support the sixty-three Black soldiers in Houston serving life sentences for the 1917 riot that led to the hasty execution of thirteen of their fellow Black infantrymen: "The game, which is for the benefit of the imprisoned [Twenty-Fourth] infantry soldiers who were given life sentences, should be well attended, as this is only one of the many ways that we can help those who stood up for their rights in Houston, Tex., a few years back. They deserve the help of every able-bodied citizen of our Race. If you can't go, buy a ticket and give it to some one who can."[85] Readers had reason for optimism since US representative Daniel Read Anthony of Kansas had recently exerted pressure on the secretary of war and the House of Representatives to consider clemency for the imprisoned soldiers. Three more years would pass before four soldiers were released, and the final thirty-four would be released or become eligible for parole by 1928.[86] Sports, especially amateur basketball, were woven into African American cultural life in Chicago and other big Northern cities in the 1920s, and athletics were part of a larger awareness of growing racial pride and political possibilities in the wake of profound national change.

Playing for the Defender AC, a team sponsored by and named for the newspaper to which he contributed articles, Butler carried the sanctioned authority of Black Chicago's sports activism. World War I, mass migration, and a dramatic rise in urbanization fueled a growing sense of racial possibilities, purpose, and Black agency, which he symbolized under the emerging cultural rubric of the "New Negro." By the 1920s, the black press played an outsized role in shaping African Americans' political conscience and agendas. Black nationalist Marcus Garvey espoused racial separatism to largely working-class audiences through the Universal Negro Improvement Association newspaper *Negro World*, integrationist W.E.B. Du Bois challenged the color line as editor through the NAACP's magazine *Crisis*, while socialists Chandler Owen and A. Philip Randolph discouraged African American participation in the war and promoted armed defense against white racial violence in the pages of the *Messenger* newspaper.[87]

These New York–based publications competed for the embrace of a national Black readership against other newspapers, magazines, and journals, most notably Robert Abbott's *Chicago Defender*, which highlighted racial injustice and the excitement of urban life epitomized along "the Stroll." This vibrant commercial and business district on Chicago's South Side where Butler operated featured business leaders—including sports entrepreneurs—peddling ideas and cultural products in sports arenas, beauty parlors, barbershops, dance and music halls, churches, and drinking establishments. According to historian Davarian Baldwin, such places were where "black consumer practices . . . converted acts of desire into a political and intellectual life of distinction and defiance against traditional ways of life."[88] Where migrants and other Black Chicagoans strolled, focused their attention, and spent their discretionary income, then, reflected a distinct aspect of the city's New Negro consciousness. Participation on an elite, all-Black basketball team that fans paid to see made Butler part of this "marketplace intellectual life," which shaped and responded to political debates steered by arbiters like Abbott of Black print culture.

While an assertive masculinity characterized the New Negro era, Black women's church and club organizations increased female political power by educating people about the political process and women's newly won right to vote and by fighting for gender and racial justice. At a time when religious and political values often aligned, Butler's connection with the Roamers basketball team, composed of young Presbyterian women who challenged racial and gender taboos, illustrated that by this time women usually worked with men for civil rights; the marketplace of urban entertainment and political engagement brought "race man" Butler and "race women" together in social uplift.[89]

Butler continued to coach the Roamer Girls, who were scheduled to play a white team from the West Side at the end of December. When their opponents failed to show, with an expectant crowd in the stands, the Roamers instead took on the lightweight men's Defender squad. "Led by Polly Rickman the girls overcame their apparent stage fright in the second half and tied the boys to a 6 all count, thereby making it necessary to play an extra two minutes." In the final minute, one of the boys committed a personal foul, and "Polly tossed in a free throw that won the game. This delighted the crowd."[90]

On January 2, the Defender AC played the white DeSoto team of the Knights of Columbus League. The two teams "gave one of the most wonderful displays of basketball ever seen" in front of a cheering throng of three thousand at the Eighth Regiment Armory.[91] The DeSoto team scored within seconds after the opening tip and went on to defeat the locals 26–15. With the help of newsman Romeo Dougherty, the Defender AC lined up another tour, where they were scheduled to "play more games in the city of New York and vicinity than any visiting team has played since the start of basketball," the *Defender* reported.[92] "Mr. Dougherty's great influence and love of good, clean games has caused him to pick the Chicago team as the exponent of everything new in clean sportsmanship in playing the greatest of indoor sports."[93]

"Clean" sportsmanship in basketball evoked the amateur game, yet Butler's experience with the white-led AAU and the vicissitudes of Black urban life revealed the fragility of his amateur status. Despite Butler's eagerness to claim Olympic gold, events suggested that this goal might not harmonize with his transition into sports entrepreneurship, which in packed basketball arenas and along the Stroll bore the impress of marketplace activism. He no longer needed to gain white approval to compete beyond track and field as he had done for all sports while growing up and in college. Even as a sprinter and broad jumper, he would soon demonstrate that opening doors of racial opportunity outshone finishing in first place or breaking records. His dynamic mobility increasingly reflected the qualities of an urban social entrepreneur. Butler was a Chicago New Negro who, following the call of sport opportunity, increasingly looked to the East.

8

Do You Believe in Mixed Games?

Spring 1922–1926

From "Black Bottom Stomp" (1925) by Ferdinand "Jelly Roll" Morton

The Defender Athletic Club Eastern basketball tour was a success. The team netted at least eleven total wins against four losses, including a victory in New York's Manhattan Casino over the Spartan Braves, a Black Fives team that, under the brilliant leadership of Bob Douglas, would soon become the New York Renaissance (also known as the Harlem Rens), one of the all-time great basketball teams. On that day, the Chicagoans more than tripled the Easterners' point total. Sol Butler scored the first basket and kept the opponents' star player, Hilton Slocum, from making any goals.[1] When rested, the Defenders won, including their third game that season, against Cincinnati's Ninth Street YMCA team, which earned them a silver cup and claim to the heavyweight championship of the West.[2] Heading home from Ohio, their train went off the rails; the crash left both the team's general manager and coach "badly shaken up," but, contrary to the expectations of the conductor, nobody on board died.[3]

Butler's primary sport at this point was basketball, and his role in the development of early basketball as both a player and a coach should not be overlooked. Basketball in urban Black communities often served as the adrenaline-charged opening to dynamic social events; after the game, players and spectators transformed the basketball court into a music-filled dance floor, where fun, friendships, and romance flourished. Despite the excitement, however, the sport could not compete in the popular imagination with baseball or even elite track and field. Butler's athletic reputation helped draw fans to basketball games, but his success on the courts did little to extend his fame. For better or worse, audiences knew him as the great all-around athlete and Olympian.

Shortly after Butler visited and then moved to New York City, an article appeared in the *Chicago Defender* celebrating so-called race men—a term, according to sociologists St. Clair Drake and Horace Cayton, that referred to "any person who has a reputation as an uncompromising fighter against attempts to subordinate Negroes":[4]

> Every Race man or boy who has become prominent at all in his chosen line has risen to the top of that line. [Alain] Leroy Locke won the Rhodes scholarship while a student at Harvard. John Taylor, Howard Drew, Hi Wheeler, Sol Butler and Ned Gourdin were track stars, record breakers every one of them . . . Read these facts and ponder them. What is there that we cannot do?[5]

The article, "Truth about Us," pointed to a growing hope within the African American community that athletics, an arena where Black men were increasingly able to compete against white men and excel, would serve as a means of achieving racial equality, an idea that scholars Patrick Miller and David Wiggins have called "muscular assimilationism."[6] As a boy and a young man, Butler embodied this principle again and again—in Kansas; in Rock Island, Illinois; in Dubuque, Iowa; and at nearly all-white meets across the country and overseas. Rising to the top, he "force[d] the white world to recognize his talent or service or achievement," as Drake and Cayton explained, and thus assumed the mantel of race hero.[7]

But as Butler began to pass the peak of his athletic powers, he increasingly ran up against the limits of muscular assimilationism. Davarian Baldwin argues that "the larger realm of sport or 'physical culture' is an important stage where the dramas of social relations are reinforced, magnified, and sometimes directly challenged."[8] Butler's vast talents and the carefully cultivated social mobility that gave him access to white spaces and opportunities enabled him to repeatedly challenge the segregated systems of white supremacy; his incredible ability was a testament to their lie, even if his achievements could not always break down barriers and promote equality. As Butler was surpassed on the playing fields by younger, faster, stronger men, with his extraordinary physical mobility starting to wane, the realm of sport began to operate for him as a stage where the dramas of white supremacy were often reinforced and magnified. Concurrently, it became increasingly clear as he entered the ranks of professional football that "white America [made] concessions to Negroes primarily from the imperatives of economic necessity and political expediency rather than from devotion to democratic ideals."[9]

Butler Suffered Great Humiliation

In Harlem, Sol and his brother Ben moved into a unit at 2348 Seventh Avenue (now Adam Clayton Powell Jr. Boulevard), a few steps from the front door of the *Defender*'s New York office. Sol expressed interest in joining a prominent New York athletic club, but according to AAU policy, he first had to maintain residence in the city for at least four months.[10] He submitted paperwork to enter the 100-yard dash and broad jump in the Loughlin Lyceum meet at McGolrick Recreation Field in Brooklyn, but, rusty after an almost two-year hiatus from track and field, he ended up competing as an unattached athlete only in the 70-, 80-, and 90-yard dashes. He finished second in each race. Two weeks later, he took first place in the broad jump at a meet on Travers Island, but his jump of over 23 feet fell far short of his own record.[11]

By June 1922, less than two months after he had arrived in New York, Butler was making headlines for something other than athletics. Unlike sports news, which tended to appear in the middle of the paper, the *Chicago Defender* placed its story about Sol Butler's new job as an automobile salesman on the front page, reflecting the prestige of salesmanship nationally and within the African American community.[12] The automobile industry in particular, historian Walter Friedman explains, "quickly became famous for great salesmen," and the industry also became sophisticated about reaching a wide range of customers, including African Americans.[13] Businesses had historically disregarded and denigrated Black people, seeing them more as objects of ridicule than consumers and appealing to white audiences by using ugly stereotypes, including iconic characters like Aunt Jemima, introduced in 1889 and discontinued only in 2020 in the aftermath of George Floyd's murder. But the Great Migration, the war, and increasing urbanization and industrialization were changing the shape of American consumer culture. Between 1910 and 1920, the Black population of New York grew from approximately 91,000 to just over 152,000. Many of these Black residents, who often referred to themselves proudly as "New Negroes," were increasingly prosperous, with disposable incomes to spend on an ever-growing range of durable goods. "Businesses big and small, black and white, began to take the idea of a 'Negro market' more seriously," Robert Weems explains.[14]

As the only Black salesman for Mahnud Auto Sales Company in Brooklyn, which claimed to provide "real leads and liberal commission,"[15] Sol Butler would have been expected to target Black customers. Like many other car salesmen at the time in this male-dominated industry, he likely went door-to-door to demonstrate his product and answer questions about the year's new line of cars, which ranged from a $319 runabout to a $645 sedan.[16] Salesmen persuaded customers to "trade up" for the latest model, pointed out differences between a Ford and the competitors' vehicles, and arranged terms of credit.[17] Butler sold two cars in his first month on the job, the *Defender* announced with pride,[18] but his new position did not keep him from competing in a track and field meet at the end of June. At Seashore Park in Bridgeport, Connecticut, Butler again jumped just over 23 feet.[19]

Shortly after this meet, Butler was summoned, along with twelve other athletes, to appear at a disciplinary hearing at the AAU's New York headquarters on July 13. Jack Masters of the *New York Tribune* wrote:

> Probably the most important case was that against Sol Butler, former Dubuque College star and onetime holder of the American broad jump record, who is accused of playing professional basketball. The charge was made by the Allegheny Mountain Association, which contends that Butler participated in a pro game in Pittsburgh about a year ago. Butler, who is making his home here and competing unattached, admitted that he had taken part in such a game, but stated that he had been tried and served a sixty-day suspension for the offense. The local committee will investigate this angle and report its decision at a later date.[20]

But Butler did not wait for the local committee to render its decision. Exhausted from the exertions required to make himself acceptable to the white gatekeepers of amateur athletics, he walked back into headquarters the next day and handed in his AAU card.[21] A week later, the *Chicago Defender* announced Butler's separation from amateur athletics, and in the same issue of the newspaper, there appeared an advertisement for Dr. Siegert's Angostura Bitters, endorsed by African American New York alderman George W. Harris and other "leading men and women of the race," including celebrity athlete Sol Butler:[22] "Gentleman: Dr. Siegert's Angostura Bitters is a winner every time. It tones the stomach and builds healthy active people. I recommend it to all my friends. Sol Butler."

His business career was fully launched, but at this point Butler was still one of the country's best-known sports stars, and the AAU was keen to keep him on the field, filling seats, so the AAU quietly reinstated Butler's amateur status. Now twenty-seven and with one foot already planted in the professional world, Butler would compete in his final AAU track and field meet, nearly the last gasp of his amateur career. On Saturday, September 9, at Weequahic Park in Newark, New Jersey, Butler placed third in the broad jump behind world record holder Ned Gourdin and first-place finisher DeHart Hubbard, the sensation of the national meet. Only eighteen years old, Hubbard, a freshman at the University of Michigan, had drawn attention the day before by claiming the junior national title in the broad jump, setting a meet record of over 24 feet. Hubbard leaped even farther in the senior tournament, stunning the predominantly white crowd of around forty thousand, "who were liberal in their applause for the work of the colored athletes."[23] For the first time in a national AAU meet, three Black men claimed the top three spots in the broad jump. Hubbard and Gourdin would both go on to Olympic glory in 1924; Hubbard became the first African American to win an individual gold medal, and Gourdin took the silver.[24]

Sol Butler's Olympic days were behind him, but his track career was not quite over. Two weeks after the historic AAU meet, he competed in an American Legion meet at Syracuse Stadium representing the all-Black Colonel Charles Young Post Number 398 (named after the first African American to rise to the rank of colonel). His few months spent in the Student Army Training Corps in Dubuque established him as a veteran, who then represented his country in France, and he now faced the prospects of representing his post domestically in racially hostile territory. After training at Fordham University with Olympic trainer Jake Weber, Butler finished first in the broad jump and third in the 100-yard dash, qualifying him to compete for the Charles Young Post at the national American Legion meet, held in conjunction with the legion's national convention, the next month in New Orleans. He would return to the city where, two years earlier at the Olympic qualifying meet, officials allegedly forced him to complete his jumps at a separate site, away from the white athletes.[25]

Since the first national American Legion convention in 1919, posts had retained the right to refuse membership to African Americans, and in 1921 the organization created an honor society, the 40 Hommes et 8 Chevaux (40 men and 8 horses), which restricted membership to whites only.[26] Members of the New York American Legion convention elected the commander of the Colonel Charles Young Post, Thomas Walters, as a state delegate to the national convention in New Orleans. Two years earlier, the NAACP had issued a public challenge to the American Legion calling for the desegregation of posts across the country, and Walters had pushed the New York convention to adopt a resolution "asking for fair treatment of colored veterans in the American Legion," which would ensure that African Americans in Southern states could join their local legion posts.[27] New York and a few other states adopted the resolution. The white commander of the New York delegation, Major William F. Deegan, took a "strong stand in favor of opening membership in the American Legion all over the country to the Negro veterans" and lost his bid for national commander.[28] On October 14, Thomas Walters and Sol Butler departed by train for segregated Louisiana. There Deegan had the opportunity to put his values into action, as his obituary recalled a decade later:

At New Orleans, the New York delegation took Butler with them to one of the most exclusive hotels in that city . . . It was reported that when they escorted Butler into the car of the elevator that the operator refused to start the car. The New York men, under Major Deegan's leadership, took charge of the elevator, running it up to their floor and leaving it there.[29]

At the convention, Black delegates had less success confronting the color line. The eight men from Missouri, Ohio, New York, and Iowa—led by J. Q. Lindsey, an African American deputy sheriff from Des Moines and captain of the Army Expeditionary Forces—were ultimately unable to pass a resolution that would enable Black veterans to organize posts through the American Legion's national offices. The committee on amendments and by-laws instead supported an amendment that strengthened state control over the granting of charters for new posts.[30]

As for Butler, conflicting accounts make it difficult to reconstruct the exact chain of events at the New Orleans meet, but all sources concur that racism prevented him from competing fairly, if at all, in the 100-yard dash and running broad jump. The *New York Age*, a Black newspaper, reported that soon after Butler and his teammates arrived in New Orleans, the leader of the New York team "was called aside and told that Butler could not practice with the rest of the athletes," and Southern officials threatened "that 'it would be folly for Butler to attempt to practice and suicide for him to attempt to compete.'"[31] In that account, Butler voluntarily withdrew from competition to prevent his outraged teammates from withdrawing in protest. A neighboring article in the same edition of the *New York Age* declared, "Southern athletes would not run in a race in which a Negro was a competitor, and Butler was barred." A Davenport, Iowa, newspaper claimed that officials settled "the refusal of southern athletes to compete with any but white rivals" by having Butler "run by himself against time."[32] And the *Chicago Defender* printed the following account:

Butler suffered great humiliation when he appeared on the field before thousands and was ejected from the ranks as he and other runners lined up for the dashes. He was forced to run by himself against time and when he attempted to make the broad jump the official with the measuring tape refused to recognize him and deliberately walked away from the pit to another part of the field.[33]

In subsequent decades, alternate versions of the episode emerged. Shortly after Butler was posthumously inducted into the Iowa Sports Hall of Fame, the former chair of the American Legion National Athletic Commission, Ray Murphy, wrote to the *Des Moines Register* and recalled that in New Orleans, a local committee had summoned him to a meeting "to demand that [Butler] be withdrawn from the competition because of his color," but Murphy "refused . . . and stated that Butler would participate in the meet if he so desired."[34] In Murphy's account, Butler did compete but was hindered by intimidation. The next day, according to Murphy, Butler "ran a bad last" in the 100-yard dash, and his best event was no better: "Along the line of approach to the jumping block and along the side and end of the jumping pit were lined up a group of men in considerable number who had nothing to do with the track meet other, I am sure, than to intimidate Sol Butler." The man who would have easily won the event under normal circumstances jumped well below 20 feet because "the appearance of the observers along the line was menacing, and undoubtedly Sol decided that he had better not win."[35]

Without their star broad jumper and sprinter, New York narrowly lost on total points to the Louisiana team and finished in second place, just ahead of Mississippi. The northern AAU-sponsored team filed a protest with the American Legion national office. By the end of the week, officials declared that first-place honors belonged to the New York team, suggesting that contemporary accounts were correct and that the team's star member was unable to compete.[36] Nearly five years after the meet, the AAU moved its championship meet out of New Orleans because the city continued to insist on excluding Black athletes.[37]

Retired from the Amateur Track

The New Orleans trip was a disheartening reminder of the compromises, frustrations, and even dangers inherent in competing on white playing fields, which in the South made no room for race men. Butler returned to New York and the world of Black Fives basketball, this time competing as both head coach and player on a new team—the Eastern Chicago Defender Five (or New York Defenders)—formed by the editor of the newspaper's New York office, Archie J. Morgan.[38] "The paper hoped to cash in on the basketball turmoil in the East while increasing its exposure and subscriptions there by forming a team," writes historian Claude Johnson.[39] It was a time of transition for amateur basketball. The Metropolitan Basketball Association, a New York league established to support amateur play and root out professionalism, dissolved over the course of the season, and the New York Defenders, billed as an amateur team, might have landed in a gray zone. Basketball historian Bob Kuska refers to the New York Defenders as professional.[40] Yet a contemporary reporter wrote that the team sought "to bring back basketball where it was some years ago," when players did not seek or expect remuneration and stuck "close to the rules of true sportsmanship."[41]

Johnson clarifies that the shift away from amateurism reflected a broader pattern of "untangle[ing] African American aspirations from previously accepted White standards of approval," represented by the accommodationist ideology espoused by the late Booker T. Washington.[42] Professional sports embodied the new spirit of Black nationalism, economic empowerment, and proud cultural flourishing in the arts that characterized the New Negro Movement, and "the natural extension of these ideas overflowed into all areas of Black business, including basketball."[43] Openly professional all-Black teams emerged in the city. Somehow Butler found the time and energy between basketball games to play on Fritz Pollard's newly formed all-Black All-Stars football team, which included Pollard, Paul Robeson, J. Mayo Williams, Duke Slater, Dick Hudson, and John Shelburne, high-achieving friends he would collaborate with over coming decades.[44]

The New York Defenders basketball team started off strong, winning their first three games in Manhattan Casino, but they generated increasingly meager fan support. With the help of Butler's late-game long basket, the Defenders defeated the team from Howard University 22–20 in "as thrilling a basketball contest that has been witnessed in Gotham for many years."[45] Butler's former Forty Club teammate Creed Hubbard refereed, and champion bantamweight boxer Danny Edwards tossed the opening jump ball. After the Defenders' exciting win, the reported "600 or more fans," including many Black club and business leaders, danced to the music of John C. Smith's augmented jazz orchestra.[46] After one more local victory over the Spartan Field Club at New York's new Renaissance Casino on January 1, 1923, the Defender Five headed west on what turned into a forgettable tour, except for one especially impressive victory. After losing to the John Roan Post of the American Legion team from Xenia, Ohio, Butler and two other Defenders teammates joined this team to challenge Pittsburgh's seemingly unbeatable Loendi Big Five led by veteran star Cumberland "Cum" Posey. Butler made a long basket toward the end of the game and on defense held Posey to only one basket, which enabled the John Roan team to win the game 30–26, thus prompting speculation on their right to claim the Black championship (a difficult title to determine in the absence of a national league).[47]

As the Defenders' losses on the road piled up, Butler was indefinitely suspended by the AAU after he failed to participate in two highly publicized indoor track and field events, one at Madison Square Garden and the other at Fordham University. Organizers for both events advertised that Butler would be racing in special sprints, but the star athlete—whose name they used likely without his knowledge and permission—never appeared.[48] His reputation took an additional hit when the *Messenger*, a politically radical African American magazine out of Harlem, charged that the Ku Klux Klan had been meeting at the home of A. Edward Wupperman, a top executive of Angostura Bitters. In response to the magazine's calls to boycott the company, Wupperman issued a statement that Angostura Bitters was "in no way connected with the Klan" and apologized for "any embarrassment" the accusation may have caused Alderman George W. Harris and Sol Butler, the company's two Black spokespersons.[49] *Messenger* cofounder Chandler Owen regarded the episode as "a clear case of Negro cash pitted against white supremacy . . . Men's hates of somebody else are seldom as great as their love for money and wealth. This company does not hate Negroes less but it loves the Negroes['] money more."[50] Owen did not name Butler and Harris in his editorial, but the star athlete would have felt added pressure to make clear his bona fides as a race man. He soon transitioned to an unabashedly professional sports career while no longer endorsing a tainted product.

After playing his final basketball game of the season in March 1923,[51] and now officially "retired from the amateur track," Butler moved back to Chicago, where he accepted a position in a new men's clothing store owned by William "Bill" Adams, who had a reputation as being one of the finest African American tailors.[52] Adams made suits "for all the big-wigs, up and down the stroll," including for *Chicago Defender* owner, Robert Abbott. *Chicago Defender* city editor Prentis Leroy Prattis (writing under the pseudonym Roger Didier) mythologized Adams and his store in a three-part advertising serial about a fictional African king, Batouala, a character borrowed from a novel by award-winning Guianan author René Maran. In Prattis's story, Adams transforms Batouala from a "primitive" outsider to a sophisticated American urbanite: "He went in a chief and came out a man of affairs; he went in a king and came out a mister."[53] Located next to the prestigious Vendome Theater and near the *Chicago Defender* office on State Street, Adams's haberdashery was billed as "an honest-to-goodness baby Marshall Fields."[54]

Butler had been in New York for less than a year, and he easily slipped back into the rhythms of Black Chicago. In June he volunteered, along with Albert Johnson and Virgil Blueitt, to help stage a track and field event at the American Giants' (of the Negro National League) baseball field. The event, organized with administrators from Wendell Phillips High School, included physical training drills for boys, a scarf dance for girls, and a performance by the sophomore jazz band.[55] Around the same time, Butler teamed up with Francis LeRoy Holmes, who nearly medaled in the 1908 Olympics in the standing high and standing broad jumps, to offer classes for men and women in swimming, tennis, and "general athletics" under the auspices of the Bethel Athletic Association.[56] Along with volunteering and teaching classes, Butler "really put on one funny dance" in the play *Look Pleasant, Please*, which the African American fraternity Kappa Alpha Psi produced; all of the proceeds from the event went to the Wabash Avenue YMCA, often referred to as the "Colored Y." Before summer ended and at the American Tennis Association's national championship in Chicago, members of this fraternity considered Sol their "active leader."[57]

I Have No Discriminations

Unlike basketball, where most teams claimed amateur status no matter how tenuous the connection, post-college football unabashedly courted professionalism. Once the Canton Bulldogs hired sports star Jim Thorpe in 1915, other teams in Ohio and across the Midwest and East followed suit by aggressively luring successful (and usually former) college players. Shortly after Butler returned from the Olympics in Belgium, representatives from professional teams met in Canton to form the American Professional Football Conference, which soon was called the National Football League. While no African Americans participated in these backroom discussions—and their ongoing exclusion as owners and organizers over the coming decade meant partial and eventually complete segregation on the fields of play—an important handful of Black players were employed in the fledgling league. Forty-year-old Bobby Marshall joined the Rock Island Independents in 1920, the opening year, along with Fritz Pollard, who helped the Akron Pros win the first championship and the next year was named co-head coach. Before Sol entered the NFL, J. Mayo Williams played for three different teams, and Paul Robeson helped pay his own way through Columbia Law School by playing with Pollard at Akron and then with the Milwaukee Badgers.[58]

Fueled by working-class fans who eagerly paid Sunday admission fees to see violent fun that embodied certain masculine virtues as it held out the promise of boosting the reputation of their small cities, the professional game paled in national popularity and prestige to the college game. "What became the NFL in 1922 was strictly an industrial and milltown league, with transient teams and transient players, scorn from amateur purists, and indifference from the larger public," writes scholar Michael Oriard.[59] The game received scant attention in newspapers beyond the communities they served, and Butler's coming professional football career represented his capitalizing on rather than building up his fame. As a strategy of muscular assimilationism, his gridiron career now held limited promise.

In the fall, Butler headed west to Rock Island. He arrived on a Sunday and signed a contract with the Rock Island Independents of the fledgling National Football League ten minutes before the Independents' game against the Chicago Bears, co-owned by player/coach George Halas.[60] When Butler entered in the second quarter, he received a lengthy cheer from the Tri-City crowd of over three thousand, many of whom recalled his dazzling play as a high schooler and collegian. After he made an interception, gained 40 yards on a reception from quarterback Johnny Armstrong, and then received another pass, the Bears "endeavored to knock him out."[61] This was an especially chilling act of calculated violence considering that one week later, and arguably due to similar calculations, Black football player Jack Trice would die from injuries sustained in a game between Iowa State College (now University) and the University of Minnesota.[62] The resulting 15-yard penalty against the Bears led to a successful field goal by the Independents. On the opening play of the fourth quarter, Sol "electrified the crowd with a hair-raising run through the whole Bear squad."[63] Contrary to general expectation, the Independents beat the Bears 3–0.

Butler told a reporter that he previously did not have much interest in professional football. "But now things look different to him" after finding a team that included former high school and college teammates Armstrong, "Waddy" Kuhl, and Vera Lowe and African American defensive star Duke Slater, who would join Butler in many future sport endeavors.[64] But the Independents used Butler sparingly,[65] and, perhaps frustrated by his demotion to supporting player, he requested a release from his contract after only a month with the team. In November he joined the Hammond (Indiana) Pros, who reportedly bought out his contract with the Independents for around ten thousand dollars.[66]

After joining his friend Williams on the field for the Pros' losses to the Bears and the Chicago Cardinals, where they drew hundreds of African American fans,[67] in the spring of 1924 Butler was once more practicing on the basketball court at the Wabash YMCA. His old team had been renamed again and was known as the Eighth Regiment. Since Butler was now a professional football player, the heavyweight squad was considered a professional basketball team.[68] The highlight of the strong season, which included two games against white teams, was a tight, "hard fought" win on the Eighth Regiment Armory courts over Cum Posey's Loendi Big Five, which a sportswriter dubbed "the greatest basketball game ever staged in the city"; this was Sol's second victory over the titan team from Pittsburgh.[69]

His football season began back on the Hammond Pros, often referred to now as the Indians, who opened with back-to-back losses against the Racine (Wisconsin) Legion and Rock Island Independents. Williams missed the second game, secretly traveling back to New York to oversee a Paramount Records recording session of the towering blues singer Ma Rainey, backed up by rising legends Fletcher Henderson and a young Louis Armstrong.[70] Butler, who was considered a "good passer" and "the leading kicker of the team,"[71] prevented a third straight loss against the Kenosha (Wisconsin) Maroons by dodging and weaving after a reception, scoring a touchdown in the final minute of play to tie the game.[72] This was his first recorded touchdown in professional football. The next week, the Indians defeated Paddy Driscoll's Chicago Cardinals 6–3. Butler "was the best player on the field" and "the only one that made consistent gains."[73]

Missing the final Hammond game in Kansas City with Williams due to Missouri's enforced segregation policy,[74] Butler spent the rest of the season working as a free agent, bouncing from team to team. The semipro Akron (Ohio) Indians, owned by Suey Welch, "imported" him from Hammond for their game against the Akron Silents.[75] Butler scored on a two-yard run in a shutout victory. On Thanksgiving, he played with the Akron Pros, "crushing through 18 yards" against the Buffalo (New York) Bisons for a touchdown, his third in four games.[76] He extended his season and touchdown streak by playing a final game with a semipro team, the Toronto Tigers, in their victory over a team from Steubenville, Ohio.[77]

The versatile sports star transitioned back to basketball in 1925 for an underwhelming season as a player on the Eighth Regiment team,[78] yet his considerable success as coach of the Roamer Girls, who, through the dominant play of Izzy Channels, trounced the white Harvey (Illinois) Bloomers in the Eighth Regiment Armory before a crowd of forty-five hundred.[79] Butler also kept busy outside of athletics, appearing in Kappa Alpha Psi's production of the musical *You'll Be Surprised*. Bolstered by his experience on staff at the *Chicago Defender*, he took a position as sporting editor for a new Black newspaper, the *Chicago Bee*, founded by Black business magnate Anthony Overton.[80]

Around this same time, on May 16, a Negro Leagues pitcher by the name of Homer Robert "Hop" Bartley helped the Kansas City Monarchs defeat the St. Louis Stars, recording his only win of the 1925 season. After the game the local newspapers recorded Bartley's name (sometimes written as "Bartlett") as the winning pitcher.[81] But due to "a typographical error or misreading in the reporting of a single game," asserts Negro League historian Gary Ashwill,[82] the *St. Louis Globe-Democrat* mistakenly entered the name "Butler" in their report of the game, which was reprinted in the *St. Louis Argus* and the *Chicago Defender*.[83] These initial errors led to the widespread belief that Sol Butler played in the Negro Leagues, which he did not. He never took baseball too seriously as an athlete, never having played on his high school teams or in enough games in college to earn a varsity letter due to commitments in track and field and even football. The fact that subsequent generations have easily accepted that he pitched this game speaks to his status as a phenomenally gifted all-around athlete who moved deftly in numerous arenas.

After a few months on the job at the *Chicago Bee*, Butler, apparently undertaking an investigative piece, sent a letter soliciting the thoughts of "prominent coaches and distinguished athletes on the relation of race and color to sports":

THE BOOK OF 1929 ACHIEVEMENT

SUNDAY
CHICAGO BEE
GREATEST NEGRO NEWSPAPER

ESTABLISHED APRIL 1925

THE BEE'S OFFICIAL STAFF AND OFFICE FORCE

Reading from left to right, top row: Olive Diggs, accountant; Marjorie Harris, stenographer; Ada Mae Gaines, subscription clerk; Irene Gallimore, proofreader; Marjorie Emery, bookkeeper. Second row: Jack L. Cooper, theatrical editor; Sol W. Butler, sport editor; Beulah M. Hill, society editor; Stewart Hedgepath, classified advertising; J. Blaine Poindexter, Rotogravure advertising. First row: Dr. E. S. Miller, health editor; O. A. Scott, general manager; Katherine E. Irvin, managing editor; Ettinger F. Smith, advertising manager; Victor L. Gray, circulation manager. Inset, left, George Sydney, city editor. Inset right: Henry D. Middleton, editorial writer.

The Chicago Bee has enjoyed a more rapid development than any other Negro newspaper has ever known.

A GAIN OF 15,000 COPIES IN THE LAST 15 MONTHS

The rapid growth of the Bee has been largely due to a fortunate connection. The fact that the son and daughters of Mr. Anthony Overton are the principal owners of the Chicago Sunday Bee has naturally given this paper the benefit of the wise counsel of his seasoned business genius. This connection at the same time has afforded an adequate financial background.

OUR ROTOGRAVURE SECTION

The Chicago Sunday Bee was the **First Negro Newspaper** to print a picture section on Rotogravure.

The Chicago Sunday Bee is the only Negro Newspaper carrying a genuine Rotogravure with every issue.

Our Rotogravure Section is prepared and printed **Exclusively for the Chicago Sunday Bee** and cannot be found elsewhere.

It is the only Negro Newspaper carrying a Sunday Edition. Four full pages of beautiful pictures.

215

Sports editor Butler on staff of the *Chicago Bee*. (Source: *The Negro in Chicago, 1779 to 1927*, ed. Frederic H. H. Robb [Washington Intercollegiate Club of Chicago: Chicago, 1927], p. 215; courtesy of Chicago Public Library.)

1. Do you believe in mixed games? By mixed games we mean two things—a. Do you believe that a white team should play against a colored team? b. Do you favor white and colored members on the same team?
2. Do you think Negroes make as good athletes as whites? If inferior or superior, give your reasons.
3. Do you favor colored athletes in some games but no[t] in others? If so, what games? For instance, it is customary to see an occasional colored member of a football or track team but seldom on the baseball, basketball, boating, boxing and tennis teams.[84]

One letter went to Knute Rockne, director of athletics at the University of Notre Dame. "Please feel perfectly free to give your unreserved opinion," Butler wrote. Rockne responded: "I have read your questions with a great deal of interest, and I wish to say that as far as I am personally concerned I have no discriminations at all against anyone on account of race, creed or color."[85] Avoiding a direct response to questions one and three, he ended with a bit of flattery, writing, "I believe the negro makes as good an athlete as the whites. In fact, men like yourself, Hubbard, and many others have stood out very conspiciously [*sic*]." But in practice, Rockne "never questioned Notre Dame's long-standing policy not to admit 'Negroes,'" according to his biographer Murray Sperber, and he excluded Black coaches from his very lucrative coaching schools.[86]

Butler sent another letter to Amos Alonzo Stagg, the athletic director of the University of Chicago.[87] In his reply, Stagg stated, "The presence of a colored boy on the usual college team presents more managerial difficulties than internal difficulties," noting that the majority of hotels would not rent a room or serve food to Black guests.[88] He went on to say, "My observation is that the white members of the teams are very fair and decent in their treatment of a colored boy who is a member of a team, and make no objection to his presence, if he is a gentleman, either in training quarters or on the trips." After acknowledging that "colored men are splendid athletes" in track and field, he impugned Black masculinity in ways used to justify the exclusion of African Americans from military service: "Occasionally, one finds a colored athlete who is a wonderful player in football, but they are less likely to be as good in that sport, where fearlessness, aggressiveness, and dogged determination play a large part in the selection of positions."[89]

Unfortunately, no issues of the *Chicago Bee* survive from this time, so what Butler made of Rockne's and Stagg's responses, along with any other letters he received in reply to his query, is lost to history. But Rockne's ready acknowledgment that Black athletes make "as good an athlete as the whites" and Stagg's praising Black athletes in track and field while excluding them

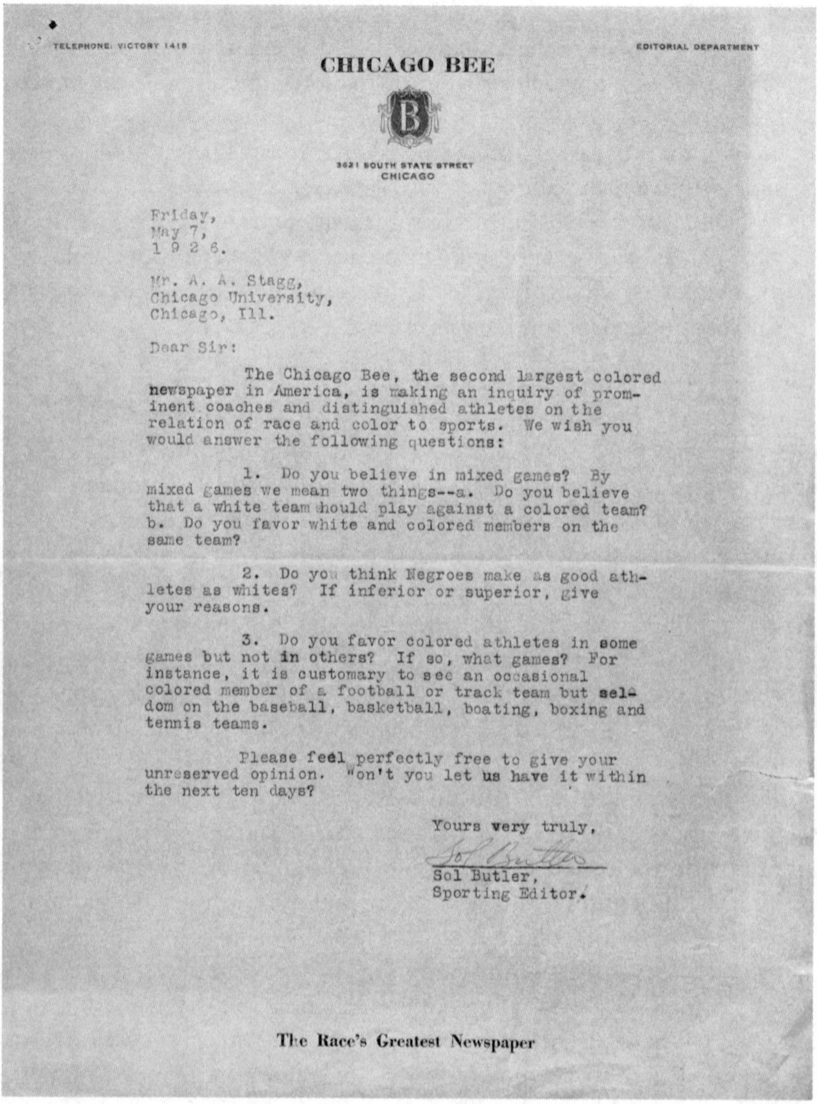

TELEPHONE: VICTORY 1418 EDITORIAL DEPARTMENT

CHICAGO BEE

3621 SOUTH STATE STREET
CHICAGO

Friday,
May 7,
1 9 2 6.

Mr. A. A. Stagg,
Chicago University,
Chicago, Ill.

Dear Sir:

The Chicago Bee, the second largest colored newspaper in America, is making an inquiry of prominent coaches and distinguished athletes on the relation of race and color to sports. We wish you would answer the following questions:

1. Do you believe in mixed games? By mixed games we mean two things--a. Do you believe that a white team should play against a colored team? b. Do you favor white and colored members on the same team?

2. Do you think Negroes make as good athletes as whites? If inferior or superior, give your reasons.

3. Do you favor colored athletes in some games but not in others? If so, what games? For instance, it is customary to see an occasional colored member of a football or track team but seldom on the baseball, basketball, boating, boxing and tennis teams.

Please feel perfectly free to give your unreserved opinion. Won't you let us have it within the next ten days?

Yours very truly,

Sol Butler,
Sol Butler,
Sporting Editor.

The Race's Greatest Newspaper

Sports editor Butler letter to Amos Alonzo Stagg dated May 7, 1926 (Amos Alonzo Stagg Papers, University of Chicago)

from his football teams reveals the hard limits of muscular assimilationism for Butler and other Black sports stars of his time. A handful of prominent Black athletes might achieve the social mobility necessary to be in a position to prove themselves as good as or better than their white peers, but, by and large, Black athletes across the United States were never given the opportunity to compete on even a nominally integrated or level playing field. Opening doors of opportunity in sports required more than brilliant Black performances in "mixed games" on integrated or against white teams; powerful white men in the sports world made clear that creating the type of durable and meaningful integration Jackie Robinson symbolized twenty-two years later upon joining Major League Baseball's Brooklyn Dodgers would require bold efforts beyond the playing fields, not only in journalism but also as coaches, managers, and organizers.

Crackers Give Lame Excuse

Butler entered his third year of professional football with the semipro Toronto Tigers in the fall of 1925. He played the deciding role with a blocked punt, interception, and long runs in a 7–0 victory over J. Mayo Williams and his old team, the Hammond Pros. Despite a perfect 3–0 start to the season and reasonably large crowds, the Tigers ran into financial difficulties and had to cancel the next game, so Butler bounced back to the Hammond Pros for one game with Williams (who in the musical realm would soon extend the popular reach of the blues by recording "Blind Lemon" Jefferson) for the team's 28–7 loss to the Chicago Bears.[90] On October 18, for the first time in his professional football career, Butler played quarterback, throwing a 39-yard touchdown pass in the Tigers' win over the Milwaukee Badgers. Still losing money despite a solid season, the owners of the Tigers decided to merge with the neighboring Steubenville Pros; Butler served as the new team's quarterback for their next game, which ended in a tie against the Canton Bulldogs, the strongest team they faced that season.[91]

Although playing a raucous, violent sport for working-class audiences, Butler found time to rehearse for a play that appealed to Chicago's Black social elite.[92] *Thais*, a four-act play by Paul Wilstach based on a novel by Anatole France, was set in Egypt during the early Christian era.[93] The play follows a desert-dwelling ascetic who travels to Alexandria to deliver the beautiful Thais from her "evil life" of performing lust-filled pagan songs. The ascetic succeeds in converting Thais to Christianity but falls prey to his own irrepressible desires. Directed by Clarence Muse and performed at the Avenue Theater, where "many beautifully gowned ladies occupied boxes on the main floor," the production won praise from "Chicago's finest," including newspaper owner Robert Abbott and celebrated tenor and choral director George Garner.[94] In prior years, this white-owned theater had reserved the main floor for whites only, but lately the Avenue had catered to Black audiences with productions ranging from minstrelsy to critically acclaimed dramas by the influential Lafayette Players.[95]

After a lackluster basketball season both as a player on the Eighth Regiment Big Five (renamed the Chicago All-Stars) and coach of the Roamer Girls,[96] on an early April night in 1926, Butler wound up at the Dreamland Cafe on

State Street. Many of the era's greatest jazz musicians performed for a show featuring the multitalented Harlem musician Nora Douglass Holt.[97] Now thirty-one, Butler was becoming "better looking" with age and also getting "serious with a certain girl," according to the society pages of a new African American weekly.[98] No longer young, perhaps newly in love, that night Holt's singing the popular song "Sweet Man" reportedly made him weep.

That fall, Butler arrived in Canton, Ohio, and signed a contract with the Bulldogs four days before the team's first game against the neighboring semipro Massillon Maroons. Coming off their worst season ever, the Bulldogs hired Butler to help them win games and fill seats.[99] A few years earlier, African American running back Ben Johnson achieved fame on the local McKinley High School team, and other Black players followed in his footsteps, so Canton fans were accustomed to seeing "mixed games" in their highly segregated town.[100] The Bulldogs battled the Maroons, a "classy sand-lot team" in Massillon, Ohio, for a 3–0 victory a week before facing their first pro team.[101] The *Canton Repository* reported that Butler at quarterback looked "like a regular."[102] The next Sunday, Butler didn't go in until the second half, but the Bulldogs were already down by two touchdowns, and they lost to the Columbus (Ohio) Tigers, 14–2. At halfback, he "played the leading role for the Dogs and his returns of punts in the final period established him as a favorite with the fans."[103]

Before the next game, the Bulldogs signed one of Butler's former Rock Island teammates, Native American football star Jim Thorpe, who was nearing the end of his incomparable sports career. Thorpe scored two touchdowns on October 3 before a crowd of three thousand at Canton's Lakeside Field in a 13–0 victory over the Louisville (Kentucky) Colonels. Butler played quarterback the entire game and made "the outstanding play," a scrambling 25-yard pass completion that led to the first score.[104] The *Canton Repository* featured a large photograph from the game of him racing laterally across the field toward the camera. In 2006, NFL Films purchased movie footage of Thorpe, and possibly Butler, from this game, the high point of what would end up being the Canton Bulldogs' final season.[105]

Butler was back at quarterback for the team's next game against the Akron Pros, coached by Fritz Pollard, the first time in professional football history that two Black quarterbacks met on opposite sides of the gridiron. The game was historic, but it was also a dud. Butler completed the only two successful passes of the game, which ended in a 0–0 tie and turned out to be the last of Pollard's NFL career. After the scoreless game, Pollard was released from the Pros; the Bulldogs took Butler out of the quarterback position and reduced his playing time.[106] Despite the historic nature of the Bulldog-Pros game, African American football fans in the area likely showed up in far greater numbers that afternoon to witness the all-Black Canton Merchants smother the former state champion Colored Giants from Youngstown at Cook Field.[107]

A few weeks later, Butler and the Bulldogs headed east to take on the New York Giants, and a scene from the Deep South replayed itself at Manhattan's Polo Grounds, where "certain Negro-hating whites from Oklahoma and Texas on the Giants . . . strenuously object[ed]" to Butler playing with the Bulldogs.[108] According to the *New York Age*, the Giants' manager, Harry "Doc" Marsh, "suggested" that Butler be kept out of the game because he "might precipitate a race riot."[109] While some of Butler's teammates protested, the Bulldogs acceded to the Giants' objections, and backfield coach Harry Robb replaced Butler with Robb's younger brother. "Crackers Give Lame Excuse for Barring Former College Star from Pro Football Game" read the subtitle of a *New York Amsterdam News* article, which reported on Butler's benching before "about forty thousand spectators" with disgust.[110] Butler suited up for a game the following week against the Hartford (Connecticut) Blues but was replaced again by Harry Robb, who released Butler and two other players before Canton's next game against the Brooklyn Lions. Robb explained that they lacked the "fight" he sought in younger players.[111] Butler's NFL career ended with a whimper.

For many years to come, Butler would test his talents on the gridiron, but from this point he would compete only *against* rather than *with* white players. As his physical mobility diminished through his thirties, he sought new and collaborative ways to make a living and open doors in the realm of sports. His attention—like that of other Black athletes excluded from white teams—increasingly focused on mixed games where African American teams showcased their talents not only as athletes but also as coaches, managers, and promoters. Butler's recent success in car and clothing sales and product endorsement spoke to his business energies synchronizing with his efforts on theater stages and playing fields. Muscular assimilationism was only a partial answer for a sports entrepreneur like Sol Butler, who operated in multiple realms as a race man. His celebrity capital—as an Olympian, cultural leader, and storied all-around athlete—and deft ability to stay relevant in the Black sporting world would soon be put to the test when the country entered an unprecedented economic crisis that would prompt him to head west.

9

Black Fury

1927–1935

From "Fantasie Negre" (1932) by Florence Price." (Copyright © 1932 [Renewed] by G. Schirmer, Inc. International Copyright Secured. All Rights Reserved. Used by permission.)

Addressing a national interracial gathering of physical education leaders in October 1924 at a conference in Atlantic City, Howard University administrator and Booker T. Washington's former secretary Emmett Scott declared that healthy desires for recreation and "physical prominence . . . have somewhat diverted the children from the perverted ideal which all the boys had when Jack Johnson won the heavyweight championship of the world, and they all wanted to be pugilists."[1] Scott identified three Olympic broad jumpers and a Rose Bowl quarterback—Sol Butler, Ned Gourdin, DeHart Hubbard, and Charlie West—who represented the "new type of ideals . . . as against the ambition of the boy who wants to be a Jack Johnson" and "the lower ideal which for so long had a hold upon [Black males'] imagination."

Sol Butler himself was a boy when Johnson won the heavyweight championship of the world, electrifying Black Americans and sending shock waves through white America. Just coming into his own as a young athlete vying for a shot at greatness in the overwhelmingly white Midwestern communities where he was raised, Butler spent his youth crafting a persona that would afford him the social mobility necessary to move and compete freely in white worlds. This persona was often at careful odds with the kind of boastful, flashy brashness that Johnson cultivated. Butler's much-noted youthful modesty and humility neatly aligned with the Washingtonian respectability politics of the Black middle class, who also championed amateur athletics for their supposed purity of spirit over boxing and other professional sports.

But the "perverted ideal" of pugilism represented more than straightforward, lowbrow vice. Jack Johnson was a self-made champion of mythic proportions: the child of two formerly enslaved people who became a world champion, the unabashed Black man who married white women in Jim Crow America, the star athlete who used his exceptional abilities not to uplift the race but to enrich himself. In that enrichment, in that flouting of convention, another kind of uplift lurked: the opportunity for Black boys and young men to glimpse a future that offered more than the ever-narrowing strictures of segregation and the ever-present threat of racial violence undergirding Jim Crow.

By the time Emmett Scott's speech extolling the "new type of ideals" appeared in print, over two years separated Butler from his amateur track and field glory. A couple more years would pass before a thirty-two-year-old Sol Butler married twenty-four-year-old Bernice Pegge in Chicago on May 18, 1927. The *New York Age* reported that the wedding "ceremony was marked by simplicity, only relatives and a few intimate friends being present."[2] The couple had known each other for more than two years, at least since Pegge played basketball on the Roamer Girls team. She grew up on a farm near the small town of Garden, Kansas, near Joplin, Missouri, not far from Sol's hometowns in Oklahoma and Kansas. The newlyweds lived in an apartment at 5604 Prairie Avenue along with Pegge's older sister and her husband.[3] Almost no record of the relationship remains, but if this marriage to a young Midwestern woman represented Butler's connection to the middle-class values of his mother and the small Black communities in which he was raised, the end of this marriage, four years later, after Butler had left Pegge behind in Chicago to try his luck in Hollywood, represented his shift away from those values.[4]

As Butler's body slowed down, the Depression settled in, quickly stripping away the fragile economic progress Black Americans had made through the Great Migration. White America's opportunities, which Butler had found a way to seize in his youth, grew ever more out of reach. Forced to find new ways to capitalize on his diminishing fame to succeed as a sports entrepreneur, Butler increasingly embraced "the lower ideal," plying his exceptional physical and social mobility in new arenas, often for cash. And yet, even as Butler hustled for acting gigs and threw himself into the colorful world of boxing at the Main Street Gym in Los Angeles, his adolescent dreams of becoming a race leader were not forgotten. So Sol Butler forged another new path for himself, following in Johnson's formidable footsteps but also continuing to find ways to intentionally work for the uplift of the Black community, even as he left many of Scott's "new type of ideals" behind.

Old Man Sol

With segregation hardening across the North, Butler no longer played on integrated teams after his unceremonious departure from the Canton Bulldogs and may have considered legitimate integration an unreasonable goal in the short term, especially at the professional level. Instead, he doubled down on promoting mixed games but strictly according to how he initially described the concept as a sportswriter at the *Chicago Bee* in his survey letter to white sports authorities: as all-Black teams versus all-white teams. He no longer played *with* but only *against* white athletes. He also played, coached, and supported Black athletes and teams who competed against other Black athletes and teams. Aggressively adopting racial separation did not mean he rejected integration; on the contrary—and like many Northern Black parents and educational activists who had pushed for separate Black schools over the past century[5]—he considered integration the ideal but now championed separation as the best option available under racist circumstances. The goal was to create opportunity, not fight for integration no matter the cost.

Despite Jim Crow's increasing strength, Butler kept moving in business, journalism, and, for the first time, party politics and on and off the fields of play in football, basketball, tennis, auto racing, swimming, golfing, baseball, boxing, and—most significantly as a coach and organizer—track and field to keep himself and others in the game. Targeting Black audiences whose appreciation did not require him to demonstrate modesty, he embraced a flashy Olympic persona stoked by a rapidly growing commercial, celebrity-oriented sport industry. His entrepreneurism now reflected the New Negro spirit flourishing in Chicago's Bronzeville and in Los Angeles along Central Avenue, where he pragmatically combined racial uplift with the sporting life for maximum mobility. An aging sports star and evolving race man, Butler now made a living and served the African American community without caring to appease white people.

When the fall of 1927 arrived, the newly wed Butler could no longer count on the NFL for employment. The league had suffered financial difficulties the previous season and responded by reducing the number of teams. The already tenuous access of Black players basically evaporated, and Duke Slater was the only Black NFL player during the season. Butler and many other should-have-been NFL players spent future seasons participating on all-Black semipro teams that played against white teams but not ones in the NFL. "The number of local teams [of any race]—all of which vied for patrons, gate receipts, and winning wages—made Chicago a player's marketplace," notes historian Gerald Gems.[6] Opportunities for competition abounded since the "city offered . . . more than forty [mostly white] semipro football teams, with over twenty fully professional football clubs in the Midwest."

William E. Trimble, a white florist and owner of the successful Chicago American Giants of baseball's Negro Leagues organized the all-Black American Giants football team.[7] Over the decades, Negro League teams played major league teams hundreds of times in exhibition games but not during the regular season; the success of the Black players, who won the majority of these games, put the lie to the notion that they lacked the requisite skills to play in the major leagues. Trimble's new football team proved this point, too. Yet, given the public's much greater interest in baseball during this era than in football, the latter sport did not develop enough teams to create its own all-Black league.

Joined by his friends J. Mayo ("Ink") Williams and Dick Hudson, whose NFL careers also prematurely ended the preceding season, Butler signed with the American Giants. Trimble named Butler the team's coach and quarterback. Six days before the American Giants baseball team won the Negro Leagues World Series in Atlantic City, the American Giants football team, which practiced on their namesake's baseball field, defeated a white team from Clinton, Iowa, on a field in Rock Island, Illinois. "The great Sol Butler was the Sol Butler of old," wrote the *Philadelphia Tribune*, "when he led his American Giants, all-colored professional football team to a brilliant 7 to 0 victory" before about four thousand fans.[8] Several more years would pass before he would again receive broad attention for his gridiron play.

The practice of Black versus white teams in "mixed games" was more firmly established in semipro and professional basketball than in football, but sports writer Fay Young identified the absence of any paid Black basketball referees as a "BIG evil among our people."[9] Noting that the Amateur Officials Association included no African Americans, Young named Butler and his former teammates Virgil Blueitt and George Duff as candidates for referee. The three men formed the nucleus of a semipro basketball team sponsored by the Fort Dearborn Elks Lodge: "The Elks have promised to use brown-skin officials in all games or at least one in all games mixing it up with one white and one of our own." In their winning game at the Eighth Regiment Armory against Chicago's white Capper & Capper fives team, two Black referees "handled the game . . . without the least bit of trouble."[10] Duff refereed a game without complaint between the Jewish People's Institute and the Roamer Girls in the Savoy Ballroom, and in March, Blueitt refereed alongside a white official for a game at the same venue between the white Chicago Bruins and a new Black team, the Savoy Big Five. The Savoys won, and no riot erupted "despite the fact that trouble has been predicted if Colored officials were used."[11]

After an inconspicuous season of playing football,[12] in late December 1928, Butler joined the Savoy Big Five (also known as the Savoyagers), Chicago's best Black team at the time, along with future NFL player Joe Lillard and two young players who previously had played on the up-and-coming Harlem Globetrotters.[13] At thirty-three, Butler was now one of the older players, and the Associated Negro Press distributed a story about his notable longevity, which ran in the *Pittsburgh Courier* under the subtitle "Old Man Sol": "Like Tennyson's brooks, Sol Butler seems to go on forever. One by one, his contemporaries in college sports have dropped out of the limelight . . . Years have meant little to Sol."[14] Butler referred to himself in the third person as "Old Sol," a sly joke, as he bettered younger men on the playing fields and courts, but the humor wore off as the Savoyagers' season dragged on and the team floundered. While the team won 85 percent of their forty-one games, they lost to the New York Rens after squandering a double-digit lead in the final minutes of play, and they failed to reschedule a rematch. Toward the end of the season, Butler rarely played.[15]

No Whites Allowed

The aging star continued to stretch his reach in the sporting arena beyond the gridiron and basketball court. Still working as a sportswriter for the *Chicago Bee*, Butler pushed for integration in a wide range of sports, including automobile racing; the American Automobile Association excluded Black drivers from their sanctioned events. "As the records fall, so too, will the barriers that keep us from the great racing traditions in America," Butler wrote about Indianapolis mechanic Charlie Wiggins after his near–world record performance in a fifty-mile race sponsored by the Colored Speedway Association.[16] Two summers in a row, Butler, along with representatives from other Black newspapers across the Midwest, traveled to the Indiana State Fairgrounds Speedway in Indianapolis for the fifth and sixth annual Gold and Glory Sweepstakes, where he served as the starter of the race in the summer of 1929.[17] "The first and the biggest" reason "the 100-mile dirt track derby is drawing the attention of the country," one paper reported, "is that this year for the first time, no white men are identified with the promotion of the game. This marks a new epoch in the annals of the colored sport world."[18]

During this same summer, Butler also served on the organizing committee for the American Tennis Association's National Lawn Tennis Championship in Washington Park, on Chicago's South Side, which talented Black tennis player and organizer Edgar Brown touted as "the first time in the history of America that there ever has been a real open 'Lawn Tennis' tournament where all comers are welcome."[19] This openness drew players from beyond the area, like sports star Ora Washington from Philadelphia, and from Grand Rapids, Michigan, city tennis champion Roger Grant, who had been racially excluded from western Michigan tournaments.[20] The Washington Park tournament produced a racially diverse array of winners, including African American Lulu (or Lula) Porter in the women's singles; Conrado Limjoco, a Filipino man who won the men's singles and, along with Latino J. A. Perfecto, the men's doubles; and a white youth who claimed the junior division title. Illinois attorney general Oscar E. Carlstrom presented the trophies, which included one donated by the governor that had been on display for weeks at a neighboring drugstore.[21]

But even as the American Tennis Association was attempting to lower barriers, white residents in the Washington Park neighborhood were raising them. By 1929, hundreds of thousands of Black Americans had fled the Jim Crow South for Northern cities like Chicago, where they were able to achieve a degree of relative prosperity. As a burgeoning Black middle class sought to establish itself in Chicago, white Chicagoans were at the vanguard of deploying the racially restrictive real estate covenants that would help create and maintain segregated communities, along with a vast racial wealth gap, across the country. In Washington Park, white residents wrote a racial covenant designed to keep Black people from owning or renting any property in the blocks just south of the park and near the University of Chicago.[22]

Meanwhile, middle-class Black urbanites across the country looked to enjoy the same leisure opportunities as their white counterparts, and Black vacation retreats, like Michigan's Idlewild (known as "Black Eden"), "increasingly dotted the rural Midwestern landscape," notes historian Brian McCammack.[23] In 1929, Butler—along with his newspaper boss, Anthony Overton; Elks member Samuel White; and fiery president of the Great Northern Realty Company, Leonard G. Outlaw—negotiated for the purchase in southern Wisconsin of a previously white-owned beach resort, which opened in mid-June under the new name Casa Loma Country Club. The 320-acre property included a golf course (today named Nippersink Golf Course) designed by US Open champion James Foulis Jr., an attractive clubhouse, seventeen additional buildings, and 150 feet of lakeshore and beach. It was located within a few miles of Lake Ivanhoe, a Black-owned summer resort community, which opened two years earlier with an outdoor concert by jazz star Cab Calloway.[24]

The new club reportedly drew thousands of Black Chicagoans, and the Windy City Golf Club held their annual amateur and open tournaments on Casa Loma's course. In 1930 the course served as the site for the national championship of the United Golfers Association (UGA), an organization of African American professional golfers.[25] This was the UGA's fifth annual championship tournament and the first one not on the East Coast, which reflected Chicago's status, in the words of historian Lane Demas, as "the capital of black golf."[26] For the first time in tournament history, women competed in their own division and a Southerner from New Orleans won the men's division. Such a setup enabled Butler to hobnob with the wealthy and social elite as a swim instructor, on the golf course, and perhaps as part owner of the club, where his celebrity status would have attracted visitors.

"Villagers and neighbors alike admit that the negroes are orderly and keep to themselves on the club premises," but good behavior did not prevent an onslaught of threats and intimidation.[27] In the resort's first month of operation, the clubhouse windows were shot out, and "a giant firecracker" was set off on the club's driveway, which prompted employees to flee in fear. When rumors surfaced of angry white residents planning to use "torch and dynamite," Casa Loma's manager equipped club guards with shotguns and pistols. In response, the local sheriff and three deputies raided the resort, seizing three slot machines.[28] Some local white residents boycotted storekeepers who sold goods to the Black vacationers;[29] African Americans retaliated by threatening to withhold "Negro labor at nearby resorts," where whites allowed Black people to work but not vacation, and, when home in the city, boycott Chicago businesses owned by local whites.[30] They also placed a sign at the entrance of the club that read "No Whites Allowed."[31]

The white residents of Powers Lake ultimately succeeded in their plans to undo Casa Loma. In October, only four months after the club had opened its doors, a circuit court judge sided with the white plaintiffs' suit to foreclose on the mortgage of property owned by the club. A few days later, the stock market crashed, ushering in the Great Depression. By the following August, the property reverted to the original white owners after Butler, who served as president of the Casa Loma Improvement Company, and John Fangrat, the secretary and treasurer, signed a quit claim deed that relinquished their rights to the property. Years earlier, Butler had traveled with white college friends to the YMCA camp in Lake Geneva, Wisconsin, just a few miles west of the doomed resort, where he had enjoyed his leisure time without incident. Then he was one of the relatively few young adults of color among hundreds of white YMCA campers, and his presence did not threaten racial power dynamics. Years later, however, the notion of Black men owning and running recreational facilities used by Black vacationers was an intolerable threat to white supremacy in this neighboring lake community, where African Americans had worked in service roles only and could not purchase and enjoy their own property.[32]

The next year, white owners of Lake Lawn Hotel in neighboring Delavan, Wisconsin, built the so-called help's quarters for the more than one hundred Black maids, cooks, and waiters who for over a decade traveled each summer from Hot Springs, Arkansas, to serve vacationing white occupants.[33] African Americans working at Powers Lake and other area resorts and for private families attended dances at the "help's quarters," which had a telephone, barber shop, dance hall, radio, piano, and showers. Even before the federal government—through policies enacted by the Home Owners' Loan Corporation, Federal Housing Administration, and Veterans Administration—dramatically increased residential segregation during the 1930s, 1940s, and 1950s, Butler and other Northern Black entrepreneurs ran into insurmountable local and state resistance to expanding Black access to leisure and recreation on real estate deemed reserved for whites only.

Ye Olde Tymers Club

After another disappointing season playing basketball with the Savoy Big Five,[34] in the spring of 1930 Sol Butler was back in the familiar world of track and field, serving as head coach for the team sponsored by the Wabash Avenue YMCA.[35] Maulden Gibbs, a World War I vet, coached hurdlers and pole vaulters; Foster Branch, a playground director,[36] worked with sprinters and high jumpers; and sprinter L. Turner served as team captain. The athletes included Albert Washington, who missed qualifying for the 1924 Olympic team in the 100-meter run and triple jump; John William Brooks, who long-jumped in the 1936 Berlin Olympics; Otis Sexton, former captain of the University of Iowa track team; and Ralph Metcalfe, a future Olympic sprinter whom Arthur Ashe suggested might have been better than Jesse Owens (and Owens declared Metcalfe "the greatest sprinter of his day").[37] With this stellar talent, Butler's team dominated the third annual YMCA track meet at Stagg Field, more than doubling the score of second-place finisher Sears-Roebuck.[38]

The Wabash track and field team inspired the founding of a new athletic organization, Ye Olde Tymers Club (OTC), which would draw upon the talents and cultural capital of the best Black athletes in Chicago to promote "clean sport" and give "colored champions an outlet for their talents when they leave college," providing the city's young Black athletes with the kind of financial and institutional support Butler had lacked in his post-collegiate years.[39] Butler was an inaugural member of the new club, which remained a force in amateur athletics into the 1960s. Other members of the OTC, composed of Chicago residents, included some of the early twentieth century's greatest athletes: Jack Johnson, Joe Louis, Jesse Owens, Ralph Metcalfe, John Brooks, and Duke Slater.

The club's track and field team became one of the powerhouses of the Central AAU. Brooks coached Theodora Ann "Tidye" Pickett, who ran the 80-meter hurdles in Berlin, the first African American woman to compete in the Olympics. OTC all-around star Louise Harris set a state record in the broad jump, captained the girls' basketball team, and led the OTC softball team to three consecutive city championships. Claude "Buddy" Young won the Junior AAU Championship in the 100-meter dash as a member of the junior OTC track team and then achieved spectacular success as a college football player.[40] After World War II, Young "assumed a directorate post" with the club and played professional football.[41] OTC junior member Robert Ryland won the Cook County table tennis championship and would eventually become the first Black professional tennis player. Ryland recalled that as teenagers he and future jazz singer Joe Williams (born Joseph Goreed) "used to check coats at the Old Timer's Club—that's where all the old timers would meet—the guys who were somebody. Joe and I used to play table tennis together when we weren't checking coats."[42]

In May 1936 the American Olympic Committee announced that the OTC was launching a campaign to raise money to cover the expenses of African American Olympians. An OTC-sponsored AAU track meet served as the centerpiece of this fund-raising effort.[43] Media attention to the campaign ceased after Roi Ottley of the *Amsterdam News* wrote a scathing editorial that presented the Chicagoans' efforts as self-discrimination and vulgar, back-slapping nationalism that stymied social progress. Ottley believed that the American Olympic Committee ought to be fund-raising for its Black athletes, as it did for other American hopefuls, rather than pushing this burden onto the backs of a frustratingly subservient and segregated community.[44] The meet proceeded as planned, with a crowd of nearly five thousand, and many African Americans participated, including Ralph Metcalfe, Jesse Owens, OTC member John Brooks, and Ben Johnson, who ran in a special 4×100-meter relay. The all-Black fund-raising event was consistent with OTC's mission to support Black athletes, most notably in track and field. They raised money for the would-be Olympians as a pragmatic response to intractable realities, not as a concession to segregation as Ottley charged. (If not the African American community, who else would take care of their star athletes of whom they were so proud?) A week later, these American hopefuls competed in semifinal tryouts for the Olympics on Stagg Field at the University of Chicago. All but Johnson, who later injured himself, went on to the Berlin Olympics, along with fifteen other African American athletes.[45]

As the Great Depression deepened and employment opportunities disappeared, Butler couldn't afford to devote his spring to coaching the Wabash Y another season. By early January 1931, he was managing and playing guard for the Gilkerson Union Giants basketball team, which maintained a rigorous travel schedule until early April. The team barnstormed through western Illinois, southern Minnesota, and, primarily, eastern Iowa.[46] Never before had Butler kept up such a hectic game schedule, and because most hotels and restaurants in the Midwest refused service to Black people, the team probably depended on the hospitality of the small, local African American communities in the towns they visited. They often attracted large crowds, but sometimes attendance was light. In a well-advertised game in Muscatine, Iowa, against another barnstorming group, the House of David (reportedly an all-Jewish squad), a sparse crowd meant that the two "teams had to be content with something like $16 apiece."[47] Unlike earlier years on the Forty Club, Chicago Defenders, Eighth Regiment, and Savoyagers, when he played for New Negro pride and with aspirations of claiming regional and national glory as Black champions, he now played on a Black Fives team out of financial necessity.

"Typical of many barnstorming teams, Gilkerson's club generally treated fans to some comedic action," notes historian Leslie Heaphy.[48] The echo of a slowly dying blackface minstrel tradition raised revenues and warded against the threat of racial violence. The team performed in a style that evoked the eventual hallmarks of a much longer-lived team from Chicago, the Harlem Globetrotters, whom the Giants played in Des Moines at the end of the season. "Thrills, comedy and humor galore are on the cards this week for local basketball fans," touted a local paper in advance of the Muscatine game.[49] But in addition to comedic chops, another Iowa paper noted that the Gilkerson team "possessed speed and lots of it, had a passing game which had the home lads guessing where the ball was a good deal of the time and its set plays were something most every coach must dream of as the perfect basketball."[50] While clowning became a main staple of the Harlem Globetrotters once professional basketball desegregated around mid-century, the Globetrotters and Giants during this period did not let such antics detract from their serious efforts to win. This unusually busy season—they reportedly won 67 games and lost 14—was the last time Butler traveled as a player with a basketball team.[51]

Have Nothing on Central Avenue

After the basketball season ended, Butler returned home to Chicago, and in May he joined Duke Slater on a float in the Chicago Jubilee Parade, touted as the "greatest and most colorful parade in Chicago's history."[52] They traveled through a multiracial crowd of an anticipated half-million people who lined the streets of downtown. A few months later, Butler led the planning of an October birthday party for actor Richard B. Harrison at the Eighth Regiment Armory. Organizers anticipated a crowd of four thousand, which included the entire cast of the play *Green Pastures*. Harrison played the lead role of God in this all-Black-cast play, which had enjoyed unprecedented success on Broadway and was attracting capacity audiences in Chicago.[53] "Old Man Sol," now in his mid-thirties, had spent more than a decade building a life in Chicago. He was widely known in the city and across the Midwest—as an athlete, a civic leader, an entrepreneur, a coach, and, increasingly, a showman. But two years into the Great Depression, up to half of Black workers in Chicago were unemployed, and Butler's options in the athletic arena were narrowing with each passing year.[54]

Seizing what may have been his last opportunity as a professional athlete, Butler decided to head west with the Chicago Black Hawks football team, also known as "Fritz Pollard's All-Stars." The previous football season he starred at quarterback and on defense with a similar group of players that he and Pollard recruited, who competed against all-white teams—one in Pittsburgh led by Art Rooney (a team that later became the NFL's Steelers) and the other in Columbus composed of Ohio State University alumni.[55] The all-Black lineup included Halley Harding, manager of the Savoyagers basketball team, and the era's most successful Black football players: J. Mayo ("Ink") Williams, recently retired Duke Slater, rising star Joe Lillard (one of the final two Black players in the NFL before the league fully segregated after the 1933 season), and Pollard, who served as coach. Yet the season fizzled after a big win in December 1931, against Duffield's West Coast All Stars (a team presumably led by USC Trojan standout Marshall Duffield) at White Sox Park in Los Angeles and games in San Diego and San Francisco.[56] Butler did not then return to Chicago and his wife of more than four years. Instead, he threw himself into Hollywood life and the glitzy promise of the booming film industry.

In February the *Pittsburgh Courier* reported on Butler's "busy" negotiations over a contract with Metro-Goldwyn-Mayer for a film "which is slated to give him and other members of the famous Chicago Blackhawks [*sic*] football team here, a big break in a forthcoming picture . . . The studio plans a colored football story."[57] Like many of Butler's other promising Hollywood leads, the film failed to pan out. Later in the year Butler joined over one hundred other "race actors" in testing for the part of Nagu, an African king in the Universal Studios film *Nagana*: "He must be 6 feet–8 inches tall, dark brown complexion, handsome but with African features, powerfully built, have a regal dominant presence and speak perfect English."[58] The role went to a former minstrel performer in his mid-fifties, Billy McClain.

Los Angeles had an appeal for Butler beyond the lure of fortune and fame on the silver screen: The city was hosting the 1932 Olympic Summer Games. Former Olympians were flocking to Los Angeles, and Butler was in his element, "flitting about as he did when he and Charlie [*sic*] Paddock were the two fastest men in the Good Old U.S.A."[59] The current crop of Black Olympians included gold medalist broad jumper Ed Gordon and 100- and 200-meter dash gold, silver, and bronze medalists Eddie Tolan and Ralph Metcalfe. Two years earlier, Metcalfe had led Butler's Wabash Y team to victory, and the *Los Angeles Times* reported that Sol Butler had trained "star Negro sprinters" Metcalf and Tolan for the Olympic Games.[60]

Despite the "remarkably durable facade of interethnic and international harmony in Southern California in conjunction with the games,"[61] Los Angeles outside the Olympic bubble was a segregated city, and Butler would have been unable to socialize with Charley Paddock and other white friends at the segregated restaurants and nightclubs where they drank and danced after the days' contests. Seeing an opportunity in the city's racist limitations, Butler the "social lion" lent his celebrity and charisma to a new business venture.[62] The evening before the start of the games, the Harlem Show Boat, "one of the after-show places of Central Avenue," opened its doors with Butler as assistant manager and director.[63] This was the third incarnation of the nightclub at the Dunbar Hotel; the second had opened the previous October under the titular management of none other than Jack Johnson. The Dunbar Hotel was the epicenter of the burgeoning Black district along South Central Avenue.[64] "Seventh avenue in Harlem or South Parkway in Chi have nothing on Central avenue in Los," a *Pittsburgh Courier* reporter noted.[65] Vocalist Caroline Harlson remembered that "all the great musicians, singers, dancers . . . migrated to Central Avenue from all across the country."[66] Show producer and choreographer Patsy Hunter added, "And they all stayed at the Dunbar Hotel, 'cause there was nowhere else to stay." The thriving strip on South Central drew not only the era's greatest performers but also members of the Black intelligentsia and many white Angelenos, including Hollywood celebrities. Butler attended the games during the day and helped oversee the hot new club at night, staging a party for Metcalfe and Tolan, but before the end of September, he had moved on.[67]

After playing the theater role of "a political boss" in the two-act musical comedy *Central Avenue* by veteran performers Alex Lovejoy and "Jolly" John Larkin at the Lincoln Theatre,[68] Butler turned his attention back to the sporting world and refashioned himself as a boxing trainer at the Main Street Gym, located just north of the Black community surrounding Central Avenue. "Jackson is a marvelous physical specimen," Butler told a *Los Angeles Times* reporter in late April 1933 about the welterweight boxer Peter Martin, known as "Young Peter Jackson."[69] His promising "protege" was on the verge of fighting the two-time welterweight world champion Jackie Fields in Olympic Auditorium, the largest and best-known boxing venue in the city. The once famously modest athlete predicted victory for Jackson with a hyperbolic boast about his own glory days: "He is in the condition now that I was thirteen years ago when I set a new world's record in the broad jump and was outrunning Charley Paddock in the 100 meters. Just as condition sets jumping and sprint records, it wins fights in the prize ring."[70] In the 1934 Los Angeles city directory, Butler listed his profession as "pugilist," though he never fought in a single recorded boxing match.

Along with Martin, Butler trained two other promising boxers: Ernest Bendy, known as "Dynamite Jackson," and Albert "Chalky" Wright. In preparation for Bendy's fight for the Colored Heavyweight Championship against LeRoy Haynes, which he lost, Butler "concentrated on teaching the big fast powerful part Cherokee how to change that long left of his into a machine gun bullet, also how to use his weight and heighth [*sic*] to advantage in every other blow and maneuver," the Associated Negro Press reported.[71] Chalky became world featherweight champion in the early 1940s and fought in well over two hundred professional fights before retiring at thirty-six. African American author and former professional boxer Jay Thomas Caldwell described the Main Street Gym in his boxing novel, *Me an' You*, which drew liberally from the experience of Chalky Wright, to whom Caldwell dedicated his book. Caldwell depicted a boxing world rife with gambling, hustling, heavy drinking, violence, womanizing, and men, both Black and white, who encouraged and benefited from the bodily sacrifices of the predominantly poor, young fighters of color making the most of their limited years in the ring.[72]

Butler's foray into the boxing world represented an ill-defined blend of exploitation and selflessness. He gained attention from the hard-earned success of the Black boxers he trained while lending them his celebrity, which helped open doors of opportunity. As a group, these boxers rarely got to fight the top white opponents for the largest prize money.[73] Never before had Butler so baldly rejected the respectability politics of his mother and adopted the sporting life persona exemplified by Jack Johnson.

Butler also busied himself with other entrepreneurial athletic pursuits in 1934. He put together a Black baseball team that he named the Ramblers. On April 24, in what the media identified as the first night game for a Black team, the Huntington Beach Oilers "slaughtered" the Ramblers 19–3, and other white semipro baseball teams canceled their scheduled games against Butler's team.[74] His sole foray into baseball was a flop, and his efforts in the city's Women's Basketball League (WBL) were fraught. A committee had organized a series of games to raise money for a YWCA in the Central Avenue district; Butler took over coaching duties of the Vitality Girls, and games began on January 20, 1934, in Liberty Hall at Eighteenth Avenue and Figueroa Street. Joining him as a league coach, Halley Harding led the Roamers, whose name paid homage to the powerhouse women's team Butler had formed nearly fifteen years earlier in Chicago. Old friends Butler and Harding also competed on football gridirons during this period.[75]

Not content with limiting himself to coaching, Butler decided to advocate for the young Black women of the WBL. He convinced the teams to agree to pay the players 40 percent of the games' proceeds, with the remainder going toward expenses and the YWCA building fund. Unfortunately, after covering player salaries and expenses, there was no money left for the YWCA fund. An uproar ensued, and Harry Levette, a sportswriter and the league's publicity manager, wrote a scathing article on the implementation of Butler's plan. If players failed to give all their proceeds back to the building fund, Levette warned, "just as sure as Christ made little apples there is going to be some very unsavory talk about subterfuge. So listen girls you had better 'bout face before it is too late."[76]

While Sol Butler, confronted with the hard economic realities of life for an amateur athlete without the support of a college or deep-pocketed booster, had long-ago embraced professionalism, his commitment to supporting the careers and livelihoods of young women athletes here butted up against the staunch middle-class Black commitment to amateur athletics as a kind of moral good. Although his mother's old women's league colleagues may not have recognized their values in Butler's hard-nosed negotiation, his dedication to earning a fair shake for WBL players points to the activism and racial uplift inherent in many of his entrepreneurial efforts. Ultimately, the players heeded Levette's warnings and returned their 40 percent.[77] African American women's basketball in Los Angeles declined in the wake of this season.

We Need a New Union!

Sol Butler was undaunted in the face of these disappointments. In March the *Afro-American* noted that he celebrated his thirty-ninth birthday "by playing a game of basketball in a fraternity series. Butler looked the picture of health and skipped around the floor with all the vim and vigor of his younger mates and opponents."[78] He had been in LA for only a little more than two years, but he was already a fixture in the African American community. In June he served with attorneys, judges, and doctors on a committee that staged a dance in Elks Hall to honor Ralph Metcalfe and other track champions visiting the city.[79] In August he announced his "intensive campaign on behalf of a number of candidates" as the head of the Progressive Democrat-Republican League (PDRL), whose name evoked the shifting allegiances of African American voters and the character of politics in the city.[80]

"In black Los Angeles," writes historian Douglas Flamming, "the guiding ideal was pragmatic activism."[81] While almost three-quarters of party-affiliated registered voters in Butler's precinct identified as Republican in 1934, the number of Democratic voters increased each year, growing to just over 40 percent two years later. Progressives represented a small but growing number of Black voters. Butler himself identified as a Democrat, but as head of the PDRL, he appeared less interested in party affiliation than in supporting candidates who kept the African American community in mind without alienating white voters. Butler remained a political organizer through 1935, when he served on a committee to plan a four-day event that featured US senator William Gibbs McAdoo as principal speaker.[82]

Butler's role in the PDRL, an organization with multiparty affiliation, contrasted with the politicking of Jack Johnson, who several years earlier had served as a Democratic committee member in New York's second district. According to Black editor A. McDonald Ifill of the journal *The Light*, "Johnson will conduct a physical culture club from which subtle propaganda of a sort will emanate on its way to the ears and heart of colored voters" who might support New York governor Al Smith in his presidential bid.[83] In response to growing recognition of Johnson's partisan work, the chair of the Democratic

National Committee publicly rejected the notion that the former champion had any pull with the national party. Johnson later threw his support behind President Franklin D. Roosevelt midway through his first term in office. In a widely publicized speech made at a Detroit meeting of the Black nationalist organization the Universal Negro Improvement Association, he praised the Democratic newspapers for making his famous fight against Jim Jeffries possible before signaling that Republicans no longer best served African Americans' interests: "Roosevelt is champion now and wearing the belt. Abraham Lincoln was a good fighter in his prime, but he can't help us now."[84]

In contrast, Butler championed local politicians from different parties, including Republican Gordon L. McDonough for Los Angeles County supervisor: "'I think Mr. McDonough upholds the true ideals of real Americanism,' Butler said, 'and for that reason, the people of our group should stand behind this public official one hundred percent.'"[85] As county supervisor for more than a decade and then US representative for two decades, McDonough received recognition for supporting the African American community and civil rights.[86] A celebrity who enjoyed the sporting life, Butler also embraced pragmatic activism.

Shortly after the 1934 elections, Butler landed his most significant film role, as an unnamed striking coal miner in *Black Fury*, directed by Michael Curtiz.[87] Film historian Colin Shindler argues that the film "is for the historian of the New Deal arguably the most fascinating motion picture to be made in America during the 1930s."[88] *Black Fury* features Jewish actor Paul Muni as an immigrant Pennsylvania coal miner named Joe Radak. After losing his would-be spouse to another man, the demoralized Radak enters his union meeting drunk and winds up leading a group of disaffected workers in a violent strike. When the member of a thuggish detective agency kills Radak's friend, Radak shuts the mine down with dynamite and threats. The upshot of the film is the revelation that a private detective agency created the union discord for its own gain, and Radak's friend's killer is arrested.

Black Fury provides perhaps the only extant recording of Butler's voice. Early in the film he appears seated near the front of a union hall amid approximately eighty miners, at least nine of whom are Black. A national union representative celebrates the modest victories the union helped secure before cautioning members to avoid "wise guys" who would foment dissent. This warning prompts several disgruntled miners, including Butler, to rise. Three men shout out in protest, and Butler chimes in saying, "We need a new union!" *Black Fury* did not foreground the narrow range of racial stereotypes (for example, the faithful servant or comic buffoon) to which the film industry usually consigned Black men, but the Black press paid little attention to the film, perhaps because it lacked a leading Black role, stereotyped or not.[89] Butler played the most significant part among the film's African American actors, who included

Butler, playing a miner in the film *Black Fury* (1935), shouts, "We need a new union!" (Warner Bros.; film frame scan courtesy of Steve and Rosemary Miller)

his former teammate Joe Lillard, Iowan Floyd Shackelford, and journalist Harry Levette, but it was slight in comparison to Paul Robeson's role a few years later in *The Proud Valley*, another film set in a mining town.[90] One article in the *Afro-American* reported that Butler and many others "barely escaped serious injury" from a fire that broke out in a shop at the Warner Brothers Studios while filming a mining scene; numerous people were injured, and a firefighter was killed.[91] Around this same time, after heeding repeated demands from the Production Code Administration to strip the story of any content critical of big business or the mining industry, one of the two screenwriters killed himself.[92]

Black Fury's screenplay was adapted from a short story by Michael Musmanno and a stage play by Harry R. Irving, both of which were based on the brutal 1929 murder of a Pennsylvania coal miner who was beaten to death by private police employed by the Pittsburgh Coal Company. Jack Warner of Warner Brothers Studios and Joseph Breen of the era's censorious Hollywood Production Code, known as the Hays Code, forced *Black Fury*'s screenwriters to remove anything that might implicate mine owners. The film also avoided any significant depiction of interracial labor solidarity. As *Black Fury* pro-

Butler (lower left) as football star Joe Lillard in *Goin' to Town* (1935), breaks character and smiles up at Mae West after she exclaims, "Sorry, Joe." (Paramount)

gresses, the handful of Black miners disappear. This on-screen exclusion mirrored the real-life reality of organized labor in the 1930s, when Black workers comprised less than 1 percent of union membership.[93]

In early 1935, Butler had reason to believe his acting career was taking off. The *California Eagle* announced that he had landed the starring role in a staging of Shakespeare's *Othello*. The *Afro-American*'s film columnist, Fay Jackson, reported that Hollywood planned to release a film version of *Othello* with Butler playing "the Great Moor," but it never came to fruition.[94] As he worked to master his Shakespearean role, Butler also appeared, along with four other muscle-laden African American men, including Joe Lillard, in *Goin' to Town*, written in part by and starring Mae West.[95] Butler and the other "Colored boys," as they were listed on a page of the assistant director's report, were paid ten dollars a day for their work in *Goin' to Town*, while white extras earned between fifteen and twenty-five dollars a day.[96]

Toward the end of the film, West's character, Cleo Borden, appears on stage to perform an aria from the opera *Sampson and Delilah*. Butler and the other Black actors, in scant costumes with glistening, oiled skin, appear on the stage as "slaves," who exit when West snaps her fingers.[97] "Is Sol Butler getting to be the head man with Mae West?" Fay Jackson wondered. "He's in all her pictures."[98] But *Goin' to Town* turned out to be the end of Butler's brief film career rather than the beginning. West's film marked the last time Butler could be clearly identified on screen; in any future roles, he appeared as a faceless extra in the background, as he did in *Show Boat*, which starred his friend Paul Robeson.[99]

A Forerunner

By the spring of 1935, Butler had abandoned his film career "to take up newspaper publishing" as the managing editor of a new Black weekly, the *Los Angeles Truth*, which released an edition each Wednesday, sold for five cents, and bore the motto "a progressive newspaper for progressive people."[100] The newspaper's office was located at 4105 South Central Avenue, the same address as the popular Club Alabam and across the street from the Dunbar Hotel. The inaugural, and perhaps only extant, issue of the *Los Angeles Truth* appeared on March 27. "Featuring SOCIETY ♦ STAGE ♦ SCREEN ♦ SPORTS" the masthead blared. Articles included hagiographies of powerful white men in the culture industry—such as casting agency head Campbell McCullough, theater manager Jules Wolfe, and humorist Will Rogers—who helped open doors for Black actors; reports on Black entertainers like Stepin Fetchit (born Lincoln Perry), Helen Hayes, William Dunn, Ethel Waters, and John Larkin; and coverage of rodeos, horse racing, boxing, tennis, track, and other sports. "The Los Angeles Truth dedicates its work to the community," Butler the "socialite" wrote,[101] promising to feature "the exact happenings of the local community concerning society, stage, screen and sports."[102]

The first issue of the *Los Angeles Truth* also included opinion pieces on a local political issue, a ballot initiative to give a franchise to a local gas company. While one op-ed argued for rejecting Charter Amendment 1A, a longer editorial, representing the newspaper's position, supported the measure. A half-page ad on the paper's back page promised seven million dollars in revenue and a host of new jobs if the ballot initiative passed. What did not appear in the first issue of the *Truth* were articles about the criminal justice system, such as the ongoing trials of the Scottsboro Boys; antilynching campaigns; housing and labor discrimination; or other topics that propelled African American activism and drew front-page attention in Black newspapers with much larger circulations. The *Los Angeles Truth* was a short-lived enterprise. Other weeklies referenced the *Truth* as late as May, after which the newspaper was not heard from again.[103]

CLUB ARABY In Gala Opening March 28th

A Progressive Paper

THE LOS ANGELES TRUTH

Featuring

SOCIETY ★ STAGE ★ SCREEN ★ SPORTS

For Progressive People

No. 1—Vol. 1 LOS ANGELES, CALIFORNIA, WEDNESDAY, MARCH 27, 1935 2

CANOPY

By SOL BUTLER

The Los Angeles Truth dedicates its work to the community. Its slogan, "The Greatest Good for the Greatest Number," is the law of society. Within these columns will be found the exact happenings of the local community concerning society, stage, screen and sports.

We will enedavor to cover the above mentioned phases in thorough manner. Along with these will be added another feature for name of the club will be Kewpie page, wherein there will be cards and memberships given to the children writing in to the Truth, with their correct address. The name ofthe club will be Kupie Klub and all members must be registered with the Truth before they are actual members of the organization.

If you are inclined toward poetry or short, short stories of not more than one hundred words, let us know about it and we will gladly publish said poems or short story every week. If you do not get your story in the first week, just remember that you must have been late and another member of the club beat you to it. So mail your stories in early.

The kiddies' page will require all of their stories in before Thursday noon of each week. If you happen to mail it late, then do not look for the story or poem until the following week. The Kewpie Klub are active members, full of energy and alert to every situation. The Kewpie Klub editor, remembering this, believes that every member of the organization will follow the rules to the letter.

There are no charges for membehship in the Kewpie Klub so get busy, members.

* * *

The sports writers of the different dailies have been singing the praises of one Joe Louis, calling him the "Back Menace" to the great Max Baer. And they have just claim for all the articles they have written about the wonderful colored boy.

But Max Baer has something that no other white fighter has had to confront, instead of one colored menace he has two. While the papers have been lauding the greatness of Joe Louis and stating that in another year he will be ready for a championship fight, right here in Los Angeles is as good a fighter as the present crop affords in the person of our own Leroy Haynes. True, Haynes is not the knock-out artist that Louis is. He is more on the order of Gene Tunney, clever, fast and heady. Like Louis, he has a colored manager in his brother-in-law, Charley Williams. Williams is a likeable fellow but he has not the od "mazuma" like the Louis gang affords, hence the reason for Haynes slow progress.

Give Haynes the same breaks and in a few months you will not know just which one to choose as

(Continued on Page 7)

CENTRAL CASTING HEAD FRIEND OF GROUP

Campbell McCullough

Campbell McCullough Engineer, Writer, Executive

Back in 1905, a young man by the name of Campbell MacCulloch graduated from the University of Toronto as a proficient engineer and went to New York, where he was given a chance to put what he had learned into practical use. In 1908 from electrical engineering he went to industrial engineering.

Although engineering was his chief interest at the time, magazine articles were written in his spare time, but Campbell did not stop with that. He wrote three plays before he became an assistant in the Triangle Film Corporation as the advertising manager, studio manager, business manager, and scenario editor.

(Continued on Page 7)

Crutchfield Made Favorite to Win In Primaries

A complete check up of the entire district by precinct workers indicates that Homer Crutchfield will be elected councilman of the 7th District in the primaries next Tuesday, April 2. In all parts of the district the citizens are rallying to the standards of Crutchfield. It is believed by political observers

(Continued on Page 2)

Style Show To Hold Month's Spotlight

The coming style show that is to be produced at Masonic Hall April 18th, by Mrs. Alicia Strickland and Miss Permelia White of Los Angeles and Pasadena respectively, is fast gaining momentum in this section. These two young ladies have made names for themselves as modistes of rare ability.

Mrs. Strickland, a graduate of

(Continued on Page 2)

Vote Yes on 1-A Means More Jobs, Says Luke McGahan

Charter Amendment 1-A, the gas franchise proposal which will increase city revenues by more than $7,000,000, shoud receive the overwhelming approval of the voters Tuesday.

The sum of $7,000,000 from an entirely new source, is sufficient even under existing conditions, to pay al expense of the city government for many months.

With this revenue the city can restore to the payrolls the workers in the street cleaning department who lost their jobs because the city was unable to continue their wages.

Many of our neighbors were the unfortunate victims of this slash in personnel. They were hard-working, substantial citizens, who

(Continued on Page 5)

CLUB ARABY OPENS WITH GREAT SHOW

Sweet Music crooning, gay laughter mingled with the sound of popping corks, sound of dancing feet keeping time to the Bobby Chapman's Arabian nKights, every body gay. It's Club Araby, newest cabaret s ensation owned and operated by the well known sportsman Johnnie Baber. The music starts again, four persons,

PATSY-HUNTER

three girls and a male singer, they tell me it is Charley Andrews, great baritone and the three shades of brown going into their number and they do themselves proud.

Patsw Hunter

Then comes that high stepping dancing chorus headed by Patsy Hunter, well known as a great great dancer and producer, following her is Ernistine Porter, Ruth Scott, Lucille Battles, Myrtle Fortune, Alice Keys and Gladys Johnson, these names need no introduction to followers of night clubs, as they are hard to beat on anybody's floor. Next the Three Broadway Flashes, dancing trio deluxe. The music becomes low again and Eddie Wright, street singer, appears. He is impersonating Gene Austin and he does a good job.

Known Artists

The stars keep sparkling and Miss Octavia Summers and Miss Alma Travers take charge of the floor and you jknow ust what happens. The guests applaud and every one is merry. Tony Collins, the manager is bound to every one, trying to see that they have a grand time.

The location is 55 and Central avenue, and it is a replica of a shiek's tent upon the desert. The decorations are bright and gay, known colors for the orient. Go out and see them.

Jules Wolfe A Benefactor To Eastside

By EDWARD R. LONG

Mr. Jules Wolf, manager of the Lincoln Theatre, has been in the amusement business for the past twenty-five years. Mr. Wolf entered the Eastside amusement section in June, 1927, taking over the Rosebud Theatre from West Coast Theatres at the time.

When Mr. Wolf opened the

JULES-WOLFF

Rosebud, it was in very bad condition, and he immediately made many improvements and was very successful in its operation. At the time, it had an entire white personnel, but he immediately began to replace the positions held by white with colored employees, and The Rosebud was the first business enterprise on Central Avenue to boast of an entire colored personnel. Many of the Eastside residents know the history of the Lincoln Theatre, and realize that this theatre was not a success when it opened.

Mr. Wolf took over the Lincoln in August, 1930, after several oth-

(Continued on Page 5)

Defeat 1-A, Says Will Anderson, Noted Attorney

Six specific reasons why on Tuesday, April 2, voters should reject Proposition 1-A, through which the Los Angeles Gas and Electric Corporation is seeking a special-privilege gas franchise, were given today by Will H. Anderson, president of the Municipal Light and Power Defense League. The League has long battled in the interests of the peopl for municipally-owned utilities.

Anderson's six reasons for voting "no" on 1-A are:

1. The present franchise pro-

(Continued on Page 7)

The inaugural issue of the *Los Angeles Truth*, edited by Sol Butler. March 27, 1935. (University of California Los Angeles Special Collections)

Even without his own weekly, Butler weighed in on a heated debate over Black athletic success. In a letter to the Los Angeles sports editor of the *Daily News*, he disagreed with "the noted physicians and coaches" who attributed the "sensational work" of African American long jumpers and sprinters to racial differences, writing, "I wonder if you would be willing to take the real reason from one of the first broad-jumpers that started the parade of colored stars forward."[104] After walking readers through an impressive list of Black athletes, he claimed that no discernible racial attributes linked them together. Their builds were different—referring to himself as "a type that looked like a weight man"—and the size of their shoes varied dramatically; this point was particularly salient given rising belief that Black athletes benefited from uniquely endowed heel bones and Achilles tendons. Historian David Wiggins notes that such racialized speculation grew in the wake of the 1932 Olympics and, in particular, Jesse Owens's towering success months earlier at the National College Athletic Association (NCAA) championship meet.[105] "No different build, as all of the men I have mentioned have varied in builds as easily as their names have varied," wrote Butler. "Right now in the grade schools are lads with their hearts and minds set on being another Owens or [Eulace] Peacock. And from that burning determination will come another black champion."[106]

Butler continued to train boxers, including light heavyweight Charlie "Killer" Coates, who received ample attention in the *Los Angeles Times* leading up to his fight against former light heavyweight title holder Maxie Rosenbloom. The newspaper featured three large photos of Coates, Butler, and Coates's white manager, Suey Welch, singing around a piano, jogging, and at rest, all smiles and confidence. The accompanying article, which bore the subtitle "Colored 'Killer' Has Chance to Flatten Hebrew in Olympic Feature," hyped the fight in racial terms during a period of increasing antisemitism.[107] The hype worked; the stadium was full, and two thousand people were reportedly turned away at the door. Rosenbloom defeated Coates in ten rounds on points.[108]

In August 1936, heavyweight Ernest Bendy traveled with Butler, his manager, to White City Arena in Chicago for his final fight, which he lost.[109] Butler stayed in Chicago, where, a few years later, he worked with a young boxer named Altus Allen, whom Butler hoped would eventually claim the world heavyweight title from Joe Louis. Butler served as Allen's trainer and manager and, along with George Halas, owned partial interest in his contract.[110] At nineteen, Allen defeated Johnny Paychek (born Pacek) by a knockout in June 1940. "Ain't that lift ["left"] a whiz?" Butler said after the fight.[111] "He only used his right twice in 10 rounds. Of course, he ain't learned to use it the way he ought to yet. But he's still young. Just a cub." Full of confidence, Butler announced his intentions to match his prizefighter against the light heavyweight champion Billy Conn, a fight that never materialized, but first Butler accompanied Allen on a two-month vacation in California. A reporter recalled seeing Butler back in Los Angeles "with a French beret, sparkling-polished nails, razor sharp creased pants, [and] a block long car with everything except shower bath"—the flashy, glitzy epitome of the "perverted ideal . . . of the boy who wants to be a Jack Johnson."[112]

• • •

Butler entered California playing football with the Chicago Black Hawks and, near the end of his West Coast stay four years later, he coached (and despite his forty-one years, probably played on) an all-Black football team, the Black Olympics. Prior to a Thanksgiving Day game against the all-white Atlantic Seals in Atlantic Boulevard Stadium, Butler predicted, "We'll fill the stadium," and appeared convinced that the reported "thousands of followers of his team" would attend.[113] "If the Seals have any fans they will have to stand up," he said. As his previous Chicago and New York basketball teams had illustrated through interracial matchups, the social significance of the games extended beyond the playing fields and into the stands, where he saw potential for social change.

His team lost the game, but a decade later Black sports entrepreneurs won a far greater battle when the Los Angeles Rams signed UCLA star Kenny Washington and, soon after, his college teammate Woody Strode to contracts that permanently reintegrated the NFL. Sol's friend Halley Harding—who was born in Wichita, Kansas, just after the Butlers first arrived and lived in Rock Island, Illinois, around the time Sol attended the local high school there[114]—was the driving force behind this civil rights victory. By then an influential journalist and editor in Los Angeles, Harding used his platform to push the Rams' executives to integrate their team by drawing attention to the stadium in which they wished to play. Speaking to the Los Angeles Coliseum Commission in early 1946, Harding laid bare the hypocrisy and injustice that he, Sol, and other colleagues had aimed for decades to redress as athletes, coaches, and organizers and through the Black press.[115]

Years later, sportswriters would fondly recall the efforts of Harding and Butler, who brought Black semipro football to Los Angeles and stayed to nurture a cultural climate where fans expected to see top Black talent on the gridiron. Journalist Herman Hill, who wrote about integration in sports for the *Pittsburgh Courier* and integrated basketball at the University of Southern California, happily quipped, "Little did [Sol and Halley] know that they were a forerunner of the things to come."[116] Even when brash and immodest, Butler demonstrated that lasting social change came through innovative collaboration.

Cooldown

1936–1954

From "Cowboy from South Parkway" (ca. 1940) by Margaret Bonds and Langston Hughes. (©2021 Videmus/Louise Toppin. All Rights Reserved. Reprinted by permission of Videmus/Louise Toppin for the Bonds/Richardson family. Hughes lyrics used by permission of International Literary Properties.)

Back in Chicago after his Hollywood sojourn, Butler found work as the bodyguard of celebrity cosmetician Marguerita Ward. "Not only is [Ward] consulted in the perfection of 'make-up' by the theatrically eminent, socially elect and fastidiously correct members of her own race, but by equally meticulous members of the white race in its theatrical and social capacities," wrote white Chicagoan Kitty Chappelle.[1] Ward provided Butler with entrée back into Chicago society. In November he and Ward attended a large party thrown in honor of actor Clarence Muse. Guests included jazz great Louis Armstrong, attorney Edith Sampson, and civil rights activist Daisy Lampkin. Ward also helped connect Butler with Chicago's drama scene. Decades earlier she contributed to the minstrel shows of Bert Williams and George Walker, first as a singer and later as the makeup artist who, responding to concerned theater managers, created makeup that ensured light-skinned dancers registered as

Black to white audiences. In 1937 she became the makeup artist for the new National Negro Theatre Guild. Butler identified himself to a Dubuque reporter as the guild's assistant director; the lack of corroborating sources suggests that this title was wishful rather than real. The company's second production, *Sugar Hill*, appeared at the Studebaker Theater in Chicago in February 1938.[2] Butler gave one of the "noteworthy performances in the cast of 47."[3]

Ward's office was located on Forty-Sixth Avenue, a few blocks from Butler's apartment on South Parkway (now King Drive) and around the corner from Ye Olde Tymers Club's elegant clubhouse at 4725 South Parkway. Ward and the wife of *Defender* owner, Robert Abbott, were both members of the club's women's auxiliary, which used the clubhouse to host events. The location also became the NAACP's headquarters for a 1939 membership campaign.[4] Before Ye Olde Tymers Club member Jesse Owens achieved international fame by winning four gold medals in the Berlin Olympics in 1936, Butler and Owens appeared together shaking hands at the NCAA (National Collegiate Athletic Association) Track and Field Championships in Berkeley, California, in a *Chicago Defender* photo below the title "Broad Jump Stars."[5] In December 1937, Butler traveled back to Dubuque, where his college teammate Dale Welch was president and his old basketball coach still had Butler's photo hanging in his office, to speak at a sports awards dinner. "You know," Sol told a Dubuque reporter, "I always figured I should have been a millionaire."[6] Twelve years later, the university invited him back to campus to speak at a banquet in Peters Commons during homecoming. The previous year, Dubuque's basketball team had advanced to the National Association of Intercollegiate Basketball (NAIB) tournament, only to be told to bench their star Black player, LeRoy Watts. Instead, Dubuque and other schools withdrew from the tournament. In response, the NAIB reversed its segregationist policy, two years before the NBA desegregated.[7]

Butler lived his final years in Chicago, no longer sought out as a star player—although he claimed to still suit up for football games into his forties—but valued as a legendary sports figure. As increasingly hopeful signs of segregation's demise emerged during the World War II era, he remained dedicated to creating sport opportunities, especially for Black youth. But he now was more an observer than driver of the cultural change he and other aging entrepreneurs had sparked.

Black Creative Destruction

Thirty-five years after Sol Butler began his sports career as a schoolboy in Hutchinson, Kansas—where he developed a preternatural social mobility in order to move freely on the white playing fields of the Midwest—US athletics were finally starting to catch up. In 1946 the NFL reintegrated; in 1947

Jackie Robinson reintegrated Major League Baseball; in 1950, twenty years after the heyday of Butler's career in Black Fives basketball, the first Black players were drafted by NBA teams. In the 1948 Olympics, high jumper Alice Coachman became the first Black woman from any country to win a gold medal. After more than two decades of Black boxers being denied a chance at the heavyweight title once Jack Johnson lost the crown to Jess Willard, in 1937 Joe Louis claimed the title, which he held for twelve years. The death knell of Jim Crow in sports sounded years before the long, violent end of de jure segregation across the country.

From the early to late 1940s, Butler had a full-time job with the Chicago Park District. Along with other duties and responsibilities relevant to "promoting, planning, organizing, and supervising all physical activities for men and boys," Butler was paid "to plan and conduct city-wide athletic contests and tournaments."[8] As a park district supervisor, he directed a "football coaching school" for over two hundred boys in Washington Park.[9] One of six teams in the Chicago Park District, they practiced "two hours three times a week [and] put emphasis on the finer points of passing, kicking, blocking and running."[10] With the help of his friend Duke Slater, in 1944 Butler's inaugural team became "known as the hardest tackling team playing boys' football."[11] Butler and Slater partnered to coach the twelve-to-seventeen-year-old boys for at least three more seasons. Butler also left his mark on women's athletics; the Harlem Globe Trotterettes, traveling across the country in a nine-passenger DeSoto van, identified Butler as their founder and trainer.[12] After he returned to Chicago from Los Angeles, Butler developed the Oberlin Athletic Club's women's basketball team, which became "one of Chicago's premier women's sport organizations."[13]

Butler remained active with Ye Olde Tymers Club through the late 1930s and early 1940s, planning formal affairs at the clubhouse and mentoring the next generation of Black athletes. The citywide pattern of racial segregation, reinforced through the threat of violence, redlining, and restrictive real estate covenants, ensured that Chicago's Black youth depended solely on the guidance of Black mentors. "No racial group in the city is so definitely confined within the limits of its own numbers for its recreational outlets as is the Negro," wrote the Chicago Recreation Commission.[14] As trailblazing stars like Jesse Owens, Jackie Robinson, and Joe Louis—and, before them, Jack Johnson, Howard Drew, Duke Slater, Paul Robeson, and Sol Butler—leaped, dashed, swung, tackled, and punched their way through the controlling sphere of white supremacy, the freedom of movement they embodied was still out of reach for most Black Americans, even long after the passage of the 1964 Civil Rights Act ended legal segregation in the United States.

Economic theorist Joseph Schumpeter saw innovation as an essential trait of capitalism and introduced the theory of creative destruction. Along with the slow death of segregation, hastened by Butler and his fellow dynamically mobile, pre–World War II Black sports entrepreneurs, came the destruction of a separate all-Black sports world that Butler helped create in Chicago, New York, and Los Angeles. As Schumpeter biographer Thomas McCraw summed it up, innovation "is very much a double-bladed sword."[15] Jobs were lost. Black expertise, ingenuity, and leadership went increasingly underutilized, woefully excluded by white-controlled businesses and leagues. The success of Sol Butler and other Black sports entrepreneurs contributed to the broader pattern of desegregating the country while paradoxically destroying the self-sustaining Black economy that helped support them. The Negro Leagues were the most notable casualty, but the destruction hit all levels of all-Black sports, including the opportunities for promising young African American athletes to receive coaching and nurturing from elders who shared their complexion and the experience of navigating a world shaped by white supremacy.

Former NFL player Sherman Howard recalled seeing Sol Butler "every day" as a teenager "because after he'd leave work he'd stop by the playground and work with us in track."[16] A junior member of Ye Olde Tymers Club, Howard and other junior members were guided by senior members, including Butler, Duke Slater, Jesse Owens, Jack Johnson, and Joe Louis. "Everything was detailed" in terms of Butler's coaching: "He'd say, you know, 'Make sure your hands are here. Make sure your foot is here,' before he'd say 'Now, get out there and run.'" In an interview with author Andy Piascik, Howard asserted, "Sol Butler was just fabulous working with kids. He had the techniques and skills to show you how to be the best," even though opportunities were limited.[17] "I found that the skills Jesse [Owens] and Sol taught us in track, you could take anywhere. It was the same thing with the football skills we learned—how to come out of the hole, how to move your body, how to use your body, everything." In a subsequent interview, Howard demonstrated a specific skill he learned from Butler:

> The thing that Sol was teaching us, he just had it naturally. Jesse Owens could come out of the holes quickly, but Sol showed us how to bring your body out of the holes first and then straighten up . . . He would demonstrate how he wants you to do it. In slow motion, you know, because he [would] say "you come out, pulling your body out of the hole" . . . you have to have strength to pull your body out in a cross position. Your shoulders help pull you most the time, like this . . . [*Howard demonstrates swinging his arms at shoulder height, perpendicular with the ground, and across his body.*] There's more strength in this cross getting up because you're getting your whole shoulders to get your body out. Before it was straight ahead . . . Sol was the type of guy who could figure that out.[18]

Howard suggested that Olde Tymers Club members' compassionate mentorship meant even more to him and his long-term success than their athletic training; certainly, other young athletes, many of whom never went on to fame in college and professional sports like Howard, benefited enormously from club members' attentive care.[19] Yet despite the eventual loss of highly influential athletic institutions behind the wall of segregation, Black athletes on balance have benefited from the creative destruction of the color line. Acknowledging the ugly racial incidents; low overall participation rates beyond basketball and track and field of African American women; and the need for far more African American coaches, managers, upper-level administrators, and team owners that persist up to the present, historian David Wiggins concludes that "overt racism in sport is now taboo." Regarding travel, accommodations, public facilities, and opportunities and safety on the playing fields, "Black athletes of today do not have to navigate the blatant forms of racial discrimination encountered by . . . great African American athletes of the past."[20]

A "Que Hombre" Sort of a Guy

After he stopped participating in competitive sports and the United States entered World War II, Butler moved further from the public eye. No longer did journalists marvel over his ageless athleticism and youthful vigor. An occasional newspaper article mentioned his past athletic exploits or listed him among the pantheon of great athletes,[21] but aside from his work with Ye Olde Tymers Club and youth football, he made no new sport headlines. In early December 1941, immediately after the Japanese bombed Pearl Harbor, Butler composed a patriotic song, "We Are Ready, Uncle Sam," with Alice and Alberta (Bert) Whitman, two of the four sisters who made up the influential, long-lived Black vaudeville group the Whitman Sisters.[22] For over a decade, the famous sisters owned a house just around the corner from Butler.

The next year, sportswriter Dan Burley noted that Butler had started an artists bureau, which he hoped would "bring him across the line at the same time with Fritz Pollard, J. Mayo (Ink) Williams and Paul Robeson, all former sidekicks."[23] Pollard had just signed a contract to work as a talent scout for the Soundies Distributing Corporation of America; Williams supervised Black talent for Decca Records, most notably boosting Louis Jordan toward stardom; and Robeson's stage career was thriving.[24] Butler's short-lived artists bureau represented a final attempt—after decades spent as a performer (from the minstrel shows of his youth to the sound stages of Hollywood) and newspaperman—to make his mark on American popular culture.

Sol Butler left behind very little record of his personal life—no journals, no correspondence—and as his celebrity waned, the record grew even more scant,

"We Are Ready Uncle Sam" (1941), written by Sol Butler and sisters Alberta (Bert) and Alice Whitman immediately after the bombing of Pearl Harbor. (Library of Congress)

so any public accounts take on outsize importance in the effort to reconstruct the final decades of the once-famous athlete's life. A confounding 1936 story in the *Dubuque Telegraph-Herald* departs so dramatically from established biographical facts that it raises many more questions than it answers. Joe Kleeman, a white man from East Dubuque, told a reporter that Butler, whom Kleeman claimed to know from playing barnstorming basketball in Iowa, told a reporter that Butler had paid him a visit while on the way to Minnesota's Twin Cities to "enter business" and "organize a professional football and basketball team."[25] Butler's wife (unnamed in the article) had died two years earlier, Kleeman maintained, after bearing two children, whom Butler was keeping "with relatives in Minneapolis." The story is impossible to verify: Berniece does not appear in the Chicago death records, although Sol's sister Josephine did identify him as widowed on his death certificate; there are no birth certificates or any other records or reports to indicate that Butler had any children (and none of the newspaper reports on the Butler divorce mention offspring); and there are no records of Butler in any Minnesota directories or reports of him around the area in the state's newspapers. But making sense of this strange, incongruous missive from East Dubuque is equally impossible.

Kleeman's tale highlights the elusive project of the biographer: the struggle to fit the messy, sometimes contradictory, often incomplete details (gleaned through myriad sources, each one fallible) of a human life into neat narratives and compelling arguments. Sol Butler's extraordinary athletic career offers a lens through which to view the American experience in the first half of the twentieth century, but he was also an individual, and his life was defined not only by the choices he made, opportunities he created and seized, restrictions and boundaries he could or could not hurdle as a Black athlete in Jim Crow America but also by countless and unknowable drives, desires, fears, hopes, beliefs, and twists of fate that remain unknowable, impossible to order into tidy conclusions. Did Butler have children whom he kept so well hidden that they simply vanished from the historical record? Probably not. But any absolute truths (even the year of Sol Butler's birth is uncertain)—along with the conversations that may or may not have transpired between Butler and Kleeman and Kleeman and a *Telegraph-Herald* reporter—are all lost to history.

On November 18, 1940, Butler's older brother, Ben, identified in the US Census as divorced and a reporter for the *Tulsa Eagle*,[26] died at forty-eight in what appeared to be a suicide: His "body was reclined in a chair and gas was pouring from an open jet in the room."[27] Over the next few years, short blurbs memorializing Ben's athletic prowess appeared in sports pages across the country. A characteristic entry read: "[Ben] was a good sprinter racing 60 yards once in world equalling time."[28] We can imagine Sol calling in favors with old sportswriter friends, honoring his dead brother with the kind of press Ben never received in life. Shortly after World War II ended, Anna's only child and Sol's only niece, Velna Mae, died in Denver;[29] and the lone nephew, Ben Jr.'s son, Howard Butler, disappeared from records around this time,[30] thus dimming present hopes of finding living descendants. On May 25, 1952, Mary Butler died at the age of eighty-four.[31] It's likely that Sol went home to Hutchinson for the funeral, but we don't know for sure.

The final years of Sol Butler's life grow even hazier. "Few who daily came in contact with Butler knew him as a former American broad jump champion and a sprinter of national note," wrote his friend Frank "Fay" Young, because "Sol never talked much about himself . . . He seemed to let bygones be bygones—and seemingly preferred to forget the days of glory."[32] He apparently put on weight, and the *Chicago Defender* reported that "he wishes folk would stop looking at his waistline." The columnist teased him by suggesting that the "cold shouldn't bother you, BIG BOY."[33]

By the late 1940s he was, for unknown reasons, no longer working for the park district. His final full-time job had nothing at all to do with athletics or recreation. He worked at a bar a few blocks east of his Chicago apartment. At the corner of Forty-seventh Street and Cottage Grove Avenue, Pappy's liquor store and bar was only a few blocks north of Washington Park, near the heart of Black Chicago's business and entertainment district. "Pappy's lounge has a very good reason for being one of the most popular spots on the south side," wrote culture reporter Dave Clark, because "it has two of the nation's top bartenders in Sol Butler and Oscar Curtis."[34] In October 1948, Clark reported that Butler was "all smiles . . . since he took the boys around Pappy's lounge for a 'killing' on the world series," where Satchel Paige (the first Black player to pitch in a World Series) and the Cleveland Indians had defeated the Boston Braves in six games.[35]

While rarely addressed in the historical record, Sol's affinity for gambling and games of chance may have stretched back to his days in Wichita as a grade school marbles champ. The impassioned debates in school and around town over eagerly awaited football games inevitably turned speculative, engaging topics like the Hutchinson, Rock Island, or Dubuque team's chances of winning and their projected margins of victory. He would have known how his vaunted talents fueled betting at local stores, pool halls, dives, and other establishments where gambling flourished. At a dinner for varsity athletes in Dubuque, Sol allegedly offered to make five-dollar bets, a sizable figure at the time, that the freshman class would not prevent him from attending the following night's junior-senior banquet (a bet he would have won after being freed from the freshmen's shackles by friends in the junior class). A year later, he reportedly brought eleven pairs of dice aboard the ship bound for the Belgium Olympics in hopes of playing wagering games, which ended up being banned.[36] By the time he worked at Main Street Gym in Los Angeles and at Pappy's in Chicago, he was already thoroughly versed in gambling culture, if not a seasoned gambler himself. His place of employment may have been one of the thousands of "policy stations" in the city, where Black residents bet on numbers as people do in the lotteries of today.[37]

On the last day of November 1954, a Tuesday, only "about six customers" sat in the lounge of Pappy's liquor store when a fifty-one-year-old man named Jimmie Hill stumbled in, already three sheets to the wind.[38] Around 5' 9" and stocky, Hill fit a general physical description of Butler himself, but the scar running from above Hill's eye down his left cheek spoke to the tough, hardscrabble life of a man who had attended school only through the fifth grade.[39] When the drunken divorcé started harassing waitress Lillian Williams and patron Corrine Brandy, two married women in their thirties, Sol—who not only served as bartender and day manager but also took on the role of bouncer—"reprimanded Hill," said witnesses, "and asked him to leave."[40] Hill threatened to come back, but Sol and the other workers laughed it off. He had lived within a few blocks of the bar for over a decade and this was not the first time that staff kicked the former coal-worker-turned-decorator out of Pappy's.

For some unknown reason, Hill was especially angry that day (perhaps the reprimand and laughter triggered some deep-seated resentment against the former sports star who appeared so self-assured), and he "returned a few minutes later, kicked the tavern door open and began firing a .45 automatic at Butler," hitting him with bullets in the chest and either the hip or abdomen, according to varying accounts. Not one to avoid a duel or shy from anyone, Butler grabbed a revolver kept on hand for such crises and returned fire; he and another manager shot Hill several times. When the "crazed gunman" hit the floor, Ollie Watkins, an off-duty waitress at Pappy's, "kicked the gun from his hand." Butler was rushed to Provident Hospital, where he was questioned by a detective as he lay bleeding.[41]

The next day, Wednesday, December 1, 1954, Jimmie Hill died from his wounds at Cook County Hospital, just a few hours shy of his fifty-second birthday. That same day, in the evening, and despite the doctors' "heroic efforts," Sol Butler succumbed as well.[42] After devoting most of his fifty-nine years to pushing the boundaries of social and physical mobility, resulting in moments of sublime freedom that his ancestors and most of his African American contemporaries could only dream about, his body now came to a complete rest.

Responding to the news of his passing, Black physician, inventor, poet, and former star athlete Henry Binga Dismond wrote:

> He was a "Que Hombre" sort of a guy
> With a quiet, reassuring power;
> But you knew at once from the look in his eye
> His final would be his noblest hour.[43]

It is unknown if his sisters were able to make it to his bedside at Provident Hospital for his final hours, but Josephine, who signed his death certificate, and Anna both escorted his body back to Wichita, after the funeral service at Metropolitan Funeral Parlors five blocks north of his residence on South Parkway (now Martin Luther King Drive). Information about his Chicago service and the subsequent one at Citizens Funeral Home in Kansas is lost, but it is easy to imagine the receptions filled with old friends and loyal fans sharing vivid stories about his extraordinary athletic feats and charismatic personality. Newspaper coverage, which acknowledged that his name and accomplishments might be unfamiliar to new generations, recounted his high school and college athletic dominance in Hutchinson, Rock Island, and Dubuque, his world-beating broad jumping, blazing speed, and professional sport successes.[44]

Many accounts got most details correct, while others—like the one that claimed he was born in Texas and served as the "tropical assistant" for the man who first played Tarzan in Hollywood films—got things wildly inaccurate.[45]

Chicago Tribune sports editor Arch Ward identified him as "one of the greatest all-around athletes who ever lived."[46] Some tributes spoke to personal bonds. "I used to sit on his lap" during dinner as a child, recalled the daughter of his college football coach; she had visited him in Chicago and spoken with him several times over the telephone. "I know that Dad is grieving as I am in Sol's passing."[47] Butler's high school, college, and professional football teammate and friend Johnny Armstrong heard the news of his death over the telephone, vividly recalls Armstrong's daughter Pixie Armstrong Freymann; it was "one of the few times I saw him cry."[48] Her typically stoic father, who took a train to Chicago, served as a pallbearer at the funeral.[49]

Sol Butler was laid to rest in Wichita's Maple Grove Cemetery, within a few paces of his mother's grave and, in a neighboring section, that of his older brother. (Ben Sr. was buried in a Hutchinson cemetery alongside other veterans.) Their remains lay in integrated soil, not relegated to an inferior section, far from the graves of white Kansans, by the segregation then practiced at other Wichita cemeteries. When Anna and Josephine died years later, they were placed in plots surrounding the one for their younger brother. Etched into the dark gray surface of his headstone and bordered by red granite, a sprinting figure—with arms spread wide—appears to have just crossed a finish line. The only text that accompanies his name and years of birth and death speaks to a title he worked passionately to claim: "OLYMPIC CHAMPION."

• • •

Each year, the University of Dubuque hosts the Sol Butler Classic, an indoor tournament that takes place under a large banner that displays some of Butler's crowning athletic feats. The broad (long) jump school record Butler set at Dubuque has survived for over a century, but nothing as clear-cut as a record exists to testify to his broader cultural impact. Had he been the first human to sail twenty-five feet in a competition or been injury-free for the 1920 Olympics to win gold in the broad jump, he might be better known today as a trailblazer. As a football player, he would have achieved greater recognition and boosted his professional opportunities by doing well on an East Coast college team, like his friends Fritz Pollard and Mayo Williams at Brown, or a large state school, like his friend Duke Slater at Iowa. Had he lived long enough to write a memoir or be interviewed by a historian, his role in helping desegregate sports might already be a familiar and cherished story.

Sol Butler's life began just before the US Supreme Court enshrined the doctrine of "separate but equal" and ended just after it was overturned. He conducted his remarkable athletic career in dynamic defiance of the constraints on Black bodies that often violently limited movement and opportunity, life and liberty. Butler's defiance evolved over the course of his life. As a young man, he honed his remarkable social mobility to claim space for himself on white playing fields; as a Black sports entrepreneur disappointed by the limitations inherent in white sport worlds, he worked to create opportunities for himself and other Black athletes in a burgeoning Black sport world; as a great athlete edging past his prime, he wielded a brasher persona as he continued to seek glory for himself but more and more often for the young people he mentored as a coach, trainer, and manager. Sol Butler lived all of his years in Jim Crow America, but his leaps—hard-won and ultimately fleeting—beyond the long shadow of Jim Crow offered a glimpse, hopeful and heartbreaking, of another world.

Preceding pages: Butler walks out of the broad jump pit at the Inter-Allied Games on July 4, 1919. (Courtesy University of Dubuque Archives)

Notes

Abbreviations

ARCHIVES AND GOVERNMENT RECORDS

AASP	Amos Alonzo Stagg Papers, Hanna Holburn Gray Special Collections Research Center, University of Chicago Library
ABC	Avery Brundage Collection, 1908–1982, Universtiy of Illinois (Urbana) Archives
BRTC	Billy Rose Theatre Collection, New York City Public Library
CHM	Chicago History Museum
HHC	Heinz History Center, Pittsburgh, Pennsylvania
HWL	Harold Washington Library Center, Special Collections, Chicago Public Library
KFYMCA	Katz Family YMCA Archives, University of Minnesota (Twin Cities)
KHS	Kansas Historical Society, Topeka
MCA	Morgan County (Alabama) Archives
MHLSC	Margaret Herrick Library Special Collections, Los Angeles, California
NARA	National Archives and Records Administration
PR	Civil War Pension Records, Department of Veterans Affairs, Washington, DC
RCMS	Reno County Museum and Strataca, Hutchinson, Kansas
SARMAR	Stuart A. Rose Manuscript, Archives, and Rare Book Library, Emory University
SCRBC	Schomburg Center for Research in Black Culture, New York, New York
UCLASC	University of California Los Angeles Special Collections
UDA	University of Dubuque Archives
UDOR	University of Dubuque Office of the Registrar

UILLSC	University of Iowa Law Library Special Collections
UNDA	University of Notre Dame Archives
USCSC	University of Southern California Special Collections
VGH	Vivian G. Harsh Research Collection, Chicago Public Library

NEWSPAPERS

AA	*Afro-American (Baltimore, MD)*
ABJ	*Akron (OH) Beacon Journal*
ADW	*Atlanta Daily World*
ALW	*American Legion Weekly*
ANP	Associated Negro Press (Chicago news service)
BDE	*Brooklyn Daily Eagle*
BG	*Boston Globe*
CD	*Chicago Defender*
CE	*California Eagle (Los Angeles)*
CR	*Canton (OH) Repository*
CT	*Chicago Tribune*
DDL	*Davenport (IA) Democrat and Leader*
DDR	*Davenport (IA) Daily Republican*
DDT	*Davenport (IA) Daily Times*
DBQDT	*Dubuque (IA) Daily Times*
DE	*Dubuque (IA) Evangelist*
DMR	*Des Moines Register*
DMT	*Des Moines Tribune*
DS	*Dubuque (IA) Student*
HG	*Hutchinson (KS) Gazette*
HN	*Hutchinson (KS) News*
HSB	*High School Buzz (Hutchinson, KS)*
IS	*Interstate Schoolman (Hutchinson, KS)*
JT	*Journal Times (Racine, WI)*
LAS	*Los Angeles Sentinel*
LAT	*Los Angeles Times*
MD	*Moline (IL) Dispatch*
MKEJ	*Milwaukee Journal*
MUJ	*Muscatine (IA) Journal*
NYA	*New York Age*
NYAN	*New York Amsterdam News*
NYH	*New York Herald*
NYT	*New York Times*
NYTB	*New York Tribune*
PC	*Pittsburgh Courier*
PDP	*Pittsburgh Daily Post*
PP	*Pittsburg[h] Press*
PT	*Philadelphia Tribune*

QCT	*Quad City Times (Davenport, IA)*
RIA	*Rock Island (IL) Argus*
RJ	*Racine (WI) Journal*
SFS	*San Francisco Spokesman*
SLPD	*St. Louis Post-Dispatch*
SLST	*St. Louis Star & Times*
TDC	*Topeka Daily Capital*
TH	*Telegraph Herald (Dubuque, IA)*
TP	*Topeka Plaindealer*
TSJ	*Topeka State Journal*
TT	*Times, The (Munster, IN)*
WB	*Sedalia (MO) Weekly Bazoo*
WDE	*Wichita Daily Eagle*
WP	*Washington Post*
WS	*Wichita Searchlight*
WT	*Watch Tower (Rock Island, IL)*

Warm-Up

1. For theory that underpins my understanding of the link between mobility and justice, see Mimi Sheller, *Mobility Justice: The Politics of Movement in an Age of Extremes* (London: Verso, 2018); on the fruitful concept of *motility*, "a more comprehensive form of mobility," which emphasizes the vital interconnections between various forms of movement, see Vincent Kaufman, Manfred Max Bergman, and Dominique Joye, "Motility: Mobility as Capital," *International Journal of Urban and Regional Research* (December 2004): 749–50.

2. Elizabeth Stordeur Pryor, *Colored Travelers: Mobility and the Fight for Citizenship before the Civil War* (Chapel Hill: University of North Carolina Press, 2016), 3, 76–102.

3. Terry Anne Scott, *Lynching and Leisure: Race and the Transformation of Mob Violence in Texas* (Fayetteville: University of Arkansas Press, 2022).

4. Koritha Mitchell, "No More Shame! Defeating the New Jim Crow with Antilynching Activism's Best Tools," *American Quarterly* 66, no. 1 (2014): 144.

5. Robert Loring Allen, *Opening Doors: The Life and Work of Joseph Schumpeter*, vol. 1: *Europe* (New Brunswick, NJ: Transaction Publishers, 1991), 132.

6. Joseph Schumpeter, *The Theory of Economic Development*, new introduction by Richard Swedberg (1911; New York: Routledge, 2021 [trans. 1934]), ix.

7. Allen, *Opening Doors*, 103.

8. Patrick Miller and David K. Wiggins, *Sport and the Color Line: Black Athletes and Race Relations in Twentieth-Century America* (New York: Routledge, 2004), ix.

9. On how Black sports entrepreneurship embodied liberatory notions of Black masculinity that defied servitude, see Davarian Baldwin, *Chicago's New Negroes: Modernity, The Great Migration, and Black Urban Life* (Chapel Hill: University of North Carolina Press, 2007), 195, 223.

10. Schumpeter, *Theory of Economic Development*, 66.

11. Chris Hanna and James Morton, "Unfinished Legacy: Kobe Bryant and His Support of Women's Basketball," *Journal of African American Studies* 25, no. 2 (2021): 312–23.

12. Schumpeter, *Theory of Economic Development*, 55.

13. Dominik Hartmann, *Economic Complexity and Human Development* (London: Routledge, 2014), 59.

14. Schumpeter, *Theory of Economic Development*, 65.

15. Clifford Murphy, *Ink: The Indelible Life of J. Mayo Williams* (Champaign: University of Illinois Press, 2024), 253.

Chapter 1. Endured Many Hardships

1. Sol Butler and Ben Butler, *Three Years of High School Athletics* (Rock Island, IL: Driffill Printing Company, 1915), 5.

2. Sallie Murphy, General Affidavit, 18 January 1910, Benjamin Butler, PR; 1830 US Census; Minutes Probate Court, books 14 and 16, MCA.

3. Minutes Probate Court, books 14 and 16, MCA; David A. Burleson, *Burleson's Heaven: Westview—Home to Six Generations of Burlesons* (Burleson Family Research Group Inc., 2019), 16; David A. Burleson Morgan County conversation/tour with author, 5 June 2019; Jennie E. Downs, General Affidavit, 18 January 1910, Benjamin Butler, PR; 1860 US Census; *The Heritage of Morgan County, Alabama* (Clanton, AL: Heritage Publishing Consultants, 1998), 172; regarding the Burlesons' church, which Ben may have attended, see Wylheme Ragland, "Morgan County, Alabama Native, Baptist Preacher, Progressive Texas Educator and Humanitarian," *Morgan Memories* (June 2019): 3–7; Mt. Pisgah Baptist Church minutes, MCA; Joseph Shackelford, *Muscle Shoals Baptist Association* (Trinity, AL, 1891), 10–13; for a negative assessment of religious instruction and life under slavery, which Ben allegedly shared with his family, see Josephine Butler, "Daughter of Slave Believes Letter Writer Is Misinformed," *WDE*, 23 July 1969, 4.

4. "Longs for Old Days," *HN*, 7 July 1910, 2.

5. James Benson Sellers, *Slavery in Alabama* (1950; Tuscaloosa: University of Alabama Press, 1994), 154, 210; Joseph W. Danielson, *War's Desolating Scourge: The Union's Occupation of North Alabama* (Lawrence: University of Kansas Press, 2012), 9–11, 94.

6. "Longs for Old Days," *HN*.

7. "Longs for Old Days," *HN*.

8. Benjamin Butler, PR; Peggy Allen Towns, *Duty Driven: The Plight of North Alabama's African Americans during the Civil* War (Bloomington, IN: AuthorHouse, 2012), 2; Danielson, *War's Desolating Scourge*, 137–38.

9. Benjamin Butler, Affidavit, 15 April 1891, PR; William H. Thrift, Roster and Records of Iowa Soldiers in the War of the Rebellion, vol. 1 (Des Moines, 1908), 162; A. A. Stuart, Iowa Colonels and Regiments: History of Iowa Regiments in the War of the Rebellion (Des Moines: Mills & Company, 1865), 77–82.

10. "Longs for Old Days," *HN*.

11. Benjamin Butler, Affidavit, 15 April 1891, PR; Guy E. Logan, *Roster and Record of Iowa Troops in the Rebellion*, vol. 1 (accessed February 21, 2015), http://iagenweb.org/

avilwer/books/logarymilsoc.html; Sarah-Eva Ellen Carlson, "They Tell Their Story: The Dakota Internment at Camp McClellan in Davenport, 1862–1866," *Annals of Iowa* 63 (2004): 251–78.

12. "A Young 'Old' Soldier," *WB*, 6 February 1906, 5.

13. Eric Foner, *Reconstruction: America's Unfinished Revolution, 1863–1877* (New York: Harper & Row, 1988), 5, 524, 553–56.

14. Benjamin Butler, General Affidavit, ca. 1895, PR.

15. Pension Commissioner, letter to Rep. E. H. Madison, 14 September 1909, PR; Benjamin Butler, General Affidavit, 8 September 1909, PR.

16. John Allison, "Roby Burleson's Diary," presentation at the Alabama Historical Association Annual Meeting, 21 April 2017; Stephenson-Burleson Cemetery Records, maintained by Dan Burleson, William Forrest Burleson (deceased), and David and Anne Burleson; Roby A. Burleson's Diary, 1866–1867, MCA.

17. Allison, "Roby Burleson's Diary."

18. Benjamin Butler, General Affidavit, 8 September 1909, PR.

19. Benjamin Butler, Affidavit, 16 October 1911, PR.

20. Declaration for Widow's Pension, Mrs. Ben Butler, 26 April 1919, PR; 1880 US Census; Titus Brown, *Faithful, Firm and True: African American Education in the South* (Macon, GA: Mercer University Press, 2002), 10–11; Sholes City Directory, Macon, Georgia, 1878.

21. Heather Andrea Williams, *Self-Taught: African American Education in Slavery and Freedom* (Chapel Hill: University of North Carolina Press, 2003), 140.

22. Brown, *Faithful, Firm and True*, vii–viii, 45, 77; "Some Interesting Facts Concerning the Colored People of Macon," *Macon Telegraph*, 20 February 1881, 1; *Statistical Abstract of the United States of America: 1880* (Washington, DC, 1881), 154; *Report of the Commissioner of Education for the Year 1879* (Washington, DC, 1881), xxxix; 1880 US Census; 1940 US Census.

23. Sharon Wright, *Race, Power and Political Emergence in Memphis* (New York: Garland, 2003), 10–11; Paula J. Giddings, *Ida: A Sword among Lions* (New York: Amistad, 2008), 52, 54, 60–68.

24. Wright, *Race, Power and Political Emergence*, 14–21.

25. Marriage License, Ben Butler and Mary Wellins [*sic*], 18 December 1888; Declaration for Widow's Pension, Mrs. Ben Butler, 26 April 1919, PR; Wiley Henry, "Historic Avery Chapel Closes after 156 Years," *Tennessee Tribune*, 3 October 2019 (accessed 10 April 2020), https://tntribune.com/community/local/memphis/historic-avery-chapel-ame-closes-after-156-years/; Giddings, *Ida*, 131, 175, 614; 1900 US Census; for Ben Butler's previous marriage to Margaret "Maggie" Hopkins and their lone surviving child, see Benjamin Butler, questionnaire, 30 March 1915, PR; Minnie Nolan, General Affidavit, 24 October 1919, PR; Maggie Butler Certificate of Death, PR.

26. Memphis City Directories: *Boyle-Chapman* 1872–1873 and 1876; A. E. Sholes, compiler, 1877, 1878, 1879, 1881; [Harlow?] Dow 1891 and 1892, Shelby County Register of Deeds, "Memphis City Directories 1849–1943, Shelby County Records, https://register.shelby.tn.us/archives.

27. Giddings, *Ida*, 176–87.

28. Giddings, *Ida*, 189.

29. Giddings, *Ida*, 58–59, 67, 157, 201.

30. Arthur Lincoln Tolson, *The Negro in Oklahoma Territory, 1889–1907* (PhD diss., University of Oklahoma–Norman, 1966), 16–20, 48–49; "Not a Negro State," *TDC*, 8 March 1890, 4; "Off for Oklahoma," *Lawrence (KS) Daily Journal*, 27 January 1891, 1; "Negro Settlers in Oklahoma," *Lincoln (NE) Daily News*, 21 December 1891, 6; also see "Complimentary," *TSJ*, 27 November 1889, 5; *Oskaloosa (KS) Independent*, 1 February 1890, 5.

31. David Chang, *The Color of the Land: Race, Nation and the Politics of Landownership in Oklahoma, 1832–1929* (Chapel Hill: University of North Carolina Press, 2010), 154.

32. Murray R. Wickett, *Contested Territory: Whites, Native Americans and African Americans in Oklahoma, 1865–1907* (Baton Rouge: Louisiana State University Press, 2000), 110; also see Jimmie Lewis Franklin, *Journey toward Hope: A History of Blacks in Oklahoma* (Norman: University of Oklahoma Press, 1982), 22–23.

33. "A Sedalian Writes to the Bazoo Concerning the 'Boom' at Kingfisher, Oklahoma," *WB*, 19 April 1892, 3.

34. "Are You Ready to Start," *Columbus (NE) Journal*, 20 April 1892, 1; "The Great Race Which Took Place at Noon To-Day—Scenes at Kingfisher," *WB*, 26 April 1892, 3.

35. "Negroes Starving," *Scranton (PA) Republican*, 12 May 1892, 2; "Enraged Colored People," *Sedalia (MO) Democrat*, 17 June 1892, 3; "Nearly Lynched Him," *Estherville (IA) Daily News*, 23 June 1892, 14.

36. Oklahoma Territory Land Tract Books, vol. 5, p. 120; *Statistical Abstract of the United States* (Washington, DC: US Department of the Treasury, 1922), 283.

37. Indian Allotment, Killing Woman, 6 May 1892, Tract books, p. 120; 1870, 1900, and 1910 US Census; Volunteer Enlistment, Battery and Muster Roll, Battery Descriptive Book, & Batt'y Muster-out Roll of Mathew Clower[s], Military service records of volunteer Union soldiers, NARA; Benjamin Butler, questionnaire, 30 March 1915, PR; Questionnaire completed by Benjamin Butler, 4 May 1898, PR.

38. "Oklahoma Land Cases," *Weekly Oklahoma State Capital*, 4 March 1896, 3.

39. Glen V. McIntyre, "Kingfisher," *Encyclopedia of Oklahoma History and Culture* (accessed 16 June 2015), www.okhistory.org; Tolson, *Negro in Oklahoma Territory*, 16–18, 21.

40. McIntyre, "Kingfisher"; Leonard B. Cayton, *A History of Black Public Education in Oklahoma* (PhD diss., University of Oklahoma–Norman, 1977), 23, 29; Tolson, *Negro in Oklahoma Territory*, 103–104.

41. "Mixed Schools," *TDC*, 1 January 1891, 1.

42. Tolson, *Negro in Oklahoma Territory*, 78–84.

43. "Full Negro Ticket," *WDE*, 23 September 1900, 10.

44. Kathleen L. Groman, "Civil War Pensions," *Essential Civil War Curriculum* (accessed 8 June 2020), https://www.essentialcivilwarcurriculum.com/civil-war-pensions.html; Declaration of Invalid Pension, 22 September 1890, PR.

45. Ben Butler Affidavit, 16 January 1894, PR.

46. Affidavits and medical examinations filed by M. V. Tierney, 1895–1901, PR.

47. E. O. Tyler and George F. Robinson, General Affidavits, 15 June 1897, PR.

48. Declaration for Invalid Pension, 13 May 1891, Shelby County, PR.

49. "Ben Butler Finds Capt. Joseph Davis and Secures His Signature," *DDR*, 13 August 1901, 6.

50. "They Fitted Him Out," *DDR*, 14 August 1901, 8.

51. Pension Claims, 1890–1901, Invalid Pension Increase Request, 13 April 1903, PR; James A. Davis Affidavit, 1 August 1901, PR.

52. 1900 US Census.

53. Increase Request Claims, 1903–1905, PR.

54. Land Tract Books, vol. 6, p. 2.

55. Dan Feldman, "Oklahoma Loaded Up on Wins over Kingfisher College," *Dallas Morning News*, 25 October 2012 (accessed 22 June 2015); Butler and Butler, *Three Years*, 52.

56. Tolson, *Negro in Oklahoma Territory*, 106–110.

57. "Colored Folks' Fair," *WS*, 15 September 1906: 2; Untitled, *WS*, 29 September 1906, 2; Untitled, *WS*, 28 September 1907, 2; *Population of Oklahoma and Indian Territory*, Bureau of the Census (Washington, DC, 1907), 11; *Abstract of the 1910 U.S. Census: Supplement for Kansas* (Washington, DC, 1912), 618.

58. Nell Irvin Painter, *Exodusters: Black Migration to Kansas after Reconstruction* (New York: Alfred A. Knopf, 1977), 184; also see 188, 190–91, 196; Craig Miner, *Kansas: The History of the Sunflower State, 1854–2000* (Lawrence: University Press of Kansas, 2002), 152–53.

59. *Statistical Abstract of the Census: Supplement for Kansas*, 13th Census (1913), 591, 596; *Kansas: A Guide to the Sunflower State* (New York: Viking Press, 1939), 294–98; Gretchen Cassel Eick, *Dissent in Wichita: The Civil Rights Movement in the Midwest, 1954–72* (Urbana: University of Illinois Press, 2001), 17; W. N. Miller, "We Are Justly Proud," *WS*, 9 September 1905, 2.

60. "Colored Grocery Store," *WS*, 12 August 1905, 1; "Colored Grocery Store," *WS*, 26 August 1905, 3; Advertisement, *WS*, 9 September 1905, 3; "Colored Grocery Store," *WS*, 23 September 1905, 4; "Something New," *WS*, 4 November 1905, 3; "James L. Harper," *WS*, 23 December 1905, 2; "Moved! Moved!" *WS*, 28 July 1906, 2; "Colored Store No More," *WS*, 8 December 1906, 4.

61. "The Clansman," *WS*, 12 January 1907, 2; "Booker T. Washington: Makes Great Speech in Wichita," *WS*, 21 January 1905, 1; "Color Line in Cemetery," *WS*, 13 June 1908, 5.

62. Grand Army of the Republic, Post Records, box 8, KHS; James L. Davenport, letter dated 14 September 1909, to Edmond H. Madison, PR.

63. "School Opens Monday Morning," *WS*, 9 September 1905, 1.

64. "Without Excuse," *WS*, 6 January 1906, 2.

65. "Made Their Protest," *WS*, 10 February 1906, 2; "A Significant Defeat," *WS*, 7 April 1906, 2; "Must Swallow It," *WS*, 28 July 1906, 2.

66. "Negro Children Barred from City Schools by the Republican School Board of Wichita," *WS*, 15 September 1906, 1.

67. "The School Question," *WS*, 22 September 1906, 1; "The School Decision," *WS*, 13 October 1906, 1; "The Decision in Full," *WS*, 13 October 1906, 6; "Colored Teachers Secured for Wichita Schools," *WS*, 27 October 1906, 2; "Shall Negroes

Have Separate Schools?" *WS*, 27 October 1906, 7; "Like the Negro Teachers," *WB*, 30 October 1906, 5; "Colored Teachers Installed," *WS*, 3 November 1906, 2; "Negroes Win School Case," *WDE*, 12 July 1907, 5; "Prelude to Brown—1907: *Rowles v. Wichita*," *Brown Foundation* (accessed 9 June 2022), https://brownvboard.org/content/prelude-brown-1907-rowles-v-wichita.

68. Physician's Affidavit, 5 June 1906, PR.

69. "A Grand Success," *WS*, 8 September 1906, 2.

70. "Sacred Program A.M.E. Church," *WS*, 29 December 1906, 2.

71. "Are Doing Grand Work," *TSJ*, 8 January 1906.

72. "Locals," *WS*, 26 May 1906, 2.

73. Helen Walker-Hill, "Western University of Quindaro, Kansas (1865–1943) and Its Legacy of Pioneering Musical Women," *Black Music Research Journal* 28, no. 1 (2006): 10.

74. "William Tecumseh Vernon," *Journal of Negro History* (October 1944): 507; "W. T. Vernon Confirmed," *WS*, 19 May 1906, 1.

75. "Locals," *WS*, 4 April 1909, 4.

76. Kim Cary Warren, *The Quest for Citizenship: African American and Native American Education in Kansas, 1880–1935* (Chapel Hill: University of North Carolina Press, 2010), 141.

77. "An Immense Crowd Heard Prof. W. T. Vernon Speak," *WS*, 8 August 1908, 1.

78. Evelyn Brooks Higginbotham, *Righteous Discontent: The Women's Movement in the Black Baptist Church, 1880–1920* (Cambridge, MA: Harvard University Press, 1994).

79. "Jolly Three," *WS*, 11 November 1905, 2.

80. "Iola Tabors," *WS*, 17 March 1906, 4; also see Untitled, *WS*, 18 August 1906, 1.

81. "Locals," *WS*, 13 June 1908, 2.

82. "Instances of Negro Success," *WS*, 2 February 1907, 1.

83. "Baseball Team," *WS*, 25 July 1908, 2; "Issues Challenged," *WS*, 31 March 1906, 2; "Notice," *WS*, 30 September 1905, 1.

84. Theresa Runstedtler, *Jack Johnson, Rebel Sojourner: Boxing in the Shadow of the Global Color Line* (Berkeley: University of California Press, 2013), 44–67.

85. Geoffrey C. Ward, *Unforgivable Blackness: The Rise and Fall of Jack Johnson* (New York: Alfred A. Knopf, 2004), 145.

86. "Johnson Defends His Title," *WS*, 23 October 1909, 1.

87. "Grand Concert," *WS*, 20 November 1909, 1.

88. Baldwin, *Chicago's New Negroes*, 196.

89. "Largest in History," *WS*, 25 May 1907, 5; 1940 US Census.

90. "Old Man Sol's Sun Sets," *WDE*, 5 December 1954, 2B.

91. Untitled, *WS*, 17 July 1909, 1; "Colored Jurors," *WS*, 1 May 1909, 1; also see Sondra Van Meeter, "Black Resistance to Segregation in the Wichita Public Schools, 1870–1912," *Midwest Quarterly* 20 (October 1978): 64–77; Eick, *Dissent in Wichita*, 18.

Chapter 2. Good Behavior and Gentlemanly Conduct

1. "Longs for Old Days: This Ex-Slave's Heart Goes Back to Dixie and the Cotton," *HN*, 7 July 1910, 2; for a discussion on the paternalistic use of eye dialect (i.e., representing speech through writing in a way meant to evoke a character's naivete or unintelligence), see Sarah Rude Walker, "'You Is Kind, You Is Smart, You Is Important': The Invention and Mediation of Black Language in *The Help*," in *Like One of the Family: Domestic Workers, Race, and In/Visibility in* The Help, ed. Fiona Mills (Newcastle, UK: Cambridge Scholars Publishing, 2016), 71–77; for an unequivocally negative view of slavery that Ben allegedly shared with his children, see Josephine Butler, "Daughter of Slave Believes Letter Writer Is Misinformed," *WDE*, 23 July 1969, 4.

2. "Their Prayers Won, They Say," *Kansas City (MO) Times*, 5 July 1910, 3.

3. "Longs for Old Days," 2; on Butler favoring Johnson, allegedly claiming, "I prayed for the old boy," see "Not the Churches," *HG*, 5 July 1910, 5.

4. Rex Beach, "Johnson and Age Defeat Jeffries," *CT*, 5 July 1910, 1.

5. Bat Masterson, "Negro Best Fighter the Ring Has Ever Seen," *St. Louis (MO) Daily Globe-Democrat*, 5 July 1910, 15.

6. Geoffrey C. Ward, *Unforgivable Blackness: The Rise and Fall of Jack Johnson* (New York: Alfred A. Knopf, 2004), 216–18.

7. Ward, *Unforgivable Blackness*, 4.

8. Jack Johnson, "Johnson Modestly Tells How He Won," *CT*, 5 July 1910, 24.

9. John Bentley, "I May Be Wrong," *Lincoln (NE) Star*, 2 February 1936, 7.

10. Booker T. Washington, *Character Building: Being Addresses Delivered on Sunday Evening to the Students of Tuskegee Institute* (New York: Doubleday, Page & Company, 1903), 127–28; on a prominent nineteenth-century Black intellectual, doctor, and abolitionist claiming that bootblacking "produced the best average colored men," see James McCune Smith, letter to Frederick Douglass, 10 April 1852, quoted in Derrick R. Spires, *The Practice of Citizenship: Black Politics and Print Culture in the Early United States* (Philadelphia: University of Pennsylvania Press, 2019), 151.

11. Bentley, "I May Be Wrong," 7.

12. "Negro Athlete's Father Is Dead," *WDE*, 20 April 1919, 8.

13. For information on Butler's competition (imitator?), see soda water bottler Thurman Bixler's entry in Sheridan Ploughe, *History of Reno County Kansas*, vol. 11 (Indianapolis: B. F. Bowen & Co. 1917), 282.

14. Minute Book and Meeting Minutes (1909–1910), Joe Hooker Post #17, Grand Army of the Republic Records, KHS; on members' views on slavery, see Ploughe, *History of Reno County*, 124–28, 203, 339; also see Hutchinson City Directory (1913), 21.

15. Pension certification, 30 August 1912, PR; Private Laws of the United States of America Passed at the Sixty-Second Congress. Session II (1911–1912), 291.

16. Sanborn Map, Hutchinson, Kansas, April 1915; Hutchinson City Directory (1913), 78; 1915 and 1925 Kansas State Census; 1920 and 1930 US Census.

17. "Negro Athlete's Father Is Dead," 8.

18. "Hutchinson News," *WS*, 23 October 1909, 5; "Hutchinson Kansas," *WS*, 30 October 1909, 1.

19. "Hutchinson News," *WS*, 6 November 1909, 4.

20. "Hutchinson Kas.," *WS*, 27 November 1909, 4.

21. Untitled, *HN*, 16 June 1911, 1; "Arrested on Girl's Complaint," *HN*, 13 June 1911, 5; "Gardner Establishes Another Record," *HG*, 16 June 1913, 11; "Guilty of Assault," *HN*, 24 January 1911, 8; "John Gardner Out on Parole," *HG*, 22 February 1911, 6.

22. "Failed to Support Wife," *HN*, 3 April 1912, 11.

23. "The Case of Ben Butler," *HN*, 7 December 1911, 5.

24. "Locals," *WS*, 2 July 1910, 4; "Wichita News," *TP*, 8 July 1910, 6; *Statistical Abstract of the Census* (1913), 569, 612.

25. Advertisement, *WS*, 15 October 1910, 1.

26. "For Sale," *WB*, 7 April 1910, 3; "Wichita News," *TP*, 8 July 1910, 6; "Hutchinson, Kansas," *WS*, 5 November 1910, 4.

27. Sol Butler and Ben Butler, *Three Years of High School Athletics* (Rock Island, IL: Driffill Printing Company, 1915), 5; "Maple-Lincoln," *HN*, 15 February 1942, 22; *Annual Report and Course of Study of the Public Schools of Hutchinson, Kansas* (1908), 13–15.

28. Justus Hall, *Hall's Outlines of United States History*, 5th ed. (Chicago: A. Flanagan Co., ca. 1908), excerpt reprinted in *IS*, March 1911, 10.

29. "Negroes in Race," *TSJ*, 10 March 1913, 5; "Colored Woman Candidate for School Board," *TP*, 28 February 1913, 4; "Mrs. Broadus Will Run," *HN*, 24 February 1913, 2.

30. David J. Peavler, "Creating the Color Line and Confronting Jim Crow: Civil Rights in Middle America: 1850–1900" (University of Kansas, PhD diss., 2008): 461; Ploughe, *History of Reno County*, vol. 1, 230–31, 382–83; Untitled, *IS*, November 1911, 26.

31. J. O. Hill, Untitled, *IS*, May 1911, 14, 25.

32. Untitled, *IS*, March 1912, 22; *IS*, May 1911, 25; *IS*, June 1911, 25.

33. Claudia Goldin, *How America Graduated from High School: 1910 to 1960* (Cambridge, MA: National Bureau of Economic Research, 1994), 2; *Negro Education: A Study of the Private and Higher Schools for Colored People in the United States*, vol. 2, no. 39 (Washington, DC: Bureau of Education, 1916), 16–17; Heather Andrea Williams, *Self-Taught: African American Education in Slavery and Freedom* (Chapel Hill: University of North Carolina Press, 2005), 174–200.

34. Jimmie Franklin, "Blacks and the Progressive Movement: Emergence of a New Synthesis," *OAH Magazine of History* (Spring 1999): 22.

35. Untitled, *IS*, July 1912, 4; "Where Kansas Stands," *Kansas School Magazine*, February 1913, 78.

36. Untitled, *IS*, January 1911, 26.

37. J. O. Hall, "The High School and Citizenship," *IS*, January 1912, 19–20.

38. Benjamin Rader, *American Sports: From the Age of Folk Games to the Age of Televised Sports*, 3rd ed. (Englewood Cliffs, NJ: Prentice Hall, 1996), 110; Ploughe, *History of Reno County*, vol. 11, 434.

39. Rader, *American Sports*, 111.

40. Luther Halsey Gullick, "Boys and the 'Gang' Spirit," *IS*, November 1911, 24.

41. Untitled, *IS*, February 1911, 26; Alden Arthur Knipe, *Captain of the Eleven* (New York: Harper & Brothers, 1910).

42. Robert Pruter, *The Rise of American High School Sports and the Search for Control, 1880–1930* (Syracuse, NY: Syracuse University Press, 2013, 67; Untitled, *IS*, March 1912, 26; Untitled, *IS*, May 1912, 18.

43. Butler and Butler, *Three Years*, 5–6; on Butler being elected captain of a team that won the grade school championship, see David K. Sebben, "*Nothing Great Is Easily Won": The Solomon Butler Story* (Self-published, 2023), ch. 2.

44. Butler and Butler, *Three Years*, 6–7.

45. Butler and Butler, *Three Years*, 7.

46. Louis T. Harlan, *Booker T. Washington: The Wizard of Tuskegee, 1901–1915* (New York: Oxford University Press, 1983); Kim Cary Warren, *The Quest for Citizenship: African American and Native American Education in Kansas, 1880 to 1935* (Chapel Hill, NC: University of North Carolina Press, 2010), chs. 4, 5; Evelyn Brooks Higginbotham, *Righteous Discontent: The Women's Movement in the Black Baptist Church, 1880–1920* (Cambridge, MA: Harvard University Press, 1993).

47. Butler and Butler, *Three Years*, 7; also see "Struggled to a Tie," *HN*, 16 October 1911, 3, reprinted in Steve Miller, *Huddle Up Hutch: A History of Salthawk Football, 1902–2016* (Hillsboro, KS: Hillsboro Free Press, 2017), 18.

48. Miller, *Huddle Up Hutch*, 17–19.

49. Butler and Butler, *Three Years*, 7, 9.

50. Butler and Butler, *Three Years*, 10.

51. Butler and Butler, *Three Years*, 10.

52. "Hutchinson Highs Were Winners in Big Event," *HG*, 28 April 1912, 2.

53. Butler and Butler, *Three Years*, 13.

54. "Hutchinson Second at Lawrence Meet," *HG*, 5 May 1912, 1.

55. "They Broke Two Records," *HN*, 6 May 1912, 5.

56. "High School Has Two Men on Naismith's 'All-Kansas,'" *HN*, 7 May 1912, 9; see also "Local Athletes to Compete for Honors," *HG*, 15 May 1913, 3; Arl Frost, "Hutchinson Will Send Three Men to Meet," *University Daily Kansan*, 25 April 1912, 3; *High School Buzz*, 1912 yearbook, 64.

57. "Hutchinson Won Third," *HN*, 11 May 1912, 8.

58. Butler and Butler, *Three Years*, 16.

59. "Grades in Big Meet," *HN*, 8 May 1912, 3; "Freshmen to Haven," *HG*, 12 May 1914, 8.

60. Untitled, *Nickerson (KS) Argosy*, 28 November 1912, 8.

61. Miller, *Huddle Up Hutch*, 21.

62. "Pratt to Play Hutchinson," *WB*, 20 November 1912, 4.

63. Butler and Butler, *Three Years*, 18–19.

64. "First Defeat," *Pratt (KS) Union*, 28 November 1912, 5.

65. "Locals Hold Kingman in Season End Game," *HSB*, 6 December 1912, 1.

66. "People of Kansas and What They Are Doing!" *TP*, 31 October 1913, 1.

67. "From the Watch Tower," *Stafford (KS) Courier*, 2 April 1914, 4.
68. "Sol Butler Breaks Record at Chicago," *HSB*, 3 April 1914, 1.
69. "Black Hand Letter," *HN*, 7 February 1913, 10.
70. Untitled, *HSB*, 1 November 1912, 1.
71. "No Base Ball Team at the High School," *HG*, 15 March 1913, 3.
72. "Hutchinson Is Easy Winner in Pratt Meet," *HG*, 27 April 1913, 1; "Highs Are at Pratt," *HN*, 26 April 1913, 1; "Busy on the Track," *HN*, 18 March 1913, 2.
73. "Track Athletes to Lawrence," *HG*, 1 May 1913, 2; "Show Butler's Trophies," *HG*, 17 April 1914, 4.
74. "Lawrence Develops Best Mud Crawlers and Wins Big Meet," *HG*, 4 May 1913, 3; "Mud Hurt the Highs," *HN*, 5 May 1913, 3; Butler, *Three Years*, 20; "Highs Won at Wichita," *HN*, 10 May 1913, 8; "Hutch Highs Again Victorious," *HG*, 10 May 1913, 3.
75. "High Schools Battle on McCook Tomorrow," *University Daily Kansan*, 16 May 1913, 4; "Wichita Won State Meet," *Manhattan (KS) Mercury*, 19 May 1913, 4.
76. Butler and Butler, *Three Years*, 21.
77. "People of Kansas," *TP*, 1.
78. Butler and Butler, *Three Years*, 21.
79. "Stafford Is Easy for Local Highs," *HG*, 12 October 1913, 5.
80. *HSB*, 3 October 1913, 7.
81. "Hutchinson Highs Drop First Game," *HG*, 18 October 1913, 5.
82. Untitled, *Great Bend (KS) Tribune*, 20 October 1913, 4.
83. Miller, *Huddle Up Hutch*, 23; also see "Highs Play Soldiers," *HN*, 28 October 1913, 3.
84. Butler and Butler, *Three Years*, 24.
85. "Highs Beat Soldiers," *HN*, 3 November 1913, 3.
86. Tom Shine, "Was Wichita State Really the First College to Throw a Forward Pass in College Football?" 8 December 2023 (accessed 1 August 2024), kcur.org/sports/2023-12-01/football-forward-pass-invention-wichita-state-university.
87. Pruter, *Rise of American High School Sports*, 93, 97.
88. Sally Jenkins, *The Real All Americans: The Team That Changed a Game, a People, a Nation* (New York: Doubleday, 2007), 6.
89. "Highs Beat Emporia," *HN*, 8 November 1913, 3.
90. Miller, *Huddle Up Hutch*, 362; "What Is Happening at the Reno County High School?" *Nickerson (KS) Argosy*, 27 November 1913, 8; "Highs Won at Salina," *HN*, 28 November 1913, 3.
91. "High School Students to Give a Football Minstrel," *HN*, 31 December 1913, 3; "Football Team to Give Minstrel," *HSB*, 16 January 1914, 1; *Allagaroo* (Hutchinson, KS), 1914); "High School Minstrel Pleased Last Night," *HN*, 7 February 1914, 10.
92. "The Colored Folks Help," *HN*, 17 February 1914, 7; also see H. H. Peters, *Charles Reign Scoville: The Man and His Message* (St. Louis, MO: Bethany Press, 1924), 6.
93. "Colored Folks Help," 7; for a subsequent singing event led by Ben Sr., see "Music and Musicians," *HG*, 17 November 1918, 6.

94. "Colored Folks Help," 7.

95. "Biggest Interscholastic Meet at Northwestern U.," *HN*, 27 March 1914, 3.

96. "Sol. Butler to Enter Northwestern Classic," *HG*, 26 March 1914, 5; Pruter, *Rise of American High School Sports*, 106, 137–38.

97. Butler and Butler, *Three Years*, 26.

98. Morris Robinson Jr., *A Place We Can Call Our Home: The Emerging Evanston Black Community Circa 1850–1930*, 2nd ed. (Evanston, IL: Shorefront, 2013), 3–8, 11, 19, 20; Morris Robinson Jr., email to author, 12 January 2019.

99. Butler and Butler, *Three Years*, 26.

100. *Syllabus Yearbook* (Northwestern University, 1916), 90.

101. "Lewis Institute," *CT*, 24; also see Butler and Butler, *Three Years*, 52–53.

102. "Sol Butler Won in All of His Preliminaries," *HN*, 28 March 1914, 2.

103. "Butler Complimented by Northwestern Coach," *HSB*, 17 April 1914, 1.

104. "Sol May Run on U.S. Olympic Team," *HN*, 23 April 1914, 3.

105. "Butler Has Chance to Enter Olympiad," *HG*, 23 April 1914, 3.

106. Sportsman, "Live Tips and Topics," *BG*, 31 March 1914, 6.

107. "Butler a Sensation in Northwestern Meet," *HG*, 31 March 1914, 5.

108. "Sol Won New Cups," *HN*, 30 March 1914, 3.

109. "Sol Had a Parade," *HN*, 31 March 1914, 2.

110. "Reception for Sol," *HN*, 1 April 1914, 3; "Big Demonstration for Triumphant Sol," *HG*, 1 April 1914, 8.

111. "Hutchinson, Kansas," *TP*, 17 April 1914, 3.

112. "Sol Butler Breaks Record at Chicao [*sic*]," *HSB*, 3 April 1914, 1.

113. "Butler Breaks World Record," *HG*, 26 April 1914, 1.

114. "Hutchinson Wins Track Meet at Pratt," *HSB*, 1 May 1914, 1.

115. Butler and Butler, *Three Years*, 28; "Boys Deserve Credit," *HN*, 4 May 1914, 2.

116. "Highs Take State Meet," *HG*, 3 May 1914, 1.

117. "Highs Are at Wichita," *HN*, 8 May 1914, 3; "Sol Butler Made a World's Record," *WB*, 9 May 1914, 14.

118. John Grover, "To a Negro Boy Goes a Great Place in Valley Sports," *Kansas City Star*, 11 October 1931, 18.

119. Grover, "To a Negro Boy," 18.

120. David Reed, email to author, 28 January 2022.

121. "Show Home-Made Movies," *HG*, 7 May 1914, 4; "Is This Man Elmer Swanson?" (accessed 10 May 2021), https://jimpotterauthor.com; "Can Pick Team Now," *HN*, 18 April 1914, 12; "Film of Short Grass Romance to Be Shown," *HG*, 3 December 1915, 3.

122. "Are After More Honors," *HN*, 9 June 1914, 2; "Famous Coach Picks Hutchinson to Win Meet," *HN*, 13 June 1914, 8; "Country's Biggest Meet," *HG*, 14 June 1914, 1; Pruter, *Rise of American High School Sports*, xvi.

123. "Business Men Send Team to Chicago," *HG*, 7 June 1914, 5.

124. Butler and Butler, *Three Years*, 30.

125. "Sol Butler Was Second," *HN*, 15 June 1914, 9; Amos Alonzo Stagg Papers, box 186, May–August 1914 scrapbook, and box 303, "Track 1911–1916," p. 136, AASP.

126. “University High Takes Prep Meet over 115 Schools,” *CT*, 14 July 1914, 24.

127. “Negro Athletes Hold First Meet,” *CT*, 14 June 1914, 24.

128. Butler and Butler, *Three Years*, 31; Robinson Jr., email to author.

129. Butler and Butler, *Three Years*, 31.

130. “World’s 100-Yard Record Is Broken,” *Austin (TX) American*, 26 July 1914, 4; “Live Tips and Topics,” *BG*, 29 July 1914, 7.

131. “Sol First in Photo,” *HN*, 31 July 1914, 10.

132. Jonathan Finn, *Beyond the Finish Line: Images, Evidence, and the History of the Photo-Finish* (Montreal: McGill-Queen’s University Press, 2020), 68, 81–83.

133. Butler and Butler, *Three Years*, 32; regarding Butler’s initial plans to attend Northwestern University, see “Sol Butler Back Wearing Chi Duds,” *HG*, 18 August 1914, 3.

134. “Coach Roe to Go to Rock Island, ILL,” *HN*, 31 July 1914, 3.

135. Butler and Butler, *Three Years*, 32.

136. Butler and Butler, *Three Years*, 22.

137. “Sol Butler May Run,” *HN*, 3.

138. Butler and Butler, *Three Years*, 32; see also “Butler to Chicago,” *HG*, 30 August 1914, 3; “Butler to Rock Island, Ill,” *HG*, 8 September 1914, 8; on Butler criticizing the Hutchinson school gymnasium and favoring the Rock Island YMCA, see Sebben, *“Nothing Great.”*

Chapter 3. Exceptional Chances for an Athlete

1. “Coach Arrives to Begin Work,” *RIA*, 3 September 1914, 5; Drew VandeCreek, “African Americans, Race and Ethnicity in Illinois and the North during the Civil War,” *Illinois during the Civil War* (accessed 22 June 2022), https://digital.lib.niu.edu/illinois/civilwar/race; Benton McAdams, *Rebels at Rock Island: The Story of a Civil War Prison* (DeKalb: Northern Illinois University Press, 2000), 143; *Statistics for Illinois*, 1910 Census; Interview with William McAdams, 2012, in MSS 291 Oral history interviews, Special Collections, Augustana College, Rock Island, Illinois.

2. Keith McClellan, *The Sunday Game: At the Dawn of Professional Football* (Akron, OH: University of Akron Press, 1998), 16, 254, 264, 266.

3. “Good Showing at First Practice,” *RIA*, 16 September 1914, 8; Doug Frazer, Rick Miers, and David Sebben, *Rock Solid: Our History: A History of Rock Island High School, Rock Island, Illinois* (Self-published, 2016), 170; “Lem Says Rock Island Will Win,” *RIA*, 5 November 1914, 10; Sol Butler and Ben Butler, *Three Years of High School Athletics* (Rock Island, IL: Driffill Printing Company, 1915), 31–35; “Aledo Walloped by R.I. 76 to 0,” *RIA*, 5 October 1914, 10; “Islanders Trim Ottawa,” *RIA*, 19 October 1914, 10; for an account of the 1914 high school football season, see David K. Sebben, *“Nothing Great Is Easily Won”: The Solomon Butler Story* (Self-published, 2023), ch. 3.

4. “Butler Placed on State Team,” *RIA*, 2 December 1914, 10.

5. Butler and Butler, *Three Years*, 36.

6. Butler and Butler, *Three Years*, 37.

7. “Team Work Cause of R.I. Victory,” *RIA*, 16 November 1914, 10.

8. “Patterson Tells of Play Made by Butler,” *MD*, 21 November 1914, 8.

9. *WT*, vol. 6, no. 4 (1915), 63.

10. "Tuskegee Singers Here Three Days," *RIA*, 3 May 1915, 12.

11. "Tuskegee Singers Please at School," *RIA*, 5 May 1915, 8; for confirmation that no record exists of Hutcherson in the Tuskegee University Archives, see email to author from Cheryl Ferguson, archival assistant, 18 July 2017.

12. "Relates Trials of Colored Students," *RIA*, 7 May 1915, 3.

13. Butler and Butler, *Three Years*, 1.

14. "A Literary Effort," *WT*, vol. 6, no. 3 (March 1915), 12.

15. "Sol's Book Out Soon," *HN*, 11 March 1915, 5.

16. "Athlete's Book Is Out," *DDT*, 29 March 1915, 9.

17. Jonathan Barz, "Butler Autobiography as Literature," unpublished essay (July 2022), 1.

18. "Tri-City Schools in Harmony Again," *RIA*, 31 December 1914, 10.

19. Untitled, *WT*, vol. 6, no. 4 (1915), 84.

20. "A Literary," *WT*, 12.

21. "Butler Brothers Are Inseparable," *CD*, 17 April 1915, 1.

22. "Sol's Book," *HN*, 5; *WT*, vol. 6, no. 4 (1915), 16; Butler and Butler, *Three Years*, 1, 3.

23. Butler and Butler, *Three Years*, 1.

24. "Sol Is Author," *HN*, 26 February 1915, 3.

25. Barz, "Butler Autobiography," 5.

26. W.E.B. Du Bois, *The Negro Problem* (New York: James Pott and Co., 1903), 45.

27. "Along the Color Line," *Crisis* 10, no. 3 (July 1915): 112.

28. Kim Cary Warren, *The Quest of Citizenship: African American and Native American Education in Kansas, 1880–1935* (Chapel Hill: North Carolina Press, 2010), 123–44.

29. Butler and Butler, *Three Years*, 34.

30. Butler and Butler, *Three Years*, 45; for evidence of Roe's literary ambitions and skill, see Herbert N. Roe and William E. Landers, *Ginger* (Kansas City, MO: Burton Publishing Company, 1927).

31. Butler and Butler, *Three Years*, 5; James Olney, "'I Was Born': Slave Narratives, Their Status as Autobiography and as Literature," *Callaloo* 20 (Winter 1984): 46–73.

32. Benjamin Soskis, "Freedoms and Fictions," *New Republic* (3 June 2002): 37.

33. Barz, "Butler Autobiography," 4.

34. Ellery Harding Clark, *Reminiscences of an Athlete: Twenty Years on Track and Field* (Boston: Houghton Mifflin, 1911), 31–32, 46, 161.

35. For the first published English translation of Jack Johnson's 1914 French autobiography, which initially appeared as a series of articles in 1911 and the Butler brothers likely did not read, see Jack Johnson, *My Life and Battles*, ed. and trans. Christopher Rivers (Dulles, VA: Potomac Books, 2009).

36. Moses Fleetwood Walker, *My Home Colony: A Treatise on the Past, Present and Future of the Negro Race in America* (Steubenville, OH: Herald Printing Co., 1908); for more on Walker, who attended a predominantly white institution in the North and later promoted racial separation, see David Zang, *Fleet Walker's Divided Heart:*

The Life of Baseball's First Black Major Leaguer (Lincoln: University of Nebraska Press, 1995).

37. Burt L. Standish [Gilbert Patten], *Frank Merriwell at Yale; or, Freshmen against Freshmen* (1903) (accessed 26 July 2022), https://www.gutenberg.org/ebooks/11115.

38. Butler and Butler, *Three Years*, 51.

39. Michael Murphy and Lawson Robertson, eds., *College Athletics: A Handbook of Instruction in the Events of the Collegiate Track and Field Programme* (New York: American Sports Publishing Company, 1894); Albert Lee, *Track Athletics in Detail* (New York: Harper & Brothers, 1896); George Orton, *Athletic Training for School Boys* (New York: American Sports Publishing Company, 1905); Arthur Ruhl, "Track Athletics," in *Rowing and Track Athletics* (New York: McMillan Company, 1905); Arthur Swazey Jones, *Track Athletes* (Boston: Small, Maynard & Company, 1912); Michael Murphy, *College Athletics* (New York: American Sports Publishing Company, 1912); James Sullivan, *How to Become an Athlete* (New York: American Sports Publishing Company, 1914); Butler and Butler, *Three Years*, 49; see also training and hygiene manuals in boxes 122, 123, AASP.

40. Michael Murphy, *Athletic Training* (New York: Charles Scribner's Sons, 1914), xix.

41. Leon Coursey, *The Life of Edwin Bancroft Henderson and His Professional Contributions to Physical Education* (PhD diss., Ohio State University, 1971), 160, quoted in Edwin B. Henderson II, *The Grandfather of Black Basketball: The Life and Times of Dr. E. B. Henderson* (Lanham, MD: Rowman & Littlefield, 2024), 111.

42. Henderson II, *The Life of Edwin Bancroft Henderson*, ch. 3.

43. "Moline Strikes a Snag in Islanders," *MD*, 23 January 1915, 12; "Play Geneseo and Cambridge," *DDT*, 27 January 1915, 16; "Game to Davenport," *MD*, 6 February 1915, 10; "Islanders Take a Rough Contest," *RIA*, 13 February 1915, 3; "Rock Island Wins from Aledo Quintet, 33 to 27," *RIA*, 15 February 1915, 10; "Referee Is Selected," *MD*, 18 February 1915, 10; "Islander[s] Take Tourney Honors," *RIA*, 1 March 1915, 10; "Rock Island to Wind Up Season for Davenport," *QCT*, 2 March 1915, 8; "Davenport Wins from Islanders," *RIA*, 6 March 1915, 14; "Basketball Year Successful One," *RIA*, 8 May 1915, 14; Sebben, *"Nothing Great."*

44. "Sol Butler in Finals in Big Chicago Event," *DDT*, 20 February 1915, 14; "First Regiment Armory," *Historic American Buildings Survey* (Washington, DC: National Park Service, 1965), 2, 7 (accessed 14 August 2022), https://tile.loc.gov/storage-services/master/pnp/habshaer/il/il0100/il0108/data/il0108data.pdf; "Sol Butler Wins Individual Honor," *RIA*, 22 February 1915, 10.

45. "High School Notes," *RIA*, 25 March 1915, 5; "Sol Butler Not Barred in Meet," *RIA*, 24 March 1915, 12; "Butler Equals World Record for 60 Yards," *CT*, 27 March 1915, 10; "Butler Is Whole Show in Chicago," *RIA*, 29 March 1915, 10.

46. "Butler Takes Meet Honors without Help," *CT*, 28 March 1915, 21.

47. "Sol Butler Alone Wins Meet for Rock Island," *Chicago Examiner*, 28 March 1915, part 3, 18.

48. "Colored Athlete in Great Shape," *DDT*, 25 March 1915, 14.

49. "Fear Islanders Track Athletes," *DDT*, 30 April 1915, 22; "Roe Picks Men for Track Team," *DDT*, 7 May 1915, 20; "Sol One Hundred Books," *HG*, 1 May 1915,

5; "Islander to Rescue," *MD*, 31 March 1915, 12; "In Tryouts for Olympics," *DDT*, 31 March 1915, 20; on Northwestern University having "more colored athletes than any other [Big Ten] conference school," see "Be a Good Sport Always," in *The Negro in Chicago: 1719 to 1927* (Washington Intercollegiate Club of Chicago, 1927), 77.

50. "Butler Is Whole Show," *RIA*, 10.

51. "Moline Falls Down," *MD*, 3 May 1915, 9.

52. Albert J. Stowe, "Davenport Wins Big Eight Meet," *DDT*, 3 May 1915, 13.

53. "Sol Butler the Star in Iowa Track Meet," *HN*, 20 May 1915, 3.

54. "Tied for Second Honors in Meet," *RIA*, 17 May 1915, 10.

55. "Tied for Second Honors in Meet," *RIA*, 17 May 1915, 10.

56. "Students Guests of Progressive Club," *RIA*, 29 May 1915, 3; regarding the Butler brothers' high school transcripts, see *Rock Island High School Records*, p. 180, Rock Island High School; also see librarian Mary Mandelin, email to author, 5 August 2022.

57. Thomas D. Snyder, ed., *120 Years of American Education: A Statistical Portrait* (Washington, DC: National Center for Education Statistics, 1993), 21; 2015 Tables and Figures, National Center for Education Statistics (accessed 14 July 2022), https://nces.ed.gov/programs/digest/d15/tables/dt15_104.10.asp; "Who Earns a U.S. Doctorate?," National Center for Science and Engineering Statistics (accessed 14 July 2022), https://www.nsf.gov/statistics/2017/nsf17306/report/who-earns-a-us-doctorate/race-and-ethnicity.cfm.

58. Regarding controversy over Butler's age and this Chicago meet, see Sebben, *"Nothing Great,"* ch. 3.

59. "Local Athletes Depart for Chi," *RIA*, 10 June 1915, 5; "Butler Defeated in Century Dash," *RIA*, 14 June 1915, 14; "Local Star Ties for Second Place," *DDT*, 14 June 1915, 16; AASP, box 303, "Track 1911–1916," pp. 152–53, box 320, unlabeled photo scrapbook.

60. "Sol Is to Start West on Monday," *RIA*, 23 July 1915, 12.

61. "Sol Is to Start West," 12.

62. "Butler Is Whole Show," *RIA*, 10.

63. "Helping to Raise Funds for Butler," *RIA*, 26 July 1915, 12.

64. "Raising Funds to Aid Sol Butler," *RIA*, 24 July 1915, 3.

65. "Fund for Butler Is Growing but Slowly," *RIA*, 27 July 1915, 5.

66. "Butler Joins Chi Party at Station," *RIA*, 29 July 1915, 9.

67. Sebben, *"Nothing Great,"* ch. 4.

68. William Pickens, *Bursting Bonds* (Boston: Jordan and More Press, 1923), 192.

69. "Butler in Frisco," *HG*, 3 August 1915, 6; also see Brown Holmes, "Outlook Dark in Expo. Meet," *Fairmont West Virginian*, 3 August 1915, 8.

70. *Panama-Pacific International Exposition, 1915: The World Meets in San Francisco*, brochure published by National Park Service (accessed 27 August 2022), https://www.nps.gov/goga/learn/historyculture/upload/PPIE-Brochure-FINAL-for-Web.pdf.

71. Delilah L. Beasley, *Negro Trailblazers of California* (Los Angeles: Self-published, 1919), 301–304.

72. Lucien H. White, "Morse, New Speed King," *NYA*, 12 August 1915, 6.

73. Frank Mortan Todd, *The Story of the Exposition*, vol. 3 (New York: Knickerbocker Press, 1921), 182; "Sol Butler Is Back from Pacific Coast," *RIA*, 4 September 1915, 13.

74. "Butler Won Junior Championship Jump," *HG*, 17 August 1915, 8.

75. "Are to Feature Solomon Butler in the Class Song," *RIA*, 23 May 1918, 13; for song lyrics, see Sebben, *"Nothing Great,"* ch. 3.

76. *The 1918 "M": A Yearbook Published by the Senior Class of the Moline High School*, 1918, pp. 94–96 (accessed 12 July 2018), https://archive.org/stream/reference_molinelibrary_1918.

77. Paul Waggoner, "HHS Yell Began Innocently Enough . . .," *Legacy* (Winter 2005): 10–12; Steve Miller, email to author and David Sebben, 4 April 2024.

78. "D.A.C. Is Offered Services of Butler," *DDT*, 7 February 1920, 14.

79. John H. Wigmore, "Campus Gossip: What Others Think" (Editorial), *Daily Northwestern*, 3 April 1914, 2; a full transcription is available in Sebben, *"Nothing Great,"* ch. 2.

80. Wigmore, "Campus Gossip," 2.

Chapter 4. Welded into One Blood

1. "Sol Butler Wins from Eighteen High Schools," *CD*, 3 April 1915, 4; "Sol Butler Will Stay with Coach," *HN*, 5 June 1915, 2; "Sol and Ben Butler Graduate from School," *HG*, 8 June 1915, 5.

2. "R.I. Will Lose Services of Roe," *DDT*, 20 May 1915, 14.

3. "Along the Color Line," *Crisis* 10, no. 3 (July 1915): 112; John Carroll, *Fritz Pollard: Pioneer in Racial Advancement* (Urbana: University of Illinois Press, 1992), 47–48; *Northwestern University Bulletin: Annual Catalogue, 1915/1916* (Evanston, IL: Northwestern University, 1916), 75; *Harvard University Catalogue, 1915–1916* (Cambridge, MA: Harvard University, 1916), 509–519.

4. "Sol Butler Is Back from Pacific Coast," *RIA*, 4 September 1915, 13.

5. Record of the Dubuque College and Seminary, 1911–1917, p. 286, UDA.

6. *DS*, January 1915, 29.

7. Cyrus McCormick, *The Century of the Reaper* (Boston: Houghton Mifflin, 1931), 1–2, 11.

8. Joseph Mihelic, "A Survey of the History of the University of Dubuque, 1846–1979," p. 28, UDA.

9. *TH*, 6 May 1917, 24.

10. *DE*, 30 April 1917, 2.

11. Record of the Dubuque College and Seminary, 1911–1917, UDA; "The Mission of the Christian College," *DE*, 2 July 1917, 3.

12. Joseph Mihelic, "Basic Material about the University of Dubuque," undated document, UDA.

13. Information culled from reports in the Record of the Dubuque College and Seminary, 1911–1917, and various issues of *DS*, UDA.

14. Cornelius Steffens, "The Genius of Dubuque," *DE*, 6 August 1917, 3.

15. Record of the Dubuque College and Seminary, 1911–1917, p. 282.

16. "The Story of Dubuque, 1852–1918," catalog, undated, UDA; also see Cor-

nelius Steffens, "Unity in Diversity," *DE*, 29 September 1919, 1; Hermann Styles Ficke, "Race Prejudice," pamphlet reprinted from *American Hebrew* (ca. 1941), UDA.

17. Steffens, "Genius of Dubuque"; Daniel J. Adams, "Koreans in Transition: Americanization at the University of Dubuque, 1911–1935," *Transactions of the Royal Asiatic Society, Korea Branch* 80 (2005): 102.

18. Untitled, *DS*, April 1916, 13.

19. Benjamin Butler, "Freshman Class History," *The Key* (1917), 56. *The Key* was the Dubuque College yearbook.

20. "Freedmen Report," Westminster Church, April 17–18, 1917, Presbytery of Dubuque, UDA; for additional anti-Black sentiment, see Andrew E. Schindler, "A Party," *DS*, June 1914, 5; J. J. Puente, "The Voice from Porto Rico," *DS*, February 1915, 7–11.

21. For campus expressions of anti-Black attitudes, see Schindler, "A Party," 5, and Puente, "Voice from Porto Rico," 7–11.

22. Untitled, *DS*, October 1915, 22.

23. Francis Hegar, "The Spirit of the South," *DS*, June 1916, 7–10.

24. Hegar, "Spirit of the South," 7.

25. David Brodnax, "'Breathing Freedom's Air': The African American Struggle for Equal Citizenship in Iowa, 1830–1900" (PhD diss., Northwestern University, 2007); Robert R. Dykstra, *Bright Radical Star: Black Freedom and White Supremacy on the Hawkeye Frontier* (Cambridge, MA: Harvard University Press, 1993).

26. Dykstra, *Bright Radical Star*, 7–13; David Brodnax, "Morgan, Nathaniel," *African American National Biography*, 31 May 2013 (online); Mohammad A. Chaichian, *White Racism on the Western Urban Frontier: Dynamics of Race and Class in Dubuque, Iowa* (1800–2000) (n.p.: Africa World Press, 2006), 76.

27. David J. Peavler, "Creating the Color Line and Confronting Jim Crow: Civil Rights in Middle America, 1850–1900" (PhD diss., University of Kansas, 2008), 150.

28. Census of Iowa for the Year 1915, census editor Ora Williams (Des Moines, IA: Executive Council of the State of Iowa, 1916), 601.

29. James Howard, "Locals," *DS*, June 1916, 17–18.

30. "Draws Color Line in Dubuque," *Dubuque Daily Gazette*, 23 October 1906.

31. "Race Equality Not Found Here," unidentified news clipping, 6 May 1907, National Mississippi River Museum and Aquarium, Captain William D. Bowell Sr., River Library, Dubuque, "African Americans in Dubuque"; also see David Brodnax Sr., "Almost Free: African Americans in Dubuque, 1830–1900," presentation, University of Dubuque, 5 April 2013, pp. 24–26; Richard Breaux, "On, Behind and Ahead of the Curve: The African American Presence at UD and in Iowa," in *Ahead of the Curve: The First Century of African American Experiences at the University of Dubuque*, exhibition catalog, ed. Brian Hallstoos and Jonathan Helmke (Dubuque, IA: University of Dubuque, 2015), 14.

32. For additional illustrations of Butler's musical activity, which included performing "Alma Mater," a piece written by recently deceased alumnus Vicente Bernal, see *DS*, January 1917, 14; *DE*, 2 April 1917, 2, 11; Vicente Bernal, *Las Primicias* (Dubuque, IA: Telegraph-Herald, 1916), 16.

33. Henry Reemtsma, letter to Ocania Chalk, 22 October 1975, UDA; also see Stephany Harvey, letter to Ocania Chalk, 15 October 1973, UDA.

34. Joseph Duke, letter to Jane Pitts, 1 August 1975, UDA.

35. For examples of criticism within the institution, see James Howard, Untitled, *DS*, March 1916, 24; "Alma Mater Died!" and "University of Dubuque Under Fire" in folder "UD Controversy 1920," box L38, Mihelic Files; and boxes 16, 32, 33, Wettstone Files, UDA.

36. Cornelius Martin Steffens and Paul Patton Faris, *Adventures in Money Raising: An Outline of Presidential Duties and Experiences for the University of Dubuque* (New York: Macmillan Company, 1930), 17–19.

37. Untitled, *DS*, September 1915, 31.

38. "Athletics," *DS*, October 1915, 28–29; Reemtsma letter.

39. *The Key* (1917), 93.

40. *The Key* (1917), 105; also see Henry Reemtsma, *Changes* (Guelph, Ontario: Self-published, 1983), ch. 4.

41. "The Season," *The Key* (1917), 105–106; on Butler playfully mocking the media for questioning his plans to remain in college beyond the football season, see David K. Sebben, *"Nothing Great Is Easily Won": The Solomon Butler Story* (Self-published, 2023), ch. 5.

42. "Chalmers' Men Score in Last Period to Break Tie," *DBQDT*, 28 November 1915, 4.

43. "Heavy Gridiron for Big Football Game," *DBQDT*, 25 November 1915, 6; also see "Stage All Set for Clash of Rival Elevens," *TH*, 24 November 1915, 9.

44. Regarding the claim that there "certainly would have been bloodshed" if the rival Irish Catholic and German and Dutch Protestant fans would have met on Dubuque streets after the game, see Reemtsma, *Changes*, ch. 4.

45. "Big Football Game Was Profitable One," *DBQDT*, 28 November 1915, 6; Neal Rozendaal, *Duke Slater: Pioneering Black NFL Player and Judge* (Jefferson, NC: McFarland, 2012), 22.

46. "Gleason vs. Butler on Field Tomorrow," *RIA*, 24 November 1915, 10.

47. "Gleason vs. Butler on Field Tomorrow," 10.

48. "Chalmers' Men Score in Last Period to Break Tie," *DBQDT*, 28 November 1915, 4; "Heavy Gridiron for Big Football Game," *DBQDT*, 25 November 1915, 6; *College Spokesman*, 1915, 79; "Captain Gleason Quits the Team," *RIA*, 13 September 1915, 7; for a lively remembrance of the game, see James Odenkirk, "Sol Butler: The Fleeting Fame of a World-Class Black Athlete," in *Before Jackie Robinson: The Transcendent Role of Black Sporting Pioneers*, ed. Gerald Gems (Lincoln: University of Nebraska Press, 2017), 143.

49. Joe Niese and Bob Dorais, *Gus Dorais: Gridiron Innovator, All-American and Hall of Fame Coach* (Jefferson, NC: McFarland, 2018), 73–76; Ray Robinson, *Rockne of Notre Dame: The Making of a Football Legend* (New York: Oxford University Press, 1999), 39–48; Gerald Gems, *Windy City Wars: Labor, Leisure, and Sport in the Making of Chicago* (Lanham, MD: Scarecrow Press, 1997), 146.

50. "Thursday's Football Game," *DBQDT*, 28 November 1915, 4.

51. Reemtsma, *Changes*, ch. 4.

52. "Hot Time Last Night on College Campus—Celebrated Victory," *DBQDT*, 28 November 1915, 6.

53. *DS*, December 1915, 19–20.

54. Henry Reemtsma, Untitled, *DS*, December 1915, 30.

55. "Stage All Set for Clash of Rival Elevens," *TH*, 24 November 1915, 9; "Big Football Game Was Profitable One," *DBQDT*, 28 November 1915, 6.

56. *The Key* (1917), 103.

57. *The Key* (1917), 96.

58. *The Key* (1918), unpaginated.

59. Breaux, "On, Behind and Ahead of the Curve," 17.

60. Joseph Duke, letter to Jane Pitts, 1 August 1975, UDA; reprinted in *Racing Past the Color Line: Sol Butler and Paul Robeson in Collegiate Athletics*, exhibition catalog, ed. Brian Hallstoos and Jonathan Helmke (Dubuque, IA: University of Dubuque, 2014), 22.

61. Brian Hallstoos, "'Excellent Work and Superior Traits of Personality': Composing an Integrated Music Department" and Richard Breaux, "'Tireless Partners and Skilled Competitors': Seeing UI's Black Male Athletes, 1934–1960," in *Invisible Hawkeyes: African Americans at the University of Iowa during the Long Civil Rights Era*, ed. Lena and Michael Hill (Iowa City: University of Iowa Press, 2016), 35–36, 42, and 145–46; Richard Breaux, email to author, 22 November 2024; Record of the Dubuque College and Seminary, 1911–1917, p. 265, UDA.

62. Untitled, *DS*, January 1916, 24.

63. Mihelic, "A Survey," 29; James Howard, "Earmark of Progress," *DS*, December 1915, 15.

64. *The Key* (1917), 74–75.

65. *DS*, January 1916, 18–19.

66. *DS*, February 1916, 20.

67. *The Key* (1917), 75; also see *DS*, April 1916, 13, and *DS*, March 1916, 29.

68. Brian Hallstoos, "Defusing Racism: Olympian Sol Butler's Serious Playfulness," *Character and . . . Play* 9 (2023): 57–77.

69. Robert van Gelder, "Robeson Remembers," *NYT*, 16 January 1944, sect. 2, x; Martin Duberman, *Paul Robeson* (New York: Alfred A. Knopf, 1988), 20; for a dramatized version of Robeson's experience making the Rutgers football team, see Brian Hallstoos, *Sol & Paul* (one-act play) (2015) (accessed online 3 July 2024), https://www.youtube.com/watch?v=9kIDI2PK9yk.

70. *The Leavenworth Times*, 28 September 1915, 8; "Held on Murder Charge," *TSJ*, 30 September 1915, 12; "Continued to April Term," *HN*, 21 January 1916, 2; Valerie Darnell, Reno County District Court, telephone conversation with author, 23 May 2018.

71. "Negroes Start Town," *TSJ*, 10 November 1915; *TSJ*, 4 February 1916, 3; "Negro Town Soon to Open," *TSJ*, 20 March 1916, 3.

72. "Program Announced," *HN*, 21 December 1915, 9; regarding Ben Butler's oratory in Dubuque, see *DS*, March 1916, 28–29.

73. On the basketball season, see *The Key* (1917), 110; *DS*, January 1916, 29; *DS*, February 1916, 22–23.

74. "Sol Butler Ties Forty Yard Mark," *RIA*, 26 February 1916, 14; *DS*, March 1916, 40.

75. *Indianapolis Recorder*, 15 April 1916, 1; "Sol Butler in Smart Set Meet," *CD*, 22 April 1916, 7; "Sol Butler Off to New York for Meet," *RIA*, 16 March 1916, 12; "Butler Passes Through City," *CD*, 22 April 1916, 7.

76. *DS*, April 1916, 21.

77. *DS*, April 1916, 22; *DS*, June 1916, 28.

78. Dave Johnson, phone conversation with author, 24 January 2014; *The Key* (1917), 116; *DS*, May 1916, 22; "Dismond Wins Second Place for Maroons in Penn Relay," *CT*, 29 April 1916, 12.

79. Johnson, conversation with author; also see Brian Hallstoos, *Gridirony: Segregated Stardom*, poster session, American Historical Association Conference, Washington, DC, 4 January 2014; Hallstoos and Helmke, *Racing Past*; Hallstoos, *Sol & Paul*.

80. Dennis Gildea, "The Penn Relays: Celebrating the 'Black Woodstock of West Philly,'" in *Philly Sports: Teams, Games, and Athletes from Rocky's Town*, ed. Ryan Swanson and David Wiggins (Fayetteville: University of Arkansas Press, 2016), 230.

81. Bob Olmsted, "Give Letters to Local Athletes," *RIA*, 18 May 1916, 10; *DS*, June 1916, 29; George Fisher, "Track," *The Key* (1918), 104; "Butler Wins Five First Places," *CD*, 27 May 1916, 7.

82. "Butler Shines in Hawkeye Meet," *RIA*, 29 May 1916, 10.

83. "Individual Star of the Big Meet," *TH*, 28 May 1916, 24.

84. Dorsey and Turfley Family Papers, 1868–2003, folder 11, box 1, HHC; "Colored Collegians to Compete," *PP*, 11 June 1916, 24; Jake Moore, "Negro Progress in the Realm of Athletics," *CE*, 16 April 1926, 1; Chester L. Washington, "Sez Ches," *PC*, 24 January 1942, 17.

85. "Sol Butler Again Stars," *Freeman*, 3 June 1916, 7; *TH*, 11 June 1916, 20; "300 Athletes from Three States Will Compete in Big Press Meet Saturday," *PP*, 11 June 1916, 1, 4; Gertrude Gordon, "Young and Old Look Forward to Press' Annual Field Meet," *PP*, 13 June 1916, 1.

86. "Unprecedented Interest in Press' Meet to Be Held Saturday at Forbes Field," *PP*, 14 June 1916, 1.

87. "Records Smashed by Stars on Field," *PP*, 18 June 1916, 4.

88. "Immense Crowd Cheers at Big Press Meet," *PP*, 17 June 1916, 1; "Athletes in Fine Trim for Press Meet Tomorrow," *PP*, 16 June 1916, 1.

89. "Great Sprinting in Century Dash," *PP*, 18 June 1916, 5.

90. "Race for Team Trophy Is Tie," *PP*, 18 June 1916, 4.

91. Jake Moore, "Negro Progress in the Realm of Athletics," *CE*, 16 April 1926, 1; *PP*, Sports Section, 17 June 1916; *PP*, Sports Section, 18 June 1916; *TH*, 11 June 1916; "Colored Collegians to Compete," *PP*, 11 June 1916, Dorsey and Turfley Family Papers, clipping in folder 16, box 1, HHC.

92. Washington, "Sez Ches," 17.

93. "Hutchinson, Kansas," *TP*, 1 September 1916, 3; "To Go After World Title," *HN*, 29 August 1916, 3.

94. "Sol Butler Runs 100 Yards for Touchdown," *CD*, 25 November 1916, 5.

95. *DS*, December 1916, 18–19.

96. For an account of the one loss of the 1916 football season and only game in Butler's college career that he did not play quarterback, see G. Heineman, "LaCrosse 12, Dubuque 3," *The Racquet*, 23 October 1916, 2; "Foot Ball," *The Key* (1918), 102.

97. Reemtsma, "Athletics," *DS*, December 1916, 20–21; also see Reemtsma, "Athletics," *DS*, January 1917, 20–21.

98. Reemtsma, "Athletics," *DS*, April 1917, 14.

99. "Indoor Interclass Meet," *DS*, April 1917, 14; Reemtsma, "Athletics," *DS*, June 1917, 20; *The Key* (1919), 109–114; *DE*, 4 June 1917, 2; "Why Butler Didn't Run in State Meet," *TH*, 22 May 1917, 7; regarding Butler declining the invitation to compete in a subsequent state meet, see "Sol Butler Barred from State Meet," *DMR*, 20 May 1919, 4; "Butler Unable to Attend State Meet," *DMR*, 21 May 1919, 9; "Butler's Absence Arouses Comment," *TH*, 25 May 1919, 28; on Butler's three Chicago indoor track meets that preceded the college season, see "Dismond Beats Meredith," *NYT*, 28 January 1917, 16; "Sends in No Alibi," *HN*, 1 February 1917, 3; "Play Teachers Here Saturday," *TH*, 7 February 1917, 7; "Chicago Athletes Win A.A.U. Title," *Ottumwa Semi-Weekly Courrier*, 3 April 1917, 3; "Kansas Kids Making Good," *HN*, 27 April 1917, 3.

100. *DS*, March 1917, 15.

101. Alvin Straatmeyer, *Child of the Church: University of Dubuque 1852–2008*, ed. Joel Samuels (Cedar Rapids, IA: WDG Communication, 2008), 79; Sol Butler, academic transcripts, 1915–1920, UDOR.

102. Clifford R. Murphy, *Ink: The Indelible J. Mayo Williams* (Urbana: University of Illinois Press, 2024), 103.

103. *TH*, 25 April 1917, 13; "Sol Butler Takes Broad Jump Event," *CD*, 5 May 1917, 8; "Red and Blue Runners Capture Two Relay Titles in Annual Carnival," *Daily Pennsylvanian*, 30 April 1917, 1.

104. "Penn and Chicago Take Big Events," *Evening Star*, 29 April 1917, part 5, p. 1.

105. *TH*, 22 April 1917, 24.

106. "Entries for Meet Small," *Grand Forks Herald*, 5 June 1917, 8; "Conference Meet Won by Maroons," *Arizona Republican*, 10 June 1917, 9; "Butler Awarded Race," *HN*, 6 July 1917, 8; Jonathan Finn, *Beyond the Finish Line: Images, Evidence, and the History of the Photo-Finish* (Montreal, Quebec: McGill-Queen's University Press, 2020), 81.

107. "Sol Butler Makes Talk," *CD*, 10 February 1917, 9.

108. *TH*, 1 June 1917, 7.

109. *The Key* (1918), unpaginated.

110. On nineteenth-century African American performer Thomas Dilward in integrated minstrel troupes, see Josephine Lee, *Oriental, Black & White: The Formation of Racial Habits in American Theater* (Chapel Hill: University of North Carolina Press, 2022), 63–73; for Black performers with blackface whites on film, see Arthur Knight, *Disintegrating the Musical: Black Performance and American Musical Film* (Durham, NC: Duke University Press, 2002).

111. "For Benefit of Church," *HN*, 23 December 1913, 9; Advertisement, *HN*, 7 January 1913, 2.

112. "Just Like Real Thing," *HN*, 9 January 1913, 10.

113. "Colored People Danced," *HN*, 22 March 1913, 2.

114. Henry T. Sampson, *Blacks in Blackface: A Sourcebook on Early Black Musical Shows* (Lanham, MD: Scarecrow Press, 2013), 1090.

115. "Home Theatre," *Cinema Treasure* (accessed 24 December 2020), http://cinematreasures.org/theaters/47079.

116. "Hutchinson, Kansas," *TP*, 7 March 1913, 3.

117. "Minstrels Made Hit," *HN*, 5 March 1913, 9.

118. "Minstrels Made Hit," 9.

119. David Krasner, *Resistance, Parody and Double Consciousness in African American Theatre, 1895–1910* (New York: St. Martin's Press, 1997), 26.

120. "Minstrels Made Hit," 9; also see William Mahar, *Behind the Burnt Cork Mask: Early Blackface Minstrelsy and Antebellum American Popular Culture* (Urbana: University of Illinois Press, 1999); Stephen Johnson, ed., *Burnt Cork: Traditions and Legacies of Blackface Minstrelsy* (Amherst: University of Massachusetts Press, 2012); Annemarie Bean, James Hatch, and Brooks McNamara, eds., *Inside the Minstrel Mask: Readings in Nineteenth-Century Blackface Minstrelsy* (Hanover, NH: Wesleyan University Press, 1996).

121. "Hutchinson, Kansas," *TP*, 7 March 1913, 3.

122. Yuval Taylor and Jake Austen, *Darkest America: Black Minstrelsy from Slavery to Hip-Hop* (New York: W. W. Norton, 2012), 3.

123. Eric Lott, *Love and Theft: Blackface Minstrelsy and the American Working Class*, 20th ed. (London: Oxford University Press, 2013); Robert Nowatzki, "Paddy Jumps Jim Crow: Irish-Americans and Blackface Minstrelsy," *Eire-Ireland* 41, nos. 3/4 (2006): 162–84; Michael Rogin, *Blackface, White Noise: Jewish Immigrants in the Hollywood Melting Pot* (Berkeley: University of California Press, 1996).

124. For further reading on Butler and blackface minstrelsy, see Hallstoos, "Defusing Racism," 66–69.

125. Undated article, Johnny Armstrong scrapbook, p. 90, private collection; *DS*, May/June 1917): 22.

126. YMCA College Catalog, pp. 20–21, box 114, KFYMCA.

127. *The Key* (1919), 175; "Lake Geneva," *Intercollegian*, October 1918, 5; Harrison S. Elliot, "Distinctive Features in the 1919 Student Summer Conferences," *Intercollegian*, October 1919, 7.

128. Nina Mjagkij, *Light in the Darkness: African Americans and the YMCA, 1852–1946* (Lexington: University Press of Kentucky, 1994), 61–64.

Chapter 5. Unusual Amount of Stamina

1. Robert V. Hayes, "Houston Riot of 1917," *Texas State Historical Association* (accessed 13 December 2022), https://www.tshaonline.org/handbook/entries/houston-riot-of-1917; Adriane Lentz-Smith, *Freedom Struggles: African Americans and World War I* (Cambridge, MA: Harvard University Press, 2009), 68, 74–78; Edgar Sandoval, "A Deadly Riot, and Then 3 Trials, 110 Convictions and 19 Executions," *NYT*, 26 February 2022, A17.

2. Lentz-Smith, *Freedom Struggles*, 4–5.

3. "Negro Troops Shoot Down Scores of Whites," *DBQDT*, 24 August 1917,

1; "Rioters to Answer for Murders and Mutiny," "Withdraw All Negro Troops," and "Court Martial Doesn't Satisfy Houston," all in *DBQDT*, 26 August 1917, 1; Alvin Straatmeyer, *Child of the Church: University of Dubuque 1852–2008*, ed. Joel Samuels (Cedar Rapids, IA: WDG Communication, 2008), 61, 79–82; Nancy Derr, "The Babel Proclamation," *Iowa Heritage Illustrated* 85, nos. 2/3 (2004): 128–44; on a campus organization happily switching from using German to the English language, see Sol Butler, "History of Philophronia," *The Key* (1918).

4. "Beg Your Pardon!" *CT*, 26 May 1917, 17.

5. Record of the Dubuque College and Seminary (1918–1923), 6–12, UDA.

6. *DE*, 10 September 1917, 2; *DE*, 12 May 1917, 2; *DE*, 24 September 1917, 2.

7. *DE*, 14 January 1918, 3.

8. *Race Prejudice* (pamphlet, ca. 1941), Misc. College and Seminary Materials, Mihelic box, UDA.

9. *The Key* (1919), 115.

10. *The Key* (1919), 116.

11. John Chalmers, "Football in Dubuque College," *DE*, 24 December 1917, 7; "Platteville Beaten," *DBQDT*, 30 September 1917, 6; "Dubuque Hits Hard," *DBQDT*, 14 October 1917, 6; "Point for Cornell," *DDT*, 26 October 1917, 14; "Dubuque Victorious," *DBQDT*, 27 October 1917, 3.

12. The *Key* (1919), 97.

13. "Dubuque and Cornell in Tie Contest, 13 to 13," *DBQDT*, 4 November 1917, 6.

14. "Dubuque College Playing Championship Saturday," *HN*, 2 November 1917, 3; *The Key* (1919), 97; *DE*, 12 November 1917, 2.

15. *The Key* (1919), 116, 152–53.

16. William H. Cumberland, *The History of Buena Vista College* (Ames: Iowa State University Press, 1966), 179–80.

17. *The Key* (1919), 96.

18. *1919 Rudder* (Buena Vista College, 1918), unpaginated.

19. *The Key* (1919), 97; also see "Playing for Title," *DBQDT*, 20 November 1917, 6; "Dubuque Will Win," *DBQDT*, 21 November 1917, 10; "Last of the Season," *DBQDT*, 22 November 1917, 10; "Off for Fayette," *DBQDT*, 23 November 1917, 12; "Chalmers Men Win Hawkeye Conference," *DBQDT*, 25 November 1917, 6; "Dubuque Gets Large Score," *DMR*, 25 November 1917, 33; "Rock Island, ILL.," *Bystander*, 7 December 1917, 1.

20. *The Key* (1919), 93.

21. "Butler to Run All Star Team," *TH*, 6 December 1917, 13; "All-Stars Gather for Soldier Game," *DMR*, 6 December 1917, 6.

22. Jack North, "Star Football Eleven Works Hard for Game with Camp Dodge," *DMT*, 6 December 1917, 13.

23. "Butler to Run," *TH*, 13.

24. "Sol Butler to Lead All-Star Team Saturday," *DDT*, 6 December 1917, 15.

25. "Des Moines Lands Big Football Game," *DMR*, 4 December 1917, 8.

26. Sec Taylor, "Grinnell Shares Honors with Ames on All-Iowa Team," *DMR*, 9 December 1917, 26.

27. Sec Taylor, "All-State Eleven Beats Camp Dodge in Chilly Contest," *DMR*,

9 December 1917, 26, 28; also see "All-State Eleven to Meet Camp Dodge Stars on Saturday," *The Courier*, 4 December 1917, 11; "All-Stars Will Practice Today," *QCT*, 5 December 1917, 7; "Squad Chosen to Play Camp Dodge," *DMR*, 5 December 1917, 8; "All-State Eleven in Fine Shape for Game with Soldier Team," *DMT*, 7 December 1917, 12; Sec Taylor, "Will Play Game Despite Blizzard," *DMR*, 8 December 1917, 8.

28. "Football," *Clavis* (formerly *The Key*) (1920), 116–20; *Racquet Yearbook* (La Crosse, 1919), 95; "Sol Butler Beats Grinnell," *CT*, 13 October 1918, 20; Sec Taylor, "Eight Hawkeyes Are Given Places on All-State Eleven for 1918," *DMR*, 15 December 1918, 14; regarding Dubuque German College's admission into a new athletic conference, see *Iowa Intercollegiate Conference-Records*, pp. 112, 115, box 160, UDA.

29. Regarding the possibility that African American player Alton Washington at Northwestern preceded Butler in quarterbacking a white college team for more than one season, see Arthur Ashe, *A Hard Road to Glory: A History of the African-American Athlete, 1619–1918*, vol. 1 (New York: Warner Books, 1988), 173–74.

30. John Adelmann, email to author, 4 January 2018.

31. Lloyd Vance, "The Complete History of the African American Quarterbacks in the National Football League (NFL)—Part I," *Coffin Corner* 27, no. 6 (2005) (accessed 19 December 2022), http://www.profootballresearchers.org/archives/Website_Files/Coffin_Corner/27-06-1102.pdf; for attention to the racism that has hampered African American access to the quarterback position in the NFL's modern era, see Louis Moore, *The Great Black Hope: Doug Williams, Vince Evans, and the Making of the Black Quarterback* (New York: PublicAffairs, 2024).

32. *DE*, 25 February 1918, 2.

33. On how his busyness in sports led to class absences and academic concerns, see *Faculty Minutes*, 26 March 1918, UDA; Solomon Butler transcripts, UDOR; *The Key* (1919), 178.

34. "Regarding the 1918 basketball season, notable for the team achieving its highest-winning percentage with Butler at the "pivot" (center) position, see *The Key* (1919), 102–104; *DE*, 25 March 1918, 2; "Two Fast Games for Local Quint," *TH*, 26 February 1918, 7; Sol Butler Will Compete in Races," *TH*, 2 March 1918, 3; *The Key* (1919), 189; "Chicago Carries Away Honors in Illinois Relays," *DMR*, 3 March 1918, S1.

35. *DE*, 11 March 1918, 2.

36. "Dubuque Meets Saints; Opener Next Tuesday," *QCT*, 4 April 1918, 7; also see "Open Baseball Season Tuesday at St. Ambrose," *DDT*, 8 April 1918, 11.

37. "Saints Drive in Two Frames Cop Game, 10–8," *DDT*, 10 April 1918, 15; "Saints Win over Dubuque College," *RIA*, 10 April 1918, 10; *Clavis* (1920), 131.

38. *Clavis* (1920), 127; "Will Compete in Drake Relays," *DMR*, 7 April 1918, 2-S; "Live Tips and Topics," *BG*, 5 April 1918, 8.

39. Sec Taylor, "Missourian's Work in 100-Yard Dash Feature of Relays," *DMR*, 21 April 1918, 1-S.

40. Ralph Wagner, "Sidelights on Drake Relay Meet," *DMR*, 21 April 1918, 2-S; *BG*, 25 April 1918, 9.

41. Regarding Butler's season ending meet in La Crosse, Wisconsin, where he

earned five first-place finishes in lieu of attending the Penn Relays, see "Sol Butler Victor over La Crosse Normal Squad," *CT*, 28 April 1918, part 2, 2.

42. "Hutchinson, Kansas," *TP*, 17 May 1918, 2.

43. *The Key* (1919), 163, 169, 178, 189.

44. Joseph Duke, letter to Jane Pitts, 1 August 1975, UDA; on Duke relaying that Ben allegedly absconded with Sol's trophies, see James Odenkirk, "Sol Butler: The Fleeting Fame of a World-Class Black Athlete," in *Before Jackie Robinson: The Transcendent Role of Black Sporting Pioneers*, ed. Gerald Gems (Lincoln: University of Nebraska Press, 2017), 151.

45. Benjamin Butler and Solomon Butler transcripts, UDOR, University of Dubuque (Ben: 1915–1918; Sol: 1915–1920).

46. "Wichita, Kansas," *Kansas City Advocate*, 19 July 1918, 3.

47. "Our Dubuque Girls," *DE*, 12 July 1920, 5; regarding the earliest female students, see *DE*, 20 August 1917, 2; Straatmeyer, *Child of the Church*, 63–68.

48. Martin Duberman, *Paul Robeson* (New York: Alfred A. Knopf, 1988), 25.

49. William Oscar Smith, *Sideman: The Long Gig of W. O. Smith: A Memoir* (Nashville: Rutledge Hill Press, 1991), 227–28; Brian Hallstoos, "'Excellent Work and Superior Traits of Personality': Composing an Integrated Music Department," in *Invisible Hawkeyes: African Americans at the University of Iowa during the Long Civil Rights Era* (Iowa City: University of Iowa Press, 2016), 38–39; for the type of social gathering that could have sparked public outcry had either Butler brother attended, see Joseph Duke, "Ice Cream, Wild Women, and Song; or, A Night at Callahan's," *The Key* (1919), 154–55.

50. *DE*, 13 September 1920, 3–4.

51. John Demos, *The Heathen School: A Story of Hope and Betrayal in the Age of the Early Republic* (New York: Alfred A. Knopf, 2014).

52. Bill Douglas, "Wartime Illusions and Disillusionment: Camp Dodge and Racial Stereotyping, 1917–1918," *Annals of Iowa* 57 (1998): 111, 127–28.

53. Brian Hallstoos, "Defusing Racism: Olympian Sol Butler's Serious Playfulness," *Character and . . . Play* 9 (2023): 57–77.

54. "Kansas Colored Girl, Army Nurse," *WDE*, 13 January 1918, 1.

55. "Graduates at Washington," *HN*, 15 June 1917, 8; *TP*, 1 October 1915, 6; "Hutchinson, Kan.," *TP*, 11 January 1918, 1; "Colored Girl in U.S. Army Nursing Corps," *HN*, 12 January 1918, 2; "Field Hospital for Wichita Is Opened by Nurses Association," *Wichita Church Chronicle*, 6 June 1924, 8; "Willie Anderson Gets Road Term in Assault Case," *Asheville Citizen-Times*, 3 May 1944, 11; "Woman Is Given Suspended Term in Assault Case," *Asheville Citizen-Times*, 1 June 1944, 6; Hassell Bradley, "Pioneering Nursing No Easy Lot," *WDE*, 10 November 1967, 24; "Retired Nurse, Daughter of Former Slave, Dies," *WB*, 29 October 1972, 54; on Freedmen's nurses breaking the racial barrier in the Army Nurse Corps in World War I and creating opportunities in World War II, see Mabel Keaton Staupers, *No Time for Prejudice: A Story of the Integration of Negroes in Nursing in the United States* (New York: Macmillan, 1961); also see *Course of Nurse Training at Freedmen's Hospital, Washington, D.C.; approved by Secretary of Interior, October 27, 1909* (Washington, DC: US Government Printing Office, 1909); *Freedmen's Hospital School of Nursing,*

1894–1973 (Washington, DC: Howard University, 1973); "Oteen Hospital Will Have 476 Additional Beds," *Asheville Citizen-Times*, 14 January 1944, 5; Maria Smilios, *The Black Angels: The Untold Story of the Nurses Who Helped Cure Tuberculosis* (New York: G. P. Putnam's Sons, 2023), 246–48, 312–14.

56. "Social Mass Meeting at Broadus Hall Monday Eve," *HN*, 6 September 1918, 6.

57. "Meeting Well Attended Progress for Race Made," *HN*, 10 September 1918, 5.

58. "Meeting Well Attended," 5.

59. "Meeting Well Attended," 5.

60. "Student's Army Training Corps," *DE*, 19 August 1918, 2; *DE*, 2 September 1918, 2; "College Opening," *DE*, 16 September 1918, 3.

61. *DE*, 9 September 1918, 3.

62. *DE*, 21 October 1918, 2.

63. C. A. Hanna, "Mars at Dubuque," *Clavis* (1920), 112.

64. *DE*, 20 May 1918, 2; *DE*, 22 July 1918, 2; Hal Chase, "Struggle for Equality: Fort Des Moines Training Camp for Colored Officers, 1917," *Phylon* 39, no. 4 (1978): 297–310; "U.S. to Establish Camp to Train Negro Officers," *CT*, 16 May 1917, 3.

65. Susan Kingsley Kent, *The Influenza Pandemic of 1918–1919* (New York: Bedford/St. Martin's, 2012).

66. Kristen Anderson-Bricker, "'Keep Germs to Yourself': Lessons from the 1918 Influenza Epidemic," *Loras Daily*, 9 April 2020); also see Kristin Anderson-Bricker, "The 'Dread Malady' and La Grippe: Surviving the 1918 Epidemics of Polio and Influenza in the City of Dubuque," presentation, Center for Dubuque History, 15 November 2018.

67. *DE*, 4 November 1918, 2.

68. *Clavis* (1920), 102.

69. *Clavis* (1920), 147.

70. *Clavis* (1920), 102.

71. *Clavis* (1920), 103.

72. *DE*, 16 December 1918, 2; *DE*, 30 December 1918, 2.

73. *Clavis* (1920), 105.

74. *DE*, 27 January 1919, 2.

75. "Noted Musician to Give Recital Here," *WDE*, 27 January 1919, 5; also see Vernon Edwards and Michael Mark, "Clarence Cameron White," *Black Perspective in Music* 9, no. 1 (1981): 51–72.

76. "A Negro Writer," *Great Bend Tribune*, 6 January 1919, 4; Pearl Bowser and Louise Spence, *Writing Himself into History: Oscar Micheaux, His Silent Films, and His Audiences* (New Brunswick, NJ: Rutgers University Press, 2000), 11; "'Sol' Butler, Famed Athlete, Slain: Fatally Hurt in a Gun Duel," *CD*, 11 December 1954, 10.

77. *Clavis* (1920), 122–24; *DE*, 3 March 1919, 2, 8.

78. *Clavis* (1920), 90, 92; *DE*, 17 February 1919, 2.

79. "Ben Butler Dies," *HG*, 2 April 1919, 2; "Deaths and Funerals," *HN*, 2 April 1919, 8; "Negro Athlete's Father Is Dead," *WDE*, 20 April 1919, 8; *DE*, 7 April 1919, 2.

80. Sec Taylor, "Grinnell Athlete Defeats Greatest Sprinters of West," *DMR*, 20 April 1919, 19.

81. Dennis Gildea, "The Penn Relays: Celebrating the 'Black Woodstock of West Philly,'" in *Philly Sports: Teams, Games, and Athletes from Rocky's Town*, ed. Ryan Swanson and David Wiggins (Fayetteville: University of Arkansas Press, 2016), 233.

82. A. C. Cavagnaro, "Legendre, Georgetown Freshman, Wins Pentathlon in Athletic Carnival at Philadelphia," *NYT*, 26 April 1919, 20; "Utah Athletes Make Good Showing in Big Penn Relay Carnival," *Salt Lake Tribune*, 27 April 1919, 30; "Western Carries Off Relay Event Prize," *WP*, 27 April 1919, 22; "Harvard Just Nosed Out in Two-Mile Relay," *BG*, 27 April 1919, 15; "Butler Wins 2 Firsts in Relay Meet," *DMR*, 28 April 1919, 14; "Sol Butler" (photo with caption), *NYT*, 4 May 1919, 67.

83. A. C. Cavagnaro, "University of Chicago Only Successful Western Entry in Western Games," *NYT*, 28 April 1919, 18; for debates over Black athleticism and high representation in certain professional sports in relation to racial attitudes regarding intelligence, work ethic, and other traits, see David Wiggins, "'Great Speed but Little Stamina': The Historical Debate over Black Athletic Superiority," *Journal of Sport History* 16, no. 2 (1989): 158–85.

84. "Butler Scores 32 Points," *Evening Public Ledger* (Philadelphia), 5 May 1919, 17.

85. "Butler Stars in Coe Meet," *DMR*, 4 May 1919, 19.

86. Waldo Norris, "Sol Butler Stars in Coe's Victory, *DMR*, 17 May 1919, 4–5; *Iowa Intercollegiate Athletic Conference—Records*, box 160, UDA, *The Key* (1921), 111.

87. "Our Track Team," *DE*, 26 May 1919, 2.

88. "Dubuque College Letter Men Enjoy Banquet," *TH*, 27 May 1919, 10.

89. "Dubuque College Letter Men Enjoy Banquet," 10; also see "Sol Butler in Farewell," *DMR*, 29 May 1919, 9; "A Week of Banquets," *DE*, 9 June 1919, 2; *Records of the Dubuque College and Seminary, 1918–23*, p. 54, UDA.

90. "May 27, 1919," *Clavis* (1920), 139–40.

91. "The Juniors," *Clavis* (1921), 146–47.

92. "Butler Rescued, Attends Banquet," *TH*, 28 May 1919, 5.

93. "May 27, 1919," *Clavis* (1920), 139–40.

94. "May 27, 1919," *Clavis* (1920), 140.

95. "The Juniors," *Clavis* (1921), 147.

96. "The Juniors," 147.

97. *Clavis* (1920), 128.

98. "Sol Butler Sails for Paris Tuesday," *TH*, 28 May 1919, 8.

99. "Sol Butler Will Go to France for Olympic Meet," *HN*, 5 April 1919, 1.

100. "Athletes to Go Overseas," *LAT*, 28 May 1919, 25.

101. "Sol Butler Sails," *TH*, 8; also see "Sol Butler Accepts Bid," *DMR*, 30 May 1919, 5; "'Sol Is Wearing a Wide Grin; He May Go to Paris," *DBQDT*, 28 May 1919, 8; "College Athletes Scatter This Week," *TH*, 1 June 1919, 24.

102. "College's Alumni Aid Booster Week," *TH*, 29 May 1919, 12; "Booster Week at College Closes," *TH*, 1 June 1919, 18.

103. "Sol Butler Sails," *TH*, 8.

104. "Sol Butler Has Big Ovation; On Way [to] Paris Arena," *DBQDT*, 1 June 1919, 12.

105. "Sol Butler Visits Defender," *CD*, 7 June 1919, 15.

106. "Sol Butler Visits Defender," 15.

107. Regarding a contemporaneous commencement address at Rutgers by a Black friend of Butler, see Duberman, *Paul Robeson*, 26–27.

108. "Commencement Exercises," *DE*, 9 June 1919, 7.

Chapter 6. The Democracy of Sport

1. "Martin, Robert L.," *Encyclopedia Dubuque* (accessed 28 January 2023), encyclopediadubuque.org.

2. "Martin, Henry A.," *Encyclopedia Dubuque* (accessed 28 January 2023), encyclopediadubuque.org; Olesia Plokhii, "Robert Martin, Tuskegee Airman Who Flew '63 and a Half' Combat Missions, Dies at 99," *WP*, 4 August 2018 (accessed 28 January 2023), washingtonpost.com.

3. Jennifer Keene, "A 'Brutalizing' War? The USA after the First World War," *Journal of Contemporary History* 50, no. 1 (2015): 79.

4. "A.E.F. Team Not Able to Sail," *Central New Jersey Home News*, 3 June 1919, 8; "Eligibles for the Inter-Allied Games," *BG*, 20 May 1919, 9; "Sol Butler to Peddle Wares in Paris Meet," *RIA*, 5 June 1919, 14.

5. Charles Paddock, *The Fastest Human* (New York: Thomas Nelson & Sons, 1933), 16.

6. "Numerous Sports Clubs in New York Are Closed to Jews and Negroes," *Jewish Telegraphic Agency Daily News Bulletin*, 14 July 1959, 4.

7. "48 Athletes on Way," *Baltimore Sun*, 5 June 1919, 13.

8. George Bronder, "To Win Big Army Meet; Is Not Sure of Javelin," *BDE*, 4 June 1919, 18.

9. "U.S. Athletes Should Win in Broad Jump," *Bridgeport Times*, 24 December 1919, 12; also see "Effect of Sea Voyage on Athletes," *Pittsburgh Post-Gazette*, 13 July 1919, 21.

10. "Sol Butler Back from Europe," *TH*, 14 August 1919, 7.

11. "Leave Areas. History" (untitled document), box 130, KFYMCA.

12. Aldrich R. Burton, 19 May 1919 letter to Ran, William Granger Papers, Schomburg Center for Research in Black Culture, New York; Elizabeth Foxwell, "Helen Hagan, Black Pianist for the AEF," in *American Women in World War I* (blog) (accessed 25 September 2018), https://americanwomeninwwi.wordpress.com/2016/01/18/helen-hagan-black-pianist-for-the-aef/.

13. "Entertainment Report—Brest Region 1919" folder, box 27, KFYMCA.

14. Cedric Robinson, *Forgeries of Memory and Meaning: Blacks & the Regimes of Race in American Theater and Film before World War II* (Chapel Hill: University of North Carolina Press, 2007), 176.

15. For a firsthand account of white Americans mistreating African Americans in France (including Brest) around the time Butler arrived, see J. E. Blanton, letter to E. C. Carter, 29 May 1919, box 2, KFYMCA.

16. "Sol Butler Back," 1, 7.

17. Joseph Hanson, ed. *The Inter-Allied Games: Paris 22nd June to 6th July 1919* (Games Committee, 1919), 127; original from Pennsylvania State University.

18. Hanson, *Inter-Allied Games*, 12–14; Elwood S. Brown interview, 9 January 1920, p. 42, box 23, KFYMCA.

19. Lou Antolihao, *Playing with the Big Boys: Basketball, American Imperialism, and Subaltern Discourse in the Philippines* (Lincoln: University of Nebraska Press, 2015), 58–59; Stefan Huebner, *Pan-Asian Sports and the Emergence of Modern Asia, 1913–1974* (Singapore: NUS Press, 2016), ch. 1; Gerald Gems, *Sport and the American Occupation of the Philippines: Bats, Balls and Bayonets* (Lanham, MD: Lexington Books, 2016), 156.

20. Elwood S. Brown interview, 5 January 1920, p. 22, box 23, KFYMCA; see also Brown interview, 9 January 1920, p. 36, box 23, KFYMCA.

21. Nina Mjagkij, *Light in the Darkness: African Americans and the YMCA, 1852–1946* (Lexington: University Press of Kentucky, 2003), 87.

22. Hanson, *Inter-Allied Games*, 140.

23. Theodore M. Brown and Elizabeth Fee, "Raymond B. Fosdick (1883–1972): Ardent Advocate of Internationalism," *American Journal of Public Health* (July 2012) (accessed online 7 October 2018), https://www.ncbi.nlm.nih.gov/pmc/articles/PMC3478029/; Raymond Fosdick, "Memorandum for General Pershing on Morale in the American Expeditionary Force," 1 February 1919, pp. 13–14, box 21, KFYMCA; Hanson, *Inter-Allied Games*, 30–35.

24. Robert Elias, *The Empire Strikes Out: How Baseball Sold U.S. Foreign Policy and Promoted the American Way Abroad* (New York: New Press, 2010), 93.

25. Hanson, *Inter-Allied Games*, 123, 176c.

26. "Sol Butler Back," 7; also see Paddock, *Fastest Human*, 22–23.

27. Undated newspaper clipping, *New York Tribune*, box 24, KFYMCA; Hanson, *Inter-Allied Games*, 41–42.

28. Bronder, "To Win Big Army Meet," 18.

29. "A.E.F. Trials Close," *TSJ*, 19 June 1919, 8; "Sol Butler, A Second Robeson," *Central New Jersey Home News*, 20 June 1919, 21; "A.E.F. Athletes Equal Records," *New York Herald*, 21 June 1919, 17.

30. Hanson, *Inter-Allied Games*, 176i.

31. Hanson, *Inter-Allied Games*, 176.

32. Paddock, *Fastest Human*, 82.

33. Hanson, *Inter-Allied Games*,176d.

34. "Sol Butler Wins in Dash," *Salina Evening Journal*, 25 June 1919, 1.

35. "Sol Butler Back," 7.

36. For visual evidence of the airplane's surprisingly low flight over the field, see Hanson, *Inter-Allied Games*, 147.

37. Brown interview, 9 January 1920, box 23, KFYMCA, 61–62.

38. Paddock, *Fastest Human*, 25; also see Judith Enright-Smith, "John Armstrong Howard, Canada's First Black Olympian" (accessed 1 July 2018), https://thediscoveryblog.com; Gerry Weaver, "From 'Army' Howard to Harry Jerome: A Trailblazing Legacy of Courage" (accessed 1 July 2018), http://www.army-armee.forces.gc.ca.

39. Paddock, *Fastest Human*, 28.

40. Hanson, *Inter-Allied Games*, 310.

41. On Butler not racing in the 4 × 200-meter relay, see "Sol Butler Back," 7.

42. Hanson, *Inter-Allied Games*, 176g.

43. Frank P. Lahm, *The World War I Diary of Col. Frank P. Lahm, Air Force, A.E.F.*, ed. Albert F. Simpson (Maxwell AFB, AL: Historical Research Division, Aerospace Studies Institute, 1970), 200; see also "Yankees Lead Field," *Sunday Oregonian*, 29 June 1919, 5.

44. Box 42, S series, Canadian War Records Office photographic collection, Library and Archives Canada, Ottawa, Ontario.

45. Paddock, *Fastest Human*, 32–34.

46. *The (New York) Sun*, 3 August 1919, 5.

47. "King Pats U.S. Negro," *The Tennessean*, 30 June 1919, 10.

48. "Americans Win Inter-Allied Games at Paris," *ALW*, 4 July 1919, 23.

49. "Bursts of Duds," *ALW*, 1 August 1919, 21.

50. "Bulletin Board," *ALW*, 15 August 1919, 20.

51. David Pilgrim, "The Tom Caricature," Jim Crow Museum, December 2000; edited 2024 (accessed 5 February 2023), https://www.ferris.edu/HTMLS/news/jimcrow/tom/homepage.htm.

52. *General Regulations Governing the Competitions: Pershing Stadiums, Paris* (Games Committee, 1919), 36.

53. "Mahoney, Back from War, to Compete for the B.A.A.," *BG*, 29 July 1919, 9.

54. Hanson, *Inter-Allied Games*, 490; on Butler inaugurating "the great tradition of Negro long-jumpers" with this victory, see R. L. Quercetani, *A World History of Track and Field Athletics, 1864–1964* (London: Oxford University Press, 1964), 248.

55. *TH*, 14 August 1919, 7; Charles Paddock, *Track and Field* (New York: A. S. Barnes, 1933), 93; Alan Gould, "Sifting Olympic Hopes," *Fort Worth Star-Telegram*, 27 May 1932, 18.

56. Hanson, *Inter-Allied Games*, 157.

57. Memorandum of Agreement between Community Motion Picture Bureau and Committee on Allied Armies and Prisoners of War, 9 January 1919, box 22, KFYMCA; also see Summary of Minutes of Joint Meeting of Executive and Finance Committees, 24 July 1919, p. 2, box 3, KFYMCA.

58. Film footage of Sol Butler in the broad jump, Paris, France, recorded 4 July 1919, UDA; "A.E.F. Films Shown at the Helena Y.M.C.A.," *Independent-Record* (Helena, MT), 20 January 1920, 2.

59. "General Pershing Awarding Medals to the Winners on the Closing Day of the Athletic Meet at the Pershing Stadium," film footage of Sol Butler shaking General Pershing's hand, 1919, Critical Past (accessed 5 March 2024), https://www.criticalpast.com/video/65675051503_Athletic-meet_people-gather_General-Pershing_awarding-medals.

60. Lahm, *World War I Diary*, 202.

61. Hanson, *Inter-Allied Games*, 336; for a photograph of Butler shaking General Pershing's hand, see page 487.

62. "Sportography," *El Paso Herald*, 25 July 1919, 10.

63. “Sol Butler Back,” 1; “Montenegrin King Knights Sol Butler,” *HG*, 20 August 1919, 8; “Old Sol’s Sun Sets,” *WDE*, 5 December 1954, 2B; on Butler defeating Paddock in 100 meters, see “Victorious Yank Athletes May Compete in New York,” *Galveston (Texas) Daily News*, 27 July 1919, 7; regarding sports played in the Tuileries, see Elias, *Empire Strikes Out*, 91.

64. “Paris Stages Greatest Victory Parade in History,” *Kingston (New York) Daily Freeman*, 14 July 1919, 1; also see “France Honors Allied Dead on Bastille Day,” *BG*, 14 July 1919, 5; “Passionate Thanks Given Soldiers of Victory in France’s Divine Moment,” *Pittsburgh Post-Gazette*, 16 July 1919, 2.

65. “Sol Butler Back,” 7.

66. “Bunch Phillips Was Also in A.E.F. Meet,” *HN*, 24 July 1919, 3.

67. Joshua E. Blanton, letter to R. B. DeFrantz, 9 September 1919, Colored Work Department Records, box 2, KFYMCA.

68. “Will Celebrate Soldier Victory,” *Detroit Free Press*, 27 July 1919, 17; “Sol Butler Returns to America from France,” *WB*, 11 August 1919, 7.

69. “Victorious American Athletes Return on the Imperator,” *NYT*, 11 August 1919, 13.

70. “Sol Butler Back,” 1; “Picked Up ’Round Town,” *HN*, 11 August 1919, 8; “Montenegrin King,” *HG*, 8.

71. *Evening Missourian* (Columbia), 6 August 1919, 2.

72. William Tuttle, *Race Riot: Chicago in the Red Summer of 1919* (Urbana: University of Illinois Press, 1996); Carl Sandburg, *The Chicago Race Riots, July, 1919* (Mineola, NY: Dover Publication, 2013); Eve L. Ewing, *1919* (Chicago: Haymarket Books, 2019).

73. Thomas Guglielmo, *White on Arrival: Italians, Race, Color, and Power in Chicago, 1890–1945* (Oxford: Oxford University Press, 2003), 43.

74. David Roediger, *The Wages of Whiteness: Race and the Making of the American Working* Class (London: Verso, 2022); Allan Spear, *Black Chicago: The Making of a Negro Ghetto, 1880–1920* (Chicago: University of Chicago Press, 1967).

75. Cameron McWhirter, *Red Summer: The Summer of 1919 and the Awakening of Black America* (New York: St. Martin’s Griffin, 2012).

76. Grif Stockley, “Elaine Massacre of 1919,” Encyclopedia of Arkansas, www.encyclopediaofarkansas.net, last updated 29 June 2024 (accessed 21 November 2018).

77. Cornelius Steffens, “Unity in Diversity,” *DE*, 29 September 1919, 1; John Jowett, “The Vision of Racial Union,” *DE*, 3 November 1919, 1.

78. Cornelius Steffens, “New Era Expectations,” *DE*, 16 February 1920, 1.

79. John H. Burma, “Young People’s Meeting, Sept. 28, 1919,” *DE*, 22 September 1919, 7.

80. Reprinted in “Leading Press Opinions,” *St. Louis Star-Times*, 7 July 1919, 12.

81. *The Key* (1921), 116; *Crisis* 18, no. 5 (1919): 255.

82. *The Key* (1921), 158.

83. *The Key* (1921), 185; also see pages 161 and 167.

84. Report of the American Olympic Committee, Seventh Olympic Games, Antwerp, Belgium, 1920 (Greenwich, CT: Condé Nast Press, 1921), 367.

85. "Indians Off for Dubuque Brawl," *MD*, 26 November 1919, 14; "Sol Butler Will Play with Legion," *DMR*, 27 November 1919, 10; "War Veterans Winners," *DMR*, 28 November 1919, 8; "Sol Butler Plays against Indians," *DDT*, 28 November 1919, 25; "Dubuque Legion Turns the Tables on Moline Indians," *TH*, 28 November 1919, 11; "Ira Davenport," *Olympedia* (accessed 20 March 2025), https://www.olympedia.org/athletes/78294.

86. "Dubuque Legion," *TH*, 11; John Armstrong scrapbook, private collection.

87. Sol Butler, academic transcripts, 1915–1920, ORUD.

88. *DE*, 1 December 1919, 1; "The People's Forum," and "City Locals," *Hutchinson Blade*, 27 December 1919, 1, 4; "Sol Butler Joins Forty Club," *CD*, 20 November 1919, 9; also see Gerald Gems, "Blocked Shot: The Development of Basketball in the African-American Community of Chicago," *Journal of Sport History* 22, no. 2 (1995): 140.

89. "In the Chip the Law," *CD*, 10 January 1920, 11; also see "Grace Lyceum," *CD*, 3 May 1919, 12.

90. "D.A.C. Is Offered Services of Butler," *DDT*, 7 February 1920, 14.

91. *The Key* (1921), 161; *Dallas Express*, 14 February 1920, 4; "Sol Butler to Try for Olympics," *TH*, 16 February 1920, 10; "Butler Will Compete," *DMR*, 18 February 1920, 10; on Butler being named to the AAU All-American team in the broad jump, see "All-American Team," *TSJ*, 1 January 1920, 3; Mark Dyreson, "Selling American Civilization: The Olympic Games of 1920 and American Culture," *Olympika: The International Journal of Olympic Studies* 8 (1999): 8.

92. Seminary Faculty Minutes 1916–1926, p. 25, UDA; regarding the Forty Club western tour, which Butler apparently missed, see "Wabash Ave. 'Y' to Have Home Coming," *CD*, 28 February 1920, 11.

93. J. W. Cobb, "Colored News," *Richmond (Kentucky) Daily Register*, 13 March 1920, 6; also see "Howard Drew and Sol Butler Asked to Boost the Event," *Bystander* (Des Moines, IA), 12 March 1920, 1.

94. Advertisement, *TP*, 19 March 1920, 3; *TP*, 26 March 1920, 3; *Kansas City Sun*, 27 March 1920, 8.

95. "Hero of Colored Youth," *HN*, 26 April 1920, 8.

96. "Personal," *HG*, 27 April 1920, 4.

97. "Howard Drew Wins Southern Classic," *Drake (Iowa) Delphic*, 30 April 1920, 1.

98. "Lawrence Boy Star," *Lawrence (Kansas) Daily Journal-World*, 3 May 1920, 6; also see "Hutchinson, Kansas," *Negro Star* (Wichita, KS), 7 May 1920, 3.

99. "Sol Butler to Try Out for Olympics," *TH*, 20 June 1920, 20; "Butler Goes to Olympics," *Evening Times-Republican* (Marshalltown, IA), 12 June 1920, 5; "Hutchinson Boy to Enter Olympic Games," *HN*, 18 June 1920, 3; "C.A.A. Stars in Events," *CT*, 22 June 1920, 14; "Crack Athletes of the Middlewest in Olympic Try Outs at Chicago," *DMT*, 25 June 1920, 16; *Iowa Press Citizen*, 26 June 1920, 6; "Results of the American Tryouts for the Olympic Athletic Games," *NYH*, 27 June 1920, 17; *Report of the American Olympic Committee, Seventh Olympic Games, Antwerp, Belgium* (1920): 185, 187.

Chapter 7. The Olympic Urge

1. "Willis Cummings," WPA Writers Program, Micro R-6544/Sc MG 24, reel 5; "Willis Nelson Cummings (1894–1991)," in *Penn People* (accessed 27 February 2025), www.archives.upenn.edu/exhibits/penn-people/biography/willlis-nelson-cummings/; for more on early Black students at University of Pennsylvania, see Wayne Glasker, *Black Students in the Ivory Tower: African American Student Activism at the University of Pennsylvania, 1967–1990* (Amherst: University of Massachusetts Press, 2002), 20–21.

2. Danny Sherr, "First Black Captain Cummings 'Ran Legs Off' as Penn Harrier," *Daily Pennsylvanian*, 7 November 1973, 16; Linda Henry, "The Life of Willis Cummings: Pride and Prejudice," *Daily Pennsylvanian*, 26 September 1979, 8; Edgar Williams, "He's Taken Some Long Strides in His Lifetime," *Philadelphia Inquirer*, 29 February 1980, 1; "Reminiscences of Willis N. Cummings: Oral History, 1974," Columbia Center for Oral History, Columbia University Libraries.

3. "Chaplain Halted in Use of Word 'Nigger,'" *California Voice*, 8 December 1922 (reprinted from the 11 November 1922 edition of the *Philadelphia Tribune*), unpaginated clipping in "Willis Cummings," Schomburg Center.

4. A. Budd, "'Our Earl' Shows 'Em before 28,000 in Harvard's Stadium," *AA*, 23 July 1920, 1; "Sol Butler to Try Out for Olympics," *TH*, 20 June 1920, 20; *Report of the American Olympics Committee, Seventh Olympic Games, Antwerp, Belgium* (1920), 187.

5. Thomas J. Anderson, "Anderson's Comments," *NYAN*, 18 May 1932, 13.

6. 1920 Final Olympic Tryouts Program, box 346, ABC.

7. *Report of the American Olympic Committee, Seventh Olympic Games, Antwerp, Belgium,* 1920 (Greenwich, CT: Condé Nast Press, 1921), 189–96; "American Records Broken in Olympic Trials at Harvard," *Ogden (UT) Standard-Examiner*, 18 July 1920, 9.

8. Allen Guttmann, *The Olympics: A History of the Modern Games* (Urbana: University of Illinois Press, 2002), 37–39; William Tutherly, *The World at Play: A Program of Practical Athletics for the Millions* (1920), box 23, and Minutes of Joint Meeting of Finance and Executive Committees, National War Work Council (31 March 1920), box 3, KFYMCA; Mark Dyreson, "Selling American Civilization: The Olympic Games of 1920 and American Culture," *Olympika: The International Journal of Olympic Studies* 8 (1999): 1–42.

9. Joseph Turrini, *The End of Amateurism in American Track and Field* (Urbana: University of Illinois Press, 2010), 16.

10. 1920 Final Olympic Tryouts Program, ABC.

11. "Live Tips & Topics," *BG*, 8 March 1922, 11; also see John Bentley, "I May Be Wrong," *Lincoln Star*, 2 February 1936, 7.

12. "Old Sol's Sun Sets," *WDE*, 5 December 1954, 2B.

13. Joseph Cooper, "Dangerous Stereotypes Stalk Black College Athletes," *The Conversation*, 20 August 2018, https://theconversation.com/dangerous-stereotypes-stalk-black-college-athletes-101655; also see Matthew Hutson, "Whites See Blacks as Superhuman; and That's Not Exactly a Compliment," *Slate*, 14 November 2014

(accessed 7 January 2019), https://slate.com/technology/2014/11/whites-see-blacks-as-superhuman-strength-speed-pain-tolerance-and-the-magical-negro.html.

14. Neal Thompson, *A Curious Man: The Strange and Brilliant Life of Robert 'Believe It or Not' Ripley* (New York: Crown Archetype, 2013), 81–82.

15. Robert Ripley, "America's Olympians," *Akron Evening Times*, 13 August 1920, 15.

16. Ripley, "America's Olympians," 15.

17. Davarian Baldwin, *Chicago's New Negroes: Modernity, the Great Migration, and Black Urban Life* (Chapel Hill: University of North Carolina Press, 2007), 200.

18. R. Earl Johnson, "Many Star Athletes Failed in Olympics," *PC*, 31 July 1948, 8.

19. "Sol Butler," *DMT*, 23 July 1920, 10; also see M. V. Morgenstern, "Athletes: Mid-Western Olympic Trials," *University of Chicago Magazine*, July 1920, 340.

20. "American Olympic Team Off for Games," *BG*, 27 July 1920, 6; "Olympic Athletes Sail for Antwerp," *NYT*, 27 July 1920, 15.

21. *Report of the American Olympic Committee*, 28.

22. "Olympic Athletes Sail for Antwerp," 15.

23. Guttmann, *The Olympics*, 39.

24. Charles Paddock, *The Fastest Human* (New York: Thomas Nelson & Sons, 1933), 65.

25. *Report of the American Olympic Committee*, 29.

26. Henry Farrell, "All Not Pleasant at Antwerp Olympic Games in 1920," *PP*, 8 June 1928, 49; for more regarding conditions on the *Matoika*, see Dyreson, "Selling American Civilization," 11–13; Thelma Payne Sanborn interview, March 1987, by Anita DeFrantz; Aileen Riggin interview, 11 November 1994, by Margaret Costa; and Walker Smith interview, April 1987, by George Hodak, all at http://digital.la84.org (accessed 22 March 2025); Charles E. Parker, "On Board the U.S.S. Princess Matoika," *Hammond (IN) Times*, 29 July 1920, 10.

27. *Report of the American Olympic Committee*, 207.

28. For a detailed account of conditions on the *Matoika* that suggests Butler may have roomed below the sick bay level, see John Hallahan, "Athletes Made Best of Poor Conditions," *BG*, 22 August 1920, 1, 16.

29. Hallahan, "Athletes Made Best," 16; also see James Meredith, "Olympic Athletes Seem Perfectly Satisfied as Matoika Sails Onward," *PP*, 31 July 1920, 6; James Meredith, "Week on Shipboard Is Good Conditioner for Olympic Team," *PP*, 3 August 1920, 6; "Duke's Sweet Music Cures Sick Athlete," *Honolulu Star Bulletin,* 26 August 1920, 4; on Butler declaring that he would not compete in a future Olympics "unless they build a bridge across the ocean," see "Never Again," *Milwaukee Sentinel*, 13 August 1920, 8.

30. "Olympic Athletes Revolt against Leaders," *Washington Times*, 13 September 1920, 14.

31. Farrell, "All Not Pleasant," 8.

32. "Earl Johnson Writes about Olympic Games for 'Afro,'" *AA*, 27 August 1920, 1; on Sol's popularity, also see "On the Cinder Path," *NYA*, 23 October 1920, 7; for a secondhand report from Pennsylvanian hurdler Harold Bannon that Butler

was the most popular athlete at the Olympics "because of his wonderful humor and all around good fellowship," see Joseph Duke, letter to Jane Pitts, 1 August 1975, UDA; *Racing Past the Color Line: Sol Butler and Paul Robeson in Collegiate Athletics*, exhibition catalog, ed. Brian Hallstoos and Jonathan Helmke (Dubuque, IA: University of Dubuque, 2014), 22.

33. Walker Smith interview, 10–12.

34. W. H. Robertson, "Eby's Fast Workout in the Half Mile," *NYH*, 10 August 1920, 9.

35. "Yank Athletes' First Workout," *Milwaukee Journal*, 10 August 1920, 14; "Live Tips and Topics," *BG*, 14 August 1920, 5; Guttmann, *The Olympics*, 39; "American Squad in Olympics to Be Well Coached," *Berkeley Daily Gazette*, 21 March 1924, section 2, p. 3.

36. R. Earl Johnson, "England Had Colored Runner," *AA*, 3 September 1920, 7.

37. Arthur Draper, "New Yorker Breaks High Jump Record," *NYTB*, 18 August 1920, 11.

38. R. Johnson, "England Had Colored Runner," 7.

39. Draper, "New Yorker Breaks High Jump Record," 11.

40. Alvin Moses, "Four Colored Athletes Hold Premier Broad Jumping Laurels," *PC*, 24 December 1927, 17; also see "Bronzed Athletes Hold All Broad Jumping Records," *AA*, 24 December 1927, 18; "Landon, Yale Jumper, Sets Olympic Mark," *NYH*, 18 August 1920, 11.

41. [Sol Butler lying on his back, clutching his left leg] ID: btv1b90342996, and [Butler being carried by two men] ID: btv1b9034300d, Gallica Digital Library, Agence de presse Meurisse, 1920 (accessed 23 February 2019).

42. R. Johnson, "England Had Colored Runner," 7.

43. Moses, "Four Colored Athletes," 17.

44. "U.S. Stars Welcomed in Gotham," *Minneapolis Star*, 3 October 1920, 37; regarding Butler's return trip, see "Sol Butler Returns," *CD*, 9 October 1920, 6; on Butler competing in London two weeks after his injury, see "American and British Athletes Tie at 5 to 5," *NYH*, 5 September 1920, 14.

45. "2 Girls of 14 Stars in Olympic Parade," *NYT*, 3 October 1920, 14.

46. Untitled, *DE*, 18 October 1920, 2; also see "New York City Briefs," *CD*, 9 October 1920, 3.

47. "Sol Butler to Study in the East," *Bystander*, 4 November 1920, 3.

48. "Sol Butler Home Again," *HN*, 22 October 1920, 12.

49. "Olympic Stars Are Planning to Quit," *Press & Sun-Bulletin* (Binghamton, NY), 4 October 1920, 17; "Sol Butler Visits Wichita," *WDE*, 24 October 1920, 9; regarding a job offer from an HBCU in Topeka, see "Want Butler as Coach," *HN*, 23 October 1920, 19.

50. James Grossman, *Land of Hope: Chicago, Black Southerners, and the Great Migration* (Chicago: University of Chicago Press, 1989), 135; on Chicago's Black population growing from 44,103 to 109,458 people between 1910 and 1920, and swelling to 277,751 by 1940, see *Thirteenth Census of the United States Take in the Year 1910: Statistics for Illinois* (Washington, DC: Government Printing Office,

1913), 612, *Fourteenth Census of the United States: 1920: Bulletin: Population: Illinois* (Washington, DC: Government Printing Office, 1921), 19, and *Sixteenth Census of the United States: 1940: Population: Characteristics of the Nonwhite Population by Race* (Washington, DC: Government Printing Office, 1943), 6.

51. Gerald Gems, *Windy City Wars: Labor, Leisure, and Sport in the Making of Chicago* (Lanham, MD: Scarecrow Press, 1997), 157.

52. Bob Kuska, *Hot Potato: How Washington and New York Gave Birth to Black Basketball and Changed America's Game Forever* (Charlottesville: University of Virginia Press, 2004), 98.

53. Claude Johnson, *The Black Fives: The Epic Story of Basketball's Forgotten Era* (New York: Abrams Press, 2021), 316.

54. "Chicago Defender Sporting Editor Asks That Western Basketball Be Cleared of Professionalism," *CD*, 18 December 1920, 6.

55. "Sol Butler Joins Forty Club," *CD*, 20 November 1920, 9.

56. Edwin B. Henderson II, *The Grandfather of Black Basketball: The Life and Times of Dr. E. B. Henderson* (Lanham, MD: Rowman & Littlefield, 2024); David Wiggins, *More Than a Game: A History of the African American Experience in Sport* (Lanham, MD: Rowman & Littlefield, 2018), 26–27; Kuska, *Hot Potato*; C. Johnson, *Black Fives*.

57. Regarding Butler's role as editor and the formation of a club that prompted Chicago's Bud Billiken Day Parade, see *CD*, 14 January 1922, 16, 18; *CD*, 21 January 1922, 16, 18; "Bud Says," *CD*, 17 June 1922, 14; Wallace Best, "Bud Billiken Day Parade," *Encyclopedia of Chicago* (accessed 19 March 2019), www.encyclopedia.chicagohistory.org/pages/175.html.

58. "Open Basket Ball Sason," *CD*, 2 October 1920, 9; "Bits of Sport," *CD*, 11 September 1920, 6; "Basketball," *CD*, 16 October 1920, 6; "Basket-Ball," *CD*, 6 November 1920, 9; "Sport Squibs," *CD*, 20 November 1920, 9.

59. Sol Butler, "Forty Club Opens Local Basketball Season Monday," *CD*, 4 December 1920, 6.

60. "Forty Club Victors over Fast Gotham Five," *CD*, 8 January 1921, 6; for accounts of other games in Chicago, see "Forty Club Downs Evanston 'Y,' 25–23," *CD*, 11 December 1920, 6; "40 Club Beats Evanston; Awaits Baltimore Five," *CD*, 22 January 1921, 6; Bernard Lewis, "Forty Club Topples the Fast Baltimore Five," *CD*, 29 January 1921, 7; William Harris, "Western Teams 'Roughed' Athenians in Western Tour," *AA*, 4 February 1921, 7.

61. Kuska, *Hot Potato*, 102.

62. "40 Club Vs. Indianapolis Monday," *CD*, 12 February 1921, 6; "Cincinnati Quintet to Play '40' Club," *CD*, 19 March 1921, 6; "'40' Club Makes Fine Record," *AA*, 25 March 1921, 7; "Chicago 40 Club Wins and Loses," *CD*, 12 March 1921, 6; E. Everett Lane, "'40' Club 39 Athenians 23," *AA*, 4 March 1921, 7; "Shots for the Basket," *PP*, 2 March 1921, 9; "Loendis Beat Chicago Five; Butler Plays," *PDP*, 4 March 1921, 11.

63. "St. Christopher to Play Forty Club," *CD*, 19 February 1921, 6.

64. C. Everett Lane, "Sport Tid Bits," *AA*, 18 February 1921, 7.

65. "Afro-American Notes," *PP*, 27 February 1921, 43; also see W. E. Clark,

"Forty Club Defeats the St. C. Machine," *NYA*, 5 March 1921, 6; C. Everett Lane, "Sport Tid Bits," *AA*, 11 March 1921, 7.

66. "Basketball Quints Rounding into Shape as Season Opens," *Pittsburgh Dispatch*, 12 December 1920, sec. 4, p. 1; "East Liberty Is to Have Big Professional Floor Team: Professional Quint to Represent City on East End Floor," *Pittsburgh Dispatch*, 6 December 1920, 7.

67. George Thornton Fleming, *History of Pittsburgh and Environs* (New York: American Historical Society, 1922), 15–16.

68. Jeremy Brecher, *Strike!* (Cambridge, MA: South End Press, 1997), 138; for more on Haddock, including his ties with the *Pittsburg Press* and as a judge at the Harvard Stadium Olympic tryouts at which Butler injured himself, see "Newspaper Man Has Big Responsibility," *Editor & Publisher* 52, no. 17 (1919): 25; Final Olympic Tryout program, box 346, ABC; Roger A. Godin, *Before the Stars: Early Major League Hockey and the St. Paul Athletic Club Team* (St. Paul: Minnesota Historical Society Press, 2005), 68–69.

69. John T. Taylor, "Notes of the Amateur Athletes," *PP*, 13 March 1921, 24 and 20 March 1921, 28; "A.A.U. Committee Deals Out Both Penalties and Pardons," *NYT*, 14 July 1922, 13.

70. For an account of a game in which Butler scored three touchdowns, including on runs of 80 and 55 yards, see "Butler and Blueitt Star as Lincoln A.C. Wins, 29–0," *CD*, 3 December 1921, 10; Ocania Chalk, *Black College Sport* (New York: Dodd, Mead, 1976), 312–13.

71. Keith Myerscough, "Women's Basketball: The 'Black Fives' 1904–1930" (29 May 2017), *Playing Pasts* (accessed 22 February 2022), https://www.playingpasts.co.uk/articles/gender-and-sport/womens-basketball-the-black-fives-1904-1930-part-4-of-7/; for evidence that Butler formed this team, see "Girl Basketeers Ask No Quarter from Boy Quints," *Medford Mail Tribune*, 2 February 1937, 7.

72. "Pollie Rickman Leads Roamer Girls to Victory," *CD*, 26 March 1921, 5.

73. Susan K. Cahn, *Coming on Strong: Gender and Sexuality in Twentieth-Century Women's Sport* (Cambridge, MA: Harvard University Press, 1994), 293.

74. Jaime Schultz, *Women's Sports: What Everyone Needs to Know* (New York: Oxford University Press, 2018), 21.

75. Dorsey and Turfley family papers, 1868–2003, HHC.

76. "Gourdin Carries Harvard to Front," *AA*, 27 May 1921, 2; "Harvard Athlete Topples Mark of 31 Long Years," *CD*, 28 May 1921, 11.

77. Frank Young, "Just Confidential," *CD*, 30 July 1921, 11.

78. "I Wish I Could Have Been There," *AA*, 21 October 1921, 7.

79. "Sol Butler to Try to Set New Broad Jump Mark in A.A.U. Meet," *CD*, 11 August 1921, 11.

80. "Athletes Out to Set New Marks in A.A.U. Title Tomorrow," *CT*, 12 August 1921, 8.

81. "Joie Ray Wins One-Mile Race on Slow Track," *NYTB*, 14 August 1921, 18.

82. "Defender A.C. Holds Banquet," *CD*, 29 October 1921, 10; Jamie Nesbitt Golden, "Black History Month Was Born at the Old Wabash YMCA," *Block Club Chicago*, 16 February 2021 (accessed 5 March 2023), https://blockclubchicago.org/

02/16/black-history-month-was-born-at-the-old-wabash-ymca-a-new-virtual-tour-lets-you-stroll-through-it/.

83. "Defender A.C. Holds Banquet," 10.

84. "Defender A.C. Will Open Basketball Season Nov. 14," *CD*, 5 November 1921, 10; also see "Defender A.C.–Evanston Arrow Game Opens Basketball Season," *CD*, 12 November 1921, 10; "Colored Fives to Play," *CT*, 14 November 1921, 22; Robert Butler, "Defender A.C. Takes Opener from Evanston," *CD*, 19 November 1921, 10.

85. "Ohio Quintet—Defender A.C. Game Monday," *CD*, 3 December 1921, 10; for an account of the game, see "Defender A.C. Defeats Ohio Quintet, 25–14," *CD*, 10 December 1921, 10.

86. "Houston Riot Case Is Revived in House," *Joplin (MO) Globe*, 17 November 1921, 5; "4 Houston Rioters Freed," *NYT*, 15 December 1924, 13; "Coolidge Cuts Terms of Negro Rioters," *NYT*, 9 March 1927, 1.

87. D'Weston Haywood, *Let Us Make Men: The Twentieth-Century Black Press and a Manly Vision for Racial Advancement* (Chapel Hill: University of North Carolina Press, 2018), 74–84.

88. Baldwin, *Chicago's New Negroes*, 5–7.

89. Bettye Collier-Thomas, *Jesus, Jobs, and Justice: African American Women and Religion* (New York: Knopf, 2010), 289–90; Patricia A. Schechter, *Ida B. Wells-Barnett & American Reform, 1880–1930* (Chapel Hill: University of North Carolina Press, 2001), 219, 222.

90. "New York Five Loses to the Defender A.C.," *CD*, 24 December 1921, 10.

91. "DeSotos Stop Defender A.C. in Fast Tilt," *CD*, 7 January 1922, 10; for more on local games, see "Defender A.C. Five Splits with Arrows," *CD*, 21 January 1922, 10; "Defender A.C. and South Chicago Whales Thursday," *CD*, 21 January 1922, 11.

92. "Defender A.C. Remaining 3 Games at 'Y.M.'," *CD*, 14 January 1922, 10.

93. "Defender A.C. Remaining 3 Games at 'Y.M.'," 10; for accounts of the Eastern trip, see "Defender A.C. Hits Road; Hard Schedule Ahead," *CD*, 28 January 1922, 10; "Defender A.C. Five Are Winning on Eastern Trip," *CD*, 4 February 1922, 10.

Chapter 8. Do You Believe in Mixed Games?

1. "Spartan Five Defeated by Defender A.C.," *CD*, 11 February 1922, 10; also see "Defender A.C. Five Are Winning on Eastern Trip," *CD*, 4 February 1922, 10; "The Defender A.C. Invades the East," *NYA,* 4 February 1922, 6; William White and Russell Caution, "Defender A.C. Takes Pair of Basketball Games in East," *CD*, 18 February 1922, 10.

2. "Defender Quintet in Wreck after Winning Western Title," *CD*, 18 March 1922, 10.

3. "Passengers Escape Injury in Bad Wreck," *Logansport (Indiana) Pharos-Tribune*, 15 March 1922, 1.

4. St. Clair Drake and Horace Cayton, *Black Metropolis: A Study of Negro Life in a Northern City* (New York: Harcourt, Brace and Company, 1945), 394.

5. "Truth about Us," *CD*, 3 June 1922, 14.

6. Patrick Miller and David Wiggins, eds., *Sport and the Color Line: Black Athletes and Race Relations in Twentieth-Century America* (New York: Routledge, 2004), ix.

7. Drake and Cayton, *Black Metropolis*, 395.

8. Davarian Baldwin, *Chicago's New Negroes: Modernity, the Great Migration, and Black Urban Life* (Chapel Hill: University of North Carolina Press, 2007), 194.

9. Baldwin, *Chicago's New Negroes*, 206.

10. "New York Society," *CD*, 5 March 1921, 3; "Sol Butler in Gotham," *CD*, 6 May 1922, 10; "New York Society Notes," *CD*, 15 July 1922, 9.

11. "Sol Butler to Compete in Loughlin Lyceum's Games," *NYH*, 14 April 1922, 6; "Sol Butler in Lyceum Games," *CD*, 20 May 1922, 10; "Farrell Star of Loughlin Games," *NYH*, 22 May 1922, 13; "Sol Butler Returns to Track Athletics," *NYA*, 27 May 1922, 6; "'Overton Cup' Goes to Higgins for Second Time," *BDE*, 4 June 1922, 47; *AA*, 26 May 1922, 9.

12. "Sol Butler Is Now an Automobile Salesman," *CD*, 17 June 1922, 1.

13. Walter Friedman, *Birth of a Salesman: The Transformation of Selling in America* (Cambridge, MA: Harvard University Press, 2004), 193–94.

14. Robert Weems, *Desegregating the Dollar: African American Consumerism in the Twentieth Century* (New York: New York University Press, 1998), 7–8.

15. Advertisement, *BDE*, 19 March 1922, D7; regarding the first African American to open a car dealership, see *A History of African American New Car Dealers* (accessed 23 March 2025), www.aacardealers.com; also see Ed Davis, *One Man's Way* (Detroit: Edward Davis Associates, 1979), 18–27.

16. Advertisement, *BDE*, 5 March 1922, section 2, p. 6.

17. Friedman, *Birth of a Salesman*, 196–97.

18. "City Briefs," *CD*, 22 July 1922, 9; for an account of an early African American car dealer, see Davis, *One Man's Way*, 18–27.

19. "Butler Wins Broad Jump," *CD*, 1 July 1922, 10.

20. Jack Master, "A.A.U. Committee Deals Out Both Penalties and Pardons," *NYTB*, 14 July 1922, 13; also see John Taylor, "Notes of the Amateur Athletes," *PP*, 27 August 1922, 30.

21. "Butler Quits; Ends Career as an Athlete," *CD*, 22 July 1922, 10; "Sol Butler's Amateur Career Ends as He Resigns A.A.U.," *HN*, 8 August 1922, 3; "Curtain for Sol Butler," *AA*, 28 July 1922, 9; regarding Butler's first meet after relinquishing his amateur status, see "McAllister Runs Hundred in 0:10," *NYT*, 14 August 1922, 9.

22. Advertisement, *CD*, 22 July 1922, 17; George W. Harris interview by Everette L. Beanne, 25 May 1939, New York Public Library Digital Collections (accessed 29 March 2025), https://digitalcollections.nypl.org/items/556e1560-55a3-0133-2346-00505686d14e#/?uuid=51286380-5e35-0133-0593-00505686a51c.

23. "De Hart Hubbard Defeats Ned Gourdin and Sol Butler," *NYA*, 16 September 1922, 6.

24. On Butler allaying Hubbard's competition jitters, see DeHart Hubbard, "Hubbard Tells of Winning First National Event," *AA*, 5 December 1925, 9; for a contrasting recounting of this event, which casts Butler as a jerk and Hunter Johnson as a timely mentor, see Chester Washington, "Sez Ches," *PC*, 24 January

1942, 17; also see Lewis Dial, "The Sport Dial," *NYA*, 28 October 1933, 6; on Butler coaching a young athlete during this period, see "Figuerosa Makes Good Showing at Senior Championship Meet," *NYA*, 2 September 1922, 6.

25. "College News and Gossip," *NYH*, 17 September 1922, 53; "Salt City Post Wins Syracuse Athletic Meet," *Democrat & Chronicle* (Rochester, NY), 23 September 1922, 21; "Represent Legion Men," *CD*, 7 October 1922, 9; "Chas. Young Post Wins Honors at Syracuse," *NYA*, 30 September 1922, 2; Edwin Henderson, "It's a Long Haul from Day When Tan Olympian Had to Broad Jump in Friend's Backyard," *AA*, 19 February 1949, 9; Dan Burley, "U.S.A.: Battle Ground of Sports Where Racial Goodwill Is Generated," *Tone*, 1 April 1960, 4; Leslie Matthews, "The Sports Whirl," *NYAN*, 30 September 1967, 36.

26. "Southerners Want No Negro American Legionnaires," *NYA*, 21 October 1922, 2; Christopher Nehls, "'A Grand and Glorious Feeling': The American Legion and American Nationalism between the World Wars" (PhD diss., University of Virginia, 2007), 209.

27. "Challenge American Legion on Race Issue," press release, 30 September 1920, NAACP, "Federal Surveillance of Afro-Americans (1917–1925): The First World War, the Red Scare, and the Garvey Movement," University of Iowa Law Library; also see Col. Chas. Young, subject file, Papers of the NAACP, Part 9: Discrimination in the U.S. Armed Forces, Series A: General Office Files on Armed Forces' Affairs, 1918–1955, University of Iowa Law Library.

28. "Major William F. Deegan, Friend to Negro Vets, Dies after Operation," *NYA*, 9 April 1932, 7.

29. "Major William F. Deegan . . . Dies," 7.

30. V. P. Thomas, "American Legion Ignored Resolution to Admit Negro," *NYA*, 4 November 1922, 5; McCrae Jones, "American Legion and the Negroes," *St. Louis Argus*, 27 October 1922, 1, 5; Nehls, "Grand and Glorious Feeling," 209–210; "Negro Delegates Cause Trouble at Legion Convention," *Daily Clarion-Progress* (Opelousas, LA), 16 October 1922, 1; "American Legion," *Marble Rock (IA) Journal*, 28 September 1922, 1.

31. "Sol Butler Not Allowed to Compete in Legion Meet," *NYA*, 4 November 1922, 6.

32. "Sol Butler Gets Taste of Dixie's Ideas on Blacks," *DDT*, 30 October 1922, 13; also see "Southerners Would Not Race Butler, Noted Negro Star," *TH*, 30 October 1922, 7.

33. "Color Line Drawn on Sol Butler in Legion Games," *CD*, 28 October 1922, 10.

34. Bert McGrane, "On the Sidelines," *DMR*, 8 April 1958, 11, 13.

35. McGrane, "On the Sidelines," 13; also see Al Monroe, "Speaking of Sports," *CD*, 31 July 1937, 20. For accounts that identify this event as an Olympic tryout in new Orleans, see: Edwin Henderson, "It's a Long Haul from Day When Tan Olympian Had to Broad Jump in Friend's Backyard," *AA*, 19 February 1949, 9; Dan Burley, "U.S.A.: Battle Ground of Sports Where Radical Goodwill Is Generated," *Tone*, 1 April 1960, 4; and Leslie Matthews, "The Sports Whirl," *NYAN*, 30 September 1967, 36.

36. "The Legion's Own Olympics," *American Legion Weekly*, 10 November 1922,

19, 21; Thomas, "American Legion Ignored Resolution," 5; "Color Line Drawn," 10; "New York Team Wins Legion Athletic Meet," *Press and Sun-Bulletin* (Binghamton, NY), 21 October 1922, 18; "Harlem News Comments on Segregation of Butler," *CD*, 11 November 1922, 1; "Chas. Young Post Wins Honors at Syracuse," *NYA*, 30 September 1922, 2.

37. "A.A.U. Takes Annual Games from New Orleans," *AA*, 30 April 1927, 15; David Wiggins, *More Than a Game: A History of the African American Experience in Sport* (Lanham, MD: Rowman & Littlefield, 2018), 88; on earlier attempts to exclude Black athletes from Southern AAU meets, see Frank Young, "Keefe Pens a Few Words in New Orleans Paper," *CD*, 30 April 1927, 9.

38. "Archie J. Morgan Marries Teacher," *NYAN*, 27 April 1932, 6; "Defender to Have 'Five' in New York City," *CD*, 7 October 1922, 10; "Defenders Start Dec. 7th," *NYAN*, 29 November 1922, 4; "Sportive Spotlight," *NYAN*, 3 January 1923, 4.

39. Claude Johnson, *The Black Fives: The Epic Story of Basketball's Forgotten Era* (New York: Abrams Press, 2021), 336.

40. Bob Kuska, *Hot Potato: How Washington and New York Gave Birth to Black Basketball and Changed America's Game Forever* (Charlottesville: University of Virginia Press, 2004), 97.

41. "Defenders Start Dec. 7th," 4.

42. Johnson, *Black Fives*, 332.

43. Johnson, *Black Fives*, 332–33.

44. Regarding professionalism in basketball, see Johnson, *Black Fives*, 316–19, 332–47; Kuska, *Hot Potato*, ch. 4; Douglas Stark, *Breaking Barriers: A History of Integration in Professional Basketball* (Lanham, MD: Rowman & Littlefield, 2019), 15–16; regarding Fritz Pollard's All-Stars, see John M. Carroll, *Fritz Pollard: Pioneer in Racial Advancement* (Urbana: University of Illinois, 1998), 155; Clifford R. Murphy, *Ink: The Indelible J. Mayo Williams* (Urbana: University of Illinois, 2024), 85.

45. "Defender Five Cops First Game," *NYAN*, 13 December 1922, 6.

46. "Defender Five Cops First Game," 6; also see "N.Y. Defenders Beat Howard 5 in a Fast Tilt," *CD*, 16 December 1922, 10; "When the East Meets the West," *NYAN*, 27 December 1922, 4; "Lincoln vs. N.Y. Defenders," *CD*, 23 December 1922, 10; Bill White, "In and Around New York," *CD*, 16 December 1922, 10; "Basketball," *NYAN*, 3 January 1923, 4.

47. "New Year's Scores," *CD*, 6 January 1923, 10; "Xenia Beats N.Y. Defenders," *CD*, 3 February 1923, 10; "Boasting Braggarts Bested by Unknown Team," *NYAN*, 21 February 1923, 4; "Loendi Beaten by Xenia American Legion," *CD*, 17 February 1923, 10; Kuska, *Hot Potato*, 119; also see "Acmes Trounce Defender's New York Quintet, 24–15," *CD*, 13 January 1923, 10; "N.Y. Defender 5 Trounces Crack Ohio White Quintet," *CD*, 27 January 1923, 10; Alexander O. Taylor, "The Buckeye State," *CD*, 3 February 1923, 15.

48. "Sol Butler Indefinitely Suspended for Not Running," *NYA*, 3 February 1923, 6; "Scholz Suspension Lifted," *Daily News* (New York), 27 January 1923, 20; "Taint of Too Much Money in Athletics," *Lincoln Journal Star*, 8 February 1923, 9; "In and Around New York," *CD*, 9 December 1922, 10; "College Relay and Sprints

to Fordhams Track Games in Gotham Armory This Evening," *Bridgeport Telegram* (Cincinnati), 20 January 1923, 19; "Amateurs Accept Lure of 'Gate,'" *Bakersfield Californian*, 7 February 1923, 13.

49. Chandler Owen, "Colored Cash and White Supremacy," *CE*, 10 February 1923, 1.

50. Owen, "Colored Cash and White Supremacy," 1.

51. "Is Sol Butler a Pro? A.A.U. Will Investigate," *BDE*, 15 February 1924, 24; also see "In Hubbard, Butler and Gaurdin [*sic*] America Has 3 Unbeatable Broad-Jumpers," *BDE*, 6 February 1924, 24; John Gleaves and Matthew Llewellyn, "Charley Paddock and the Changing State of Olympic Amateurism," *Olympika 21* (2012): 6–7.

52. "Sol Butler Now with the Adams' Clothing Co.," *CD*, 9 June 1923, 4.

53. Roger Didier, "Batouala's Underwear," *CD*, 26 May, 2 June, and 9 June 1923, 5.

54. "A New Men's Shop," *PC*, 23 June 1923, 10.

55. David W. Kellum, "Freshmen Women in Phillips High School Field Day," *CD*, 9 June 1923, 10.

56. Advertisement, *CD*, 23 June 1923, 4.

57. Edgar G. Brown, "Around Chicago," *PC*, 23 June 1923, 10; about this tournament, see "Chicagoans Win Two Tennis Titles," *CD*, 1 September 1923, 10; Cecil Harris and Larryette Kyle-DeBose, *Charging the Net: A History of Blacks in Tennis from Althea Gibson and Arthur Ashe to the Williams Sisters* (Chicago: Ivan R. Dee, 2007), 106–109; "Society Smiles on Tennis Finals," *PC*, 8 September 1923, 5.

58. Marc Maltby, *The Origins and Early Development of Professional Football* (New York: Garland Publishing, 1997), 184, 198; Keith McClellan, *The Sunday Game: At the Dawn of Professional Football* (Akron, OH: University of Akron Press, 1998), 17–19.

59. Michael Oriard, *King Football: Sport and Spectacle in the Golden Age of Radio and Newsreels, Movies and Magazines, the Weekly and the Daily Press* (Chapel Hill: University of North Carolina Press, 2001), 5.

60. "Hooked to Contract," *RIA*, 1 October 1923, 12.

61. "Independents Batter Famous Bears, 3 to 0," *RIA*, 1 October 1923, 12.

62. Jaime Schultz, *Moments of Impact: Injury, Racialized Memory, and Reconciliation in College Football* (Lincoln: University of Nebraska Press, 2016), ch. 1; John Rosengren, "A Football Martyr," *SBNation*, 25 November 2014 (accessed online 11 April 2019), www.sbnation.com/longform/2014/11/25/7275681/jack-trice-iowa-state-football-profile.

63. Pat Patton, "Place Kick from Thirty-Yard Line Decides Contest," *MD*, 1 October 1923, 15.

64. "Look for 'Sol' Today," *RIA*, 4 October 1923, 14.

65. "Neither Side Ever Really Near Scoring," *DDL*, 8 October 1923, 7; "Independents Await Cleveland Invasion," *MD*, 6 October 1923, 15; "Dry Field Hope of Rock Island in Clash Today," *DDL*, 14 October 1923, 28; Art Williams, "A Line on Sports," *RIA*, 22 October 1923, 16; "Sidelights on Hibbing-R.I. Game," *DDT*, 22 October 1923, 17; "From Sidelines at West Park," *RIA*, 29 October 1923, 14;

"Independents Have Tough Time Stopping Mere Boy, but Defeat Omahans 20–6," *DDT*, 29 October 1923, 15; "Omaha Team Books Independents for Game on Oct. 28th," *DDT*, 18 October 1923, 18.

66. "Sol Butler Is Released," *RIA*, 31 October 1923, 16; "Chicago: What the City Was Like at Birth of Defender," *CD*, 13 August 1955, 10A; "Sol Butler Sold to Hammond Pro Football Team for $10,000," *CD*, 10 November 1923, 6; Johnny Armstrong scrapbook, p. 38, private collection.

67. "Big Game of Year Looms Up," *The Times* (Munster, Indiana), 8 November 1923, 16; Frank Schreiber, "Hammond Throws Scare into Cards, but Loses 6 to 0 Battle," *CT*, 12 November 1923, 18; "Chicago Cards Beat Hammond by 6–0 Count," *QCT*, 12 November 1923, 7; Frank Young, "A Few Words to the Sporting Editor of Chicago American," *CD*, 9 February 1924, 10; "Bears Win Hot Tilt with Hammond, 14–7," *RIA*, 26 November 1923, 16; Murphy, *Ink*, 103–105.

68. "Our Sports File of 12 Years Ago Says," *CD*, 27 February 1937, 13.

69. David Kellum, "Eighth Regiment Defeats Loendi, 29–22," *CD*, 5 April 1924, 10; also see "Evanston Downs Eighth Regiment by 20 to 8 Score," *CD*, 9 February 1924, 11; David Kellum, "Grenadiers Drop 34–17 Game to Eighth Regiment," *CD*, 16 February 1924, 10; David Kellum, "Wilberforce Is Beaten by 8th Regiment Five," *CD*, 15 March 1924, 10; "Pittsburg Loendis Play 8th Regiment, March 28," *CD*, 29 March 1924, 10; "Evanston Beaten by 8th Regiment '5'," *CD*, 19 April 1924, 12.

70. "Sol Butler Come[s] to R. I. Park with Hammond Gridders," *DDT*, 8 October 1924, 16; "Islander Score at Will in Sabbath Contest with Hammond, Winning 26–0," *DDT*, 13 October 1924, 15; Murphy, *Ink*, 119–20.

71. "Hammond Tilts with Paddy's 11," *The Times* (Munster, IN), 24 October 1924, 27.

72. "National Pro Grid Notes," *Journal Times* (Racine, WI), 24 October 1924, 19.

73. "Hammond Indians Down Chicago Cardinals," *Buffalo (New York) News*, 27 October 1924, 20; also see Riley Murray, "Hammond Indians Too Much for Paddy Driscoll's Cardinals," *CT*, 27 October 1924, 28.

74. "Sports Brief," *CD*, 8 November 1924, 9; Murphy, *Ink*, 120.

75. "Welch's Indians Take Silents across to Tune of 22 to 0," *ABJ*, 24 November 1924, 20; on the Akron Silents (also known as the Goodyear Silents), an all-deaf team that won 80 percent of its seventy-five games between 1917 and 1923, see Cheri Goldner, "Akron: 'The Crossroads of the Deaf,'" *Past Pursuits: A Newsletter of the Special Collections Division of the Akron-Summit County Public Library* vol. 9, no. 2 (summer 2010): 5 (accessed 22 March 2025), www.akronlibrary.org/images/SpecCol/pursuits92.pdf.

76. Jack Gibbons, "Powerful Lineup of Pros Stops Buffalo Team in Its Tracks," *ABJ*, 28 November 1924, 28.

77. "Toronto Tigers Win Title by Trouncing Steubenville, 26–0," *Pittsburgh Post-Gazette*, 8 December 1924, 10; "Sport-Pickups," *PC*, 20 December 1924, 12.

78. "Notes of the Game," *CD*, 6 December 1924, 6; David Kellum, "Maroons in 17 to 15 Win from Eighth," *CD*, 17 January 1925, 10; J. Wm. Jesse Lovell, "8th

Regiment Cops 27-to-22 Cage Contest," *CD*, 7 February 1925, 10; "Athenians Win Seven Games," *AA*, 7 February 1925, A6; "8th Regiment Five Beaten after 25 Straight Wins," *CT*, 9 February 1925, 22; "Leondi Quintet Stops 8th Illinois," *AA*, 21 February 1925, A7; "Chicago Loses to Leondi '5'," *PC*, 21 February 1925, 6; G. L. Mackey, "Sports Mirror," *AA*, 11 April 1925, 7.

79. "Roamer Girls Win in Third Overtime Period," *CD*, 24 January 1925, 10; "Basketball," *AA*, 21 February 1925, 6; "Phillips Takes Basketball Game from Armstrong by 25–15 Score before 4,500," *CD*, 21 February 1925, 10; "All-Around Athlete," *The Light* (New York), 5 November 1927, 30; "Fay Says—," *CD*, 4 February 1928, 8; "Woman Executive of Eastern Paper Is Popular in New York," *PC*, 13 February 1932, 5; on the Roamers' star player, "one of the greats" in basketball and tennis, see Robert Pruter, "Isadore Channels: The Recovered Life of a Great African American Sports Star," in *Before Jackie Robinson: The Transcendent Role of Black Sporting Pioneers*, ed. Gerald R. Gems (Lincoln: University of Nebraska Press, 2017), 179–203.

80. Phillip G. Smith, "Sing Kappa Sing," *Kappa Alpha Psi Journal*, December 1953, 212; J. M. Howe, "Sport Sidelights," *PT*, 18 July 1925, 11.

81. "Monarchs Win Fast Game," *Kansas City Star*, 17 May 1925, 17; "Monarchs Make Clean Sweep of St. Louis Series," *Kansas City Call*, 22 May 1925, 6.

82. Gary Ashwill, email to author, 16 May 2023; for author's initial proposal that Butler did not play for the Monarchs, see Brian Hallstoos, "Baseball Bona Fides: Sol Butler and Black Sport Entrepreneurship," Baseball in Literature and Culture Conference, Ottawa University, Kansas, 16 July 2021, author's collection.

83. "St. Louis Stars Fall before Team from Kansas City," *St. Louis Globe-Democrat*, 17 May 1925, 12; *St. Louis Argus*, 22 May 1925, 2; "Monarchs in Triple Win over St. Louis," *CD*, 23 May 1925, 9.

84. Sol Butler to Knute Rockne, 7 May 1926, box 1a, University Athletic Director's Records 8/44, UNDA.

85. Knute Rockne to Sol Butler, 11 May 1926, box 1a, University Athletic Director's Records 8/44, UNDA.

86. Murray Sperber, *Shake Down the Thunder: The Creation of Notre Dame Football* (New York: Henry Holt, 1993), 227–28.

87. Sol Butler to Amos Alonzo Stagg, 7 May 1926, AASP.

88. Amos Alonzo Stagg to Sol Butler, 10 May 1926, AASP.

89. Amos Alonzo Stagg to Sol Butler, 10 May 1926, AASP; for more on Stagg's racial views and an instance when he fought discrimination, see Paul Emory Putz, "Amos Alonzo Stagg and Trump's America," *Sport in American History*, 2 February 2017 (accessed 31 March 2023), https://ussporthistory.com/2017/02/02/amos-alonzo-stagg-and-trumps-america/.

90. "Butler and Nesser to Play with Toronto," *ABJ*, 11 September 1925, 30; "Tigers to Open Season Sunday," *Evening Review* (East Liverpool, OH, 19 September 1925, 12; "Tigers Victors over Columbus," *Evening Review*, 28 September 1925, 10; "Toronto Tigers Beat Hammond Pros 7–0," *TT*, 5 October 1925, 11; "Former Olympic Athlete Plays Pro Football," *PT*, 17 October 1925, 11; "Bears Pile Up 28–7 Victory," CT, 12 October 1925, 31; Murphy, *Ink*, 123, 129–33; on Butler scoring the

only touchdown of the game on a punt return, see "Toronto Defeats Hammond," *Herald-Star* (Steubenville, OH), 5 October 1925, 11.

91. "Toronto, Buffalo, Milwaukee Beaten by Tigers," *PDP*, 19 October 1925, 10; "Toronto-Stub Elevens Merge," *ER*, 22 October 1925, 14; "Butler's Injuries to Keep Him Out," *Detroit Free Press*, 31 October 1925, 15; "Steubenville Holds Canton to Tie," *PDP*, 2 November 1925, 10; "Steubenville Ties," *PDP*, 9 November 1925, 10; "Bait for Bugs," *Decatur (IL) Daily Review*, 27 November 1925, 23.

92. "'Thais' Holds Spotlight in City's Dramatic Circle," *CD*, 5 December 1925, 5.

93. Paul Wilstach, *Thais: A Play in Four Acts* (Indianapolis: Bobbs-Merrill, 1911).

94. "'Thais' Holds Spotlight," 5; for more on the cultural climate that George Garner helped shape, see Brian Hallstoos, "Windy City, Holy Land: Willa Saunders Jones and Black Sacred Drama" (PhD diss., University of Iowa, 2009).

95. Baldwin, *Chicago's New Negroes*, 96.

96. "Basketball," *AA*, 12 December 1925, 9; "Stars Beat Wilberforce," *AA*, 2 January 1926, 7; Frank Young, "Lindstrom's Team Victors in Fast Game," *CD*, 30 January 1926, 8.

97. Samantha Ege, "The Curious Case of 'Naughty Little Nora,' a Jazz Age Shape Shifter," *NYT*, 12 November 2024); Samantha Ege, *South Side Impresarios: How Race Women Transformed Chicago's Classical Music Scene* (Champaign: University of Illinois Press, 2024).

98. "Clubs Is Trumps," *Heebie Jeebies*, 8 May 1926, 20.

99. "Sol Butler Here to Fill Halfback Position on Bulldog Outfit," *CR*, 15 September 1926, 17.

100. Tut Allen interview by Ronald L. Robinson and Larry Robinson, 2 December 1972 and Lillian Bean interview by Aldonia Small, ca. 1974, *Canton Black Oral History*, Stark Library, Canton, Ohio; for memories of experiencing and counteracting racial exclusion and oppression in Canton during the 1920s, see *Canton Black Oral History*, an eleven-volume project completed in the 1970s, in particular the interviews of Allen, Bean, Kathleen Barboza, Austin Andrews, Rev. Beaumont, Otis Bell, Daniel Gray Bonds, Clarence Bonner, Alvin Calhoun, Rose Ellis, Mr. And Mrs. Fenrick, Annabelle Jones, Mr. and Mrs. James Jones, Merod McDonald, Bertha Pullin Turner, Laree Turner, Houston Taylor, Elnora Stevens, Aldonia Small, Lewis Smallwood, Pearline Parker, Mrs. Motely, Beaula Wilder, and Nealie Watson, Stark County District Library, Canton, Ohio.

101. "Grind but Some of Timber Looks Fine," *CR*, 20 September 1926, 9.

102. "Grind but Some of Timber Looks Fine," 9.

103. "Bulldogs Outplay Tigers by Wide Margin but Lose Tough Game 14–2," *CR*, 27 September 1926, 11.

104. "Bulldogs Look More Like Themselves as They Smear Colonels 13–0," *CR*, 4 October 1926, 9.

105. "Butler Made Things Dark for Colonels" (photo), *CR*, 4 October 1926, 9; Steve Doerschuk, "Film for Sale: Only Known Footage of Thorpe," *CR*, 21 June 1981, unpaginated clipping, UDA; Travis Vogan, *Keepers of the Flame: NFL Films and the Rise of Sports Media* (Champaign: University of Illinois Press, 2014), 87.

106. Carroll, *Fritz Pollard*, 178; "Battle with Akron Today Should Show if Bulldogs Can Fill Bill," *CR*, 10 October 1926, 41; "Great Forward Wall Hold Stage as Bulldogs and Akron Draw 0–0," *CR*, 11 October 1926, 11; "Pollard Dropped by Akron; Showed No Class Sunday," *CR*, 13 October 1926, 19; Paul Waggoner, "When Local Talent Hits the NFL," *HN* (posted online 1 January 2016); for reports on the next four games, including two that Butler played in their entirety, see "Buccaneers Display Great Offense to Win over Bulldogs 16–13," *CR*, 18 October 1926, 8; "Thorpe, Robb and Calac in Backfield with Him for Conflict against Jackets," *CR*, 20 October 1926, 18; "Yellow Jackets Hand 17–0 Defeat to Bulldogs at Philadelphia," *CR*, 24 October 1926, 44; "Adverse Break Contributes to 16–13 Defeat of Bulldogs Crew," *CR*, 31 October 1926, 40; "Muller's Team Improves," *LAT*, 1 November 1926, 38; "Two Field Goals by Sonnenberg Defeat Bulldogs at Detroit 6–0," *CR*, 1 November 1926, 14; "Bulldogs Invade Eastern Sector with Lengthy List of Cripples," *CR*, 2 November 1926, 15.

107. "Merchants Bring in Colored Team for Sunday Game," *CR*, 6 October 1926, 23; "Merchants Play at Home Sunday," *CR*, 16 October 1926, 8.

108. "'King Sol' Not Allowed to Appear in Line-Up Here," *NYAN*, 10 November 1926, 13.

109. Lewis Dial, "The Sport Dial," *NYA*, 30 November 1935, 8; also see Carroll, *Fritz Pollard*, 179.

110. "'King Sol,'" *NYAB*, 13; for a subsequent account of Butler's benching, see Romeo Dougherty, "Sportopics," *NYAN*, 23 March 1932, 12; regarding racial discrimination at the polo grounds, see Buster Miller, "The Sports Parade," *NYA*, 4 November 1939, unpaginated clipping, Grover C. Buster Miller Scrapbook, SCRBC; also see "Not All Well on Grid," *CR*, 28 October 1926, 19; "Color Line in Football Also," *CR*, 29 October 1926, 48; "Late Touchdown Gives Bulldogs 7–7 Draw with Giants at New York," *CR*, 3 November 1926, 18.

111. "Bulldogs Are in Brooklyn Today with Three Gone," *CR*, 14 November 1926, 8; also see "Hartford Blues Tame Bulldogs in Scrappy Game on Eastern Grind," *CR*, 8 November 1926, 10; "Bulldogs Lack Scoring Punch and Lose to Steam Rollers 21–2," *CR*, 12 November 1926, 12; James Weldon Johnson telegram to Curtis Wilbur, 26 October 1926, Papers of the NAACP, Part II: Special Subject Files, 1912–1939, Series A: Africa through Marcus Garvey, UILLSC.

Chapter 9. Black Fury

1. Emmett Scott, "Leisure Time and the Colored Citizen," *The Playground* 18, no. 10 (1925): 595; for an account of the conference where Scott delivered his address, see "America Will Shortly Have Native Drama," *Atlantic City (NJ) Daily Press*, 18 October 1924, 1, 22.

2. "Sol Butler, Ex–Broad Jump Champ, Marries," *NYA*, 2 July 1927, 6.

3. 1910, 1920, and 1930 U.S. Censuses; Kansas State Census, 1915.

4. "Sue for Divorce Mrs. 'King' Sol Butler," *AA*, 3 June 1933, 3; regarding the suggestion that Butler was unfaithful to Pegge within their first year of marriage, see "It Wouldn't Do to Tell," *The Light*, 24 March 1928, 14.

5. Zoë Burkholder, *An African American Dilemma: A History of School Integration and Civil Rights in the North* (New York: Oxford University Press, 2021).

6. Gerald Gems, *Windy City Wars: Labor, Leisure, and Sports in the Making of Chicago* (Lanham, MD: Scarecrow Press, 1997), 157.

7. "Owner Chicago Giants Organizes Football Team," *CE*, 30 September 1927, 8; "Chicago Plans All-Star Pro Grid Outfit," *PT*, 29 September 1927, 11.

8. "Sol Butler's Eleven Downs White Pros," *PT*, 20 October 1927, 11; for additional reports on American Giants games, see Lloyd B. Cain, "Wash-ings by 'Wash,'" *JT*, 15 October 1927, 18; "Racine Regulars Tackle Chicago Colored Giants Here Sunday," *JT*, 11 October 1927, 19; "Racine Pros Give Giants 12–6 Beating," *CD*, 22 October 1927, 9; "Wash" Cain, "Racine Regulars Beat Giants, 12–6," *JT*, 17 October 1927, 15–16; "Mills Eleven to Battle American Giants Tomorrow," *CT*, 22 October 1927, 20; "Local Eleven Grabs Another Victory," *Suburban Leader* (Cicero, IL), 27 October 1927, 9; "Schwarzel's Cicero Boosters Defeat American Giants 7 to 0," *Suburban Leader*, 3 November 1927, 11.

9. "Fay Says," *CD*, 21 January 1928, 8.

10. "Ft. Dearborn Elks Victors over Cappers," *CD*, 4 February 1928, 8.

11. "Fay Says," *CD*, 10 March 1928, 8; also see "Fay Says," *CD*, 4 February 1928, 8; "Fort Dearborn Elks Quintet Opens Season," *CD*, 28 January 1928, 9; "Ft. Dearborn Elks Beaten by Finucanes," *CD*, 18 February 1928, 9; regarding an influential early Black referee, who managed and coached a women's basketball team in New York, see Chris "Dutch" Huiswood Scrapbook, SCRBC; on Butler playing stellar defense in a fraternity game victory, see "Savoy Topics," *The Light*, 3 March 1928, 15.

12. "Sport Observations: Old Man Sol," *PC*, 5 January 1929, B4.

13. "Buffalo Is Walloped by Savoy Five," *CD*, 29 December 1928, 8; "Davis All-Stars Have Two Tough Games Scheduled," *TT*, 4 January 1929, 27; "Red Pepper," *TT*, 9 January 1929, 15; on Butler exchanging barbs months earlier with a Savoy player, see "Savoy Topic," *The Light*, 18 February 1928, 7.

14. "Sport Observations," B4; also see "Elks Fall before Cohn Jewelers in Hard Fought Game," *The Light*, 10 March 1928, 3.

15. "Fiall Halted as Savoy Falls before Fast Five," *PC*, 26 January 1929, B5; "Savoy Wants to Play Rens," *Inter-State Tattler* (New York), 11 January 1929, 12; Susan J. Rayl, "Smilin' Bob Douglas and the Renaissance Big Five," in *Separate Games: African American Sport behind the Walls of Segregation*, ed. David K. Wiggins and Ryan A. Swanson (Fayetteville: University of Arkansas Press, 2016), 22–23; Francis, "Renaissance on Tour," *NYAN*, 6 February 1929, 6; "N.Y. Renaissance Club Trims Savoy," *AA*, 9 February 1929, 11; "Rens Claim Nat'l Title," *PC*, 9 February 1929, A4; "Savoy Big '5' Grabs Opening Series Fracas," *CD*, 14 March 1929, 11; "Savoy Five Loses, 31–9 to Nationals," *CD*, 16 March 1929, 9; P. L. Prattis, "Questions Renaissance Supremacy," *NYAN*, 13 February 1929, 8; regarding segregated seating and George Halas, see "Goldes and Savoy Game Unfinished," *CD*, 12 January 1929, 9; "N.Y. Renaissance Club Trims Savoy," 11; "Bruins Put Skids under Savoy Big 5," *CD*, 10 February 1929, 8.

16. Todd Gould, *For Gold and Glory: Charlie Wiggins and the African-American*

Racing Car Circuit (Bloomington: Indiana University Press, 2002), 95; for more on Wiggins and the Gold and Glory Sweepstakes, see Todd Gould, "Gold and Glory Sweepstakes," in Wiggins and Swanson, *Separate Games*, 109; "Colored Racing Classic Set for Fourth of July," *Journal & Courier* (Lafayette, IN), 2 July 1928, 11.

17. "Auto Drivers Invade Indianapolis—Lincoln Giants Beat Bacharachs," *CD*, 29 June 1929, 8; also see "Crowds Flock to Auto Races," *AA*, 7 July 1928, 13; "Thundering Speedsters Set for Indianapolis Gas Grind," *PC*, 22 June 1929, A4; "10,000 See Anderson Win Race," *AA*, 13 July 1929, 15; "Grice Fatally Hurt in Auto Race," *CD*, 13 July 1929, 8; Gould, "Gold and Glory Sweepstakes," 122.

18. "Drivers Ready for 100-Mile Grind," *CD*, 30 June 1928, 9.

19. Bill Gibson, "The Passing Review," *AA*, 13 July 1929, 14; for more on Brown and the tournament, see "Illinois State Officials Support Nationals Lawn Tennis Tournament," ANP, July 1929, UILLSC; "Next Colored Tennis Champion May Be a Filipino," ANP, August 1929; "Everything Set for Chicago Tennis Tournament," ANP, July 1929, UILLSC; *Journal of the Proceedings of the South Park Commission* (Chicago, 1931), 242; for a history of the American Tennis Association, see Sundiata Djata, "Game, Set, and Separatism," in Wiggins and Swanson, *Separate Games*, 165–78; for contemporaneous discrimination by the US Lawn Tennis Association, see NAACP Administrative File: Subject File "Discrimination Sports 1929–30," UILLSC; on how Washington Park and the tennis tournament served as a battleground along both racial and class lines, see Brian McCammack, *Landscapes of Hope: Nature and the Great Migration in Chicago* (Cambridge, MA: Harvard University Press, 2017), 44–50.

20. "Chicago Lawn Tennis Tournament Attracting Stars of First Magnitude," ANP, July 1929; "Grant Barred from Michigan Tournament," ANP, July 1929, UILLSC; regarding Grant fighting discrimination in Grand Rapids, see Randal M. Jelks, "Making Opportunity: The Struggle against Jim Crow in Grand Rapids, Michigan 1890–1927" (accessed 15 May 2024), https://dutch-americans.org/wp-content/uploads/2017/02/1993_05_jelks.pdf.

21. "Filipino Net Star Humbles Edgar Brown," *PT*, 8 August 1929, 11; "Illinois State Officials," ANP.

22. Truman K. Gibson, Jr., *Knocking Down Barriers: My Fight for Black America* (Evanston, IL: Northwestern University Press, 2005), 41–51; McCammack, *Landscapes of Hope*, 35–36.

23. McCammack, *Landscapes of Hope*, 71.

24. "Move to Oust Negroes from New Resort," ANP, August 1929, UILLSC; "Hold Service for Taxicab Executive," *CD*, 20 July 1940, 4; "Shotgun Guards Patrol Negroes' Country Club," *MKEJ*, 1 August 1929, 1, 2; Frank Young, "Fay Says," *PC*, 22 August 1931, 13; Diane Bezucha, "'What I Felt There Was Free': State to Commemorate Black-Founded Resort Community and Haven," *Wisconsin Public Radio*, 2 June 2022; for information on a notable golf professional at Casa Loma, see "Northwestern Celebrates Pioneer Horace McDougal" (accessed 19 May 2024), https://nusports.com/news/2023/2/20/northwestern-celebrates-pioneer-horace-mcdougal; regarding Outlaw, see "Hold Service for Taxicab Executive," *CD*, 20 July 1940, 4.

25. Marvin Dawkins and Graham Kinloch, *African American Golfers during the Jim Crow Era* (Westport, CT: Praeger, 2000), 47; "Eastern Golfers Set for Big Title Tourney," *PC*, 28 June 1930, A5; Young, "Fay Says," A5; "Chicago Awarded National Links Tourney for Third Year; Honor 2 Philly Men," *PT*, 29 December 1932, 7; Edwin Bancroft Henderson, *The Negro in Sports* (Washington, DC: The Associated Publishers, Inc., 1939), 200–201; Ralph Chilton, "Boston National Golf Meet Looms as Challenging Item," *ADW*, 12 August 1941, 5; George Adams, "FORE!" *PC*, 5 May 1956, 34; on University of Iowa golfer George Roddy, the first Black captain of a golf team, winning the amateur championship at Casa Loma Country Club, see Richard Breaux, "'Tireless Partners and Skilled Competitors': Seeing UI's Black Male Athletes," in *Invisible Hawkeyes: African Americans at the University of Iowa During the Long Civil Rights Era*, ed. Lena M. Hill and Michael D. Hill (Iowa City: University of Iowa Press, 2016), 213.

26. Lane Demas, *Game of Privilege: An African American History of Golf* (Chapel Hill: University of North Carolina Press, 2017), 41.

27. "Shotgun Guards Patrol Negroes' Country Club," *MKEJ*, 1 August 1929, 1, 2.

28. "Seize Slot Machines at Resort for Negroes," *La Crosse Tribune and Leader-Press*, 5 August 1929, 6.

29. "Shotgun Guards," *MKEJ*, 1 and 2.

30. "Move to Oust Negroes," ANP.

31. "Wants to Oust Negro Colony," *RJ*, 3 August 1929, 22.

32. "Casa Loma Club Griefs [*sic*] in Court," *RJ*, 23 October 1929, 8; *H. M. Wisland v. Casa Loma Country Club*, Kenosha County Circuit Court, 24 July 1930; "Negroes' Country Club at Kenosha Abandoned," *Minneapolis Tribune*, 17 August 1930, 6; "Negro Country Club Is Near Abandonment," *Manitowoc (Wisconsin) Herald-News*, 16 August 1930, 12; "Casa Loma Is Extinguished by Quit Claim," *Kenosha News*, 15 August 1930, 1; for more on unjust real estate practices, see Mehrsa Baradaran, *The Color of Money: Black Banks and the Racial Wealth Gap* (Cambridge, MA: Harvard University Press, 2017), ch. 3; Richard Rothstein, *The Color of Law: A Forgotten History of How Our Government Segregated America* (New York: Liveright Publishing, 2017); for information on Casa Loma Country Club's presence in Chicago, see "Young Host Gives Pretty Dance Party," *CD*, 24 May 1930, 7.

33. Francis Hatcher, "Around the Resorts," *CD*, 1 August 1931, 15.

34. "Savoy Big Five Foe of Davis Sports Five," *TT*, 27 December 1929, 23; "Davis Cagers Sport to Beat Savoy 33 to 21," *TT*, 30 December 1929, 14; J. W. Ramsey, "On the Sport Trail," *RIA*, 3 January 1930, 28; "DeHart Hubbard Quint Beats Savoy '5,' 22–15," *PC*, 11 January 1930, 14.

35. "Windy City Stars Form Track Team," *PT*, 6 March 1930, 11.

36. McCammack, *Landscapes of Hope*, 87–88.

37. Arthur Ashe, *A Hard Road to Glory: A History of the African-American Athlete 1919–1945* (New York: Warner Books, 1988), 88; Jesse Owens, *I Have Changed* (New York: William Morrow, 1972), 67.

38. "Sears-Roebuck Wins State 'Y' Track Crown," *CT*, 23 June 1929, 26; "Metcalfe Stars as Wabash Wins Y. Track Meet," *CT*, 22 June 1930, 26.

39. "Chicago Cagers See Big Season This Year," part 1, Associated Negro Press

News Releases, Claude A. Barnett Papers, CHM; also see Chicago Recreation Commission, *The Chicago Recreation Survey*, vol. 3 (Chicago, 1938), 94, 118, 120, 133.

40. Ron Grossman, "Tidye Pickett: Chicago Track Star Was First African-American Female Olympian," 19 August 2016, ChicagoTribune.com (accessed 6 January 2019); "Old Tymers Club Loses Its Star Girl Athlete," *CD*, 6 February 1943, 21; "Six Jr. Champs Featured in National AAU Meet," *NYAN*, 26 June 1943, 13; for more on Pickett, see Robert Pruter, "Tidye Pickett: The Unfulfilled Aspirations of America's Pioneering African American Female Track Star," in *Before Jackie Robinson: The Transcendent Role of Black Sporting Pioneers*, ed. Gerald R. Gems, 237–61 (Lincoln: University of Nebraska Press, 2017).

41. Joe Bostic, "Sports Extra," *NYAN*, 29 March 1947, 13.

42. Robert Ryland as told to Darlene Powell Garlington and Eileen Harris, *My Story: Robert Ryland, First Black Professional Male Tennis Player* (N.p.: EH Graphics, 2019), 27.

43. Al Monroe, "Speaking of Sports" and "Olympic Stars to Clash Here Under Olde Tymers," *CD*, 23 May 1936, 13.

44. Roi Ottley, "Hectic Harlem: Self-Discrimination," *NYAN*, 6 June 1936, 13.

45. Dan Burley, "No Records In 'Olympics': Stars Shine," *CD*, 13 June 1936, 13; Wilfrid Smith, "Owens Wins Four N.C.A.A. Titles; Records Fall," *CT*, 21 June 1936, 25 and 28.

46. "Negro Cagers to Play Intercity Contest," *SLST*, 14 January 1931, 14; "Argus Bulldogs Nose Out Chicago Union Giants Five, 18–16," *SLPD*, 15 January 1931, 22; "Gilkerson Champion Negroes to Clown for Clear Lake Spectators," *Mason City Globe-Gazette*, 22 January 1931, 21; Leslie A. Heaphy, *Black Baseball and Chicago: Essays on the Players, Teams, and Games of the Negro League's Most Important City* (Jefferson, NC: McFarland, 2006, 38; "Union Giant Court Quint Billed Here," *QCT*, 28 December 1931, 7; "Dubuque Blackhawks Will Meet Gilkerson's Colored Giants' Five," *TH*, 1 March 1931, 14; "Colored Cagers to Play Blackhawks Wednesday Night," *TH*, 3 March 1931, 8; "Sports from the Wings," *MUJ*, 5 February 1931, 8.

47. "Sports from the Wings," *MUJ*, 5 February 1931, 8.

48. Heaphy, *Black Baseball*, 38.

49. Irish O'Leary, "Colored Team vs. House of David Tuesday," *Mid-West Progressive* (Muscatine, IA), 2 February 1931, 5.

50. "Gilkerson Five Spanks Tractors in 56–24 Battle," *Courier* (Waterloo), 17 March 1931, 13; regarding the team's two best players, Tommy Brookins and Randolph Ramsey, see Murry Nelson, "Tommy Brookins: Pioneer in Two Worlds," in Gems, *Before Jackie Robinson*, 205–235; also see "House of David and Union Giants Ready for Battle Here Tuesday," *MUJ*, 2 February 1931, 6; "Lovers of Basketball to See Game as It Should Be Played," *Nashua Reporter*, 18 February 1931, 1.

51. For a report of Butler soon after traveling as a manager with a women's basketball team, see Sec Taylor, "Sittin' in with the Athletes," *DMR*, 24 January 1931, 9.

52. "Formation of the Jubilee Parade," *CT*, 11 May 1931, 2.

53. "Chicagoans in Business Jubilee," part 1, Associated Negro Press News Releases, 1928–1964, Claude A. Barnett Papers, CHM; "Chicago Fetes Star of Green Pastures," *PT*, 1 October 1931, 6; Green Pastures scrapbook, BRTC; Walter C. Daniel, *"De Lawd": Richard B. Harrison and The Green Pastures* (New York: Greenwood Press, 1986), 114.

54. Tracey Deutsch, "The Great Depression," *Encyclopedia of Chicago* (accessed 29 May 2019), www.encyclopedia.chicagohistory.org/pages/542.html; "Negro Weeklies Mirror Progress," *AA*, 17 August 1929, 5; for information on how the Great Depression impacted Butler's boss Anthony Overton, see "The Chicago Bee Has Five Planks," *PC*, 10 August 1929, A2; William Jones, "Business and Industry," *AA*, 22 March 1930, A18; "Oust Victory Life Officials," *CD*, 19 March 1932, 1.

55. "State Alumni to Face Negro 11 for Charity," *Dayton (OH) Daily News*, 30 October 1930); Tom Young, "Pollard, Butler & Co. to Meet All-Star Ohio 11 at Columbus Nov. 27," *PC*, 8 November 1930, 16; Tom Young, "Gala Holiday Planned as 'Pro' Grid Stars View on Neil Park Stadium," *PC*, 15 November 1930, 15; Paul Kurtz, "West View May Eliminate Burns from Titular Race," *PP*, 20 November 1930, 36; Paul Kurtz, "Burns Loses to West View; Majestics Trim Chicago," *PP*, 24 November 1930, 32; Rob Ruck, Maggie Jones Patterson, and Michael P. Weber, *Rooney: A Sporting Life* (Lincoln: University of Nebraska Press, 2010), 73–74; "Ohio State Stars Beats Pollard 12–0 in Mud," *PC*, 6 December 1930, 15; for an account of these games, see Clifford R. Murphy, *Ink: The Indelible J. Mayo Williams* (Urbana: University of Illinois, 2024), 175–76.

56. "All-Stars Win Coast Tilt, 20–6: Sol Butler Sprints 20 Yards to Score," *CD*, 2 January 1932, 9; Murphy, *Ink*, 179–81; "Football Stars to Go to Far West," *ADW*, 9 December 1931, 6; "Lillard, Slater, Star as Pollard's '11' Wins," *PT*, 31 December 1931, 10; "Longshoremen to Clash Today," *LAT*, 3 January 1932, 68; "Negro Grid Stars Play," *LAT*, 25 December 1931, 31; "Bombers Lose Hard Tussle," *NYAN*, 10 October 1936, 16; John Carrol, "Fritz Pollard and the Brown Bombers," *The Coffin Corner* 12, no. 1 (1990): 1–4; on Butler coaching a Knights of Columbus football team two seasons later, see "Social Knight," *CE*, 8 December 1933, 4.

57. Lawrence LaMar, "Sol Butler in Movies," *PC*, 12 March 1932, 17; on sporting films during this era serving as metaphors of segregation, see Thomas Cripps, *Slow Fade to Black: The Negro in American Film, 1900–1942* (Oxford: Oxford University Press, 1993), 274–75; for a history of Black representation in film, see Donald Bogle, *Toms, Coons, Mulattoes, Mammies, and Bucks: An Interpretive History of Blacks in American Films*, 4th ed. (New York: Bloomsbury Academic, 2001).

58. "Sol Butler Seeks Job in Talkies," *PT*, 4 February 1932, 11.

59. Landis Buford, "Doing the Avenue," *Hollywood Filmograph*, 30 July 1932, 5.

60. "Garcia Kayos Sparring Foe," *LAT*, 3 April 1934, 30.

61. Sean Dinces, "Padres on Mount Olympus: Los Angeles and the Production of the 1932 Olympic Mega-Event," *Journal of Sport History* 32, no. 2 (2005): 139.

62. Bob Boardman, "Our Reporter at the Olympics," *Oregon Statesman*, 2 August 1932, 7.

63. "Former Jump Champ Opens Night Club," *AA*, 6 August 1932, 15; also see

"Show Boat Opens," *CE*, 26 August 1932, 9; "Press Men to Entertain at Club," *CE*, 5 August 1932, 9.

64. "Press Men to Entertain at Club," *CE*, 5 August 1932, 9; Ralph Eastman, "'Pitchin' Up a Boogie': African-American Musicians, Nightlife, and Music Venues in Los Angeles, 1930–1945," in *California Soul: Music of African Americans in the West* (Berkeley: University of California Press, 1998), 82; Douglas Flamming, *Bound for Freedom: Black Los Angeles in Jim Crow America* (Berkeley: University of California Press, 2005), 306.

65. "Davis Plans Brand New Stage Show," *PC*, 13 August 1932, 16.

66. Johnny Otis, *Upside Your Head! Rhythm and Blues on Central Avenue* (Middletown, CT: Wesleyan University Press, 1993), 26.

67. Harry Levette, "Upper-Cuts and Blocks," *CE*, 19 August 1932, 9; "Big Gamble," unidentified and undated clipping, "Jolly" John Larkin scrapbook, SARMAR; Jeremy White, "The Los Angeles Way of Doing Things: The Olympic Village and the Practice of Boosterism," *Olympika: The International Journal of Olympic Studies* 11 (2000): 79–116; "An Olympian's Oral History: Aileen Riggin," 1 November 1994, 53 (accessed 22 July 2024), https://digital.la84.org/digital/collection/p17103coll11/id/660/; Harry Levette, "Hollywood Backer Leaves Show Flat," *PT*, 29 September 1932, 11; "White and Peters New Showboat Club Head," *NYAN*, 19 October 1932, 8.

68. *Central Avenue*, original farce comedy presented by Edmund Heath, Lincoln Theatre, Special Midnight Show program, 9 November 1932, Larkin scrapbook, SARMAR; "'Central Avenue' Musical Comedy Opens on Coast," ANP, Barnett Papers, CHM.

69. "Butler Recruited by Peter Jackson Forces," *LAT*, 27 April 1933, 26.

70. "Butler Recruited," 26; for more on Peter Martin and his white manager Wirt Ross, see J. Cullen Fentress, "Young Peter Jackson Knocks Out Garcia," *ADW*, 19 April 1934, 5; Henry Armstrong, *Glove, Glory and God: An Autobiography* (Westwood, NJ: Fleming H. Revell, 1956), 145, 156–60, 165–67; also see "Coast Boxing," *AA*, 6 May 1933, 16; "Sol Butler Now Bosses Fighters," *AA*, 22 July 1933, 18.

71. Harry Levette, "Western Sports," ANP, Barnett Papers, CHM; for more on Wright, see "Chalky Wright" statistics, BoxRec.com, https://boxrec.com/en/box-pro/9596 (accessed 28 March 2025); "Albert 'Chalky' Wright: Plain Fact and Pulp Fiction from Mae West to the Featherweight Title to Boardwalk Empire," Ringside Report, https://ringsidereport.com/?p=56987 (accessed 24 July 2019); for discussion on Butler's role as a trainer and boxing in California during the mid-1930s, see "Sol Butler: Trainer, Manager . . . and Boxer? (1930s in LA)" post and replies, May–August 2019, BoxRec.com.

72. Jay Thomas Caldwell, *Me an' You* (New York: Lion Book, 1954), 5, 7–8, 115, 118; see *Me an' You* p. 41 for a passage that evokes W.E.B. Du Bois's notion of "double consciousness" when the protagonist describes Main Street Gym as "the only place, except for the Avenue, he did not have to think about being a Negro"; for discussions on California boxing and race, see Jim Tully Papers, box 52, Special Collections, UCLA; Louis Moore, *I Fight for a Living: Boxing and the Battle for Black*

Manhood, 1880–1915 (Urbana: University of Illinois Press, 2016), 140–41; Tracy Callis and Chuck Johnston, *Boxing in the Los Angeles Area, 1880–2005* (Victoria, BC: Trafford Publishing, 2009), 37–38.

73. For reports on Bendy sparring with white boxer Max Baer in preparation for his heavyweight title fight against Primo Carnera, see "Local Omegas Can Really Rejoice Now," *SFS*, 5 April 1934, 2; "Boxers Getting Ready for Big Season This Year," *CE*, 19 January 1934, 9; Lawrence LaMars, "Gallery Cracks," *PC*, 12 May 1934, A4.

74. "City Rivals Battle at Bowl," *Santa Ana Register*, 24 April 1934, 6; "'Cats' Defeat Stars in 11th, Square Series," *Santa Ana Register*, 25 April 1934, 6.

75. Madelene Hunt, "Interest Booms in Games for New 'Y.W.' Building," *CE*, 17 November 1933, 12; "Girls' Loop Ready in Los Angeles," *PT*, 23 November 1933, 10; Madelene Hunt, "Girls All Agog for Basketball Games," *CE*, 19 January 1934, 9; "Colored Girl Cagers Clash in Twin Bill," *LAT*, 19 January 1934, 32; "Vitalities and Athenas Play for Championship Sat. Night," *CE*, 23 February 1934, 9; "Down in Front," *CE*, 24 November 1937, 3B; for a report of a Knights of Columbus football team Butler coached immediately before coaching the Vitality Girls, see "Social Knight," *CE*, 8 December 1933, 4; for reports on the Los Angeles Hottentots, a football team for which Harding played and the media announced Butler would coach, see Byron Reilly, "Sporting Spice," *SFS*, 2 November 1933, 3; Byron Reilly, "Sporting Spice," *SFS*, 14 December 1933, 5; "Lillard's Hottentots Boast 51 in Row," *ADW*, 18 February 1934, 7; "Coast Basketeers Make Great Mark," *PT*, 22 March 1934, 10.

76. Harry Levette, "Upper Cuts and Blocks," *CE*, 9 February 1934, 9.

77. Levette, "Upper Cuts and Blocks," 9.

78. "Sol Butler 37 Years Old," *AA*, 17 March 1934, 18; on Butler coaching Kappa Alpha Psi basketball teams, see "30 Years of Inter-Frat Cage Highlights," *LAS*, 25 June 1959, SM37; Herman Hill, "Do You Remember When?" *LAS*, 9 July 1959, 39.

79. J. Cullen Fentress, "Fentress' Gab Stuff," *CE*, 15 June 1934, 10; "Track Champions to Be Honored Guests Here," *CE*, 22 June 1934, 1; J. Cullen Fentress, "Fentress' Gab Stuff," *CE*, 29 June 1934, 4B.

80. "Progressive League Opens Headquarters," *LAS*, 23 August 1934, 7.

81. Flamming, *Bound for Freedom*, 193.

82. Index to Register of Voters, Los Angeles Precinct 225, 1934, and Precinct 385, 1936; Frank Harris, Norwalk reference librarian, email to author, 27 April 2019; "Democrats to Fete Party Chieftains," *LAS*, 11 July 1935, 1.

83. A. McDonald Ifill, editorial, *The Light*, 24 December 1927, 10–11, box 48, George P. Johnson Negro Film Collection, UCLASC.

84. "Li'l Arthur Swings Towel in Corner of New Deal Champ," *Fort Worth Star-Telegram*, 1 November 1934, 10; Geoffrey C. Ward, *Unforgivable Blackness: The Rise and Fall of Jack Johnson* (New York: Alfred A. Knopf, 2004), 430–31.

85. "Butler for McDonough," *LAS*, 1 November 1934, 6.

86. "McDonough Fair Says Study Club," *LAS*, 11 July 1935, 1; Gordon McDonough, 6 January 1947 letter to Helen Samuels, executive secretary of National Negro Congress, box 75; Lorenzo Bowdoin, 12 April 1949 letter to McDonough;

McDonough 19 April 1949 letter to Bowdoin, box 69; Sherman Adams, Assistant to the President, 4 May 1954 letter to McDonough, box 70; Donald McLarnan 20 May 1954 letter to McDonough, box 70, all in Gordon Leo McDonough Papers, USCSC; "G. McDonough Gets L.A. WPA Jobs Approved," *LAS*, 19 September 1935, 1; for information on the candidate for sheriff that Butler and the PDRL supported, see Ruth Lavell, "Sheriff Eugene W. Biscailuz: An Administrative Biography" (MA thesis, University of Southern California, 1960), 28, 32.

87. Michael Curtiz, dir., *Black Fury*, Warner Bros., 1935.

88. Colin Schindler, *Hollywood in Crisis: Cinema and American Society, 1929–1939* (London: Routledge, 1996), 169.

89. Cripps, *Slow Fade to Black*, 266.

90. Lawrence LaMar, "Star Stuff," *SFS*, 23 November 1934, 3; "Behind the Scenes with Harry," *CE*, 25 January 1935, 6; for more on the 1940 film *The Proud Valley*, see John Cunningham, "A Second Look," *Cineaste* 22, no. 2 (1996): 40–41.

91. "Sol Butler and Movie Extras in Studio Fire," *AA*, 15 December 1934, 9.

92. Schindler, *Hollywood in Crisis*, 169–89.

93. Schindler, *Hollywood in Crisis*, 169–89; Paul Frymer, *Black and Blue: African Americans, the Labor Movement, and the Decline of the Democratic Party* (Princeton, NJ: Princeton University Press, 2008), 24, 28; Paul Moreno, *Black Americans and Organized Labor: A New History* (Baton Rouge: Louisiana State University Press, 2006), 169–71, 195.

94. "Sol Butler Heads 'Othello,'" *CE*, 26 December 1934, 7; Fay Jackson, "Hollywood Star Dust," *AA*, 19 January 1935, 8; for information on the director, producer, and lone white actor in an otherwise all-Black cast and his connections with *Othello* and African Americans, see Luke Cosgrave, *Theatre Tonight* (Hollywood, CA: House-Warven, 1952), 81, 103–105, 117–24, 142.

95. Alexander Hall, dir., *Goin' to Town*, Emanuel Cohen Productions, 1935.

96. *Goin' to Town*, Paramount Production Materials, MHLSC.

97. *Goin' to Town*, Paramount Production Materials.

98. Fay Jackson, "In Hollywood," *AA*, 18 May 1935, 9.

99. "Robeson Completes Film, Leaves for London," *PC*, 11 January 1936, A6; "Jolly" John Larkin scrapbook, circa 1914–1932, SARMAR.

100. Associated Negro Press News Releases, 1928–1964, Barnett Papers, CHM; *Los Angeles Truth* 1, no. 1 (1935), box 50, George P. Johnson Negro Film Collection, UCLASC.

101. Louis V. Cole, "Chatter," *LAS*, 28 February 1935, 9; for Butler in the public eye, also see John Fowler, "Spreading Joy," *CE*, 8 March 1935, 8; Harry Levette, "Upper-Cuts and Blocks," *CE*, 1 March 1935, 7; Louis V. Cole, "Chatter," *LAS*, 28 February 1935, 9; "Ethel Waters Given Royal Welcome Here," *LAS*, 4 April 1935, 4; "Democrats to Fete Party Chieftains," *LAS*, 11 July 1935, 1; "'Green Pastures' Stars Entertained," *CE*, 21 February 1936, 5.

102. Sol Butler, "Canopy," *Los Angeles Truth*, 1935, 1, 7.

103. Louis V. Cole, "Chatter," *LAS*, 7 March 1935, 10; Roi Ottley, "Hectic Harlem," *NYAN*, 20 April 1935, 9; "Sol Butler New Editor," *AA*, 27 April 1935, 21; untitled advertisement, *LAS*, 21 March 1935, 5.

104. R. A. Cronin, "As the Crow Flies," *Daily News* (Los Angeles), 25 July 1935, 12; for a complete transcription of Butler's letter, see David Sebben, *"Nothing Great Is Easily Won": The Solomon Butler Story* (Self-published, 2023), ch. 9.

105. David Wiggins, "'Great Speed but Little Stamina:' The Historical Debate over Black Athletic Superiority," *Journal of Sport History* 16, no. 2 (1989), 160; for an example of ideas about Black physical superiority that Butler rejected, see "Negro Has the Winning Heal," *Sporting Globe*, 2 March 1938, 5; regarding a trailblazing Black sport organizer's assertion that the "native muscular development and vitality of the Negro of the South, if directed in channels of athletic activities" would produce superior results, see Edwin B. Henderson, "The Colored College Athlete," *Crisis* 2, no. 3 (July 16, 1911), 115, quoted in Henderson II, *The Grandfather of Black Basketball*, 111.

106. Cronin, "As the Crow Flies."

107. "Wise Money on Veteran," *LAT*, 26 January 1936, 25; also see "Doll Nelson, Coast Welter, Wins Twice," *AA*, 25 January 1936, 23; "Moment of Relaxation," photo with caption, *CE*, 31 January 1936, 7; "Coates Faces New White Hope," *CE*, 28 February 1936, 8.

108. J. Cullen Fentress, "Coates, Aggressive All the Way, Loses Fight," *CE*, 31 January 1936, 8.

109. Braven Dyer, "The Sports Parade," *LAT*, 20 August 1936, 31; for reports of blindness shortening Bendy's career, see Robert Ripley, "Believe It or Not," *SLPD*, 7 February 1936; 47; "Salt and Pepper," *PC*, 26 September 1936, 15; Chuck Johnston, "Re: Classic American West Coast Boxing," 21 November 2019, BoxRec.com; on Butler guest editing a column in the *St. Louis Argus* on the Olympics, see Sebben, *"Nothing Great,"* ch. 9.

110. "Altus Allen to Fight First Pro Bout Thursday," *Freeport (Illinois) Journal-Standard*, 16 May 1939, 9; Lanita Morris interview with author, September 2019; John Bentley, "I May Be Wrong," *Nebraska State Journal*, 9 May 1940, 11; "Altus Allen Signs to Box Johnny Paycheck [*sic*]," *Freeport (IL) Journal-Standard*, 24 May 1940, 11; for Butler representing a boxer named Walter White, see Russ Cowans, "They Set a Record That Will Never Be Equaled," *Detroit Tribune*, 18 April 1942, 7.

111. Bill Collins, "Dark Battler New Sensation," *Lincoln (NE) Star*, 11 June 1940, 11.

112. Earl J. Morris, "Grandtown Day and Night," *PC*, 17 August 1940, 21; regarding Butler and Allen sitting ringside at a heavyweight fight, see Herman Hill, "Martin Kayoes Indian Fighter," *PC*, 20 July 1940, 17.

113. "Postponed Game between Black Olympics and Atlantic Seals to Be Played Turkey Day," *CE*, 25 November 1935, A6; also see "Atlantic Seals Play Dusky Foes," *LAT*, 28 November 1935, part 2, p. 13; "Seals Trim Negroes, Book L.A. Club Team," *New Pilot* (San Pedro, CA), 29 November 1935, 9.

114. "Halley Harding," Seamshead.com (accessed 29 March 2025), https://www.seamheads.com/NegroLgs/player.php?playerID=hardi01hal; Rock Island, IL High School, *The Watch Tower* 10, no. 3 (1919), 70; *The Watch Tower* 11, no. 18 (1920), 23; 1910 US Census, Rock Island, Ward 7, Roll:T624_321; p. 7a; Enumeration District: 0127; Family History Library microfilm: 1374334.

115. Alexander Wolff, "The NFL's Jackie Robinson," *Sports Illustrated*, 12 October 2009 (accessed 12 May 2023), https://vault.si.com/vault/2009/10/12/the-nfls-jackie-robinson; Thomas G. Smith, *Showdown: JFK and the Integration of the Washington Redskins* (Boston: Beacon Press, 2011), 65, 73, 113, 126; Gretchen Atwood, *Lost Champions: Four Men, Two Teams, and the Breaking of Pro Football's Color Line* (New York: Bloomsbury USA, 2016), ch. 9; Keyshawn Johnson and Bob Glauber, *The Forgotten First: Kenny Washington, Woody Strode, Marion Motley, Bill Willis, and the Breaking of the NFL Color Barrier* (New York: Grand Central Publishing, 2021), 130–34; Nathan Fenno, "In Football Stadiums and Ballparks, He Fought for the Rights of Black Athletes," *LAT*, 18 January 2021 (accessed 29 March 2025), www.latimes.com; A. L. Smith, "Football's Pioneering Racial-Equity Game Changer," *The Crusader*, 14 September 1922 (accessed 29 March 2025), https://chicagocrusader.com/footballs-pioneering-racial-equity-game-changer/.

116. Hill, "Do You Remember When?" 9 July 1959; also see "Southland Mourns 2 Sports Figures," *LAS*, 6 April 1967, A1.

Cooldown

1. Kitty Chappelle, *Colored Culture in Chicago*, box 47, Illinois Writers Project, VGH.

2. Earl J. Morris, "Grand Town Day and Night," *PC*, 26 September 1936, 6; "Morris Eat Shop Mecca for Fans," *PC*, 24 October 1936, A8; "Clarence Muse Keeps Date in City; Is Feted," *PC*, 21 November 1936, 2; Roi Ottley, "Solve Negroes' Cosmetic Problems," *CT*, 29 August 1954, part 3, 7; "Negro Guild Theatre, Inc. to Present Drama in Sept.," *NYA*, 14 August 1937, 9; Ken Murphy, "The Sports Clinic," *TH*, 19 December 1937, sect. 2, 1; George B. Murphy Jr., "'How Come Lawd?' Fails to Please; Show Closes," *AA*, 16 October 1937, 24; "'Sugar Hill,' Satirical Comedy, Presented in Chicago Loop," *ANP*, Barnett Papers; "'Sugar Hill' Opens Run in Chicago," *PT*, 3 February 1938, 14.

3. "'Sugar Hill' Is Big Sensation in Chicago," *ADW*, 8 February 1938, 5.

4. "Honorary Memberships for 3 in Olde Tymers Auxiliary," *CD*, 16 April 1938, 6; "All Set for $5,000 Goal," *CD*, 29 October 1938, 14; "N.A.A.C.P. in Campaign for Members," *CD*, 25 November 1939, 8.

5. Frank Young, "What Has Become of Our Olympic Heroes?" *CD*, 9 September 1939, 13.

6. Murphy, "Sports Clinic," sect. 2, 1; also see "Sol Butler, Dubuque 'U's Negro Four-Sport Athlete, Competes in France as Broadjumper," unidentified clipping, dated 7 January 1937, UDA; *The Key* (1939), 105; "Butler Speaks Tonight at U. Football Fete," *TH*, 16 December 1937, sect. 2, 1; John Fuhrman, "Dubuque Loses to Knights in 49–44 Contest," *TH*, 17 December 1937, 11.

7. "Butler to Speak at Homecoming," *TH*, 10 October 1949, 21; "Gala Weekend Slated at UD," *TH*, 18 October 1949, 12; *The Key* (1950), 70; *University of Dubuque Bulletin*, July 1946, 6, UDA; Richard Breaux, "On, Behind and Ahead of the Curve: The African American Presence at UD and in Iowa," in *Ahead of the Curve: The First Century of African American Experiences at the University of Dubuque*, exhibition

catalog, ed. Brian Hallstoos and Jonathan Helmke (Dubuque, IA: University of Dubuque, 2015), 18; "Racial Ban Lifted Too Late for U. of D.," *The Cue*, 11 March 1948; Kurt Kemper, *Before March Madness: The Wars for the Soul of College Basketball* (Urbana: University of Illinois Press, 2020), ch. 5.

8. *Proceedings of the Civil Service Board, Chicago Park District*, vol. 4 (1942), HWL; also see Marri B. Johnson, "With the WACS," *ADW*, 19 November 1943, 3; Lorraine Flood, letter dated 13 July 1989 to Mary Ann Latham, UDA; for a salary scale of park employees, see *Earning and Wage Practices in Municipal Governments of 15 Cities, 1944: Bulletin of the United States Bureau of Labor Statistics, No. 848* (1945), pp. 17–19 (accessed 12 January 2020), https://fraser.stlouisfed.org/title/4316; for white park employees seeking work waivers because their "position offered [was] in a colored district," see *Proceedings of the Civil Service Board, Chicago Park District*, vols. 7 and 9 (1944).

9. "200 Youths Listed in Sol Butler School," *AA*, 13 October 1945, 22; regarding Butler's reputation regionally as a leader in programming youth athletics, see Forrest Flewellen, "Flew's View: Community Spirit Paves Way to Amateur Sports Program," *Ohio State News*, 17 December 1949, 22.

10. "Grid School for Youngsters," *LAS*, 4 September 1947, 23; also see "Washington Grid School Is Open," *PT*, 3 September 1946, 13; Sam Lacy, "Bankhead Chased in Major League Start," *AA*, 6 September 1947, 13.

11. "200 Youths Listed," *AA*, 22.

12. "Stars Set Game with Girl Five," *Daily Chronicle* (Centralia, WA), 26 January 1951, 2; "Negro Women Will Play VFW Stars," *The Independent* (Helena, MT), 4 March 1951, 13.

13. "Sports Round-Up," *AA*, 16 March 1935, 20.

14. Chicago Recreation Commission, *The Chicago Recreation Survey*, vol. 3 (1937): 94.

15. Thomas K. McCraw, *Prophet of Innovation: Joseph Schumpeter and Creative Destruction* (Cambridge, MA: Belknap Press, 2010), 255.

16. Sherman Howard interview by Brian Hallstoos and Gordon Musel, 28 February 2015.

17. Andy Piascik, *Gridiron Gauntlet: The Story of the Men Who Integrated Pro Football in Their Own Words* (Lanham, MD: Taylor Trade Publishing, 2009), 74.

18. Howard interview.

19. Howard interview; "Olde Tymers Club Women Plan Affair," *CD*, 8 April 1939, 17; "Olde Tymers, Chicago Packers to Stage Clinic at U. of C.," *CD*, 30 September 1961, 20; Howard interview; see also Vietta L. Robinson, *Sherman J. Howard: Football and Beyond: The Legend and Legacy of an African-American NFL Pioneer* (Orlando, FL: Dominion House Publishing & Design, 2015), 23–47; and Piascik, *Gridiron Gauntlet*, 71–73.

20. David Wiggins, *More Than a Game: A History of the African American Experience in Sport* (Lanham, MD: Rowman & Littlefield, 2018), 198.

21. Untitled, *ADW*, 19 January 1935, 5; "Sport Question Box," *CE*, 24 December 1936, 10; Frank Young, "What Has Become of Our Olympic Heroes?" *CD*, 9 September 1939, 13; Chester Washington Jr., "Sez Ches," *PC*, 24 September 1938,

16; P. L. Prattis, "Exposition to Immortalize Names of World's Greatest Negro Athletes in Reviewing Achievements of Race in Sports World," *PC*, 6 July 1940, 16; Daniel, "Confidentially Yours," *NYAN*, 14 December 1940, 18; "They're Still Talking . . .," *SLPD*, 8 August 1937, Comic Section, 7.

22. *Catalog of Copyright Entries 1941, Music New Series* 36, pt. 2 (Washington, DC: Library of Congress, 1941), 2014; for more on the Whitman Sisters, see Nadine George-Graves, *The Royalty of Negro Vaudeville: The Whitman Sisters and the Negotiation of Race, Gender and Class in African American Theater, 1900–1940* (New York: St. Martin's Press, 2000).

23. Dan Burley, "Crowds in East Eclipse Chicago's Sport Classic," *NYAN*, 5 September 1942, 11.

24. John M. Carroll, *Fritz Pollard: Pioneer in Racial Advancement* (Urbana: University of Illinois, 1998), 212–13; Clifford R. Murphy, *Ink: The Indelible J. Mayo Williams* (Urbana: University of Illinois, 2024), 209–18; Martin Duberman, *Paul Robeson* (New York: Alfred A. Knopf, 1988), chs. 12–14.

25. "Sol Butler Visits in East Dubuque," *TH*, 22 May 1936, 8; for a similarly vexing report about two alleged family members (including one who completed her military training at Fort Des Moines), see Johnson, "With the WACS," 3.

26. 1940 U.S. Census. "United States, Census, 1940," FamilySearch (https://www.familysearch.org/ark:/61903/1:1:VB2F-XR8 : Fri Jul 12 06:06:13 UTC 2024), entry for Benjamin F. Butler, 1940.

27. "Deaths," *HN*, 23 November 1940, 6; also see "B. F. Butler Is Dead," *WB*, 21 November 1940, 13.

28. "City Briefs," *Negro Star*, 31 January 1941, 4; also see Al Moses, "Beating the Gun," *ADW*, 1 September 1941, 5.

29. *Negro Star*, 8 November 1946 (accessed 21 July 2024), genealogytrails.com/kan/Sedgwick/abitse.html; "Miss Velna Mae Gardner and Mr. Fred Edgar of Denver Are United in Marriage before Many Friends," *The Call*, 20 October 1939, 11.

30. "B. F. Butler Is Dead," 13; for information on when and where Velna Mae Gardner Edgar was interred in Fairmount Cemetery, Denver, Colorado, see Robin Brilz, email to author, 14 March 2025.

31. "Funeral Notices," *WDE*, 27 May 1952, 25; "Mrs. Elizabeth Butler, 85, Dies at Home Here," *WDE*, 26 May 1952, 9.

32. Frank "Fay" Young, "Fay Says: Sol Buter [*sic*]," *CD*, 11 December 1954, 10.

33. Ole Nosey, "Everybody Goes When the Wagon Comes," *CD*, 27 December 1952, 10.

34. Dave Clark, "Windy City Chatter" (September 1948), *ANP*; also see Ocania Chalk, undated letter, UDA.

35. Clark, "Windy City Chatter."

36. "Old Man," *Wichita Morning Eagle*, 2B; "May 27, 1919," *The Key* (1920), 139; "No African Golf on Olympic Ship," *Hammond Times*, 29 July 1920, 10; Charles Paddock, *The Fastest Human* (New York: Thomas Nelson & Sons, 1933), 65–69.

37. Elizabeth Schraeder Schlabach, *Dream Books and Gamblers: Black Women's Work in Chicago's Policy Game* (Champaign: University of Illinois Press, 2022);

Nathan Thompson, *Kings: The True Story of Chicago's Policy Kings and Numbers Racketeers* (Chicago: Bronzeville Press, 2006).

38. "'Sol' Butler, Famed Athlete, Slain," *CD*, 11 December 1954, 10.

39. James "Jimmie" Hill, World War II draft card; Cook County death certificate; 1940 U.S. Census, "Cook, Illinois, United States records," images, FamilySearch (https://www.familysearch.org/ark:/61903/3:1:3QS7–89MB-ZSYN?view=index : Mar 29, 2025), image 80 of 944; United States National Archives and Records Administration.

40. "'Sol' Butler, Famed Athlete, Slain," 10.

41. "'Sol' Butler, Famed Athlete, Slain," 10; on Butler carrying a gun as early as the 1920s, see "It Wouldn't Do to Tell," *The Light*, 11 August 1928, 15.

42. "'Sol' Butler, Famed Athlete, Slain," 10.

43. Russ J. Cowans, "Russ' Corner," *CD*, 8 January 1955, 10.

44. Coroner's Certificate of Death, UDA; "Ex–Rock Island Athlete Shot, Dies at Chicago," *DDT*, 2 December 1954, 1–2; "Ex–Canton Star Sol Butler Dies," *ABJ*, 2 December 1954, 68; "Butler, Star Athlete, Is Gun Victim," *RIA*, 2 December 1954, 1–2; Sec Taylor, "Sittin' In," *DMR*, 3 December 1954, 21–22; "'Sol' Butler, Famed Athlete, Slain," 10; "Former Athlete Dies in Chicago," *WDE*, 3 December 1954, 16; "John O'Donnell's . . . Sports Chats," *QCT*, 3 December 1954, 21; "Sol Butler, First Tan Pro Is Killed," *The Call*, 10 December 1954, 11; "Sol Butler's Death Recalls Athletic Feats," *AA*, 11 December 1954, 19; "Milestones," *Time*, 13 December 1954 (accessed 21 July 2024), https://time.com/vault/; Sec Taylor, "Sittin' In," *DMR*, 13 December 1954, 17.

45. "Sol Butler's Death Recalls His Talent as Early Film Star," *CD*, 11 December 1954, 6.

46. Arch Ward, "In the Wake of the News," *CT*, 6 December 1954, 73.

47. Mrs. J. R. Youngquist, "What the People Say," *CD*, 1 January 1955, 9.

48. Pixie Armstrong Freymann, telephone conversation with author, 8 February 2018.

49. Pixie Armstrong Freymann, emails to author, 6 and 8 July 2024.

Index

BRIAN HALLSTOOS is a professor at the University of Dubuque.

The University of Illinois Press
is a founding member of the
Association of University Presses.

Composed in 11.5/13 Adobe Garamond
with Gotham display
by Jim Proefrock
at the University of Illinois Press
Manufactured by Sheridan Books, Inc.

University of Illinois Press
1325 South Oak Street
Champaign, IL 61820-6903
www.press.uillinois.edu